MW00365765

FLEEING
THE SWASTIKA

FLEEING
THE SWASTIKA

Faye Cukier

To order additional copies of this book, contact:
Xlibris Corporation
1-888-795-4274
www.Xlibris.com
Orders@Xlibris.com
27093

To my beloved parents,
Sofie and Jakob Cukier,
and the six million others
who were not as lucky—
and Serafin Torres, M.D.,
my very special angel.

Chapter 1

"*L'Indépendance! L'Indépendance!*" The hoarse baritone shouted. Layered atop were the pubescent screams of "*Nieuwe Gazet! Nieuwe Gazet!*" His official hat was obviously too big for the newsboy's still growing head. The monotone repetitions of "*Le Soir! Le Soir!*" completed this *a cappella* ensemble of the evening carriers. The unmatched unison of the vendors' trio—not unlike a paper war— was audible until the witching hour. Glancing at the headlines in bold letters, the word "Hitler" stood out against the unfamiliar "*La Guerre! Oorlog!*" This was the corner of *Pelikaan Straat*, the world center of diamonds and *de Keyserlei*. Yes, the elegant Avenue de Keyser.

There was so much vitality. One didn't know where to look, listen or smell first. Only hours away from Cologne, Germany, where I was born and which I had to leave, possibly forever, for this intriguing port-and-diamond city, Antwerp, Belgium, there was a marked difference.

The girls in their teens, ever so beautiful, attired in haute-couture suits or coats with matching frou-frou fox-trimmed hats shaped like large pompons coquettishly tilted onto the right brow, demurely peeked underneath the furry hair to flirt with the male passersby, who tipped their hats. The long mascara lashes, fuchsia lipstick, and rouge made them look like true miniatures of the French femme fatale. Here I was in my brand new German double-breasted beige suit with long jacket, short skirt and brown high felt hat, with no make-up, taking pride in my *teint naturel*. I was very busy observing these demoiselles *à la Parisienne* promenading with their parents, some with their less than gorgeous husbands or fiancés (those were diamond bedecked) or the ones standing in groups. I overheard their tri-lingual discussions in Flemish and French. When English was spoken, I knew this linguistic *manoeuvre* was all about an overt envy of the engaged ones, bemoaning their ripe age of 17, one even 18 and still no prospects in sight.

What nostrils' delight, the real French perfume, mingled with the whiff of steak and *pommes frites*. This seemed to be a national comfort food here in Antwerp. Also, one could enjoy a certain lingering scent of cleanliness.

There was something so warm in the architecture, possibly French Gothic as opposed to the austere, dark grey modern of our recent, unpleasant years in Germany.

In the mid-1930s our situation deteriorated dramatically. It was a tormenting decision and heartrending sacrifice to leave Koeln and everything we loved. Thus came about Mutti's and my first day on September 11, 1938 in exile.

"Why must you amble like a peasant who comes to the big city for the first time in his life? I'm ashamed of you gazing at the very top of these houses instead of listening to the practical points I am now presenting!" shook me completely out of my interesting observations.

"Are you aware that all we have is what we took along for our four weeks' tourist stay, our so-called vacation, and then what?" Mutti demanded.

"You have your diamond jewelry with you!" I answered.

"So, that won't last forever! Do you realize they stuck their famous 'cuckoo' on everything: our beautiful cherry furniture, the Bluethner Piano and even the Mercedes, not to mention trucks, trailers and tractor."

"But Vati sold the contents of the warehouses such as the profile iron, copper, brass, bronze and tungsten."

"Yes, but for 'peanuts' while the booming business itself was confiscated. By the way, were you aware of the following: while the sale was going on, and you were sitting at the desk of our office, you broke down sobbing and sobbing, burying your head on top of your folded arms, that there were no dry eyes around you? Even the hearts of the most rugged Aryan buyers were touched by this scene of a fifteen-year-old having such sensitivity, understanding this was the first tremendous step into the unknown abyss forced by the Nazi government."

"Yes, of course, it didn't go unnoticed through my veil of tears. Although I felt always ashamed to weep publicly, that time, I was overcome by emotions of 'Farewell, my young Life!'" While saying this, I did not want to delve into the sad reality and continued people-watching. What a gorgeous day it was, that eleventh of September 1938!

All these beautiful, young, lively crowds were passing us by. How wonderful for them that their happy lives continued without interference. As I was thinking this, a large group of young, tall, good-looking males and females walked by, chatting in the unmistakable Viennese accent. Ach so, I thought, other refugees from Austria! It came to mind that in four short weeks, after our tourist visa will be up, that's what I'll be, "a refugee!"

There wasn't a cloud over Antwerp but oh, so many on my mind. Will Vati liquidate everything in Koeln? How will he get here? Certainly not by first-class train, as we were the last, very lucky recipients of a Belgian visitor's visa for Polish citizens. Even I, though born in Köln, was Polish because there, your nationality is your parents' blood and not the country of your birth. To be both, a Polack and Jew, thus "a Polish Jew!" was really subhuman. Therefore, Vati could only escape with the aid of paid smugglers through the forest, which formed the Belgian-German border. This always had an element of danger.

They confiscated everything. Of course, they tried to do it still in a gentlemanly fashion. Yes, I remember that German IRS agent being there each and every day, maybe for one-and-a-half years. Whenever I returned from school, that "vinegar face" greeted me. His final decision: "more tax was owed than there were assets." This was a measure to justify their confiscation, in reality, called thievery!

It was good that Vati made his occasional short trips to bring the money here. Since this was understandably a high-risk undertaking on the part of the smugglers, half of the amount went to them. But better to be left with 50% than zero and the Nazis with everything. To take marks out of Germany was a life-threatening business. "Currency Devisen," men caught with this, were thrown into the infamous concentration camp of Dachau to be tortured there. We knew first-hand from the only lady dentist that her fiancé, a German Jew of means, tried to do it without the expertise of the professionals and, ended up in that place of terror.

Thank heaven that there was some cash in this city that was ours for security, plus the relatives. These were "black sheep" on each side of Vati and Mutti's families. His poor, elder baker, half-brother, was married to Mutti's older sister. That was how my parents met. It was a miracle that this couple produced three such beautiful, intelligent children. Because of this family, Vati was able to arrange all formalities in their name.

While walking, architecture and people-watching, all these thoughts, whirled through my mind, when the most optimistic one lifted me—tomorrow, first thing, to the U.S. consulate!

We finally obtained statements through our American, rich relatives. They were "dug-out" through Uncle Max, a hard-working contractor, who was just not affluent enough to substantiate an affidavit, which guaranteed that the U.S. government never had to support us.

As I was euphoric in this city of fascination, the dictorial pragmatic voice of my mother invaded my rosy images: "That's enough amusement—now, off to the humblest section of Aunt Hella!"

As an only child, I couldn't understand the coolness, yes, sometimes hostility, between the siblings.

The visit would have been quite a bleak prospect if I wouldn't have recalled my handsome cousin with smoldering green-blue eyes whom I met two previous times. The first, when I was ten years old, wanting him for my brother. The second trip, one-and-a-half years ago, wishing he wasn't my cousin at all, poor and proletarian.

I had an aversion toward communism. The reason being, overnight, the most ardent of them converted into fanatical Nazis, when they became successful.

We just followed our noses, and the smell of the candle factory led us to the lowliest section of Antwerp named *Borgerhout*, indeed a poverty-stricken sight. However, the cobblestones imparted a charming quaintness to the place.

The sisters embraced, my Robert Taylor look-alike cousin was in the process of drying his hands upon our arrival, while boring his eyes deeply into mine. The more vigorously he used the towel, the more profound became his gaze. I was embarrassed when I felt myself blush, as all good virgins would. Without relinquishing his stare, he threw the towel into a corner. He walked up to me with spread arms, greeting me warmly with his wonderful American English, which bewitched me. He didn't act at all like a seventeen-year-old, poor communist of *Bourgerhout*.

The neighborhood odor didn't bother me, nor did the heated dispute of the two women from the background. Maurice's welcoming cousinly kiss built into such passion, which stirred-up mixed emotions within me. But the bewilderment of innocence released me from my feelings. We were just two young happy silhouettes as this beautiful Sunday slowly turned to dusk.

We had a lot to tell one another. I then became practical when I stated: "Tomorrow, first thing, to the U.S. Consulate . . . !"

"Forget it, forget it!" Maurice said with so much compassion in his eyes.

"But Maurice, why, it's my only chance . . ."

He interrupted with: "Every day, when I go to work, up the Avenue de la France, I see thick lines of refugees. They can't even get near the doorman! They extend from before the open portals of the U.S. Consulate's building. There are queues a few meters out on the sidewalk."

Then it all became so hopelessly sad. Even the charm and warmth of Maurice couldn't entice me anymore. Still protesting, I tried to make light of it, mainly fooling myself, "But Maurice," I said, "here is the affidavit!" It consisted of many signed notarized documents and bank statements. "Wasn't it nice that our Uncle Maxie endeavored to get these after he sent us his own, several times improved, but no dice, it wasn't good enough to show

sufficient financial support. The fact that we could verify our own
economic solvency was meaningless. Do you know that funny story
about him? He was two years older than Vati. Our grandparents
from the *Shtetle* in Poland forgot to record his birth, but when Vati
was born, they registered them as twins on Christmas 1896. Later
on, they were even dressed identically, amusing, eh?"

My cousin was right. Monday we left our pleasant clean Hotel
Locarno and walked to the Consulates-Embassies-tree-lined Avenue
de la France, *Frankrijklei* in Flemish, and the big crowd indicated
the exact location of the U.S. Consulate as described by Maurice.
We formed the long line's tail and couldn't even see the registration
desk, let alone the doorman.

I recognized the same good-looking males and females with
their unmistakable Viennese accent. I felt flattered when the most
impressive, handsome one flirted with me even though surrounded
by these beautiful tall girls. When asked whether I was new in
town before I could answer, Mutti pulled me—as though his eyes
would lessen my chastity, while mine caught a mature man biting
into a lemon, defensively saying in German: "It calms my nerves,
it calms my nerves. You are new in Antwerp, aren't you?"

"You mean to tell me," I said in astonishment, "everyone
escaping from Hitler to Antwerp winds up in this queue?"

"You catch on very fast, *gnaediges Fraeulein*," answered the
Viennese, ever so politely, while the other gentleman was busy
taking another nerve-calming bite. "This is like a full time job,"
the citrus-sucking one chimed in. "You are lucky your first day is
in the sunshine."

"What are you so terribly nervous about?" I inquired.

"I'll tell and show you, *Fraeulein*."

"I'm Hermann Rinsky," and he tried to get in front of the
rows, clumsily stepping on many a toe, until he reached his object,
pulling a charming blonde out of the crowd, who was socializing
at another part of the line. "This is Frau Rinsky." While studying
this incongruous pair, he said, "O.K., I showed you and now I'll
tell you: I am a native of Poland, which sets me into the Polish
quota meaning I have to wait years for my U.S. visa. My Trudy

here was born in Germany, which translates to Americans: German quota, putting her in the faster lane, assuming between now and two years, she is considered for an entry."

"So that signifies I'll have the same problem with my parents! But how can the most democratic country have such absurdity of law?"

"Because they really and truly don't want us," answered the tall Viennese. "They are using the same trick as did the Nazis. By the way, I am Dr. Koenigsmann."

Even his name is impressive, I thought, Dr. Koenigsmann!

"When I graduated law school, I didn't go any further. Right after the Olympics in Berlin, Germany 1936, the first anti-Jewish law was firmly established: keeping Aryan patients/clients out of Jewish medical and law offices. With the smart Jews leaving, how many Jewish patients/clients were left? In a way, the Jewish doctors of both medicine and law were extremely blessed winding up in the U.S. prior to the strict quotas. Let's face it, *gnaediges Fraeulein*, the large bulk of the Jewish population under Hitler is Polish-born, so the Americans have to make it tougher on them by years of waiting till it'll be too late. The influx of German Jews is smaller, so duration while still long, isn't quite that ridiculous. I venture to say that a native Belgian might get his immigration visa within weeks, because Belgians don't have to leave Belgium. Even after Hitler coming into power, Germans still swore by Jewish doctors and lawyers. Their popularity was overwhelming. So *raus,* out with them and Americans wouldn't let us in as the going got tougher. Very, very serious, indeed," he emphasized in English, spiked with that waltzing accent. His face grew more bitter with each explanation.

I was glad to show off my English by summing up: "Our future looks so frightening, so threatening!"

Whereupon, he asked with a softer expression: "Were you aware, that in English you sound so much more arrogant than in German? Do you know what that means?"

"Look at my mother now, and I shouldn't know that word?"

We both burst out laughing, and I was glad to get back at her for acting so disgustingly high and mighty. Why couldn't she be a little glad for the few moments of innocent and yes, informative pleasure I had? Promptly, she tried to quell my laughter while shaking her head.

"Mutti, this isn't exactly a funeral yet!"

"How dare a daughter talk like that to a mother," she accused me in the third person.

"Such a million-dollar smile, such wonderful English and so smart!" he exclaimed.

"You are very gallant, Herr Dr. Koenigsmann, a million Belgian francs would suit me fine (about $20,000)." I ate up every flattering word after Mutti's criticism of me. Great . . . ! I thrilled inwardly.

"It is a real job coming here every day, but at least now, it was sheer fun. It's so much of a chore that I even got a small furnished apartment on the Avenue *d'Amerique*, a few long blocks over there. Same street, only the name has been changed."

"Hmm!" I raised my brows.

"No, it's just a basement. That's what became of me: a penny-pinching-would-be lawyer! I couldn't afford to invite you to a cheap restaurant for dinner, but I might swing a *café au filtre*." He offered sheepishly.

Suddenly, a very dry voice said in both English and German: "This office is being closed, come back tomorrow."

"How many tomorrows?" Dr. Koenigsmann sighed.

The dry voice came out of a very narrow mouth, placed in a gaunt face, topped with a white Naval Officer's type hat.

Before the line of people broke, Mutti pulled me away. Like a restrained child, I waved bye to Dr. Koenigsmann and Mr. and Mrs. Rinsky.

We again were walking on the Keyserlei, a splendid pastime! I was in deep thoughts of both, the light and serious side of Dr. Koenigsmann.

"Do you realize that you didn't hear one word I said? I bet you are musing on that Austrian child molester," Mutti said harshly.

"Isn't that carrying it a bit too far?" I asked. "Besides, no one takes me for my age. Everyone assumes me to be in my late teens. Why not stretch these most wonderful years?"

"Are you Fanni, Fanni?" a strange voice in foreign German, inquired.

"Yes, but . . ."

"I am Sacha Horovitz," this middle-aged, breathless man, in a fine Brummel hat, declared. His eyes were full of mischief.

"Oh yes, I recognize your name. In fact, I typed a note for Vati thanking you for your hospitality to him. How is your kind wife and two boys? How did you know who I was?"

"Your father so proudly showed off your photos. You are even prettier in person. Follow me, follow me, please," gracefully leading us to his family. The boys were nine and ten years old, both of their birthdays being July 11, 1929 and '28, respectively.

"Why don't you have lunch with my family tomorrow? We live within walking distance."

Every destination seemed to be so, which made Antwerp even more charming. He handed us his card, reading, underneath his name: "*Courtier des Diamants.*"

It was a lovely, light-colored house, with a huge, white, lacquered door, near the park, on the *Plantinlei*. I remembered the monument depicting freedom from Spain in Medieval times. (I have a picture with my cousin, in front of same.) This work of art could be seen from their home. While waiting for the door to be opened, again I made a mental comparison to the austerity of the dark gray apartments in Nazi Germany. How anxiety-provoking! Though the one we left, was one great exception: a white round house with circling red flower beds.

We were greeted promptly by a pretty blue-eyed blonde, also a native of Koeln, from a prominent intelligent family. She was their niece, *Fraeulein* Stern. Her uncle, a middle-aged tax lawyer from Koeln, locally well known, could have passed as a jaded brother of Charles Boyer. He paid little attention to us, four females.

When the conversation abruptly turned to the U.S. consulate, Rosa didn't even want to discuss matters. Her prosperous brother did get to the U.S. two years ago, but wasn't a citizen yet, therefore unable to sponsor her.

She declared, "I'm actually going to marry a well-to-do American that my brother arranged. I hope I'll love him when he comes for me."

I felt very fortunate to have found this family. They were most supportive, especially when the third week of the visitor's visa was up, they advised us to look for another hotel already just to be prepared.

This change was a far cry from the pleasant "*Locarno.*" One had to enter a large boisterous brasserie, run by a lovely Flemish family. The daughter was a few years older than I, the son about my age. I explained our situation in English to these two peers of mine. Also that we are expecting Vati soon. Their parents had to think it over. When we returned, they were afraid to do anything illegal, since it was against the law to have anyone living there without registration at City Hall and the Police. I went from moderately priced, to cheap hotels, making almost dizzy rounds of them, and finally coming up with "*La Scala*" at *Statie Straa*t, a section of rather ill repute. They didn't ask many questions being too busy with the adjoining night-club and movie-house.

I didn't mind the all night sound of that wonderful American jazz I heard on my first day here. Our new place looked actually quite plush with its royal blue carpeting.

Then after one week, our fifth in Antwerp, we were asked whether we registered. When the answer was negative: "You'll have to leave by tomorrow," we were told.

Back to the "Billiard Palace," begging the daughter in English to rent us a room, then the father—taking a minute out of his beer-tapping-suggested: "Go to the *Stadhuis* (City Hall), say that we would like very much to have you here, would they extend your visitor's visa for six weeks."

We did just that. The prospect of being without a roof over our heads was frightening. What treasures of monuments we passed glancing at them from the corners of our eyes hastily to get there before noon. The *Stadhuis* (City Hall) itself was a daintily built jewel of Medieval architecture. My heels made the rush through narrow streets quite difficult. Looking for the department

"*Vreemdelingen*" (Foreigners), we found a policeman with a longish face, peeking underneath a helmet similar to a London Bobby's. He reminded me somewhat of the *portier* from the U.S. Consulate, but older and more approachable. All around were benches taken by people speaking German and Jewish above a whisper. I stated my problem and at least felt relieved when the officer registered us and made us wait, indicating a possibility for an extension. There was standing room only, because we were late risers and barely made it on time.

Right after us this adorable, overdressed lady came with four equally adorable children. Her high spirits and elegant black fox-trimmed suit could signify that she was stepping out in style somewhere exciting—hardly, as she too waited for a prolongation. She came from *Passau* and *Graz*, towns where anti-Semitism was rampant, especially since the *Anschluss* to Austria. One night she packed her children, who suffered the most, being harassed constantly, and put on her best suit, leaving everything behind. While referring to the children, she kissed each one, and not unlike Vati, her husband also would liquidate the business and join his family in Antwerp later. That certain sparkle made her look so young and vivacious which was quite infectious. She had the befitting paprika name of Mitzi.

I learned there were two like—"regular jobs:" the U.S. Consulate and City Hall. We were too late. The following day was a replay of the first; but on the third, Mitzi and I clickedy-clogged happily with our stylish high heels on the old cobblestones, for we made it! Not six weeks, but at least four we did receive.

Joyfully bursting into the room of "*La Scala*," taking off my shoes and stockings, it felt great to dig my nude feet into the deep pile of the carpeting, as I gleefully exclaimed: "Look Mutti!" showing her my *faît accompli* with great pride.

"What, only four weeks? You could and should have gotten six! Now, let's not get lazy! They don't want us here any longer, not even with the extension. Now, off to the 'Billiard Palace!'"

"Give my poor feet just ten minutes and I'll be all right." My tired aching toes protested: "Then go alone."

"—but I cannot talk to them."

"Then wait, please!"

"No, right now!"

I could barely get into my shoes, dragging myself and rationalizing, that when seeing the suffering expression on my face, they surely will rent that large comfortable room, the bath only a half flight up. They will have compassion for me. They did. We returned with our one large, elegant, genuine pig leather suitcase.

The view was lovely onto the *Koningin Astrid Plein*, named after the Scandinavian-born beloved Queen of the Belgians, who died in a car accident, (the auto being driven inattentively by her royal husband, King Leopold in the early 30's, at *Kusnacht, Switzerland*). The landscaping of this large square was exquisite. The purple and yellow flower hues forming a symmetric design all over this place were leading towards Keyserlei and into an entirely different world to the far other end of this elongated Plaza.

The weather got brisk, which necessitated wearing my warmer, brick-colored, seven-eighth, smart-looking walking suit. Mutti added her twin silver foxes, worn separately on each shoulder on top of her pin-striped one and donned her cloche.

I loved to indulge in the European favorite pastime, "*La Promenade*," wandelen in Flemish on the avenue, here *de Keyserlei*, of course. But no longer could we afford to sit in the only enclosed terrace of the "*Londres*" nor the adjoining café windows.

The full-time U.S. Consulate "job" was reduced. I hated to admit that these visits were of less and less value. Only once did I get inside the front portals which led to a garage driveway flanked by miniature sidewalks. These were furnished with long benches, filled to capacity with immigrant hopefuls, better said "hopeless." The "inner sanctum" connected with the actual waiting room. Whether seated or standing in line on the street, the last famous words were always: "This office is being closed now, come back tomorrow." I thought with envy, do these fortunate native U.S. citizens know how very lucky they are, they were just born there, just simply born there! One day, I took my courage and asked the tight-lipped doorman, in English, "Does one ever get inside these portals and actually see an officer?"

He bent a little sideways without looking at me, bouncing from heel to toe, and back to heel, in order to literally throw his weight around, "someday," was his curt answer.

"You mean as 'someday my prince will come?'" I dared to retort, hoping I might stand out from the sheep in line. That little humor fell on deaf ears.

This is how I spent my days. Evenings were filled with smart conversation and laughter at the Horovitz's, which were charming and informative. How happy I was that Vati looked them up during his various, short smuggling trips. Mrs. Horovitz, née Stern, was of a prominent family, whose brothers did business with him in Koeln.

After one such night, as we got through the boisterous brasserie to take our key, I realized it was gone, I ran up the steps, and there he was, my Vati, trying to wash his feet in the basin of our room. He looked so exhausted, his big, green eyes grayish and bloodshot.

"My dear Vatichen," I kissed him, never having been separated this long.

Mutti arrived, planting herself at the door, with a mocking look on her fine features, proudly waiting for Vati to make the first move, which he obligingly did, embarrassed, trying to dry his foot. Mutti complained that was her towel, not to use it! I helplessly watched this awkward scene.

"Vati, tell us, tell us, sit down here in this easy chair!"

But Mutti insisted about the towel.

I could've done as Walt Disney's "Mickey Mouse," bouncing my head against the ceiling. I couldn't take the tension, visualizing myself as this up and down "roof-hitting" cartoon and gladly handed him mine. Once this was out of the way, he told us how daringly and illegally, he sold the "Cuckoo-labeled" cherry-wood furniture, the Mercedes, and the *Bluethner* piano.

In his story, just minutes before the Gestapo came to arrest him; he was in the new apartment house upstairs, in the maid's quarter of Gretchen, a lovely "Hummel figurine-looking" girl on her *Landjahr*. A Nazi law which saved Vati's life provided that each German female graduate was assigned to do housework for a family in another city.

Gretchen was the landlord's maid, intelligent, anti-Nazi, and in contact with the boss of money smugglers, for liquidation of clothes, furs and other personal belongings. Everything had to be done swiftly, before the Nazi machinery went into motion.

Then he finagled himself through the woods with a German farm-house on one side and a Belgian one opposite as the two objectives. There were German shots in the dark. With fear, courage, and the other man's knowledge, they made it into Belgium. This was not Vati's first experience. In his teens, he, Uncle Maxie, and friends, were drafted by the Russian-Polish army. Jews suffered greatly through the pogroms there, and my paternal grandfather endured just as much, even though he was in the cavalry, and died as a consequence of the services for his fatherland. He was a scout and the frozen lake burst underneath the weight of his horse. He succumbed to pneumonia, which he contracted during his mission, and left a poor young widow with many small children without any means of support. It was "Evrei, Evrei (Jew, Jew)!" anyway, so the two brothers and others deserted before registering, sneaking themselves over the Polish-German border, with their aim the U.S. They all did make it to the States. My father, however, fell so in love with the beauty and gaiety of the Rhineland where he remained by choice.

This time around he was no longer a teen-ager, so he surely needed his nap after the forest experience. We all slept in the same very large room. I used the couch.

After Vati's good long rest, the three of us took our first walk as a family. He, as always, was the life of the party, at the Horovitz's, and they were happy to see him again. Their huge comfy apartment turned into a private welcome center of sorts, a home away from home for the newly "forlorn." There were intellectuals from Germany and Austria, the Antwerp bijoutiers, and those connected with the diamond industry. It turned into a kind of petit salon of *"La Belle Epoche Parisienne."*

Already past 2 A.M., on our way back to the hotel, on *Pelikaan Straat*—as we passed the Excelsior,—across the street from the very old, impressive railroad station, two tall strangers came running breathlessly and agitatedly toward us, obviously spotting our being refugees. In native German, they told us: "We just came off the train, after having escaped something terrible!" As fate would have it, they were not home but upon entering their hallway, they heard a lot of commotion, policemen yelling and commanding Polish-Jewish families to come along to Police Headquarters at once. The two brothers continued walking up, up, to their apartment, acting as though they had nothing to do with the entire matter.

After their Polish-Jewish neighbors were herded into chocolate-colored prison trucks like common criminals, the brothers just grabbed their coats and money, and left. They finally caught the last electric thirty-minute Antwerp Express. Not only were they saved by their presence of mind, but also by their Aryan appearance.

The three of us looked at each other. What a stroke of luck for Vati—and us—to have fled in the nick of time!

The younger brother added, "When they take you out of your dwelling, forget it, it's torture and death! This had happened tonight at 8:00 P.M. We didn't know exactly what, but it was sure something awful, and here we are together, alive and free!"

The following evening, the news we received from the "horse's mouth," the siblings, was all over "L'Indépendance," (the baritone), "Nieuwe Gazet," (the boy's voice), "Le Soir," (the monotone): "ON THURSDAY, OCTOBER 27TH, TWENTY O'CLOCK POLISH-JEWISH FAMILIES LIVING IN GERMANY, DRAGGED OUT OF THEIR APARTMENTS TO POLICE HEADQUARTERS."

On Monday, the 31st of October, the headlines continued: "SAME POLISH JEWS FROM GERMAN CITIES WERE DROPPED OFF IN 'NO MAN'S LAND,' BETWEEN GERMANY AND POLAND, AT THE POLISH CORRIDOR. THEY HAD NO FOOD FROM THURSDAY NIGHT UNTIL SATURDAY."

On Wednesday, the 3rd of November, "'NO MAN'S LAND' NOW GOT A NAME, 'ZBONSZON.'"

Seven months prior to our sudden departure into exile.
February 1938 Bad Godesberg, Germany.

Again, the newspaper war, "SAME POLISH JEWS FROM
GERMANY IN MILITARY STABLES IN ZBONSZON." Thus
came about the first mass deportation. The world looked on!

During 1938, Chamberlain met Hitler at one of his favorite
places, which was a pet of mine too, the romantic "Dreesen Hotel,"
in Bad Godesberg. There I dined with my parents and even was
invited to dance at fifteen in the open air swanky terrace-
restaurant-café, overlooking the Rhine River, facing the
Siebengebirge, the seven hills, backdrop of some "Wagnerian"
operas.

It was at the same Hotel Dreesen where the sign, "Juden Zutritt
nicht gestattet," Jews not admitted, met our disbelieving eyes! We
wanted to relax and have a drink. Well, we didn't have to be quite that
elegant, so we went to a less fabulous place. It also read "Juden und
Hunden, Zuttritt Verboten (Jews and Dogs Admittance Forbidden)."

Becoming panic-stricken, we wandered from place to place, realizing we could not sup anywhere, in the adorable, beloved, so familiar Bad Godesberg.

On our previous visit to the Dreesen, Hitler made an appearance there. The entrance was mobbed. The whole city was filled with frantically cheering crowds. My young feminine curiosity got the best of me. I wanted to see him in person in the worst way. But how Vati steered his Mercedes with such fury and passion against the wildly excited, waiting mass, I shall never know.

I entertained myself, reminiscing about the beginning of 1938. We stood in another line on Lange Leem Straat at HIAS: "Hebrew Immigration Association for Shelter," which proved lucky. In one week, there would be no more Billiard Palace for the second month-long prolongation visa would end in a mere eight days. In addition, not having any prospect for income, we could no longer afford to stay even in the most meager hotel.

The entire day's visit paid off though. They did get us a two-room apartment because some young husband had a sick wife and would sublet for the winter.

It was, of course, fully furnished; two plain clean rooms; a kitchen and one bedroom. What's more, no registration at City Hall nor police was needed.

After we packed our few belongings to move, we tried to get a little uplift of the *Keyserlei* walk, where a big crowd was gathered around the three yelling paperboys.

The baritone shouting, "LA NUIT DE CRISTAL!"

The boy's voice, "DE KRISTALNACHT, DE KRISTALNACHT!"

The monotone reiterated a whole story about "LA VENGEANCE DE HITLER!"

As typical of a sixteen-year-old, there flashed through my mind the fun-filled days and nights, starting officially the 11th of the 11th each year, to celebrate in great fashion the Mardi Gras season in Koeln. It culminated into the true mad days called "*Karneval Sonntag,*" "*Rosenmontag,*" and the actual Mardi Gras, "The carnival Sunday," "Monday of Roses," and "Fat Tuesday," followed by the atonement of "Ash Wednesday." What a farce! This was atonement too? But were these the same Germans with the cross on their foreheads on Ash Wednesday as the brutes of *Kristallnacht*? The 11th of the 11th also meant two months being a refugee, the eternal Jew, moving from place to place, not belonging anywhere, not wanted anywhere, not to live nor enter any place.

Oh, despair!

Chapter 2

Dull, desolate, and destitute my young life had become. Enormous emptiness befell me. The days got cold and dark. How I hated it—maybe because I was born smack in the middle of the year when spring turns into summer.

I was smart to have taken my fur along, which was the envy of my classmates. It was unusual for a young girl to possess a pinkish-beige full-length Spanish lambcoat, custom-made by the best Koeln furrier; right now, how I appreciated its warm softness!

Upon entering the Horovitz's, I heard all "*ah's*" and "*oh's*," giving me an instant lift from the depth of all those sorrows that have been clutching my soul these last weeks of utter boredom.

Well, there was a party going on with schnapps, champagne, assorted goodies, and even pineapple! Only the very rich could afford such fruit. I was the first and only one to tell my friends in elementary school, the experience of tasting the heavenly aroma of *ananas*. One tiny piece could have bought pounds of apples and pears.

I saw a new face; a baldish, mid-thirties man who spoke American English! Rosa was by his side. They were both deliriously shining with happiness.

At once, I realized that her "Pinkerton" did drop anchor, fell in love with her, and proposed marriage. But unlike "Butterfly's naval hero," he took her to America joining her brother, living happily ever after.

One day, there was a knock at the door. It couldn't be the Belgian police? Mutti and I quickly conferred.

"No one knows our address here without registration. Also, the tap was too gentle, more like that of a woman," I consoled Mutti and myself.

I opened, ever so carefully. A young blonde appeared, introducing herself as an offspring of the large Hungarian-Jewish family downstairs.

"So you are the German refugees that sub-leased Mendel's apartment for the winter? Why don't you come downstairs and visit?" she proposed warmly.

I had never met Hungarian Jews before. This family of seven adults, plus a widowed mother, did not resemble each other, not even vaguely. A very tall attractive woman said, "Oh, enter, young Pola Negri."

The assortment of faces agreed, noddingly, "Oh yes, she does look like her!"

Their friendliness made me feel so free, that I emulated the Hollywood actress's first line of "Mazurka."

"Sometimes you must sing the whole song! How about New Year's?" suggested the woman who originally invited me.

It was difficult to match the faces with the names. Just the lovely, tall, and eldest girl, Eta, was very Magyar, matching her outgoing personality. The youngest, shortest sister was a very studious, Orthodox scholar. She gave me the best advice: "Go to evening school! There is an excellent instructor, they ask no questions and I never heard this class being attended by any refugees. The Flemish just want to study their second language in case they need jobs in Brussels, and what's more, it's free!" So, I now was a French student, and I liked it.

In the process, I learned Flemish too, since that was the source language.

"Last year I never wore my fur coat, but now it is such a harsh winter that I have to use it," said Ilona, another sister.

" — and I can't even look forward to spring, because again we shall be without a roof over our heads!" I exclaimed in great dismay.

While expressing this to her, the motivating thought of making the "consulate rounds" on *Frankrijk-Lei* shot through my head. My parents wanted to come along. This consisted of repeated tries at U.S. Immigration, most sought-after, still mobbed, and the British Embassy where many ardent Zionists, eager to start a tough pioneer's life in Palestine were no longer accepted.

Strolling alongside the Rhine river with Mutti. How well
this much admired coat served me in exile! Cologne age 14

"What about any country in the vast British Dominion?"

"We'll have no more immigrants from a country, we might prepare to fight."

"What irony! Here we are Germans—at home we were Jews; after all, we do have family in Montreal, Canada."

"All right, have your sister get in touch with the authorities at the capital, Ottawa," we were told.

France was overflowing with over 250,000 refugees. In addition to us Germans, were those souls from Spain's civil war.

There was also the alternative of Madagascar, Tanganyika, Ethiopia, Orinoco Valley or other ridiculous, unsuitable suggestions for Jews who were not wanted any place.

The three of us were tired and disgusted. We went to sit at a café. The room was filled with smoke and Jewish people discussing politics and Hitler. The owner, the intelligentsia, who seemed well versed in these matters, came to the conclusion that there will be a war.

Vati, out of the blue, asked us: "Do you remember all these strange geographical places, one of which was called Tanganyika? Well, they still have untapped sources of various mines. So," he said clearing his throat, "I bought stock in Tanganyika."

"You bought what!" Mutti shrieked with raised eyebrows.

I was appalled too. Vati dared telling this venture only in a crowded café. Mutti wasn't afraid to make a scene anywhere. Even though business matters were so minor in comparison with the refugee life, this was a dangerous bite into our already shrinking, very last financial reserve. That's where Vati spent his days, wheeling and dealing at as small cozy brokerage firm, rubbing elbows with successful diamantaires! He then started raving about a wonderful Mr. London, actually from London.

"Mr. London," Vati continued, "is the most remarkable man . . ."

"Never mind Mr. London! What about those Tanganyika shares?" Mutti interrupted, "Can we afford to gamble on the Stock Exchange?"

Ashamed, I left their table and started talking to a girl, a couple of years older than myself. She answered in English, "It seems we always meet under disagreeable circumstances." Lili introduced herself as the daughter of the intelligentsia. Her protruding teeth added to her friendly charm. "You don't remember me," she went on, "from the *Keyserlei*, when you asked what the excitement of the paper boys meant. I was the first to tell you about the *Kristallnach*t."

"So, I also saw you on September 11th!"

"Oh, am I that important to you that you still recall the exact date?" she laughed with her thumb-sucking mouth. Thereafter, I explained that this was my first, not refugee, but tourist day, and she was one of the pretty fox-trimmed-clad girls I admired. "Oh, so you saw me dressed-up twice, and not in this white smock," she said, somewhat flustered.

My embarrassment was so much stronger at Mutti's loud voice shouting about Tanganyika, which before this day, I never heard of, and had become such a disagreeable name.

"Why don't you come to The Dancing with me on Sunday afternoon? I'll treat you. Don't worry, my father pays me well. I don't want to sound snobbish, but Papa doesn't really need this café. It's his hobby. He is so gregarious and loves to be the center of attraction with his political views. Also, the refugees have a gathering place where they can just sip a glass of tea for hours on end. Do step in whenever you pass our Café Riga! Pop hails from there and claims it to be the diamond of the Baltic countries. Don't forget our date . . . I'll see you!"

"I, a little German refugee, dancing?"

"Yes, you little refugee, you do have a right to live your young life!"

On that day at four, Lili was all "dolled-up," and led me to her private quarters. I apologized for not having anything more suitable to wear than this royal-blue "Angora" outfit. It was the first to be called "Ersatz," which was to become an international expression for substitute.

Lili went on about my all too-natural face and hair. Her sweet mother, a nice babushka type, was in total agreement with her.

She even explained that Antwerp-Jewish men are very fussy about their women's looks, because they can offer a lot more than just financial security, a life deluxe fit for a queen. So, it's all right for them to dress haphazardly.

"You must have noticed our many gorgeous, Jewish girls," said Lili's mother. "You are a little beauty too. Why not make the most of it? Why don't you put on a bit of rouge?"

"Me, rouge? I was known as 'the girl with the red cheeks,' in Koeln."

"That's not the point!" they both retorted. "It's to accentuate your high cheek-bones. Add some mascara to your lashes, to make your eyes look even larger."

" — but I was called 'the girl with the big dark eyes'," I protested.

"So, make them more dramatic," the two chimed in. "Your face is too shiny. Put on some powder!"

"What are you going to do to me? I'm only sixteen!"

"Only, that's precisely the prime time to look for a husband! Permit me to say, that for you it's twice as important. You might possibly escape that refugee mess," Lili's mom said.

I left with my face *au naturel*.

The Dancing was a charming place, with a great American band. They played the wonderful sound I heard the first day of my arrival here. It was surprising the beginning lyrics of some songs actually started in Yiddish. The atmosphere and orchestra were enchanting, but that was the only time I ever felt alone in a crowd.

Lili was known and liked by everyone. She couldn't even take a breather to introduce me around. Besides, in Europe people aren't that quick to present each other. The music was the sole soothing factor to my bruised ego. The warm room and the royal-blue Nazi Ersatz Angora made me feel uncomfortably hot and itchy, all of which added to my irritation. I recalled how boys and men were always standing in line to get a dance or at least my attention. Generally, I was complimented profusely on my looks and graceful dancing.

There was always fun with Vati whether taking this photo in front of his first warehouse, or at home telling me biblical stories or years later teaching me how to drive (here to his annoyance).

A couple of years earlier we stayed with Mutti's friend Hennie
and family in Düsseldorf. Decades later the three of them
were deported from Holland and perished.

Mutti's childhood girlfriend from Chestochowa, Poland and familiy visiting us. Her Bubie and I have just been punished.

On Monday, I truly had "the blues." How grateful I was for Mutti's visits to the Lang family. Her absence gave me the opportunity to sort things out for the future and to reminisce about the past, such as the wonderful Sunday mornings when I was a small child, sitting on Vati's lap. He prepared his specialties of dumplings and latkes, while narrating biblical stories. Queen Esther had the greatest impact upon me. He was better than any Sunday school in the world! Also there was fun with his versions of pseudo-French. They were merely words from his imagination, but pronounced exactly like French. Then he did the same with English and American. The latter was my favorite.

He actually used the English words when trying to impress upon me: "'Time is money, and money is time,' say Americans. But, my own slogan is: '*Zeit ist Leben, Leben ist Zeit,*'" added Vati in German. "Each minute in life counts. Even every moment has to be most productive. The rest is to be reserved for amusement. Never sit around idly because a waste of time equals a waste of life."

I understood. What's more, I agreed. Therefore, my first English words as a pre-schooler were "time" and "money."

At the present, I couldn't go to school, couldn't work, though I was full of energy and ambition. Yes, I must continue my French studies.

Flemish is a language like Yiddish for me. They both have a pleasing yet funny sound to my ears. The Koeln dialect, called Koelsch, is not very distant from Flemish. I speak this patois very well. In Koeln, as Cologne is known in German, they even named their beer "Koelsch," meaning "from Koeln."

I had to advance myself. I needed clothes in order to mingle with the Antwerp Jewish people. I would never dare ask my parents for money. Again, memories of one-and-a-half years ago wandered through my mind, but now they were of a commercial nature: doing my homework in the office while observing the workmen in order to prevent theft of valuable metals—which had been a frequent occurrence in the past, I created the idea of retailing profile iron to the many do-it-yourselfers. Vati's business was strictly selling scrap steel to rolling mills. Being good in arithmetic, I used this by having an apprentice put "T's" and "U's" on a scale, charging the customers the appropriate price. Whatever profit I made, I gave to my parents because I didn't want for anything. Could I use that money now!

It was a brisk afternoon, "bright" as can be during the winter in Europe with a weak, short-lived sunshine. I just had to get out for the now long walk downtown. It always seemed cozy at the "Café Riga." The men by now unanimously agreed with the owner about the looming war.

My two cousins Frima and little Sara flanking my aunt
Hella. Spring 1938.

Lili's smile grew broader and more oriental upon my entrance.
She took such an interest in me and my appearance that she had
someone else take over her duties as cashier. We again went to her
private quarters where I was received warmly by her mom. This
time I agreed to a makeover. They both went to work like
professionals, attacking my face and hair. I felt they were right. For
I liked the results I saw in the mirror, especially the coif: sides up,
curls on top, somewhat falling on the forehead, full and long over
the shoulders. I felt like Greta Garbo in *"La Dame aux Camilles."*
This prompted me to see her partner, my Robert Taylor look-a-

like cousin. Lili had to give me a pep talk to rid my feelings of guilt not having visited them for three months and that Maurice especially would be delighted to see the updated me. After gulping the last of my *café au filtre* and armed with nice apologetic words, the new me followed the candle smell to *Borgerhout*, being a bit nervous as my high heels echoed on the cobblestones, before stepping into their house.

Strange, again my cousin was wiping his hands for quite some time. All the while, his eyes, defiantly proud, didn't let go of mine. It was different than on that lovely September day. This time, he didn't walk up to me with open arms, but instead scolded me for not having seen them sooner.

As I was about to prepare my defense, using the excuse of the consulate rounds and other refugee-related problems, his two sisters entered. The youngest, a ten-year-old with sunken eyes and cheeks and a mop of blond hair causing the other children to call her "little Marlene Dietrich", was happy to see me. It's amazing how Sara was such a beautiful child. She resembled her father, a nondescript slight man. He was hovering in his corner, shaken by his baker's cough, getting ready to work all night long. He would return to sleep most of the day, waking up to his hacking.

Enter Frima, my prima (cousin in Spanish) who, although small of stature, had that aura of arrogance, not unlike her Aunt Sophia. This was emphasized by her squinting eyes and tiny uplifted nose. Upon seeing me, her nostrils flared, as though smelling something pungent. Like a sergeant upon seeing his general, I jumped to my feet, with a welcoming gesture. This was answered by a forced smile, and an automatic embrace.

"Ah, cousin Fanni, my Hebrew namesake!" she exclaimed.

Our common, long deceased Grandmom, which neither of us ever knew, was also "Fruma," meaning "the Pious one." This was quite ironic for both of us. Jews are rarely named after a living person.

Before I could engage into any conversation, she interrupted with her obsessive Communism; experiencing such ennui, being placed in a defensive position I tried to explain that I was pauperized now.

"Does that make you feel better?" I questioned Frima.

"No, it's the same as to have loved and lost, as opposed to having never loved."

I complained: "When I was a mere pre-schooler, the whole neighborhood of Communist children tormented me, running after me with their sing-song of 'Jew, Jew, we'll stick his nose into a ladle, and when the Jew has died, we'll throw him into an eggbox.' They were always serenading me with this wretched rhyme in Koelsch. It didn't seem like such a fun language to me then. I feel similar to that now—and you, Maurice . . . ?" I requested support.

Frima stopped him cold when he wanted to walk towards me. It was the same way when Mutti prevented Vati from giving me any consolation.

Why do these witches always succeed? I asked myself with bitterness, but continued aloud: "Do you know what it means to suddenly be a refugee? Do you realize how frightening it is, not knowing under which roof you'll be sleeping tonight?"

"Do you know how frightening it is, not knowing where tomorrow's bread is coming from?" Frima mocked me snappily, Mutti style.

"Your father is a baker," hoping that a bit of humor could steer me out of this disagreeable situation.

"Ha, ha, ha . . . !" she sneered sarcastically.

Since I couldn't fight anymore, I took to flight. A biting frigid wind blew against my burning cheeks.

There was a party going on. Again, schnapps, champagne, goodies, and even pineapple! It actually was a quiet wedding celebration. Rosa's brooding uncle's usual stone face had a beaming glow of happiness.

It was good, laughing with friends, rather than being on the defensive with relatives. As always, I was the recipient of such warmth, both emotionally and calorically. Mrs. Horovitz rubbed my icy hands, and even my feet.

Strange, Mutti never did that, not even when I was a toddler. Instead, she complained, "What is it with these cold feet and hands?"

I missed Rosa, but was glad for her good fortune. This was a
time for joy.

Everyone asked me to sing and I obliged. The audience, as
well as the performer relished the entertainment thoroughly. The
diseuse-cabaret style with my deep voice, à la Dietrich, was the
fashionable trend.

Since, in those hard times, no honeymoon took place for
refugees I was invited to Mr. and Mrs. Stern's apartment in the
Lange Leem Straat.

We talked business in their cozy dwelling about where, in a
world which was oblivious to us, we could settle.

"No one to my knowledge but you made the complete
'Consulate Rounds,' as you call them," said Mr. Stern. "Now let's
try a different approach!" He interrupted himself, banging his
forehead with his fists, tears in his eyes, he lamented, "Why, oh
why, didn't I do like my niece and listen to her brother? We could
be in New York with them now. Most of us didn't take the Nazis
seriously, thinking it was a political fad. How could I have given
up such a good career in tax law? My whole life was invested in
that practice!"

Mrs. Stern's fiery eyes flared open. They softened when she
consoled her groom: "Don't turn back, look forward!"

After a grateful nod to her, he asked whether I was willing and
able to write many letters. "I'll dictate in German; please translate
them and with my approval, the final copy will be done. Here is
my method: to correspond with officials, former clients and friends
in Britain, Canada, and America."

"I'll try my best, my *darndest* best," I assured them.

The next day I typed in English for the first time. This was
followed by a fine dinner, interesting conversation and the insistence
on a nice fee. I sheepishly accepted after many rhetorical objections.
I needed the money and truly didn't like to type, thus earning my
first pay by working rather than doing business as had occurred in
the past.

This turned out to be in vain, just as were my consulate rounds.
The answers were polite, but all ended on the same sour note:

" . . . however, we are sorry to inform you that at this time, etc., etc."

Now that I could compose and write English I concentrated that winter on communicating with my Canadian cousin, Ida, and her parents, the object: emigrating to Canada. They had to negotiate with the authorities in Ottawa. If we sent them a considerable amount of currency to ensure our independence, there would be some hope for immigration. In order to meet with their request, Vati had to sell his Tanganyika shares taking a heavy loss in a "bear market," "*La baisse*" in French. It was the last of our resources but still inadequate for the Maple Leaf.

We did what we could and sat tight as far as our entry into Canada was concerned. During this waiting period, a slogan became popular among the refugees: "Wait and drink tea!" We lived from day to day waiting and waiting.

One Saturday evening we went back to the *Keyserlei.* There was a large crowd in front of the Century Hotel, but this time a cheering one. When we approached, limousines pulled up in front of the lobby. Out of each descended a royal-looking beauty in a flowing party gown, accompanied by parents. They made their grand entrance to the Gala Ball. This was Chanukah time. These affairs were connected with Jewish holidays, the Purim festival, Jewish Mardi Gras ending the season. Purim commemorates Queen Esther, who saved Jewish lives during Haman's (a biblical Hitler) terror. Everything was so glamorous! There were plenty of diamonds, the genuine blue-white glitter. The young people played subtle mating games under the watchful eyes of chaperones, culminating in the selection of Queen Esther. This served an important Zionist purpose. While the bedecked belles were being whirled around, the voters donated trees to Palestine for the girl of their choice, the winner with the most pledges in her name thus becoming Queen Esther, Hamalka.

I was in awe of all this. How these girls lived here. Simply fabulous! They were a tightly-knit Jewish community. The only other time I saw this was in Koeln during the three high holidays in September. I was both envious and sad for I wanted this life for myself.

These were Jewish girls too, but from Belgium where there was no Hitler, as opposed to the Germans and Austrians who had to flee to Nazi-free countries. How I would have loved to stay here, to belong and taste these new wonders—but the Belgian government would not allow us. We were the underdogs of society everywhere. Since Chanukah runs parallel to Christmas, New Year's Eve 1938-1939 approached. We were invited to the Horovitz's and our neighbors, the Langs. It was a bitter cold night so everyone understood that we were going to celebrate in the same house, avoiding the long frigid walk.

The Langs' usually unused living room was heated for the occasion. I provided rather unlikely cocktail music for the arriving guests. "*La Valse de Musette*" by Puccini and the "*Habañera*" by Bizet. Previously I had sat in a then-freezing room learning these pieces, driven there by boredom because the others were speaking Magyar which I didn't understand, a tiresome language with its dropping monotone. Their music, by contrast, vibrates with brilliant, passionate sounds interspersed with sensuous melancholy gypsy strings. Once again there was champagne, schnapps, Hungarian wine, paprika goodies and goulash.

They were all such lively people. One young woman with impeccable olive skin stood out, her black hair and almost black eyes contrasted with her white boa-trimmed dress. She could have passed for one of those Gala belles at the Century. Her young husband played a Czardas. He was a hard act to follow, but I matched him with a Mazurka. It fell perfectly in place with the lyrics, "I feel in me, I feel in you the same wild blood. I love you and you love me, which fills me with frenzied courage." Indeed, since my blood filled me with frenzied courage, I could not help improvising a dance. This was accepted with enormous applause and enthusiasm. I felt like a star when people approached me suggesting that if I ever, ever get to America, to try Hollywood. An energetic Hora was done by all. Marika absolutely outdid herself. Her liveliness reminded me of Mitzi, my City Hall friend.

The only other refugee there was Erika from Erfurt. I thought this to be funny but she was serious and withdrawn. While I was starting a conversation with her, she got up to help herself to some piquant morsels. Sincerely surprised to see how erect she stood, I complimented her. She thanked me ever so faintly and back she went into her shell, just showing her impressive classic profile. Her husband who had stayed in Germany in order to try liquidating the rest of their belongings, he himself was liquidated. A Sbonzin victim, who was never heard of again, it was presumed that he committed suicide at the barbed wire, as many others did there.

This was the very first crime en masse the Nazis perpetrated. I felt sorry for her. I could relate to that for whenever I was little, and my parents were just so involved with themselves, I had that "alone-in-the-world-feeling."

The Hungarian mother, being a real matriarch, had all her offspring together in one evening. There was blond Ilona, the first to knock at our door. Then came a taller one yet, the eldest daughter named Eta. The third, very slim one, Eva, was in a constant rush like her youngest studious Orthodox sister. I felt I owed my French studies to the latter. Three sons along with their friends could have been a party by themselves. I, as an only child, marveled at these seven siblings. They had two things in common: they were very kind and typically Nordic.

So much had happened in 1938, yes 1938, the turning point of Jewish lives. The lucky ones that escaped Europe in time were on one side. On the other, we, the unlucky ones, were made both to stay and to run, simultaneously. For there was no place to stay, no place to run to.

The world was closed to us, and, at the same time, was closing in on us. I felt I had lost my roots, possibly forever. These thoughts ushered in the year of 1939.

Chapter 3

The early spring of 1939 was the ever so gradual awakening of life, typical of Western Europe. It felt great after a long sad winter.

Sorrow was emphasized by the ubiquitous sounds of "*J'attendrais*," a popular takeoff of "*Madama Butterfly's*" aria, expressing our waiting period as did the slogan "Wait and drink tea!" Even at the *Sarma,* the 5 and 10, the lamentingly wistful ballad was heard. Yes, we were waiting. Some for husbands and fathers—who never returned—all refugees were praying for favorable winds to carry us to a safe, new harbor.

One afternoon—leaving the *Sarma,* the rain really came down. Fortunately I had my umbrella. In Europe one always does. I heard such a friendly voice: "May I come underneath your shelter?" It was Mitzi, all smiles. Her diamond-shaped face was framed by bobbing curls.

"Aren't you afraid of ruining your black foxes, especially if it is still the only wardrobe you possess?" She just waved her hand as to say: who cares?

"My husband has arrived," she beamed. "He is there with two of our children underneath the large umbrella. I just couldn't resist sharing my good news with you."

"I feel so flattered that you came running in your high heels, jumping over all these puddles."

She beckoned her family to meet half way across the street. The husband seemed like a quiet person, which sort of complemented the liveliness of Mitzi. However, in the "good looks" department, I must say, he did not rate high. He told us how many individuals died or committed suicide as a result of the *Kristallnacht* and *Sbonzsin* incident. I mentioned, briefly, Erika's husband from *Erfurt*. Mitzi's Fred went on: "No matter how hard times are now, it is still better to endure this wretched refugee life than be in Germany."

"But we are hunted there and every four to six weeks by police here," I objected while studying his face to find Mitzi's strong attraction to him.

He continued: "Listen: this past January, for the first time, Hitler announced in his important long-winded speech, that he definitely is ordering the annihilation of each and every Jewish life under his rule. This is the very first time he made a public statement to that terrible fact in his ugly German." The magnitude of his threat made us shudder.

On our brisk walk home, there was a downpour. We found shelter in a recessed doorway, and heard running footsteps. A tall, broad-shouldered man entered our area.

"Dr. Koenigsmann!" I exclaimed in agreeable surprise.

"*Gnaediges Fraeulein* from the U.S. Consulate queue." He greeted me.

"Line, in American." I corrected.

"No, for me, it's going to be queue or whatever it means in Hebrew."

"You are going to Palestine!"

"Yes, *gnaediges* fast thinking *Fraeulein*, it's the Holy Land for me!"

"Your bitterness is all gone."

Only a residue of it was left when he said: "I would have preferred the U.S. because pioneering and heat are really not for me."

"It's very hot in the U.S. too," I tried to console him.

"How about celebrating this, *gnaediges Fraeulein*? I won't be here for very long."

I just loved his pleading expression. Unfortunately, he wasn't fast-thinking or else he didn't try hard enough to say all of this in English so Mutti would not have said abruptly, "Come on, let's go," pulling me out into the cold rain.

I objected, but she was adamant about leaving. She couldn't stand my having any pleasure.

I tried to mask that sorrowful winter with the joys of friendships: the Langs, Horovitzes, Sterns, and Lili with her Mom. The latter had the right idea after all. It taught me at an early age, when in Rome do as the Romans and also, to be flexible. In this case it concerned a very feminine issue, hairdo and makeup. On Ilona Lang's insistence I wound up every Saturday night at a dance.

Guys did stand in line to whirl me around, the most likeable one with blond wavy hair named Ben caught my attention. His green sporty suit matched his eyes, as did his *carte d'identité*, the most enviable one, but totally unreachable for us. Only Belgian natives could possess it. Naturalization was an extreme rarity. Then there were the yellow IDs for permanent residents, most desirable, but unattainable. The white ones, for one or two years, were a somewhat realistic dream. I enjoyed dancing and talking to Ben and he seemed flattered that I turned down others in his favor. His fussing over me put me at ease, and his sometimes slightly cross-eyed look strangely enhanced his amorous glances. I appreciated his gentlemanly-like behavior when he accompanied me home.

During the week my spring fever camouflaged my strong dislike for flat-hunting, how depressing. The many signs of *"te huren"* in Flemish have quite a vulgar connotation in German. Underneath each it said *"Geen Vreemdelingen,"* that ugly word first seen at City Hall—"No Aliens." There were many furnished apartments available but not one sans *"Geen Vreemdelingen,"* not a single abode without those damned handprinted words! Such apartheid! We were running out of time. The flat we now occupied would soon be claimed by Mendel with his convalescent wife.

But came Saturday, Ilona Lang begged me, as always, to go with her to this nice place since it was the end of the season. O.K., let the dancing and male attention cover up my downcast mood of the *"Geen Vreemdelingen."* This was the first mild starlit night with Ben walking me home. I must have bent his attentive ear about the "No Foreigners."

"I have a great idea! Take it for what it's worth. There is a lovely house with clean, cozy rooms, and a touch of luxury. They call this a pied-à-terre—meaning put a foot on the ground. Tired businessmen go there, as do couples to make clandestine love. For some it's a heaven. Why can't it be one for an unwanted refugee family? It's also well located, almost in the heart of the city you like so much. Let's walk there now and I'll show you," Ben suggested.

I protested, "But it's the opposite direction!"

"The night is beautiful with the first spring breeze caressing our young faces. It is perfect for a long walk," Ben convinced me.

We arrived. "Indeed it is a quiet street, yet close to the diamond hustle and bustle, and, as you said, an attractive house," I agreed.

"Let's go in!"

"But, Ben, I'm grateful for your suggestion. Now that I see that the place is on *Lange Heerenthal Straat*, I know where to go." The more he wanted us to enter, the more paranoid I got. "Say, for an eighteen-year old, you're sharp!" He gave me his special brand of cross-eyed glances. "Now, don't press me, I won't step in there with you and not even alone. It is perfect to go with my parents at a decent hour. The night is charming, so are you, but walk me home now," I insisted. The moon was mellow as was his good, juicy kiss. My depression was gone.

"We'll take it! We'll take it!" I said jubilantly, with Mutti's and Vati's approval. There was a touch of elegance after that plain linoleum-covered Mendel apartment. This was the first time I ever saw a bidet. I didn't want to appear unsophisticated and inquire about a toilet and a similar one in the same room. The interior reminded me of the *Locarno*, with that wonderful clean smell. Best of all, the youthful and friendly landlady did not ask a single question. The only drawback was the rent, quite steep for us . . . This meant looking again for a flat soon, which would be our sixth "home" between September and Passover. Though we had such few possessions, there would be too much lugging. Besides, space was scarce since it was more of a hotel accommodation. The storage place would have to be that of the relatives.

I hated to visit them. However, that certain curiosity about Maurice always beckoned me. Also, I was ashamed that Mutti never saw them. At least I tried. The three of us arrived and Maurice again gave me his lingering looks. I understood and answered his cool body language. "Well, why didn't you object to your sister's aggression? Not only that, I actually felt you, too, were against me."

"I'm all for you, my darling cousin, but as an only child you don't know the respect a sibling gives to the eldest," he stated defensively. "It is not worthwhile starting with Frima for her remonstrations are endless."

"You remind me of the German anti-Nazis. They were so afraid of repercussions, they became Nazis themselves."

"Look what happened to some of them, same fate as the Jews!"

Our two mothers sure made up for our fathers' silence. The two half-brothers were just sitting there, for they had absolutely nothing in common. The sisters started up their heated discussions. The reasons were sheer nonsense. "Isn't it terribly annoying?" I asked Maurice.

"No, I find it amusing. Just listen how one is outdoing the other with sarcastic remarks," Maurice pointed out. I did and, indeed, just as he said, it wasn't at all about the argument at hand, but rather a contest of cutting comments.

Enter Frima, my prima, God, I shuddered. "Do not fear, my little one, she'll barely notice you. She'll join the fighting mothers and win yet," Maurice reassured me.

"Yes, it is a matter of attitude. Instead of being enraged and ashamed, I do find it entertaining," I agreed and emphasized, "If you allow yourself to be Maurice, you do turn my visits into a nice encounter." I put my arms happily around his neck to express my appreciation, for he saved the day, after all.

Frima did join the fighting sisters just as he predicted. As soon as Vati detected the embrace, he jumped to his feet and very angrily showed his disapproval. He, no flower of virtue, was strict and overprotective, whenever there was a soupçon of something *quasi risqué*. We sat there like good children, making faces about his overreaction.

"I am so glad your things are here. Good, there is hope to see your pretty face more often. Also, for the time being, you don't live far away anymore," he said with a gleam in his eyes.

Since there was no kitchen, we were forced to have our meals out. A three-course lunch was unbelievably cheap, even for us. Mr. Unger always had something great at a special rate for us three daily diners. What he and his wife created from the most unappetizing sounding organs such as lung, liver, *miltz*, and tripe incredible, if one would see, smell and taste the finished product, especially after the daily fares of cabbage, potatoes, sauerkraut, and red beet borscht till now, one could go crazy from delight.

Our new place was pleasant and quiet. However, there was a large double bed so the three of us had to sleep together—strange, but feasible, if not for Mutti's winged elbows. Why couldn't she ever lie laterally as did we? Also, she was restless. I wouldn't dare to move for fear that I might wake her and never hear the end of it. So I moved closer to Vati for he was peaceful. It was paradise; however, when he arose at dawn I fell into a real slumber, only then, causing me to get up at noon. Since there was no bathtub, the bidet was truly handy. This was followed by our three-course main meal. Sometimes our entertainment consisted of taking turns reading the modern Jewish Russian Ilja Ehrenburg. His novel about cars— sounds boring, but it's so well written that I was fascinated.

I would drop into Lili's restaurant for a second cup, no, glass of coffee. She was delighted that I lived so close by again. "So right here in *the Lange Heerenthals Straat,*" she nodded approvingly, "then you can go to the *Korte Heerenthals Straat* to have a Passover Seder. That charming restaurant is offering holiday specials for refugee families."

This particular fête, a favorite for most, arrived. There was a refined refugee crowd. The nicely-set tables with all the traditional amenities imparted a homey atmosphere. A Rabbi from Frankfurt officiated at the services. In Germany, this was strictly observed *en famille.* For lots of us, this usually joyous feast was the first away from home. There were many tears being shed from some Mommies at the sad realization that what used to be existed no longer. Everyone talked German here. The *après-dîner* was on a happier note. And the second generation got together, exchanging opinions about what it meant to be a young refugee.

"It means to be in a small boat in a big ocean without any rudder," said one young man.

"It means to have no future," stated another.

"To me, it means wasting my precious youth," I volunteered.

"What would you like to do?" asked a well dressed one who did not express his feelings. He seemed pragmatic and lively.

"I would use my time effectively. Of course, I would study. We refugees aren't allowed anything," I sighed.

"How would you spend your time?"

"I'd play the piano, dance and sing, which is more style than voice."

"Can't do anything with that here," he evaluated quickly.

"I take shorthand and type with ten fingers."

"So, sure, they are going to hire a German stenographer without any papers," he said sarcastically. "Continue with your qualifications," he demanded.

"I speak English fluently."

"You do?" he questioned with glistening eyes. "Now there you have got something terrific. Could you teach it?"

I thought for a moment and I pictured how well I know the structure of my favorite language. My answer was affirmative. I was trying my very best not to sound too hesitant.

"Alright! Then," he slapped his hand emphatically on the white tablecloth, "I'll be your first student. I'm ready when you are. Who else, gentlemen?"

"Oh, yes," each of them said one by one.

"Hey Smendrick!" he yelled over to the waiter balancing a full tray. "You'd like to learn English or know anyone who wants to?"

"Sure, sure, everyone plans to emigrate to the US, Canada, or Palestine!"

"There is only one problem, where would I give private lessons?" I asked.

"No, I want an individual one!" insisted the interviewer. All the other young gentlemen desired the same.

I realized that I was in a small male harem. "I'm David," said the fast talker. Then he proceeded with, "Hey Smendrick, ask your boss whether during off hours he would allow Mademoiselle to teach here—over tea, of course?"

David was in a real rush to study. I was then in a hurry to find a primer. I don't even have money for a used manual, so I devised my own method whereby the student could answer my English questions in English—the first time, a great accomplishment! I was there after lunch. Of course, there were always some people at the restaurant. I handprinted my well-organized syllabus in David's notebook. He paid five francs and thanked me. It was still Passover, when I taught him each and every afternoon and others once per week. The "classroom" became a problem. Since none of the refugees lived presentably enough to have anyone over, so I got another two hours after dinner. I was delighted.

This time I didn't mind Mutti's nagging about not being able to afford "our" luxury room any longer. My meager income could not remedy the situation. Again I looked for a furnished apartment. Not only did they want just one or two people, not only didn't they want foreigners; now I was shocked out of my wits to see that underneath the *"Geen Vreemdelingen"* it read: "No Jews!" Rage gripped me upon spotting the malicious, evil, and hateful brazen words of Hitler: "No Jews!" Both stupefied and stabbed by those letters, I raced to the *Keyserlei*, in great despair!

"What is the matter, mine *Fraeulein?*" I heard. Feeling some relief, I could share this with Mr. and Mrs. Rinsky, my U.S. consulate-line acquaintances, though their sympathy brought tears to my eyes. Listening to me, Mr. Rinsky grew pale and nervous. He was searching desperately for something in his pockets. Poor man who does not have his lemon on hand! Then I told them of my happier news: the English classes. Her little girl face lit up.

"It looks as if I can leave for New York this year. I will take the lessons right now." Mr. Rinsky's face got more somber by the minute. "We'll study together, Herman," she kept consoling him by stroking his hands. "So if you need an apartment and you don't mind a real healthy walk, Herman's relatives have a comfortable one in *Berchem*, a suburb of Antwerp. They are an elder devout couple, living there since their youth."

Everything was just as Trudy Rinsky described. They were so religious that the landlady Rinsky even wore a wig, an Orthodox custom and law, so as not to seduce other men. I had heard of this but had never seen it before. Of course, Mr. Rinsky sported a beard and Yarmulke. Everything seemed fine until it came down to the main thing, the official registration. They were adamant, feeling that since this was a suburb where we hadn't lived before there would be a better chance. They would never ever do anything against the law so as not to jeopardize themselves. "But we have to go to City Hall first," I objected, "and then to the local police precinct."

"God will help," he answered with a pious gesture.

"God will give us four to six weeks," I said sarcastically, "Then God will come up with another six," Mrs. Rinsky closed her eyes a minute while approvingly nodding with an angelic smile underneath her reddish blond "*sheitel*," assuring and reassuring us of the Lord's help. The three of us conferred: we would have to buy beds and be forced to sell the first jewel, whether we stayed at the semihotel or moved here. We were very far from center city, which I loved from the start. Our small family considered this a major drawback.

Mr. Rinsky did not agree and he raved: "People from all over town come here for the weekend. They get fresh air in the nearby park. Vis-à-vis you have the trees, which are starting to blossom. They *shmecken* so good."

I had to smile sadly. For "*shmecken*" is taste in German as opposed to Yiddish smell.

"Most importantly, we didn't have to register at the other place. Maybe that was included in the high rent," we deduced.

The fear of just living from the gradual sale of her jewelry made Mutti very frugal.

Brown furniture of light weight metal, imitating wood, was bought. I had a comfy couch for sleeping all to myself. It faced the "well tasting" trees in bloom. Now, I did enjoy the wide-open window, when the soft spring breeze kissed me. I fell asleep while planning my method of teaching English to German-speaking people.

First, off to City Hall! The Orthodox Rinskys convinced us that God will help.

It looked as if they were pasted around the walls, these foreigners, unwanted refugees, begging for a few weeks of living extensions. Some nodded, knowing me from the U.S. Consulate or the HIAS "Hebrew Shelter"-line or having met me before here on these same benches. Even the policeman recognized me already. At least, he became friendlier each time, while his tight-lipped younger counterpart on *Frankrijklei* did the opposite. He discouragingly used body language as if to say. Oh, not you again! Didn't you give up on us yet? Don't you see you are bothering us?

After checking in with the officer, we had to wait our turn. Two hours was considered a short span.

A bit later, the sound of tired dragging high heels was audible. My mental prediction was correct: it was Mitzi with her husband. They had to roam from one place to another, also pleading for an extra four to six weeks as did all these people sitting in discomfort. After they registered with the authorities, Mitzi and Fred squeezed between us.

She seemed like the embodiment of springtime in the pastel outfit that she had made herself. So did I. That is how we continued our friendship during the winter at the craft's shop, we mutually admired our respective creations. Both the confiscation of our entire wardrobes and the lack of income or present funds compelled us to knit our clothes now.

" . . . first time minus the black foxes!" I teased her.

"Enough with this woman talk!" Fred objected. "I'm just thinking of my father and uncle Otto, the two illustrious heroes of the Great War. They argued, time after time, 'We should get our colonies back! How unfair to have taken all of them!? . . . '" Fred exclaimed, shaking his fist, 'our' German colonies, huh! These two men are still in Germany, still thinking Hitler is a political fad. Can you believe this, how incredibly trusting they are? Being in their fifties and not senile, they are just German before being Jewish. The world is not at war. Yet there is a war against us Jews from Germany and Austria. Look at all of us, able-bodied people sitting here, wasting all our days, pleading for what, to have our lives spared! We cannot return to our homeland Germany. They will kill us for sure. 'Welt!' where are you?!" Fred questioned in despair. We were next and got our "living extension."

Our papers, shredded from all that folding, looked beautiful with big letters "SIX WEEKS" which meant we could stay in this roomy apartment till mid-July without any residence permit worries. Hurray! Hurray! We wished the same good fortune to Mitzi and Fred. I saw a lot of Maurice. He hauled most of our immediately needed belongings from his home to our flat. Each encounter was so pleasant. I missed seeing him daily and when he gazed into my eyes there were still waves of craving for his kisses now denied me because of our separation.

It was delightfully satisfying to finally use my time effectively during the week and on Sundays. There were more merits to teaching than I ever imagined. The much-needed money was the catalyst. It was a nice bright approach to my existence for not only did I learn more about the language, but also about myself. I had not been aware of the enormous patience I was blessed with. It was particularly needed for Mr. Rinsky. At every class he brought two lemons. What a pair of pathetic students! He was a drop-out from the start, not hearing one word I said. Nothing registered in his mind, just trying mechanically to repeat the words. Trudi Rinsky was the exact antithesis. She, and my very first student David, who got me into this, were the best of the lot. They soaked it all up like a sponge. I suggested, then insisted, the Rinskys study apart. Strange, I couldn't separate them for the lesson, yet soon, they would be parted by the Atlantic Ocean.

I was content in *Berchem*. It was like a soft melody by Chopin I used to play on the piano in Koeln replacing the sad *"J'attendrais"* and Tchaikovsky's "Chanson triste." I liked the idea of being admired as a very efficient sixteen-year old teacher using my own method. Many of my male students ever so carefully inched toward asking me out. It was flattering. Yet David, my first and best, gave me a complex by being strictly business-like. He studied, and his homework was as immaculate as his dress. It made me wonder.

The only fascinating boy was my cousin Maurice. His Hebrew namesake Moish, one of my regular students, aimed for weekend dates at the end of each lesson. He suggested a foursome, along with his quasi-engaged friends. If only for six weeks, here was my chance to be productive and have fun the rest of the time just as I was taught at a young age by Vati.

Indeed, the following Saturday nights were filled with pleasure: chatting, dancing, sipping Brandy Alexandre, and walking in St. Anneke beside the Schelde.

Though the surrounding scene of this river was a far cry from the breathtaking beauty of the Rhine, I enjoyed the present moment. I felt almost the same delight in my early teens, crossing the *Muelheim* bridge daily in order to reach the Jewish school. Initially, I was forced to attend there, since I felt swept into it by Nazi laws. Then I was swept off my feet looking forward to my studies, classmates and last but not least, my teacher, Rektor Kahn, this complete, insightful human being. The consternating long trip turned out to be a delectable experience. I never got tired gazing from tram 26 at the famous silhouette of the early Gothic cathedral. Stretching to the sky like gargantuan pointed praying hands as though protecting the medieval houses and churches surrounding the Dom of Cologne, the city, which until recent years, I foolishly considered as "mine." Then Father Rhein, as the Germans call the Rhine River, rolled upstream to Bonn, Beethoven's birth place. The more southward, the more beauty on both sides was revealed. I was overcome by pangs of nostalgia when the last rays of this late Saturday afternoon threw shimmering reflections onto the small waves of the Schelde. I fought back my tears, not wanting to ruin four people's pleasant summer evening. After all, I was so glad to be part of this foursome; it gave me an instant feeling of belonging. Esther was as fair as her boyfriend was dark, a reversal of my parents' complexions. These thoughts, plus the attention of Moish, helped to quell my mistiness unnoticed. Now, I could really enjoy the last flickering sun sparkles on the *Schelde* to the left and the happily walking people to my right. All of a sudden, Beethoven's "Ode to Joy" was thundering majestically and jubilantly through my being for in this moment, at last I realized that I was a teenager.

One evening, after classes, my parents and I took an extremely long walk from *Berchem* to Center City. We had a nightcap at Lili's. She expressed her desire to celebrate during this coming weekend a bon voyage party. Moish, my would-be boyfriend, did not like the idea when I broke the news to him after the lesson. Already he acted like a junior jealous husband.

When the time came, I picked up Lili who found my group dating perfect for Antwerp, especially since I was getting to be known mainly as an English teacher, even though I had a lot of competitors: Viennese professors. Yet my avant-garde method made me so popular—not my gender nor age.

Lili stated in all seriousness: "If one is not engaged to be married, one is not supposed to kiss. So your romanceless fun is just right. Here we are convinced that boy-girl relationships and even marriages work better and are happier when the male feels more strongly for the female. As you describe Moish, this seems to be the case," emphasizing her statement with an approving nod.

By now, we reached the busiest spot, where my two favorite streets form a corner. Many hats were being tipped by the passersby. Lili changed the subject, acknowledging them. "I went to the US Consulate to apply for a visa."

"But why?" I exclaimed in honest surprise, "You have neither the desire nor necessity to immigrate, though you are very interested in American culture."

"Out of curiosity!"

"Yes, so, so?" I pressed in suspense.

"They are really mean! Not to me, mind you. They gave me instructions as to what my American sponsors would have to prepare, mostly all references and bank statements."

"We had to obtain those too. This guarantees the US Government that we won't be any burden."

"But this is the clincher," Lili pointed out opening her Oriental-looking eyes wide, "No waiting period whatsoever!—None!—Upon receipt of the affidavits, they'll issue my visa instantly. That goes to show you, for the ones that don't really need it, like myself, they still have room in the US. I am not going back there! I had to find out for myself," she concluded.

We seemed to have arrived. I was perplexed: this cozy dancing spot was housed in the Scala Hotel, our brief residence number two. By comparison, I felt happier now. Almost one year later, I realized the source of that soft American music.

Some people knew me, and those that didn't were standing in line trying hard to make my acquaintance, just as they did at the Rhine Hotel Dreesen in Bad Godesberg, a fading memory. It felt so good to know so many and be so much in demand, especially after such a long dull winter.

An adorable young gentleman, René, whom I noticed in "The Dancing" on the Queen Astrid Plaza while struggling with my itchy Angora Ersatz dress, reserved most of the dances in advance, when he saw that others beat him to it.

It was a fun-filled evening, though it didn't serve its original bon voyage purpose. We could not help that men flocked around us, as did women with Maurice Chevalier.

It was nice of René to escort me on such a very long walk and then, return by himself. He and I had so much to talk about that it seemed far shorter than expected.

Upon our arrival at the apartment, I saw a pacing male shadow. If it wasn't Moish! They faced each other for the longest time. I managed to introduce them, reluctantly. After thanking René for having accompanied me, I was glad to shut the door from inside, wondering whether I lost a student. I didn't.

Well, I thought with resignation, I guess that was the end of my St. Anneke foursome. It was.

As I entered the apartment, Mutti burst out laughing, exclaiming: "How about those two roosters, ready to fight like the real feathered ones in some villages!"

I loved her at that moment. By now, we were laughing so hard that tears were running down her hollow cheeks. I seized this opportunity to embrace her. So moved was I by this extended mother-daughter hugging, that my tears of laughter changed into those of a certain sadness. I had to get all my feelings and love into this one huge embrace. How I wished this moment would last forever. It felt wonderful being so close to her, actually touching her ecru satin smooth skin and inhaling her natural fresh clean scent. The child in me awoke; the child that longed for her love so much. My heart was always an open door for Mutti's love. Yet it was as though I was forever searching for that golden key to unlock the door to her heart. When would I get this close to her again? How long would I have to wait for the next chance? In her amazing affinity for the mundane and the pragmatic, she abruptly slackened our embrace. In her characteristic way, prior to expressing her practical thoughts into words, she put her fingers against her temples, and her mood changed.

"That beautiful bracelet has to go first even though it was the last gift he gave to me," she sighed. "I recall when you both returned from *Duesseldorf*" she reminisced: "He bought it from my childhood girlfriend's dealer-husband Abe. It was a nice surprise, I must admit, when he put it on my wrist with such a clumsy kiss on my hand."

"No, Vati's act was full of gallantry, love and wooing!" I dared to interrupt, feeling hurt for his sake.

She shook her head in disapproval: "Always the same old story, forever sticking up for your father. Two against one!"

Yet in a way I felt sorry for her. I saw her pondering over this exquisite piece, stroking it, crying again while gazing at it so lovingly from all angles giving it her last adieu.

The following day, we entered a charming store on *Pelikaan Straat*. It was recommended by Mr. London, Vati's new crony of the brokerage firm. His explanation about city names and Jews was correct again. Mr. Bialystok, (a Russian city) paid more for mounted jewelry than his competitors. Most of the diamantaires dealt in cachets of loose stones.

With a loupe stuck into his eye, he carefully examined the bracelet encrusted symmetrically with large and small diamonds interspersed with sapphires. His face expressed the universal gesture of approval. He looked from bracelet to Mutti, from Mutti to bracelet. She must have blushed right down to her toes. Then the silence, slowly building up to a point of utter suspense, was broken with the verdict. Mutti thought the price was low. He offered somewhat more. Mutti was quite dissatisfied. A heated back-and-forth hard bargaining took place. It was like on a Persian market. Zils, dumbek and the oud, the pregnant forerunner of the guitar, would have created the proper musical ambience. The colorful Turkish carpets and the oak showcases and glistening counters filled with incredibly beautiful mounted gems would have befitted an Emir and his harem.

I knew why Mutti picked this particular piece. It was one of the many gifts Vati bestowed upon her insatiable appetite for fine jewelry. This one scratched her tender wrist.

The tough negotiating session was briefly interrupted by some compassionate understanding on Mr. Bialystok's part. What hardship it must be to find oneself suddenly in the throes of poverty!

I got acquainted with this only employee, eighteen-year-old Rosalie Lipshutz. She didn't look like a Lipshutz at all. Miss McShane or even *Fraeulein* Schmitz would have been more congruous with her Aryan looks; the same could be said about her profession. She appeared more like a dairy farm girl than a diamond saleslady, her ruddy complexion and bigness suggesting health and physical strength.

The bargaining between her employer and Mutti resumed. His bald head was shining, thus competing with the glimmer of his merchandise. Mutti's cheeks were flushed. It made her ever so pretty in an interesting way. After all this *"Mideastern souk"* haggling, Mutti wanted to think it over. At this point, I was so embarrassed! I turned to Rosalie, shrugging helplessly with an accompanying quizzical expression. She in turn waved her hand palm down in a "let-them-be-what-do-you-care-gesture!" From that moment on, Rosalie became my friend.

Strange, I thought, wasn't Lili's friendship born out of the same reason: embarrassment about Mutti's behavior? Only there was a variation to the story: "The Tanganyika Scene."

The "thinking it over" consisted of us covering most jewelry stores. The wind-up was that, after a week, Mutti and I returned hoping Mr. Bialystok's offer would still be honored for it was the best in town. It finally was consummated when Vati joined us later.

At the same time, the closing of the deal between my parents and Mr. Bialystok gave me the opportunity for another encounter with his healthy country-looking employee.

Rosalie took Lili's place being my company. As all well-to-do Jewish people here, the latter was preparing for an entire summer at Knokke, an elegant Belgian seashore resort. How I would have loved going there, not only for the fun-filled days, but—I had never seen an ocean before—never! Some beautiful day I would behold the billowing foam of my dreams!

Rosalie was second generation Belgian—born to one of the finest well-known families in Antwerp: an only child, living with her widowed mother, in the mansion-like home of relatives. They both had to earn a living—a rather unusual situation here for women.

Rosalie's inner delicacy belied her robust exterior.

On Saturdays, she showed me the outskirts of the city. We both enjoyed our friendship which was enhanced by our English conversation. I was amused by the male passers-by stolen glances while walking amidst the well-manicured lawns. She proceeded to give me some pointers about the local society: "It is only façade cosmopolitan but insidiously provincial. For instance, if you date this or that student, your reputation is at stake. A girl's as well as a man's good name is more important than education, intelligence, culture, and appearance combined. If you are seen with one person of the opposite sex many times, you must announce your engagement."

"If not, you are considered a fallen woman?" I asked sardonically.

"Correct!" answered Rosalie, dead-serious. "Doesn't an invitation by a man to Brussels sound like fun?" she wanted to know.

"Yes, the mountainous city, but it has no river!"

"Never mind the geography! It is an invitation for only one thing, a naughty something."

"You mean, it signifies?"

"Yes, it does!"

"It implies going to bed with the host."

She shook her head affirmatively while her Aryan face was blushing like Mutti's in the store. "They wouldn't dare such escapades here in Antwerp. They might, they just might be discovered," she stated in earnest.

" . . . and that might have, just might have dire consequences?" I inquired playfully.

"The reputation of both parties involved would be at stake, of course!"

"The reputation!" I repeated with some malice and malaise, "the reputation! Then this is a most hypocritical society!"

"It is very hard for us young girls, and here I am eighteen already," she sighed.

"I am in enough trouble with my refugee life. I forgot about growing into a teenager—except for last Saturday. I have only six weeks clear ahead. What comes thereafter, I don't know, I shall delight in every moment!" I told her about Moish, how attentive he was, but then how jealous he turned out to be. Perhaps it was "sour grapes" when I continued: " . . . but he lacked my cousin's dash or that of Dr. Koenigsmann or even Ben's."

One warm day, Rosalie insisted that I meet her school-chum and friend Charlotte. The three of us would go to a carnival. The entire expanse of the Avenue de la France and de l'Amerique would be lined up with the usual amusements.

"You said you wanted to really live it up. You have only half the time left, come on!" Rosalie coaxed.

"Of course, that is true. I love people and enjoy crowds, but 'la kermesse' as you call it here reminds me so much of the vulgar drunken masses in Germany that were Communists turned Nazis. I never like to be swallowed up by a mob." I still objected.

"We have no drunkards. Germans are known to outdrink anybody. They are proud of it. In many countries it's something to be ashamed of. Belgium is one of those. It's different with us," Rosalie pleaded.

I always felt I should go whenever and wherever I am wanted that strongly.

Indeed, this Sunday night, I did meet Charlotte and did see "*la kermesse*." Charlotte was very intelligent. Generally, I like raspy voices, but I had to get used to her scratchy one and hyena laugh. What she had to say though was witty and interesting. Even though the honky-tonk atmosphere was not to my liking, the evening and company turned out to be pleasant. But by no means did it make up for my lost St. Annekes Saturdays.

"Hey, you two, how am I going to get home?" I asked when I realized that it was getting late.

"Don't worry, there is a trolley you can take," was their answer.

"I am totally unfamiliar with transportation. I have been using my feet since my arrival here. Most people seem to do the same," I explained.

"Yes, in fact, that is right. In an emergency or urgency, we do take an occasional one. We don't even know about taxis," Charlotte answered. How I missed our Mercedes that Vati managed to sell though it was confiscated by Nazis along with all our possessions from tractor, trucks down to my clothes. The auto he succeeded unloading on an eager Aryan since it was almost new and the price was so low.

At this point I had to accept the sad fact that there was no Daimler-Benz or tram. We found out that past a certain hour, none were available after we arrived at the street-car stop.

"God!" I exclaimed while growing anxious.

"Voila the start of *Lange Leem Straat* . . . ! You just walk to its very end," instructed Charlotte.

"Oh, God, that is where the ancient fortresses are. They looked so frightening during the day. I remember them when we went to register with the Police. God, they were so menacing!" I shrieked.

"That was because you had to go to the Police," Charlotte retorted.

"Yes, and all those empty fields surrounding the fortification. However, now I would be glad to be there already with still quite a walk ahead of me," I lamented.

Rosalie was crushed. Obviously, they were sorry, yes, sorry, but it was I, who all by myself had to undertake the longest walk in high heels.

I dashed past familiar places. As the landmarks vanished, so did my courage. Now, it was as though everything was deserted. There was just the sky, the endless *Lange Leem Straat* and me, racing. How I wanted already to be on *Pretoria Straat* where we lived. There was a South African patriotic song: "To Pretoria, Pretoria!" I suddenly got very pious. Whenever I am in danger, I become religious. I guess, I am not the only one. "On, on to Pretoria!" Oh, my garter broke. I had to hold my stocking now, while running, running to that vaguely known marching tune. I was angry at Rosalie, cross with Charlotte but furious at myself: only three more weeks of authority's repose. Did I need this self-imposed fear and flight through night and fog? I asked myself reproachfully. There, finally the long tunnel lay before me. When I was a child, Vati always warned me: "Never cross a tunnel or a bridge! You'll get lost in another part of the city." He was right. However, this time it was to my advantage, being that I lived in *Berchem*. It was on the other side, after all.

"Dieu, mon Dieu," I prayed in French before entering the dark lone underpass. It required more courage still. What noise my heels made dashing through it! Running, marching, fuming, praying, childhood-reminiscing, Pretoria-mind-humming, stocking-holding, I finally saw the weird-looking towers of the fortress stretching ominously against the night sky.

Breathlessly, I made the first left. Then, at last, there were just fields, the blackness, and me. The only sounds: the rustling of spring, my shoes, my breathing.

"Oh, God!" I became religious again. This time for gratitude upon making my second left, at last, at long last I trotted on *Pretoria, Pretoria Straat*!

My parents were in dreamland. How wonderful! Not only could I sleep all alone comfortably, I even had the whole living room to enjoy. I stopped scolding myself when I saw the sofa all prepared for bed, which I did before leaving for the *"kermesse,"* where it all started. It felt heavenly to be between the clean sheets and take in that aroma of the trees. I fell into a sound slumber.

"La Police!" heavy knocking. *"La Police!"* heavy knocking . . ." *Ouvrez la porte* (open the door)!" *"De Politie!"* heavy knocking. "Fannichen,

get up!" I heard Vati pleading with me. Again came heavy knocking on the door.

Nightmare, nightmare, go away! Vanish! Leave me be and bring me sweet oblivion! Something within me was entreating.

"Daughter, on your feet, at once!" I heard Mutti commanding.

Reality! It was reality, not a dream! Yes, a real-life nightmare!

In a daze, I brushed my hair, got into a robe. On the way to the corridor, I tried to free myself of my fear and stupor so I could act with composure. My heart was pounding right up to my throat while my shivering hands were fumbling to open the latch, in order to face the inevitable: . . . two policemen were standing before me and as though sentencing: "In the name of His Majesty, King Leopold III of the Belgians, you, the Jakob Cukier family, consisting of three persons, are under arrest!"

Though frightened as I was, the wording, pompously, conjured up visions of the historical, bordering the theatrical.

"*Mais pourquoi* (but why)?" I questioned.

"Your stay in this country is illegal," was their brief answer.

Though in a highly emotional state, Mutti produced the worn official documents at once. She and I pointed proudly to the "SIX WEEKS" in large print. The two officers conferred with each other. "There must be a mistake," they said while shaking their heads in concern. The error was not in our favor.

"Get dressed quickly and come with us!" we heard in disbelief. More incredulity: I never saw handcuffs other than in movies and what's more: they were going to put them on my wrists as well the others onto my parents'.

"*Je vous en prie! S'il vous plaît!*" I pleaded with them while trying to control a feeling of hysteria and an outburst of tears: "Please, please, we won't run away, we promise you!"—thinking to myself: . . . if so, where possibly to? "Just follow us . . . Don't put these on our wrists!" I continued my plea.

After a brief, private, conference, they said: "Off the record— we can see you are a decent family. Though it is highly irregular, we'll grant you that favor, and we'll let you walk ahead of us a fair distance without handcuffs."

I thanked them profusely.

We had to rush to get dressed. Since I possessed only this broken garter-belt, I had to go stockingless. Though almost summer, at 6 a.m., it was cold when we started our sad *cortège*. In my mind I heard the brass playing Chopin's "*Marche Funèbre*" behind us.

This time, to the left, we passed by those looming towers of the old fortress again with my earlier Marathon still lingering through this misty dawn.

The three of us were duly checked into the Berchem Police *Precinct*. As a result of the fresh chilly morning air and my bare legs, I had to use the bathroom. I was more than amazed when a policewoman did not let me out of her sight during my brief toilet break. How ironic, we had to hurry to sit here for hours on end until the youthful Captain arrived. At least we felt protected and were not particularly worried because of our six-weeks extension document. Yet during the long waiting, we worked ourselves up to a certain suspense; but now relief was near because this episode was soon to be over—so we thought. He studied the respectfully submitted papers approved by both, this, our very precinct and City Hall. Nodding negatively to himself, he went on to explain that there was a mistake in that no extensions whatsoever were given to refugees any longer. In addition, he pointed out a paragraph of the law concerning illegal aliens dating back ca. 100 years.

"The duration of your stay is long overdue. You must return to Germany!" was his "wise" decision.

"To Germany?" I exclaimed in dismay.

Studying our case further, he had yet another "marvel" of advice: " . . . well, or to Poland since you are Polish citizens."

"Not since last fall, not since the Polish 'No Man's Land' Zbonszon deportation we became stateless," I retorted.

"You certainly cannot stay here!" He firmly repeated and added: "You must leave this country within three days."

"*Mais Monsieur, l'Officier!*" I objected, "you can't do this to us!" sizing up the seriousness of the situation.

"You know very well what will happen to us upon our return to Germany or Poland . . . no life . . . !" I pleaded with burning cheeks.

"Then go to America!" he suggested.

Try to explain that story to him! I thought to myself, while telling him, "that's precisely what we are waiting for: our quota. That's exactly why we are here: to bide our time!"

"I am very sorry and can sympathize with you, but that is really none of my concern. My job is to merely inform you that you are undesirables in this country and you must leave at once," he repeated. "I am compassionate enough in that I am not detaining you here and expulsing you, because from what I can tell, you seem to be a respectable family. However, I further must warn you, that if you don't leave Belgium, you will be deported forcibly. Such is our duty. *Je regrette*," he said for the third time.

Since there was an edict already, I tried to fight for our three remaining weeks, which were rightfully ours. But it seemed the more I bargained, and I thought justifiable so, the more adamant he became about his decision.

We left in utter dismay and sadness, passing those wretched towers again. They appeared to be echoing in laughter our verdict.

Chapter 4

Upon our return to *Pretoria Straat*, the elder Rinskys seemed deeply moved regarding our plight. Mrs. Rinsky sobbed, accompanied by compassionate and encouraging Jewish expressions, tinged with a little guilt. I wallowed in self-pity, wondering what my new life's adaptation might have been before this last twist of fate. As I took my fourth long walk, I bade farewell to these surroundings, which just started to feel familiar.

After a brief rest, the three of us were on our way to the relatives—a boring matter after such a devastating one. Shortly after our arrival at their place, Maurice came home for lunch as most people did in Europe. This was the only part I liked. Even my usual he-man appetite subsided completely. Of course, we had to stay with them, but for how long, no one knew. Maurice had a friend with access to a van. My cousin would meet him after dinner to plan the moving. Until then, the afternoon seemed endless, filling me with apathy. Like a fugitive in the dark, we felt safe for me to go along with Maurice and meet his friend. Michel was a burly, jovial sort of a fellow in his late teens. He was one of those rare human beings taking delight in doing someone a favor. It seemed stimulating to his good nature and lent him a sense of importance. The balmy summer air in the park felt great. The three of us sat on a bench and discussed the method and time allotted to vacate the apartment.

A large group of young, blond, straight-haired males were passing by. They were rattling their Flemish, looking alike: medium height and slight. Bell-bottoms were worn by all. After they passed, I inquired whether they were sailors, judging from the flared pants.

"No, they call themselves 'Jeffkes.' They are groups of Jew-haters and philo-Nazis. In a way, your presence protected us," explained Michel. "Their nocturnal outings in the area are purposeful. They are on the lookout for Jewish individuals. But we young ones got wise to them after they attacked enough of our people, as we formed our own gangs to fight them," Maurice continued Michel's ghastly story.

"Oh, that's terrible," I sighed in honest amazement. "How eerie it must be, when it is a dim, moonless night!"

"Would you not have come, the two of us would never have met here, in the darkest of places, even though we now are organized and many have joined us," Michel informed me.

I couldn't stop myself from repeating how terribly revolting this was, especially since we Jews are not great fighters. They both chuckled at my remark.

"You'll be surprised when aroused, how much damage our fists can do when pushed to the edge, while we burn with rage! We actually adopted some of their tricks. One of them: wearing a big, heavy ring on each finger thus adding more pain to each blow."

"How awful you male creatures always fighting, fist fighting! I hate it!" I expressed my disgust.

"We must!" they both hastened to add.

The end of a short-lived satisfying existence in a spacious apartment was nearing. This brought Maurice and me the following evening to *Pretoria Straat*.

After a job well and quickly done, he spruced himself up a bit. While we were waiting for the van, we helped ourselves to the cups of sour milk. It was just left outside and a yogurt-like refreshment was the result.

"This is the last time I'll be enjoying our adorable terrace. What a shame God did not help us according to the Rinskys' vain prayers," I sighed with regret. "God gives no guarantees," answered Maurice with a shrug.

"I remembered my literature class at the only Jewish school in Koeln with my favorite teacher of all time, Principal Kahn. I had a crush on him. Perhaps, he had a small one on me," I explained, stirring my 'yogurt' slowly, and continued: "Sometimes, a tragedy turns into triumph. I was forced by the Nazis to leave the neighborhood schools. They didn't want me to mingle with Aryans. Therefore, we thought of the Jewish Schule on Luetzow Strasse. Even though it was very far from where we lived, I loved going there. Everything about it was fascinating: most teachers, students, especially my friend, the big, beautiful Inge Kasper. I was impressed by the depth and dedication of the faculty. It was like college by comparison to all others."

Maurice listened very attentively. He stirred his thick sour milk fast and furiously while uttering: "Well, I too have a crush on you like Mr. Kahn."

"Oh?" was all I managed to say for I felt too bewildered to enjoy his statement. "Oh!" I repeated while rising to my feet.

He slid off the chair and languorously took me in his arms. I might have been swept away, but I resisted. The intensity of his beautiful eyes fixed deeply into mine, making me feel uneasy, yet forcing me to linger in his embrace. This surely knocked me for a loop. I didn't quite know how to handle it. He was breathing more rapidly, and his eyes were half closed, making him look more sensuous. With my chin lowered, I didn't dare meet his amorous gaze again. I felt somewhat relieved when he said softly: "*Shshsht!*" as though to lull his troubled child. Now, embarrassment was overcome by euphoria. My initial reaction was quickly dispelled by the tender passion of his first gentle kiss. His caresses were ever so gradual. I felt limp. Even though I wouldn't allow myself to let go, I discovered that my body had feelings I never had thought it could or would have. They put a new kind of fun and joy into me, whisking away all my woes.

On the same evening, the temporary cramped living circumstances with the relatives started all over again. What a harsh comedown! The bittersweet interlude of youth and innocence could not obliterate reality after all.

On the following morning, my little cousin's huge blue eyes were sparkling while she announced: "You should see these two kings: Uncle Jakob and my brother! One person per bed!"

Her naïveté amused me in a sad way while thinking that we five females had to manage in only two. I probably suffered the most as a result of Mutti's winged elbows, leaving me barely any room in a single bed. While struggling to finally doze off, the biggest, busiest, buzziest, blackest mosquitoes prevented me from getting some precious sleep. Those nights were endless, as were the days, which till now, had always been too short. What became of Vati's instilling: "Time is life? Every moment has to be savored with the utmost intensity!"

However briefly, I saw Maurice in the mornings before he dashed off to work. Our little romance was all the sweeter that it was our secret and ours alone. There was the yearning for him to come home for lunch. Then, the span of the never-ending hours for him to return in the evenings, when again, like a fugitive, Maurice took me to the park after dusk. When that happened, I felt like jumping and barking for joy like a doggy that was left indoors all day long. Maybe that's why the cocker spaniels and basset hounds have such mournful eyes. I felt sorry for them and—myself. I would never have survived this pool of sorrowful inactivity without the joys of our flirtation. That's exactly what it was, no more. I had a real need, a desperate desire, to listen and talk to him. His sympathetic company eased me through the languid boredom. Outwardly, it seemed as though we were walking like other young couples, inhaling the aromatic air. To me, it was a summernight's dream.

"You are such a bundle of vitality! This instant change of lifestyle, the ever-growing depravations are tough enough for anybody, but for you, my dear cousin . . . with your sensitivity and yearning for beauty and joie-de-vivre, I know, you, especially, must be overwhelmed with profound sadness," stated Maurice compassionately. "Is my presence bringing you just a little bit of happiness, just a tiny bit?"

"Yes, these are precious moments I shall never forget. You are my oasis in the desert!" I vowed.

The following day was a beautiful, very warm Sunday. It was fun to have breakfast with a large family. At home—whatever home was for us, there were just the three of us forming a triangle. Vati and I were trying to please Mutti. The latter and I were vying for Vati's attention. Physically Mutti was in the middle. Psychologically, Vati was at the center of two women playing a ferocious game of tug-of-war. Of course, Mutti pulled harder, leaving me the loser, while she won the prize of Vati's undivided attention. All I wanted was a mere fraction.

The coffee would have been tastier without the chicory the Belgians added. I enjoyed this sunny morning, yes, the brew too, the eggs, the ever-so-often stolen glances across the table from Maurice, and the adoring ones from little cousin Sara, and even the conversation for a change.

"Let's go swimming!" suggested Frima enthusiastically. This was the best thing she ever uttered as far as I was concerned. We all gathered our attire. I was frantically happy to find my packed bathing suit, not having used it for so long. In Germany, Jews were not allowed in public places, such as pools, during the last years. I loved summer fun. How I missed it! Sara and I danced joyously in a circle. It was all right for her since she was only ten. Then again, I suppose, it was proper for me in anticipation of such pleasure after the few years' denial. "Oh, look, Sara, it still fits!" I exclaimed, twirling around in my red two-piece to show her. "Sara, I hope, you'll grow after you reach twelve, I did not. As you can see, that's the way I was as a pre-teen, when I wore this the last time," I said wistfully.

I could still remember that weekend—I recalled the clear lake that served as a daytime adventure. Though scantily clad, the people seemed so refined amidst the scenic beauty surrounding that part of the limpid water. At sunset, this was followed by a lovely ride on the idyllic country road. Still now, in my mind, I could clearly hear the peace being disturbed by boys who seemed to be after us on their noisy motorcycles. My parents and I grew anxious. The fear though, was quickly dispelled when I realized the reason for them chasing us was not at all because we were Jewish. Would they have known this fact, there might have been cause for concern. What relief when I saw the playful expressions on their faces! I was

seated alone in the back of our open convertible. Most people took
me for an eighteen-year-old.

"Where do you think you are going?" insisted Mutti, blocking
my way, "We are not supposed to be in this country at all, let
alone having summer fun!"

"Who will recognize me on the outskirts of the city?" I
questioned, making a fast mental comparison to the boys on the
motorcycles five years ago. "Do you really think anybody will
demand an ID at an outdoor swimming facility?" I asked indignantly
and somewhat mockingly, thinking: She can't be serious? Spending
money and the pleasure I would get from it must be the matter she is
irked about. I was desperately anxious to go.

"You never know," Frima fanned the instigating fire, snapping:
"Policemen of Berchem have the right to enjoy an outdoor pool
too—on their Sunday."

"She has a point. They just might go there on their day off
duty," Vati stressed.

This suggestion upset me.

"Oh, come on, let her be with us, I'll protect her," Maurice
pleaded to my delight.

"Don't get involved, Maurice! Mind your own business!" his
mother and sister interjected.

"But it was all right for you to mind mine?" I asked Frima.

"It is for your own good. You are still a typical capitalistic
pleasure-seeking wench. Your situation hasn't taught you a thing!
Has it?" She spat.

"Yes, my little daughter always had the amusement sickness,"
said Vati to my great disappointment. He was not on my side.

I allowed my gaze to travel in Maurice's direction. He shrugged
as he had, when he said: "God and religion give no guarantees!"
. . . And I thought to my dismay: "Neither does a young
romance!" He did say initially: "Oh, come on everybody, let her
join us!" Outnumbered, he simply left sheepishly, shrugging again
in surrender.

On her way out, Sara made one last attempt tugging my elbow
gently, looking so compassionately at me as though she felt my

hurt. Besides, she was the one who shared and conceived my joyous anticipation, seeing it turn into such frustration. Her incredibly beautiful blue eyes pleaded poignantly and wordlessly with the adults who were as adamant as the police officer in Berchem.

I was flabbergasted and disgruntled at all of them, except Sara, but particularly, I was shocked by Maurice's behavior. How disappointing! Why couldn't he assert himself and stand up for me? Even little Sara made more of an effort. I tried to fairly analyze the position Maurice was in. I expected to hear from him: "I'm not going, not without my cousin" I wanted him to fight for me or stay and keep me company.

The three adults launched into a conversation about old times in Poland. Uncle Manuel came home and went right to bed. Their chatter lessened so as not to awake him from his "good day's sleep." Why was the sky so blue, cloudless, bright and warm? It aggravated me even more that the sun was shining. What a perfect pool day! What a terrible hot long one for me to be indoors and feeling so alone. Other than Marxist books, there were none. This must be the first time that I lay down for I didn't usually nap unless I was having monthly troubles. This time it was to soothe my emotional pain. I felt like a young child whose favorite toy had been taken away. Tears choked up inside.

Ha! I laughed sardonically, the secret sweet romance turned sour like the milk we had, when it all started. After the initial pain, I pulled myself together to control my thoughts. They were jumping like monkeys from tree to tree. Stop, monkeys with the wild thoughts! Stop Basset hounds and Cocker spaniels with the sadness and self-pity! Such frustration! There is plenty of time to sort things, think and assess my situation.

It is a crazy idea, just to live hidden: for how long? Nobody stops anyone for IDs in the streets. How to get out of this trap? If only I would have kept my earnings! What an impossible dream! We were not permitted to be here in the first place. I would have gone to Ostend or any Belgian seashore and given lessons there. That's where the few fortunate refugees passed the summer—the ones that were able to support themselves from the sale of their jewelry. They could get lost in the international vacationing crowd and none would be the wiser. Our luck was supposed to be two-fold: having the diamonds to financially survive from their proceeds—and our relatives near. What a torment of longing I felt, to be alive . . . staying at the coast, possibly with Lili.

Hm, I haven't bothered the U.S. Consulate for a while—nor seen the arrogant one for quite some time! This will be on my agenda tomorrow! Thoughts were milling in my head.

I continued thinking: Where can I live? Official registration is out! Ben suggested the charming house of dubious repute, is really the best and safest idea. That particular one, where we did spend last Passover, was a swanky type, probably for "*la poule de luxe*" as they called that kind of cocotte nowadays. There must be other places, lower-priced, although they still would be characterized by that shady reputation. This will ruin a girl's good name, but it's fine for survival since there is hardly any interest in legality. This sure wouldn't meet Rosalie's approval!

I'll move there with my parents, and be protected . . . but what'll "they" say? As long as I know who and what I am. Besides, I can't belong to this society. How unfortunate for them and even more so for myself! After this endless day of total abandon, I learned, to be my own best friend!

Monday morning, after a sleepless night caused by worries, "wings," Mutti's elbows and mosquitoes, I finally dressed and made up, after one week, for the first time. Just prior to my confinement, I noticed in fashion magazines that turbans were in vogue. I took a scarf and with flair draped it into a toque. Having the intention to present myself at the U.S. Consulate, I wanted to look as American as possible.

It was just after lunch. Maurice offered to accompany me. I huffily declined: "I know the way very well."

"Don't be that way, my darling cousin! Besides, I really didn't know you wanted to go that badly. Also, you are not exactly thrilled with Frima's company."

"Yet, it would have meant the world to me," thinking what insensitivity!

On the way out, Frima yelled at her brother: "Aren't you ashamed to walk with her, look at that thing on her head!"

"Au contraire, I'm proud to be seen with her!" Maurice finally objected after it was too late—as far as I was concerned.

"Why does she hate me so much?"

"Oh, it's just that old Communist grudge against the Capitalists, caused by jealousy not unlike the blind envy the anti-Semites carry against the Jews. Even though we are related, there is this vast gap of ethnic, cultural, social and last but not least, economic background."

That explanation was plausible and appeased me after having wondered for so long why I was the object of such strong resentment.

The three adults were still, or again busy with their tales of yesteryear's Poland. How I wished it had happened on Sunday! I could have just walked out as I did now while Maurice was pleading to forgive and forget.

"This fugitive life is enough chastisement; I need yet a broken romance to boot!"

"Why must the romance be shattered?" Maurice shook in obvious disbelief.

"Don't ask me, ask yourself!"

"I thought they were right, under your circumstances," he apologized and tried to convince me further by pointing out: "Look, you do attract a lot of attention. It must feel great for a girl not to go unnoticed, but it's bad for you right now. It's downright dangerous!"

"There is more peril for me to be in solitary confinement," I snapped, feeling great, that for once I could act like Mutti and Frima. I emphasized this by my swaggering with hips forward, shoulders back, head held high. It was easy for me to be convincing, for I was not playing games.

As we were approaching the Ave. de la France, Maurice exclaimed: "Look, no more lines in front of the U.S. Consulate!"

"Well, everything comes to an end, especially when things are hopeless, such as America for most and a romance for some. Bye,

Maurice!" and before he could answer, I disappeared through the large portals.

There were still a lot of people in the second garage-type entrance, sitting patiently on the two-sided benches. I entered the third set of huge doors. There he was, the guard in his white Navy-style hat, a trifle less arrogant. Maybe because he did not feel like such a satrap anymore minus the lines, he motioned for me to sit. Drink tea and wait! I thought.

A lady stared at me. She mustered her courage to walk over, asking: "Excuse me, you are from Koeln, aren't you?"

"Yes, do I know you?"

"No, not really, but as you see, I know you." She grew very serious as she continued: "My brother, my baby brother, he liked you so much, so very much." Tears started welling in her eyes as she opened her worn handbag to look for something. I tried to guess whether mistiness embarrassed her or was she really searching for something important.

"Here it is!" she exclaimed with a faint smile through her tears as, indeed, she did produce a photograph with enormous pride.

I recognized this adorable face in the picture at once. I confirmed, and not without surprise: "Of course. I was destined to meet him: first at an Embassy of sorts after we finally had received our U.S. sponsorship affidavits. He was employed there and very helpful. Then I met him regularly at the Berlitz School when we both continued our English studies, but not in the same class."

"Yes, your father always picked you up with his Mercedes. He only once or twice permitted you to spend the rest of the day with him after the lessons."

"True, he took me rowing both times, and then we went to the *Stadtwald,* the beautiful suburban park and fed the deer that were roaming around freely. They were lovely afternoons," I reminisced.

"Then your parents forbade you to see him because you were too young. He was quite heartbroken about this . . . my little brother."

"I was very sorry too. It was something I would look forward to. But tell me, what makes you so sad about him now?"

This really shook her up. Then her story began: "I begged him not to go. Through this minor diplomatic job, he found out that tickets to Cuba could be purchased on a first-come-first-served basis on a ship called 'St. Louis.'" Rumor, that its German Captain, Gustav Schroeder was anti-Nazi stemming from his fair play nature, proved to be true. On May 13, 1939, she sailed for Cuba, carrying nearly 1000 passengers including my brother.

Upon finally arriving in Havana, Cuba after two weeks on the high seas, they were forbidden to drop anchor, even though huge amounts of dollars were collected per person by the Cuban Government. The truly great Captain Schroeder was forced to steer his vessel northbound to Florida. No entry was permitted there either. Rejected by both countries was proving to the world that Hitler was right. Nobody wanted Jews.

He did his utmost by steaming back and forth between the two cities for one week. Yet on June 6th, there was no other way but to head back to Europe, possibly Germany, and in that case, the entire human cargo would be unloaded into concentration camps."

The sister of my acquaintance, I knew briefly in Koeln, got hysterical. One could hardly understand her words amidst her sobs: "I wished so much that he would be amongst them but they wouldn't even leave him on shore right here in Antwerp. I couldn't get on board either. We were so close and yet so far! We have only each other in this world. He liked you so much and thought so highly of you, Mademoiselle," she sobbed again.

Though she was practically a stranger to me, I put my arms soothingly around her shivering shoulders, while urging to regain her composure. I noticed that most of the persons waiting to be called as I entered had been seen already, and she most likely might be "next." In order to reverse that somber mood, while curious as to how she recognized me after a couple of years, I asked for an explanation. Again, she was smiling through her tears when she related the following: "he once pointed you out, leaving the Commercial College of the City of Cologne on *Burgunder Strasse.*"

"Yes, I was the only Jewess (it was a school for girls only) in the entire college. I passed their most rigorous entry-exams."

She continued: "Then, perhaps a year later, he directed my glance to your open convertible where you were seated with your parents. Each time he was raving to me: 'There she is!'" trying to accompany these three words with a gracious up-palm-sweep to authenticize the occurrence.

This was a pleasant ego trip for me, enhanced by my momentary success of pulling her up from the depth of sadness.

By now, my acquaintance controlled her voice somewhat, for she must have felt compelled to share the following under the strain of her emotions: "They handed me and everyone on the *quai* printed pamphlets that read: 'We want to help the Jews. If they call our offices, each will receive gratis a rope and a long nail.' The Belgian police chased the '*Jeffkes*' with their leaflets away. But how am I to find out where my brother is?" she asked in despair and added: "I wrote the Joint Executive Committee in New York, still hoping for their answer."

Nobody minded the long waiting period. The ones to register after me shared the grief equally. One of them sighed: "Imagine, to have been non-stop on the high seas for an entire month and ten thousand miles, and now they are just 300 miles away from their original starting point, Hamburg."

When my acquaintance was called in, all of us wished her the best of luck. We then talked about her despair and found it most distressing that she was completely without her brother's whereabouts.

My turn came. For the very first time, I was allowed to enter the "sacred" consular main office where some officers worked individually behind large desks. I was seated at the very first one. A big bespectacled man heard my best English. All the other refugees were speaking German. At long last and at least, this very first real American I ever talked with was listening to me and what's more, he actually understood. He was carefully studying the affidavits with the attached financial statements, the ones that were sent over a year ago from Uncle Maxie in New Jersey. While doing so, all of his fingers met, forming a Gothic tower which touched his closed lips. As he was leaning back, comfortably, his elbows were resting on the arms of a swivel chair. Having never seen such fun furniture, I was somewhat distracted by it. As he was thinking and explaining, that thing rocked and swiveled to all sides, diminishing the seriousness of the matter at hand. After opening and closing his steeple, he concluded: "You may return here next spring. After proper processing, you might be issued an immigration visa to the United States of America."

I had to control my enthusiasm. It was as though all the violins descended from heaven playing only for me. When I inquired about my parents' quota, my total joy was dimmed by his answer: "No, not them for they are Polish. It is unforeseeable when their number will come up, sometime in the early 40's, possibly '42," he said very calmly with a friendly: "O.K.?" From that moment on, I learned that this 2-letter-question by an American signals: "Your time is up!"

Later, I found myself strutting down the *Keyserlei*. This atmosphere fitted in the realm of my up-beat mood. I heard in back of me: "*Gnaediges Fraeulein, gnaediges Fraeulein!*" Knowing who the caller was, did something to me. I had time to recover from whatever it was that affected me. I turned around: sure, there he was, a vision, tall, virile, and handsome!

"Dr. Koenigsmann!" I exclaimed, not quite successful in concealing my delight seeing him for the very first time sans Mutti.

"*Gnaediges Fraeulein!*" he repeated, facing me now. Our greetings sounded musically "allegro."

"You practice wearing your Palestine wardrobe already: an open-collared short-sleeved shirt, and sea-breeze tan!" I remarked while further suppressing my pleasant surprise at running into him.

I envied his tan, his openness, when he said: "Once more I have the great pleasure of seeing you, just once more," adding "Yes, it's this week-end that I leave for Palestine," nodding to the last words, as though in disbelief of them. "Let's celebrate our last being together! Now that my future is taking shape, I need not be that frugal at such an auspicious occasion. May I invite you for a drink?"

It was wonderfully charming and deliciously sinful to walk with this striking six-footer. He led me into the elegant terrace café

of the Century. As we were seated in the comfy chairs surrounded
by glamorous people, we looked at each other wordlessly, not only
in mutual admiration but in awe of our lost lifestyle which we
were only allowed to recapture for this fleeting moment.

"Try *Dubonnet!*"

This *apéritif* was as bittersweet as was this first and last
coincidental get-together. It also enhanced the warm and cozy
feeling I experienced in his company. I felt very grownup and
distinguished as we tried to appear in a merry way.

From the hotel-café's interior, the sounds of the piano music
could be heard, playing the latest hit: "Tonight, I must not think
of her, music, Maestro, please!" How busy my mind and my whole
being have been kept so I forgot Maurice and yesterday. What a
terrible and lonesome Sunday it has been, par contrast, what a
Monday!

I thought to myself: I have been to the Consulate, to Havana,
back to Antwerp, where I finally received a flicker of hope for the
U.S., and now, I'm having this enigmatic *tête-à-tête* at a spot I
could only admire from afar. When he gently kissed my hand, two
thoughts crossed my mind: "My reputation!" and: "I shall dream
about this hour!"

"Here's to Palestine—after all! I shall relive there this day with
you!" lifting his glass. When mine touched his, I confessed my
feelings.

Our conversation got so animated when I told him about
Rosalie's warnings. We had a lot of fun with this story. When I
imagined, however, tomorrow's self-imposed agenda, to look for
apartments in those questionable houses, he grasped my fingers
with genuine concern asking: "What shadows flitted over you just
now?"

I was ashamed and instead reported yesterday's disappointing
happening, omitting the cousin-romance.

For a moment, I expected him to say that I made too much of
it, but no: this time, he kissed my hand again as though to express
his compassion: "No, I understand very well, you felt abandoned,
and that is our general feeling right now: "The earth has abandoned

us, all corners of the world have abandoned us, and to boot, you felt the very personal abandon by your own people as well."

Then I told him about our arrest leading up to our staying with the relatives again.

He related his similar "6 AM police story." Since he could produce a bona fide visa to Palestine, unlike us, the Belgians did not take him to their precinct. That is when he went to the shore: Ostend, Blankenberghe and Knokke.

"You would have loved it there!" he exclaimed while appearing to amuse himself with his own imagination and continued: "Not only would it have served the glorious summer months some fun— and peace of mind, as to your fiesta concept, you would have liked dancing to live music at midday and the constant movement everywhere and anytime!"

"Of course, as much as I relish gaiety and the quality of fresh air that surrounds that kind of life, I would really enjoy the sight of an ocean for the first time!" I said starry-eyed.

It really bothered me that my parents would not do this for me or—for themselves. He seemed to notice every slight nuance of my thought or mood and was curiously inquisitive. Instead of revealing my ennui, I told him about my friendship with the *"Riga Café's"* daughter Lili, how I frequented there, and above all, how I would have adored joining her in Knokke.

"Ostend is really not that expensive, and think of it, an entire season without fugitive worry and, wonder of all wonders, a festive world—can you beat that!?" he exclaimed.

He must have sensed that I was looking for a last straw where living quarters in Antwerp were concerned when he said as though apologizing: "After the police incident, my landlord would not want any part of refugees again. He grew weary of the aggravation, helpful as he tried to be."

"So, in a way, I don't feel quite as bad about the *'pre-Berchem'* time, when I felt so rejected after I saw the 'to let'-signs with 'No Aliens! No Jews,'" I consoled myself and Dr. Koenigsmann agreed that they did not just act from pure anti-Semitism but for the sake of self-preservation.

Suddenly he exclaimed with pathos: "Don't you anticipate doom, that dark cloud hanging over us? Don't you catch the current of unrest, the fear of an ominous happening about to present itself, the anguish that is befalling the refugee community of Antwerp, while the Jewish-Belgian citizens are still dancing at the shore, unheedingly?"

With strong passion in his voice, and pressure on my fingers obviously underestimating his physical strength, he got so carried away with his questions of our fate that he answered them himself: "I sense the coming of something terrible! I smell gunfire! I hear the Nazi warriors shouting: '*Los, los*! On the double! Get going! *Achtung!*" Now he slackened his grip on my hands for a moment, but then again grabbing and shaking them as if to awaken me from a deep sleep, repeating his question: "Well, don't you, don't you?"

I felt embarrassed with my selfish answer: "When I first arrived here, I realized how closed the world really was for us. There will be war because the Allies want that the Russians and Germans, their two biggest enemies, the Communists and Nazis, kill each other before they, the Allies, eventually will step in . . . if— absolutely necessary . . . but lately" I interrupted myself with a sip of *Dubonnet t*o avoid his steady gaze, and I was somewhat ashamed, when I continued: "but lately, I have been so busy circumventing the various messes, while trying to leave the country. Besides, I am not one for morbid thoughts and somber sentiments though I share your feelings. Nobody tried as hard as I: visa-hunting from consulate to consulate, from embassy to embassy."

"Go anywhere you can! Just leave Europe! But Palestine? That's our hope, our future as it was our past! There is a parable to nature: wherever there was a stream, it surely will return to that spot. So shall we: the Jews to Palestine!" he concluded emphatically.

"You sound like Theodore Herzl, like . . . Zealots." I said timidly as I was taken back by such sudden Zionist fervor on his part.

"As you said: 'They accepted me, I accepted them fully,'— thus making the best of my situation setting out to create my optimal position."

I went on to tell him about Koeln, Hamburg, Havana, Miami and my jubilant success to finally be able to sit vis-à-vis a real American, and what's more, a real American consulate official. After we shared the tragic odyssey of the "St. Louis," and especially that I knew one of the passengers personally, this ocean drama was even more touching. My funny account of the swivel chair led us to the momentary glamorous, amorous present.

"I do not wish to spoil our last hour together," he said defensively, "but will you really go to the U.S. alone? Observing your Frau Mutter (Mrs. Mother, politely in German) she will hold on to you as she did, when we first met in the queue; the other time, she preferred running out into the pouring rain!" With this, we burst out laughing. He seized the opportunity to hug and kiss me—to my surprise. For a while he had the most wistful expression. Then he continued: "As I mentioned before I saw you right there at the corner, when you stood near the little guy in the big '*Nieuwe Gazet*'-hat yelling about Czechoslovakia being incorporated into the Third Reich. I was in back of you and your Mutti, but knowing her reaction and hearing another Hitler victory, I just walked away in total disgust."

"It seems the "baddies" always win," I mumbled, feeling I had lost some cherished, interesting hours or even moments I could have shared with this enchanting man.

I did not want him to walk me to the relatives' house—just the gateway of poor *Borgerhout*. Now the sad bidding adieu had arrived. It was as though an impenetrable mist of emotions subtly and suddenly was forming between us as we gazed into each other's eyes for the longest and last time, when he said with a changed soft voice: "I shall weave endless fantasies about this first, last and only *rendez-vous* of ours. I shall pine for you!" as he was shaking my hand for a finalizing farewell—again underestimating his strength— I felt my fingers slowly and gently slipping out of his strong hand.

There was a distance between us now—after I walked away, he cupped his hands around his mouth and shouted: "I shall weave endless fantasies about this afternoon!" and repeated: "I shall pine for you!"

When I literally reached the wrong side of the tracks, a train rushed by above. Its whistle intensified the feeling of wanting to be far away and safe. As I was still walking underneath the railroad bridge, I turned around one final moment to wave back at that handsome Gestalt whose image was to remain with me a long time for what it was: a bittersweet memory.

As I continued to walk, I realized that a beautiful day, an interesting hour, yes, just a fleeting fascinating moment is a gift from and to life.

Chapter 5

I felt immense emotional relief that I was able to steer Maurice back to a cousin-friend relationship. There was value and virtue in it, holding very special importance for my immediate plans. They consisted of finding living quarters in or around the district of ill repute as a very last resort, thus being in the clear with registration. Maurice was the only one to whom I could reveal my scheme. Even that was a challenge! It took a lot of persuasion to convince him of my idea. On our way he expressed his skepticism by asking: "So you really want to go through with this?" "Do I? What a question? Want to? Have to! There is no other way!" Mockingly I continued: "I finally got you to go downtown with me and now, midway, you are getting second thoughts before arriving at Statie Straat. First we'll canvass door to door on Astrid Plein!"

As usual this entire Plaza was decked out with marvelous colorful floral arrangements. Why on that very same place these sleazy houses could be found was beyond me. Though at this moment, after I had just decided to live here, it did feel much better to be surrounded by beauty. Also, *Astrid Plein* sounded not nearly as bad as *Statie Straat*. We didn't have to look hard at all. An old pipe-smoking fisherman-type showed us a furnished large studio with a door leading into a small room that barely had space for a comfortable bed. I pictured myself finally sleeping alone without Mutti's elbows disturbing me. I would be able to get up at a reasonable hour—and all this heaven without legalities! Of course, I didn't expect such luxury as a bathroom but a plain sink with running water I did! To my dismay there was only a tiny one on the landing with no door for privacy. That would present some problems but with a room all of my own I shall adjust to any inconvenience! I consoled myself. When I showed the flat to my parents a few hours later, they were happy to take it. The nocturnal arrangement was pure delight: The good rest showed in my face and demeanor and helped me over the entire situation. I did not see anything bizarre going on in the house although it was a neighborhood of whores. In the mornings I had to wash with a watchful eye and ear and many times had to dash back to our flat. When it was quiet again I rushed out to finish.

I resumed my classes and, through Rosalie's contacts, acquired many new students. The last summer weeks passed quickly. On my rare spare time, I went out with her or sometimes Charlotte. One evening I introduced them to Lili at the "Riga" when she handed me a letter from Palestine. Recognizing the sender, I opened it nervously. Starting facetiously with "*Gnädiges Fräulein*" he explained that he had to take out time from hard physical labor to write the brief message. One of the "endless fantasies he was weaving" was the wish that I could be by his side to share the sight of the blue Mediterranean. But he also stressed that I would not like the arduous life of the settlers. He concluded: "*Pages of hard work are written on my face. Just as I predicted, many mountains must be climbed here. I feel such nostalgia for a Nazi-free Europe, such longing for a Mutti-free you, such yearnings for the very last glamorous, amorous hour we spent together at the terrace. I leave while embracing you with my tender affections and a strong Shalom!*"

Teenage girls will always be avidly interested in romance. They insisted I share my story with them. I had to start from the very beginning with the US-consulate-line, followed by the tribulations Mutti caused at subsequent chance-meetings. The night was no longer young when I bade them good-bye after they had listened in awe. In a few minutes I was "home". At the corner of *Astrid Plein* and *Statie Straat* were a few "dames" clad in silver foxes and pure silk stockings. Their dresses were fluffy and seductively décolleté. They were batting their long false lashes accompanied by a few French words shamelessly addressed at the male passers-by.

I was so happy that it was Vati who opened the door upon my three knocks. I used the father-daughter privacy to show him the letter and refresh his memory.

The following morning, a stranger's voice had awoken me. The man was talking in broken German to Mutti in the adjacent studio. I listened and caught the gist of what was being said. He sounded like an officer. Mutti in her bravura denied my giving lessons illegally, in fact, she denied my being in the apartment altogether, stating that I was at the shore. Now my secret was out! But how had it reached the precinct? Who would possibly squeal on me? I had never taught in this flat and only given lessons to "my people". It had not even occurred to me that my teaching English was illegal—maybe because my whole life was. Now, of course, through the policeman's sudden appearance, our unlawful stay was discovered. We had to move on like an old refrain: "Back to the relatives!" And that after only one month.

This time Maurice came up with a workable idea: "Let's try a totally Gentile neighborhood, where nobody is aware of Jewish refugees from Germany." "Yes Maurice, we must always be one step ahead, just like seasoned criminals. Look how prepared we are now with only a minimum of belongings so that moving does not represent as grave a problem as it did the many previous times. Of course, Maurice, I shall be ever so grateful to follow your clever suggestion and I trust we won't fail," I answered while we carried the barest essentials to his house.

Always eager to exchange opinions and advice with other refugees my parents and I went to my favorite corner of *Pelikaan Straat* and *Keyserlei*, from where the squeaky voice of the boy from the *Nieuwe Gazet,* the old baritone from *L'Independance* and the usual sober monotone of *Le Soir* emerged particularly aggressive tonight. We hastened our steps. The vendors had a field-day. They were surrounded by the largest mass of people ever. ON SEPTEMBER 1 AT 0445 HOURS POLAND WAS INVADED BY NAZI FORCES WITHOUT A DECLARATION OF WAR!

We were all stunned and in severe panic about the future. The crowd dissolved, as we were walking with heavy hearts. Suddenly Vati said in a whisper: "There, at the corner of *Vesting Straat* in front of the Diamond Exchange, the tallest in that group of men, that's Mr. London!" "That's Mr. London?" I exclaimed, dropping all distressing thoughts about Poland, the war and Hitler. The cluster flocked around him. They listened to him as one would to the sounds of a heavenly harp. He exuded compassion and charisma. Though everyone looked up to him, but he had no trace of arrogance in him. I was impressed: "You talked so much about him, Vati, but you never mentioned how handsome he is!" As we passed I heard some of his comforting words: "It's just a Nazi bluff. Wait until the British and French ultimatums will arrive in Germany! We shall see what will happen then!" I approved of what was said, how it was said and especially of the person!" The image of Mr. London played tricks on me: "What a man! What a fantasy!" I reflected while trying to conjure up Dr. Königmann's tanned smiling face. Sadly enough, it was growing more distant.

Later on that night, I had the yoghurt-style sour milk with my three cousins. Maurice stirred his slowly while looking meaningfully at me. I lowered my eyes, trying both to avoid yet another romantic entanglement, and a political conversation with Frima. I broke the silence to ask Maurice about his schedule, in order to pursue his idea for a flat in a neighborhood I had never seen before.

Again Mutti's inconsiderate manners made it so difficult to fall asleep. How I missed the privacy of my own small room with that large bed! How I missed Dr. Königsmann! How I missed knowing someone like Mr. London—I figured that he must be twice my age at least. But his graying temples only enhanced his distinguished appearance. I scolded myself: What are you doing? There's a war going on and here you are reflecting on handsome men. Plus, Mr. London didn't even look in our direction, he was so absorbed consoling his friends.

A few days later, Maurice led me to what at this moment was to me "The Promised Land." On the way there, upon arriving at the *Plantinlei,* we stopped cold—overwhelmed and open-mouthed we grabbed each other's hands. The entire length of the center island was covered with tanks and all types of combat equipment. This historic event unfolded in front of our very eyes right now, right here. We looked at each other in bewilderment. Maurice exclaimed: "Oorlog! La guerre!" and I: "Krieg, Krieg!" All of it meant: "War!" I had read these words as headlines upon my arrival in Antwerp, not knowing their meaning. But now, I did not only understand these foreign words, but I also felt their foreboding and doom. It was just as Dr. Königsmann had predicted. After my initial shock at the sight of the war supplies, another realization deepened my fear. I shared it with Maurice: "What anachronism!" "Please, I'm not in the mood for your fancy words now! What is anachronism?" he questioned impatiently. "This military material is so obsolete and outdated compared to that of the Germans, which I saw in their numerous show-off parades. These tanks look as if they were leftovers from 1914-18." "They probably are. We were not prepared. These were most likely taken out of storage", Maurice tried to defend his country. Not getting over the antiquity of the 'panzers,' I joked: "One could think they even hailed from our grandfather's Crimean War."

As though conquered already, we continued our long walk that had started so briskly at a slow pace. In my mind this was accompanied by the sounds of fear: *La Finlandia*. Without a word we proceeded on *Pelikaan Straat's* right side underneath the railway bridge, watching all the busy diamond-dealer traffic across the street. It was satisfying, that at least business went on as usual. After we passed the Station entrance the beautiful flower beds on the Queen Astrid Place lay before us. I had never walked on the square's right-hand side. Here too was one lively café next to the other. I saw the "Billiard Palace" and, a few houses down, our unsightly last domicile. Shabby or not, how I wished that once again I would experience the glorious feeling of sleeping in a comfy bed in a room of my own. We turned into *Karnot Straat* and passed the "five and ten Sarma." This is where I bumped into Mitzi when she was beaming with joy despite the pouring rain. That's when I met her husband Fred and their beautiful children. Previously, I had classified him as the quiet sort. By now, I could understand what she saw in him. I missed running into them, chance meetings were the only way for get-togethers since, like criminals, we had to constantly change addresses. For a moment I forgot the military equipment and remarked: "This busy street with its nice, low-priced fashions surely is a woman's paradise." Maurice answered with a faint smile as he led me onto *Kerk Straat*. Some shops spilled over from *Karnot Straat*, but then the street became residential. The architecture was unlike anything I had ever seen. It looked like I had imagined the center of old Dutch or Scandinavian cities. After passing "Sarma"—never had I gone beyond—a whole new world! I could only fervently hope that Maurice was right and we could complete our mission. We started our quest on the cleanest, coziest, quaintest streets.

Unfortunately, there were no "leads" whatsoever for no "te huur" (for rent) signs were in sight. Though we accomplished nothing concrete, I knew at least where to "put my feelers out". On our way back we saw that a large crowd had gathered around the news boys. Their voices took a rest, while they were busy handing papers and money to and from eager readers. Upon getting closer we saw numerous important headlines:

> WAR HAS BEGUN!
> BRITISH AND FRENCH ULTIMATUMS EXPIRED AT
>   1100 HOURS AT 1115 HOURS WAR WAS
>   DECLARED BY GREAT BRITAIN, AUSTRALIA
>   AND NEW ZEALAND!
> ON THE SAME AFTERNOON, SEPTEMBER 3 AT
>   1700 HOURS THE FRENCH ANNOUNCED THE
>   BEGINNING OF A STATE OF WAR AGAINST
>   GERMANY!

"Oh my God, Maurice! It looks like a real war is brewing all around us—both East and West!" I exclaimed clutching his arm feeling personally threatened. I thought of Mr. London's consoling words to his friends about the ultimatum.

The following day, I took Mutti on the same long, but interesting walk. As we went further looking into each peaceful little street, the only people we saw were food merchants with pushcarts or horses and buggies. Mutti ordered me to inquire whether there was a flat for rent. I chose a green grocer with red cheeks, white horse and yellow buggy. He actually gave me a complete address: *Groenvinck Straat 79*. What a pleasant contrast to the somberness of the day before! A friendly tenant showed us the cozy apartment and described the way to the owners. We fervently hoped that since the landlords did not live on the premises, they might not require registration. Vati and I went to see them the next day. We had almost forgotten what rich neighborhoods looked like, forgotten that a maid in uniform would open the door, take Vati's hat and announce us. Nostalgia for our lost past enveloped us.

A big, jolly, good-looking blonde with a florid complexion wearing a floral print descended the wide curved stairway. It was quite a relief to see how friendly she was. A bit later, the husband joined us and the maid served coffee and pastries. Madame Van Houten tried her best to converse with Vati in German. I was afraid that she took him for one and would not give us the *quartier* if she knew we were Jewish. How dare people be so kind to Nazis, I thought. My malaise was lifted when Mr. Van Houten took a strong stand against them and their world shattering actions. "You are such nice people, we would be happy to have you as our tenants!" Madame Van Houten beamed. When she accompanied us to the front door, she volunteered the promise to add more finishing touches to the already lovely *rooms*. "And remember," Mr. Van Houten concluded, "whatever I can do, that the anti-Semites don't want me to do, I will most definitely do with the utmost pleasure!" He laughed while rubbing his palms.

We used our good fortune by moving immediately. Having the flat-hunt off my chest, mind and feet, I was finally free to make use of what my present life had to offer. Unlike in *Berchem* the daily walk downtown was pleasant and interesting. One morning someone addressed me with: "*Gnädiges Fräulein!*" It was Mr. Rinsky. I was glad to have run into him and his wife Trudy. She made arrangements to take up English again. When they arrived, they admired our flat and remarked that no other refugees lived as comfortably. Since her emigration to the U.S. was forthcoming, Trudy studied very hard. Driven by the fear of being left without his wife, Mr. Rinsky was even a more fierce lemon-sucking nervous wreck than before. Through them, Rosalie and recommendations from others, I was soon swamped with students. I enjoyed my growing popularity as a teacher.

On September 6, 1939, there was again a lot of hectic activity at the news casting corner with:

CHAOS IS SPREAD IN THE POLISH REAR BY
LUFTWAFFE!
GERMAN U-BOATS SINK 53 ALLIED SHIPS!

Aside from the Poland campaign these headlines were the talk of the day:

U.S. PROCLAIMS NEUTRALITY
SOUTH AFRICA DECLARES WAR ON GERMANY

Yet three days later they looked a bit better. There was a first victory for the suffering Poles. Strangers around the news stand smiled at each other. I was the object of glowing glances that I reciprocated with glee. And then: what a pleasant coincidence! The four familiar faces of the Horovitzes! They looked marvelous! Being so busy playing host to many stray refugees, it was rare, indeed, that the entire family was out together. After I had told them about my present good fortune with the nice apartment and the successful teaching, they gave me the address of a young Parisian who wanted to learn English.

The following day, I met Anette, a milliner, at her own hat shop. A tall slim 24-year-old with a ready smile, she looked exactly as I had imagined a Parisian: beautiful and sophisticated—except for her large, round, innocent eyes. She was bursting with anticipation to study. Although she was neither a refugee nor in dire economic straits, she desired to immigrate to America. Her husband manufactured the hats which she and most other shops in Brussels and Antwerp sold. They were the happiest couple I ever met, constantly laughing at their many private and public jokes. I had some spare time that Anette wanted to utilize for her first lesson. She paid me quite a few *francs* over my usual charge. She wished to take a class seven nights a week. I had to change the phonetics for my only French-born student. Her rapid understanding of English amazed me. Her accent was bewitching, but there was no way for her to pronounce the letter "h" which was silent in her mother-tongue. I took a deep breath to show her how to exhale it into the "h". After another fruitless effort she remarked: "Oh, this reminds me of my dancing class, especially belly dancing, when we do staccato breathing which makes the diaphragm quiver." I could not believe my eyes: her stomach muscles seemed to perform their own passionate rhythm. Alas, it did not help Anette with the "h." I stopped trying and decided that this flaw only enhanced her charm. Anyway, I needed no more persuasion to join her class. After our lesson, we exchanged opinions on Terpsichore. Her parents had made her take ballet but she considered it to be too rigid and constricted in movement and creativity. She loved the classes at the *Quellin School* which offered rhythmic interpretative modern and international stage dances. I briefly described my experience: "Just as I can't recall when I started walking, I do not remember when I performed for the first time. I was told that I danced and sang as a three-year-old to the tune of '*Valencia*' placed on a table top of the famed restaurant 'The Golden Carriage' on Cologne's right bank."

"This will be your first formal training then!" Anette exclaimed. "You are the right age", she added. "But how can I afford to cancel all of my Thursday night English lessons?" I asked skeptically. "You'll find a way. Even if you have to switch to Sundays!" she encouraged me.

On the way to my next student I saw a crowd gathered around the paper boys. I heard the bilingual yelling: "CANADA DECLARES WAR ON GERMANY"

Returning home, I was delighted to see the apartment spruced up. "Madame Van Houten did keep her promise!" I applauded in admiration. Having been in such a rush the previous day, I had neglected to tell my parents what had happened. They were pleased to hear about the Horovitzes. I told them about Anette and the dancing class and my regretful decline fearing a financial loss. It touched me deeply, when Mutti talked me into taking the course regardless whether I could move my students to Sundays.

I loved every moment of the dance class! Seeing Anette and meeting so many other Antwerp girls was a delight. I was the only refugee there. Prior to the actual beginning, a blonde was rehearsing for a show. When the pianist started to play the "Polonaise" by Chopin she opened in a warrior-like fashion, artistically emulating the devastation in Poland in her interpretative modern style. I was mesmerized by her skill and stirred by the subject she so masterfully embodied. She resembled my beautiful half-Jewish friend of the school in *Lützow Strasse* in Cologne, Inge Kasper.

I could not get over the fact that Mutti had actually been better to me than I had to myself. Every Thursday night I was grateful to her for the enormous joy I experienced in each class, especially when I excelled in belly dancing. Records were used to accustom the Western ear to the strange, mysterious sounds of the Middle East. To my Jewish ear, however, they were not alien, but reminded me of the cantors, the chants and the *shofar*. Perhaps it was through my childhood reminiscences of synagogue, these wailings, at times happy melodies, stirred my blood.

September 11th, the first anniversary of our arrival in Antwerp was marked by the following headline: FIRST MEETING OF ANGLO-FRENCH SUPREME WAR COUNCIL!

In comparison to last year I felt so established. On my way to teach a young Hungarian, whose fiancé was waiting for her in the U.S., there was another surprise: I stumbled into Eta, the eldest daughter of the former neighbors, and her very tall, lean and bald husband, who had finally returned. Mr. Kenner, the ex-Spain-fighter tried to modulate my German pronunciation of the "ng" endings into true French nasals. It was almost like a vocalist's course. Grateful for his help and proud of myself I playfully consoled him that there was at least one great battle he had won: eliminating some German by killing the enemy sound in my French.

Since the move to *Groenvinck Straat*, I had settled into a routine of a kind that suited my temperament because it had many daily, even hourly variations. While most people tormented themselves with the question of whether the West would be Hitler's next prey, my only link with the war was the news corner and some of the politically informed people I encountered. Vati thought an attack would be most likely to happen in spring, because then a whole summer could be fought.

One day, September 25th our news stand was surrounded by people. I rushed over to read: "HITLER WISHES FOR A SWIFT COUP DE GRACE OF WARSAW BY TERRORIZING THE CIVILIAN POPULATION WITH BOMBARDMENTS UNTIL COMPLETE SUBMISSION!" Everyone was frightened. So was I! Two days later even a larger crowd was milling around the yelling paper boys:

WARSAW WAS TAKEN BY THE NAZIS UNDER
CONSTANT FIRE!
150,000 POLISH PRISONERS! EACH ONE BRANDED
ON THE BACK LIKE CATTLE!

We stood aghast! Unrest and angst were visible on everyone's face. Dr. Königmann's phrase of doom resounded in my ears. What could I, one young girl, do? I could only go on deluding myself about what was happening, trying to, yes, enjoy my daily activities. What else was there for me in this locked up world? Tell me, Dr. Königsmann, tell me! Now what? I could scream! Thinking of him, I passed the terrace of the "Century" to glance at the table where I had heard his words and where the beginning and end of our "almost romance" had taken place. Our farewell still touched my heart. The gray sky and slight drizzle only added to my sadness.

At this moment I felt my sleeve being tugged from the back. No, not by Dr. Königsmann, but by Mitzi and Fred! They had just returned from Ostend, Belgium's main coastal city, where they had spent the entire summer gazing in the direction of Dover, England. "Yes, we had a wonderful time and were able to block out our worries. For our children it was sheer paradise! Upon our return to this city, however, the same trouble started all over again. We wished the summer in Ostend had lasted longer. Among the international crowd we managed to get lost, but now only the locals remained, which spells danger! After the end of the season a seashore town can get depressing when it is empty, windy and rainy—even more so when the white cliffs of a dream-land such as England seem to beckon you from across. Yet there is nothing, absolutely nothing you can do!" They went into detail about their desperate, yet vain, apartment hunt encountering only shame and humiliation from the "No Jews!"—rejections.

So I told them about our good fortune and recommended our nice, Gentile neighborhood. Fred thanked me but declined to take my advice, explaining: "Good fortune you say! It's not just good fortune! Your parents don't know how lucky they are to have you with your languages, *savoir-faire* and youth. "Yes", he continued, not being able to suppress his bitterness and anger, "We'll ring the bell, they'll hear our speech and slam the door in our faces, thinking we are Germans. Asking in Yiddish the same will happen only with more impact."

Just at this moment—as happens often when talking about someone—my parents were coming down the *Keyserlei*. I spotted them before they noticed me. They looked so well, and their clothes from the year before still seemed new. How proud I would have been of them! However, Mutti's body language revealed her bickering. Vati was so happy at the first eye contact. As they came closer, Mutti answered Mitzi's friendly greeting condescendingly. She then turned to me and snapped: "One hardly sees you at home! The apartment is used by you like a hotel!"

Her harsh words suppressed my impulse to embrace them. Although deeply embarrassed, I was still able to do the introductions. Mutti seemed in a rush to walk on. Then it hit me: She wanted to get Vati away from Mitzi's good looks. The drizzle turned into a steady rain, and Fred pointed to a small café. All eyes were on Mutti, who accepted. After we had comfortably settled down there, Fred's amiable way put even Mutti at ease. He asked each one of us: "Do you know who Adolf Schicklgruber is?" Mutti looked at Vati and back to Mitzi—as though to check the effect of her innately coquettish way—and answered: "I know who Adolf is, but Schickl—what?—I never heard." "You got close enough", Fred said, "Yes, Adolf Schicklgruber is none other than Adolf Hitler. What a mixed-up family constellation in that Hitler household!" In awe, we listened to this twisted, true tale.

Later on, before falling asleep, I reflected on an ancient Latin saying: *There is no better medicine for man than man.* How true this was! After today's headline, a sadness bordering on depression was budding within me. But it subsided completely after the encounter with Mitzi, Fred and my parents.

Chapter 6

On the last Thursday of September 1939, I walked with great glee to my dancing class. I still felt grateful to Mutti for what I considered a very generous idea: relinquish teaching English and indulge in a course of rhythmic international stage dancing.

The shrill sound of the "Nieuwe Gazet" boy hit my ears even before I reached "my corner" with: "Extra! Extra! IT'S ALL OVER! THE POLISH RESISTANCE IS OVER! SOVIET-NAZI TREATY BEING FORMED!" His cheeks, and those of his elder competitors, were glowing with excitement. The rest of the news concerning the Soviet splitting of the Baltics, as predicted by Lili's father, amazed me.

My joyful state dissipated as I continued my walk. Upon entering the hallway of the school, I heard the soft, elegant piano music of a Chopin Valse. My original enthusiasm returned when I saw all of the friendly familiar faces. Some busied themselves with warm-ups and others ran to me, almost in a chorus, begging for a solo of Middle Eastern dancing. I was flattered that such a talented group considered me gifted enough to perform for them.

Though I heard the recorded poetic music of the oud, the pregnant forerunner of the guitar, the Elizabethian lute, the vibrating of the dumbeki, and the sorrowful, almost human wailing of the clarinet, I began to dance with snake-like undulations, which my classmates found mesmerizing. I felt revitalized with each lustful move and gentle tremor, imagining myself a priestess gliding through my palace. The music was highly emotional; its enigmatic attraction affected me. I had a natural knack and feel for this ancestral art form.

As the music grew more frenzied, so became my state of total abandon to the drumbeat. This duet I formed with the dumbeki had a vocabulary all its own. It also could be interpreted into moods and feelings. Mine, at this very moment, defined a longing for my inherent joie de vivre that produced such ecstasy within me. My performance unfolded like an ancient rhythmic prayer that my life would remain status quo. This Moorish dance slithered into earthy sensuality as I dreamt I was dancing for Dr. Königsmann. However, the dramatic lamenting sounds emphasized my utter despair.

When the music changed into happy instrumental playing, so did my spirit and body language, revealing a légère merry-making side of the dance. While undulating, I fancied myself performing for Mr. London, another inconceivable notion, since I saw him only once, and fleetingly at that.

The finale approached and I slid one leg forward, resting forehead upon knee, arms and hands back, signaling the closing scene. I enjoyed the cheers immensely. Invigorated, my emotions, desire, and body could have gone on forever.

As I left the school with an entourage of fans, we felt the crisp evening air, heralding autumn. The excitement aroused me to such a level of euphoria that, for the moment, the war was non-existent. Since my parents were still out, I had an urgent need to share my feelings with someone. With a burst of energy, I proceeded to start a long overdue letter to Dr. Königsmann telling him my news.

Suddenly, I was inspired to condense my individual lessons into a book. Since everyone liked my teaching and learned so rapidly under my system, I decided to create a primer based on my own phonetic method. Maybe it would be worth publishing. Regarding pronunciation, English is the hardest. There are no set rules as in French nor is it spoken the way it is written. Therefore, non-English speaking people must have a sense for which syllable is accentuated. I liked that indefinable feeling which could be linked to music and interpretive dance. As I approached my "Lesson One," I actually enjoyed formulating it and became so engrossed in the writing I resented the interruptions of Mutti's bickering as she entered the house.

"You should not have said that to my sister Henna! That was wrong!" Mutti shouted, muffling her voice in view of the late hour.

Without waiting for Vati's answer, she continued, "Now we know for a fact that we cannot immigrate to Canada. We want our money back! My sister Pauline, in Montreal cannot or will not send the thousands of dollars back we had to deposit. She could at least reimburse us in dozens of foxes" she finished, while inquiring, "Aren't Canadian foxes supposed to be the most sought-after furs here in Belgium?" I burst into hearty laughter, hearing about foxes.

"What are you laughing about? You don't even know what it's about and already you are taking your father's side!" She objected.

Vati just nodded with a sarcastic expression. We looked at each other and understood that we both were playing the role of powerless peasants, as we did when Mutti was in her mad moods.

"By the way, Maurice sent his regards to you and inquired about you and your classes while some Flemish wench wrapped herself unashamedly around him." Mutti hastened to add.

My natural high sank one notch lower. I concentrated further on my English method while Mutti accused me of being insensitive concerning a matter of such vital importance to all of us. "Why can't you appreciate my cleverness in having the immigration deposit returned?" She asked with inner fire.

I began to take her more seriously, but after a brief pause she added, "and that should be done with foxes!" I was not able to suppress a smile.

"Just once be serious and wipe that grin off your face!" She commanded imperiously and inquired, "What is so funny about Canadian foxes? You enjoy wearing mine. Besides, not only will we get our money back, but with the sale of them, we might even make a profit. I think it's a clever idea on my part, as are all my thoughts. They ought to be always admired," she concluded. "What's the matter with you? Why don't I get your respect and attention? What are you scribbling there anyway, you school girl?" She wanted to know, as her eyes wandered briefly over my notebook.

I explained my English system to her.

"Oh, sure. No professor ever devised such a brilliant theory! All these philologists from Vienna would never think of such masterful linguistics!" She exclaimed haughtily and continued in her inimitable way as she pulled a chair close to me. "I am talking about big money here, our money, while you are making an important deal with your penny-worth of classes."

By now, my vitality was converted into gloom, because my efforts were not recognized. Why should I not get the credit when I was the sole breadwinner? Furthermore, outrageous injustice brought on a bellyache. This always happened when Mutti wronged me. She knew that all the earnings from my classes went for food and shelter, the rest for my own clothing. In other words, I, a teen, in order to avoid digging into our meager savings, supported our family completely. There was no use in discussing this with her as I knew that it would be a no-win situation.

Wanting to recapture my earlier state of mind, I ran into the bedroom for privacy and indulged in cobra undulations, this time in a lingering dream-like way. I was rudely awakened out of my fantasies when I heard Mutti calling, "Fanni!" As she barged in, she commanded me to write an English letter to my cousin Ida. I complied, as she busied herself with a Yiddish one to Ida's Mom, Pauline. Both letters emphasized, as expected, the foxes.

Sometime after this, everything went smoothly. I actually enjoyed life with my popular classes, Thursday night dancing course, occasional dates, and continuing my English primer. Each brought a special kind of delight. The greatest happiness was that there was very little business for the paperboys. One could finally concentrate on people rather than the news.

In Antwerp, one could divide the residents into two social categories. The first were the affluent indigenous ones with their marvelous deep tan that they acquired from Ostend, Blankenberghe, and Knokke. The other class being the pale people and the refugees who did not have the means to enjoy such vacations.

For the first group, mastering the English language became a status symbol. Being in a far better position, they sensed the pressure on me and offered far more than my usual fee.

Before long, winter came, turning quickly into a bitter season. I felt brave trotting through the icy Sunday morning snow. Each step squeaked so strongly that I was afraid I would awake someone. It was my busiest day, so I left early, fitting each student into my geographical plan, working my way up into the heart of Berchem. When I passed the house of the old Rinsky couple, I could visualize the police arresting us at dawn. On the way, I saw that menacing silhouette of the ancient fortress' towers that were so fear inspiring on previous occasions. How much more content I felt now by comparison!

The compensation for this lone, cold, windy walk was the warmth I received from each of my various pupils on my long route. Each student was a welcome interruption and made my tedious Sunday haul appear far more pleasant. I enjoyed them regardless of their level of competency or reason for studying my favorite language.

Those that had to learn English for survival were composed of a whole bevy of wives without husbands with a lower quota. The men were fortunate enough to reside in the U.S. already, leaving their loved ones behind to fend for themselves until they would some day join the men. I could not understand that of all nations, the family-oriented Americans would have so cruel a law that separated whole families and imposed such harsh regulations on people already harassed and tormented.

Once, I saw one of my student's children being reprimanded by her mother for simply acting like the child she was. They should have left the country one month before and the Belgian authorities no longer allowed them to stay here. The mother crammed her own fist into her mouth, with eyes widened for fear of being found out. The girl understood and defensively kept her flat little palm against her lips, realizing her cardinal sin of talking slightly louder than she should. I felt a bit guilty because, when she saw me, she wanted to impress me with how well she had remembered her English and shouted, "hello, teacher!" This jeopardized not only her and her mother, but also her neighbor-friends and their children. They would literally be on the icy streets should their illegal status be revealed.

How fast we forget, I thought, recalling my own plight as an illegal refugee before meeting our present landlords, the van Houtens. I was in a state of selfish gratitude that my life had improved so dramatically.

Some Sundays, my parents would pick me up at my very last stop, which they referred to as "The waiting wives with children in Berchem." This was nice, for I would not have that very long walk back through the night, wind, and snow all alone. They did not seem to mind spending so much time in that winter scene. I felt warmth toward them for so sweet a gesture. Although, this happiness was short-lived upon realizing that I was to be the arbiter of their childish arguments. Each tried to make me feel very important. In the meantime, we had established a daily routine which desensitized us from the fear of the war's prelude. Everyone else filled their empty lives with keen awareness of dread at the looming "Krieg," trying to figure out in which geographical direction Hitler's deadly arrows of destruction would aim for next.

One day, two letters arrived for me. How disappointing to have spotted my own handwriting on the envelope. The one addressed to Dr. Konigsmann in Palestine returned undelivered with the postal mark "UNKNOWN." I was very hard on myself with constant reproaches for not having answered him much earlier. Now there was no chance in ever contacting him again. This distressed and depressed me.

The other one was from the U.S. It was primarily a thank-you note from Trudy Rinsky, a satisfied student who made it to the U.S. Of course, she was happy to be there, but had a tremendous amount of adjusting to do in her new surroundings. *"It is not just another country; the lifestyle is like another planet,"* she pointed out, and went on, *"Though people have much less time here than in Europe, they are most helpful and go out of their way to show me the manner of living here. For you, my dear, life here would be sheer paradise."* Needless to say, I ate my heart out but wished her well.

Thereafter, everything continued at a modified pace. Along with the winter, however, came a sense of confusion. The ongoing dread of war caused negative mood changes in most of us, and quite especially in Mutti. She had fits of passionate hysteria over miniscule refugee inconveniences. This provoked a dramatic reaction. For instance, Sunday evenings in Berchem became most disagreeable. We lived in a far better state (thanks to our landlords and my classes) than did our co-refugees. Mutti seemed to suffer more than all of the others and expected us to commiserate. By now, I would have preferred to trot back through the snowy nights all by myself to keep my head and mood up high. I managed to do so over the entire season. My throb for life just went on and on. Involved in many projects during my waking hours, the cold came and went. Now, it became known as "The Winter of the Phony War." At the French front, soldiers were dying—of boredom. They had lunch in the forest, and played cards. The only war going on was a battle of propaganda. English leaflets bombarded German troops. The Nazis were broadcasting across the French Maginot Line.

Spring came early, bringing a fragrant excitement in the air. The long icy Sunday walks to Berchem turned into a wonderful experience every time. I was in touch with Mother Earth's refreshing scenic view which created a great "by-product" for me: acquaintances and friends, who walked there for an outing into the budding nature. For me, this was an incidental joy within an idyllic setting. Which up to now, I could never appreciate due to the disagreeable circumstances.

As the weather grew more beautiful, I ran into all my lost friends as I was crossing Berchem Park. This elicited many invitations to the house of my favorite Antwerp family: the Horovitzes. Also, after Sunday's classes, there were get-togethers with Lili, Rosalie, and Charlotte.

Since my time was limited, I introduced all of my girl friends to each other so that we became one jolly group winding up at the "Dancing" or another dansant. En route to my Berchem students, quite a few hats were tipped and raised politely, which I acknowledged. I enjoyed all the attention and flirtations. It was as though I suddenly was transplanted from blustery strict Russia into sunny, free California. Encountering all these smiling friendly faces, I felt as though I was in Hollywood. This made me blossom simultaneously with the nature surrounding me, all contributing to my forgetting that I was a refugee. In my optimism, I voiced my very own thoughts that maybe, just maybe, Hitler's insatiable appetite was assuaged. Upon this, everyone posed the same brief key question, "For how long?"

I had just left the office of a new lady student when I walked to the nearby "news-casting corner." It appeared now as it did in the past. A crowd was gathered around the boys screaming of Denmark and Norway. My curiosity quickened my pace as I pondered why they would invade the North, when they pride themselves so much on their Nordic race. I thought of Sweden being next, while imagining the "Scandinavian Dog" on the map. With these consoling thoughts, I reached the newsstands. After many "excuse me's" gliding through the crowd, I read breathlessly.

"QUISLING BETRAYED HIS COUNTRY, NORWAY AND HIS KING HAAKON." I remembered the name Quisling mentioned, along with other Hitler bootlicking traitors, by Lili's father and mine. Vati was right in his claims that the Führer would attack in early spring so the concentration would be on the war efforts rather than the elements. The article continued:

"NAZI WARSHIPS ARE ANCHORED IN THE PORT OF COPENHAGEN. BY NOON, ON THE DAY OF THE ATTACK APRIL 9TH, 1940, THE ENTIRE COUNTRY OF DENMARK WAS OCCUPIED. THE FOLLOWING EARLY MORNING, NORWAY'S CAPITAL, OSLO, WAS ALSO OVERPOWERED. BEFORE NIGHTFALL, ALL OF THE MOST IMPORTANT HARBORS SURROUNDING NORWAY WERE SEIZED."

My own reaction upon grasping the news was the same as those around. "Sweden would be next, thus alleviating us from immediate danger for at least some time. Maybe forever since an 'American miracle' might happen in the meantime. With that optimistic thought, I headed home, since there were still a few students lined up to take their lessons.

Arriving at Groenvinck Straat 79, where I lived for the longest and happiest time in Antwerp, I noticed a black man passing by everyday at noon. I had never seen a Negro before. Except once, when I was a child and a circus came to town. There were very old, shriveled little black men rolling up the carpets. But, I had never seen a specimen like this! He carried a white stick indicating he was blind, and loaded with as many of the largest bars of chocolate his big, strong hands would permit. My curiosity about this strange passer-by intrigued me to such a point that I felt compelled to ask my neighbors about him.

The husband was most anxious to impart information. As though wanting to share a personal secret, they called me inside behind closed doors to tell me the following: "His name is Ralph, and he is a famous boxer!" Mijnheer Schriver, my neighbor, and father of two little girls, continued in a childlike excited manner, "The poor fellow was very popular all over the U.S. and Europe until he came here to Antwerp. He was knocked out and blinded by his vicious adversary. Since he could no longer move about, he made Antwerp his home. He never returned to his native country, the U.S., to stand the disgrace. He is married to a local candystore owner. His fans tried to give him their hard-earned Belgian francs. But Ralph refused to accept donations. So after much persuading, Ralph's wife convinced him to sell chocolates. Now, he has a thriving sweet business."

I thanked Mr. Schriver and said, "I must talk to this Ralph. Though, I am afraid because I have never spoken with a black American."

"One is always fearful of the unknown," he encouraged me.

So, the following day, I mustered up the courage to approach him on the street. His enormous hand shook mine, the minute I said, "Excuse me, I wish to chat with you for I have never spoken to an American and I would like to check out my English." As I said this, I was shocked to discover that his palms and fingernails were almost white.

He was delighted, answering with a warm smile of snowy teeth. He spoke very soft English, which was alien to me. It was reminiscent of the American Jazz I heard when I first arrived with Mutti in

Antwerp. There was a connection between that music and his accent. In an amiable way he said, "I feel in my bones that you are beautiful."

"Well, how can I reply to that? I like the way you say the word 'bones'."

He then proceeded to state what I did not expect at all, "Within the next few weeks, a terrible disaster will happen. It will be horror the world has never seen. There's going to be an outcry, an awesome earthquake, a genocide or an inferno in this part of the globe. It will be like the end of the world, I feel it in my bones. Just as I feel that you are a young, fine, and beautiful lady. You judge for yourself whether you fit that description. You mark my words. You will remember this brief encounter for the rest of your life! Within only weeks, this awful happening will occur. I wish you all the luck in the world. You must believe me!"

Again, I shook this handsome giant's hand, and walked away with mixed feelings. This bizarre meeting took a totally different direction than I had expected. His prediction was frightening. I consoled myself in the thought that when he got knocked out, not only did he lose his sight, but he may have suffered mental losses as well.

Nevertheless, I continued enjoying every day of my interesting semi-routine life. This spring was exceptionally glorious. At the end of one exuberant, lovely day in May, my last stop was at the diamond washer's. Madame Zandmeer and her niece were there. I heard so much about how smart, nice, and beautiful she was. Some people even walked up to me on the Keyserlei, asking whether I was Miss Zandmeer. Now that I saw her, I felt extremely flattered and hoped she did also. Both of us looked in the mirror, and when our eyes met, each of us seemed to know the other's thought. We burst out into an embarrassing giggle so characteristic of young girls. Hours later, I fell asleep, still smiling about the pleasant scene in the mirror.

Sometime between the night and the wee-hours, a steady strange noise awoke me. Those annoying thud-like singular sounds seemed to come from the sky, but they did not sound heavenly at all.

"Vati, Vati, tell me is that really shooting?" I suddenly found myself dashing out of bed and asking him hysterically and repeatedly that same question.

"Yes, yes mein Kind, these are real shots. Now, they are coming to get us. It will be the greatest disaster for mankind but quite especially for us." Vati nodded with great sadness.

In the meantime, people from neighboring houses were looking to the nocturnal skies, yelling from their windows in frenzy, "Les Boches! Les Boches!" "La guerre! De oorlog!" Now I understood that this meant "war."

The night became another beautiful May Day. The repeated gunshots made small puffs of smoke in the break of dawn. Vati nodded sadly again, "Yes, Fannichen, it's our turn now. It's the beginning of the end of our world!"

I remembered that black, blind man, who felt this in his bones only two short weeks ago.

Chapter 7

It was May 10, 1940, another sunny, balmy day, the type that is ever depicted in poetry. Since we lived in a Gentile neighborhood it was of dire importance to learn what was really happening. We quickly dressed and rushed downtown. The streets looked drastically different from the time when Maurice and I were looking for an apartment. In September of 1939, when the Nazis attacked Poland, business here still had gone on as usual. Now, when it hit home everything came to a halt. Shops and offices were closed. Our most important link to the outside world, the newsboys, were missing. THIS TIME WE WERE THE NEWS! IT WAS THE HERE AND NOW MAKING HISTORY! An atmosphere of fear and confusion prevailed. People were swarming like ants into the train station. Some were walking aimlessly, others running purposefully. There were small groups huddling around. Some individuals and families were just milling about.

I noticed the pathetic silhouette of a man sitting on a big brown trunk. As we came closer, we saw him bite into a lemon with a vengeance. Of course, the tragic figure was Mr. Rinsky, the worst student I ever had. So glad was he to see us, that he quickly rose to embrace us. He was full of self-pity and anguish, but weren't we all? He sobbed: "What am I going to do without my Trudele? Were am I going to go?"

"What are we all going to do, where are we all going to run?" we asked. He continued a little firmer: "I know one thing though. I'll leave this city. Even a suicidal person like me does not want to fall into the hands of the Nazis. I just don't understand anything any more—not even my Trudele." Shaking his head, he began to search his pockets. He produced a worn, crumpled letter and handed it to me: "I received this ten days ago. Please look at this part here, Fräulein!" Since there was so much going on around us, I read under duress. It said: "*Though there is no language barrier (thanks to our very young teacher) I feel very alien and alone here. It's like being on a different planet. Everyone is in a rush. Everybody is assigned a definite task. The evenings, when the relatives return from work are pleasant. So are the weekends. I must learn how to adjust. Above all, I must learn a trade. At my age-*"

"For heaven's sake, what's going on here?" a man behind me snapped. Before I could turn around to see who it was he went on scolding me: "You have nothing better to do than read a letter at a time like this?" Tomorrow all of us are leaving", Fred stated resolutely and passionately urged us to do the same: "What are you waiting for? Go West or maybe North West! Get out of here! Run for your lives!"

"The gentleman knows what he is talking about." Mr. Stern, a relative of the Horovitzes, looking even more jaded than usual, agreed. There was a tall lanky man with him whom he introduced as his nephew Mendel. Mr. Stern told us that Sasha, his brothers and their families had left already. "As for myself, I am too old and weary. My wife of 18 months doesn't want to go either. But everyone in his right mind should and must leave!" he warned. "Forgive me," his nephew interjected, "but uncle Manny you just admitted not being in your right mind. How can you possibly insist upon staying here especially in light of everything I told you?" "Neither of us has the strength nor desire to flee," Manny persisted. I remembered his glowing Dutch bride and the smile on Mr. Stern's usually stern face at their makeshift wedding at the Horovitzes. "Tell them, tell them, Mendel, what these nice people can expect if they stay!" Manny encouraged him and explained: "Yes, my nephew had his experiences with the concentration camps of Sachsenhausen and Dachau. He was one of the first Jews at the "correction centers" that were mainly intended for Aryans who dared to oppose the regime and wanted to be just free humane Germans. They were intellectuals, professors and students. The university concierge, a Nazi, denounced their writing and circulating anti-Nazi leaflets. They were executed in mediaeval style on the chopping block."

Then Vati said with desolation: "Ja, ja! Little did I think it was meant literally when my own workers were doing the singsong: 'Heads must roll, heads must roll!' every Friday night when I provided all fifty with a keg of beer. 'Not yours, Boss' some added timidly in fear of the others."

"Let Mr. Stern continue", Mutti said impatiently. We all listened attentively as Manny told us his nephew's story: "What he saw, and what he lived through! The combination of his being hero and Houdini at the same time facilitated his recent escape. His 'crime?' He was caught 'smuggling' his own money from Germany into Belgium." Oh my God! I thought to myself, Vati was guilty of the same offense and was spared that terrible punishment. As a warning to us, Mendel set forth: "At the beginning they made us pull barrows loaded with wet earth up and down the muddy hills. This was a pointless task intended to torment and humiliate us. They did not want a Jew to feel satisfied for having accomplished useful work. My 'free' time was spent amusing and training their SS rookies-rowdies." He had to pause before he was able to continue in a quivering voice: "I'm still embarrassed when telling this dumb story: They made me crawl between the legs of a chair. Sitting on it, they yelled: 'Los, los, schnell, schnell', hitting and whipping the parts of my body that had not yet slid through. And they hated me less than any other prisoner."

"What he means is that he was their favorite", explained Manny looking at his nephew with admiration and love: "I am so happy you survived, my boy. Although I knew full well what a fighter you are, I had given up all hope. I am so proud of you for having liberated yourself against all odds."

Fred stated emphatically: "Before I run along to prepare for our departure, I have these last thoughts to share. I hope they will leave an impression on you. Following the news very closely I have detected this pattern in Hitler's operations: attack a country, create chaos, round up the Jews for annihilation." Turning to Vati he asked: "What do you have to lose now? You already lost everything two years ago: your business, your Mercedes, your trucks, tractor and trailers, your fine home with its lovely furnishings, your dignity. You don't have to invite your fifty workers to a keg of beer any more." Then Fred advised Mr. Rinsky, who stood a bit in the back: "Go home, unpack your big trunk and travel light tomorrow!" Shaking hands with Mendel: "Well, you are so much more experienced in these matters than I am. I know you'll make the right decision. I am mighty proud of your escape and curious how you pulled a stunt of such magnitude. I hope that there'll be better days when we will sit in peace and you will relate your odyssey. May we all stay well!" With these words he hugged me closely and bade an emotional farewell to my parents.

On our way home I tried to make sense of what we had just heard from Mendel. If he had indeed been their favorite the humiliations inflicted on him must have been of a comparatively minor nature. As everyone else, I had heard a lot about concentration camps, but Mendel was the first person I met who had been through that ordeal. While my parents were weighing their two options, I was conditioning myself to consider it an adventure. Instead of giving in to the utter despair and fear that I shared with the local Jews, and all fellow refugees, I began to feel excited focusing on the prospect of going to Paris and using my recently learned French. I was the first one to pack, tucking into my small suitcase dictionaries and music sheets, thinking that playing the piano might be my only means of support. With heavy hearts and worried heads we hardly slept that night.

The next morning was a copy of the previous one. Again we rushed to the train station. There were Belgian soldiers with machine guns and chains of bullets around their necks. Now and then we heard the crackling of guns in the distance, but it did not feel like a real war yet. Great confusion prevailed inside the station. There were none of the usual scenes of happy arrivals or tearful good-byes. All families and groups would either leave together or stay. Outside, passing cars loaded to the hilt with baggage, gadgets and household items on top, the back and both sides, projected a uniformly uncanny sight.

There was no Mr. Rinsky! My parents and I looked at each other and understood our silent question. Did he leave with his big trunk or did he listen to Fred? Even at a time like this, I loved our being so harmonious. Two fellows walked towards us at a fast pace. As I was trying to recall them, they exclaimed in unison: "You are the last people we see leaving Antwerp and you were the first ones we spoke to upon our arrival after we barely escaped the *Kristallnacht*." "You are the Bressler brothers who so daringly fled at the very last minute, yes, I remember", I stated. "I feel so flattered you do, Fräulein", said the taller, young, quite handsome one with a gleam in his eyes. In view of the present situation and their rush, I appreciated his attention even more. Mutti noticed the little interlude and sent me a disdainful glance. That look diminished the tenderness I had felt for her. Especially at times like these anything good must be cherished, I thought long after they had vanished in the crowd.

Still looking in their direction I saw Frima emerge from a group at the far end of the station, figuring out whether this little person was indeed she, I spotted Maurice. Neither of them saw us. I waved and jumped up to make them notice us, but Mutti commanded: "Stop that!"

Maurice pointed us out to his sister, then they pushed themselves through the mob. It was sheer delight to see Maurice's enigmatic face again. Since we had not been together for quite some time, we felt joy amidst all this fear and sadness. After the initial happy greetings, Vati turned to his niece and asked: "So what do your comrades have to say about this Nazi invasion of your country?"

"They and I know that the capitalistic Allies gave the Nazis the power to fight the so called dangers of Bolshevism. This, in turn, will weaken both sides so that the Allies can win easily over two drained forces and emerge as heroes. Clever, uh?" she answered glibly. I hated to admit that I admired her for being politically informed and fervently standing up for her belief. I could not take my eyes off of her until Maurice's piercing stare compelled me to look at him. Under Mutti's watchfulness he took my hand and said softly: "Realize that from now on you will be forced to continue running for your life like a fugitive criminal. No more affluence for you, my beloved cousin. We talked about the gathering clouds of war. Voilà, here's the storm! It's frightening while it lasts, but it will be over and remembered as just another page in history."

At this point a whole group of people interrupted the thoughts that Maurice had stirred up in me. Two were our former Hungarian landlords, the eldest daughter and her husband, who had been a "freedom fighter" in Spain. He was the very tall, lanky, bald man, who had improved my French considerably: "Now you'll see how well this will serve you in France, where so few speak Yiddish."

"At least you killed the enemy accent," I joked.

He addressed the whole group: "I know that you're all running to save your lives." "So you are my comrade, comrade!" Frima exclaimed. "Not really," he answered and went on to explain: "any Jewish freedom fighter is automatically considered a communist, whereas our prime purpose was to fight Franco's fascism." "I beg your pardon!" Frima snapped.

We were saved from further remarks by the arrival of the statuesque Erika from Erfurt, whom I had met at the 1938-39 New Year's party—mesmerized by her noble profile. It was then that her husband had been deported by the Nazis to Sbonzin and committed suicide at the barbed wire. This time, however, there was a sparkle in her eyes as she waived her train ticket to us, urging me to leave as well. We bade farewell to our relatives and friends. Maurice gave me a lingering, warm hug, murmuring: "Until we meet in far better times!"

On the way back to the apartment I was pleasantly surprised to learn that both of my parents shared my decision. "Here I thought it would take a lot to convince you to flee!" "No, we are not going to be sitting ducks", Vati replied. "Not exactly," I said, "because the rounding up of the Jews can only occur in Jewish neighborhoods and we are living in this Gentile place and—" "—and we'll be standing out like a sore thumb," Mutti finished my sentence and Vati concluded: "There's a far better survival chance here than in a Ghetto, though." Once more, we agreed, and our harmony increased my inner strength.

"What do you think of our relatives wanting to stay?" Vati asked. "Well they are too poor, Manuel is too sick with his constant cough and, like all Belgian Jews, they don't feel threatened by the Nazis," Mutti pointed out. "That's what the indigenous Jews are erroneously thinking," Vati shook his head in sympathetic disbelief. It was amazing how this animated conversation, though sad, made the long walk from downtown appear short. As we arrived for this last night, a mournful feeling befell us. We clutched each other and knew instantly that our sole resistance to fleeing was this cozy apartment, the only one which felt like home.

The next morning my parents packed our beige, elegant genuine pigskin suitcase. I asked myself fearfully: Where will I wake up tomorrow? What to leave and what to take so the bag will not be too heavy? "We must also keep in mind that even with money there will be nothing, virtually nothing available!" Weighing the luggage with a hand scale, Vati stressed, remembering the Great War, "therefore, we must be selective now."

"—unlike poor Mr. Rinsky with his big trunk", Mutti said, half in jest—half in pity. We downed our breakfast nervously. Suddenly, we were in such a rush, as though we had an important appointment. The farewell to our home made us choke. It was like saying "bye" to an old reliable friend not knowing whether we'd ever see him again.

For the first time we allowed ourselves the "luxury" of a trolley. It was another poetry-inspiring spring day, which greatly helped with my "adventure conditioning". There were still many of these strange looking fully packed cars leaving Antwerp. The owners were considered rich, because autos were not a necessity in the diamond business. Nobody wished to stay and experience first-hand what life would be under the Nazi yoke. That very thought enticed us to make our decision in time.

The inside of the train station looked the same as on the two preceding days: various groups milling around, some running in a definite direction, others pacing back and forth as if in a cage, worriers brooding and walking with fear and hesitance. Soldiers, perched with machine guns and chains of bullets, had been reinforced. There were some tearful good-byes this time. Apparently, the confident Belgian Jews were staying while their refugee relatives took off. Although we knew that our evacuation allowed my cousins no knowledge of our departure, it felt strange that there was not a single familiar face at the entire station. It was as if we were the last to go after all friends had left. What a lonely, scary feeling!

At this moment, I recalled fragments of past night's dream, depicting three people. Sometimes they were my parents and myself, sometimes fictitious, but there were always three tied with ropes onto a huge sleigh without rudder sliding down tremendous icy rocks. Facing the unknown was my interpretation of the nightmare.

My parents arrived with the tickets. Destination: Ostend! A new excitement obliterated the dream and misgivings. It was precisely where I was dying to spend the previous summer instead of having experienced the police chase. It was the wrong time but certainly the right place. Finally, I would see the ocean!

I was glad that we were part of those people who walked with a purpose. It was amazing how punctually the train arrived. Everything was perfect: we neither had to rush nor did we have to wait; there was no mob of people as one might expect during war time—the Flemish comprising the main population of Antwerp were not running from the Nazis because most of them were anti-Semitic—and finding seats for the three of us together was no problem.

We had mixed feelings when the train pulled out of the station rolling slowly alongside the familiar, usually lively and international *Pelikaan Straat* that now was so inactive. Then we passed the proud wide *Belgielei*, past *Mercator Straat* until its first stop in Berchem, the suburb we had lived in briefly with the old Rinskys. Many a memory, good and bad stirred within me.

Our compartment was soon full. Everyone was loaded with cumbersome baggage. As the escape-journey continued everything looked and felt delightful in the glistening late afternoon sun. Fragrant air entered through wide windows displaying the charming countryside in full spring splendor. "Everything looks so peaceful. Why can't it be so?" I asked my parents. They just shrugged and Vati nodded mournfully. They, too, seemed to be mesmerized by the serenity of the landscape, the simple farmhouses and the old barns and were lulled by the steady sound of the railroad track. Just as I was thinking that this was the trip I had been longing for the previous summer, the train stopped. There was no station. We had no idea what was happening. Needless to say that everyone grew impatient except Vati who kept his calm. He had prepared sandwiches—just as he used to do so lovingly in my school days. He thought this was the perfect time to eat. While unwrapping them he pointed out that the opportunity to consume food would be scarce from now on. I felt hedonistic, enjoying the snacks, the view and the spicy aroma of the spring air.

A couple of hours had passed already and the train still halted. "We should be in Ostend already!" the Berchem man exclaimed, checking his watch constantly. The sun was reduced to the last blinking between bushes and trees looking like a winking eye, reassuring us: "Everything will be all right!" Twilight in this part of Europe is a very gradual process, turning day into night. Since we did not move, restlessness seized all of us. Passengers came out of their compartments craning their necks to look at either side of the wide corridor windows. Suddenly, there was a jolt and—hurray!—the train started huffing and moving at a slow pace.

By now, the scenery was veiled in darkness. A train official in uniform appeared, pulling down all shades, requesting us to be quiet. Even the dim light inside was turned off. In the distance were deep sounds of cannon thunder.

"These are guns!" the Berchem man exclaimed. "Actually, this is heavy artillery," Vati corrected. The train moved towards the frightening noises. I was overcome by a feeling of great uneasiness which was compounded when the train came to a screeching stop. Talking about sitting ducks, I thought, here we are in the middle of nowhere surrounded by weapons—But at least we are not approaching the danger. But what if the peril comes closer? The question was burning in my mind.

Starting with Vati, everyone around me was dozing off and soon fast asleep. I felt so alone with all my fears and endless: "what ifs". The war noises scared me. There! What was that?! I exclaimed in my mind. Explosions!—was my answer. They were far enough to sound muffled but they seemed deadlier than the steady artillery. Isolation on this lonely train evoked panic I could not share— being the only one awake. How I wish to escape from these never ending hours into a deep slumber from this blackest of darkness! Imagining the peril unfolding in the distance was worse than being outside and seeing the danger. It was a night of dread in dense obscurity and I could only sit and let life happen to me. I never experienced two opposite feelings, fear and boredom, at the same time.

At last, morning came and everyone was up, relieved that we were finally moving again. "I am so happy to talk to you!" I cried to my parents complaining that I had not slept at all, or had I? "Who pulled the shades up?" I asked in amazement. "Of course the same person who pulled them down last night!" was their answer. "Also that recurring nightmare!" I told them about the three people in the dream while Vati unwrapped sandwiches for breakfast. If not for that, I could have sworn I had not slept. The beaming morning gave me new life, although there were still distant disturbing sounds. An hour later we passed fertile fields with cattle lying down. To our horror we realized they were all dead. Each passenger stared silently ahead harboring the same thoughts. This was my first-hand trauma with war. Death was in the air.

But by contrast the inside of the train was no longer quiet. It was as though land had been sighted after a long sea voyage. Starting with the Berchem man who exclaimed: "At long, long last! We made it!" looking at his watch nervously again as he left his seat, everyone busied themselves with the happy yet worrisome activity of leaving their compartment with their loads of baggage.

Within the hour, the three of us were walking the streets of Ostend. Even though the wind was howling against us with unbelievable force, it felt great to move through the avenues of the summer resort, a fishing—and port city. We looked for a hotel to relieve ourselves of our luggage. After that, we approached busy *Lang Straat* to look for other fleeing Jews. Since we had no idea where to go from here we needed others more knowledgeable of the territory. The sidewalk of the narrow main street was lined with shops and café-restaurants. We noticed other refugees that once again had to escape the Nazis. Speaking with them they appeared to be diligently preparing to embark on a ferry to Dover, England. This time, being strictly joiners, we were grateful and glad that they included us into their plan. In the following hours, while devouring the remaining sandwiches, we learned that these people came from all over Belgium, though most of them hailed from Germany. They explained that Ostend was geographically the best choice because one could escape by sea and if that failed one could always continue into France. "—and if that would fail?" I echoed with sudden fear. "Yes, we must always consider two disturbing factors: Will the British be able and willing to take us? Remember they were as impossible as the Americans when it came to issuing visas!" a heavyset lady explained. "But in an immediate emergency like this?!" I objected. "Do you recall the ship to Cuba named St. Louis?" She inquired.

At this point, one of the men continued: "The second factor is life threatening: at any given moment the *Luftwaffe* might attack because even though it is only a secondary port the ferry goes straight to Dover, England."

"Just as essential it is for us to get there, it is for the Nazis to prevent any activity between here and England." The lady concluded.

With only one thought in mind, nobody had any patience for introductions. All that mattered was that they were receptive. The jolly woman got closer and said as though imparting a secret: "Tomorrow, with God's help, we will all use our utmost efforts to get on the ferry to Dover. Why don't you join us?"

That idea absolutely thrilled us! We were even more encouraged by another man with a short white beard and an impish face who invitingly addressed Mutti: "By all means stay here with us so we will be able to leave together at the same time. Mutti blushed from this sudden attention and explained that we already had a hotel room since we had sat the whole night in the train. "What, you wasted all that money on a hotel!" The heavy lady exclaimed. Then she simmered down and said approvingly: "Well, since you paid already you might as well take advantage of such enormous luxury. Who knows when you'll see a bed again?!" We looked at each other in shock and fear. "It sure beats struggling in these hard chairs the whole night." "Whitebeard" said looking at Mutti. "Could we order any food?" Mutti asked in her little girl style. "Could we order any food?" mimicking her, he sheepishly explained: "This was a Kosher restaurant until a few days ago, but the owners took the same sea route we are intending tomorrow. Each summer I used to enjoy eating here—well, certainly not this year!" He apologized bowing and smiling politely at Mutti and disappeared only to reappear minutes later with some assorted morsels and even an aromatic cup of coffee. He shrugged defensively at Vati and me while putting it in front of Mutti with his naughty smile.

A lot of chatting, planning and packing was going on around us. When it was time to leave, "Whitebeard" and the heavyset lady offered to accompany us. When they mentioned that our hotel was near the ocean, I got wild with desire to see it for the first time in my life. Our hosts ceded reluctantly and made me promise that we would not stay longer than ten minutes in view of a suspected *Messerschmitt* attack. In great anticipation I walked with them to the sea. The tranquil immensity stretching into infinity made me feel a piety that wanted to pay homage to such eternal beauty and ancient mystery. We captured the perfect moment when the gigantic, red sun sank low defining the horizon where the sky began and the ocean ended and where it was mirrored in the sea. I was savoring this superb real life canvas of my first seascape vision, when Mutti's voice awoke me from my meditative mood: "C'mon let's go!"

My admiration for what unfolded in front of me conquered my annoyance and I dared to look, think and feel: The wind and water gave birth to the swells and waves that traveled far and long, sent from where I had been yearning to go for so many years. An eerie feeling overcame me when gazing at the ends of the universe, or rather: the gateway to the world, the symbol of hope and freedom which lay across the North Sea. I had only read about it in Heinrich Heine's poem where he likened the White Cliffs of Dover to a woman's bosom. At this moment it was my instant desire to get there. What an intrusion on the stillness of my thoughts when I heard pleadingly: "Please, Mademoiselle, we've got to leave because of the *Messerschmitt* menace!" The heavy lady warned.

I could barely tear myself away from all this dazzling maritime beauty, my mind still being on the sea, sky and sun. What a way to experience such exquisiteness under those circumstances and such pressure! Then I heard the reproaching chorus: "You promised! We must leave now! The German planes might attack any minute!"—and with that all four of them pulled me away. Only then I realized: "Oh my God! What if they would indeed come?!" It would be my fault—mine alone! The thought made me rush. As we were running, catching my breath, I apologized for my absorbed selfishness and thanked them for their kind patience.

That night my racing thoughts and restless heart prevented me from sleeping no matter how much I kept telling myself that this might be the last chance to do so in a bed. When I finally was in deep slumber it was time to rise and get ready to drag our big suitcase to the ferry port. When we arrived in the huge hall, I was astonished at how long and wide the rows of people were. They reminded me of the line at the US consulate in Antwerp almost two years ago. But at least that queue had moved ever so slowly, while this one was stationary. No ship, not even the ocean was in sight, only the orderly, unmoving, stoic mass and a British uniformed official. The crowd was too large to detect any of yesterday's acquaintances. The solid, human column seemed unreal. One could peel anxiety off their faces. There was a minimum of speech and a somber mood of fear prevailed. Bored and tired we stood there for hours until dusk dispelled us. I felt like a tiny dot within that disappointed assembly.

Upon entering the restaurant, I heard a lot of discussions that
revealed anguish and frustration. Everyone had just returned. Since
I always felt I had to be the catalyst of conversation, I exclaimed:
"Weren't these lines amazingly huge; they were so closely packed
that we didn't even catch a glimpse of one another at the dock!"
Somewhat embarrassed when no one bothered to answer I realized
that they had other things on their minds. This was a restaurant
without any food. True to the nature of most obese people, the
heavy lady was the first one to show concern. The most elementary
problem of mankind: hunger! Everyone chipped in whatever tidbits
they could scrounge together.

"Whitebeard" was absolutely exhausted, and before falling into
a profound sleep on the hard chair, he made sure that Mutti got
his portion. She gave me a tiny piece. I wish she never had, for it
was such a tease, so much so that I could not think of anything
else but that heavenly morsel—desiring more, a lot more! That
night I realized how painful hunger can be and the tremendous
fear it can bring when one does not know where one's next meal is
coming from.

The following day was a repetition of the preceding one:
running to the docks, standing in that wide line, going back to the
same nice people followed by an endless night on merciless chairs.
Since "Whitebeard" had had plenty of rest he was poking fun at
anything and everybody. Each person present was at the end of
their rope, yet laughing at the other's stupid remark. I realized
that night that extreme fear and despair can turn into uncontrollable
laughter and cheromania. I, usually a joiner, was just an amazed
onlooker at that psychological spectacle. It seemed to help them
and after a while everyone was sound asleep.

It was another struggle to doze off. This time my demanding
stomach cried out like a hungry baby. I tried to appease it by
visualizing two copies of oil studies that were hanging on the far
wall. One was a still-life by an unknown. Because of the protective
black-out-shades, I could not even see the outline. Nevertheless
my eyes were wandering to the spot where I knew them to be,
vividly remembering the fruits on the canvas. I was savoring each

grape, removing its kernel off my tongue, tasting every bite of the luscious pear—which made me almost apologetic before its beauty, though it was all a play of my imagination. In reality, my elbows were propped on the table as I lapsed into a short nap. In passing, I admired the other painting. It was Max Liebermann's *Jooden Straat*. It depicted Jewish life at a busy street market in Amsterdam—as I had witnessed in the Yiddish center of Antwerp when visiting our poor relatives. *Leuverick Straat* was typical of such a quarter. To some it was Eden, bustling with life, the finest foods, and the freshest, greenest vegetables. My nostrils were filled with the wonderful aroma of good cuisine and the clean scent of waxed floors. Everything "koved" in honor of the oncoming Friday night, the Sabbath. My palate actually tasted the cooked version of the produce laid out on long tables in Liebermann's piece. My stomach jumped for joy. A warm and happy feeling streamed through my entire being—not only from the strange "dining experience" but also from nostalgia for our pre-refugee time in Cologne.

Since all three of us could neither fall asleep nor stand this nocturnal sitting any longer, in whispers-careful not to awake the "cheromaniacs"—we decided to try our luck with the Channel crossing once more. On tiptoes we took our baggage and marched through the still dark, cool spring morning to the docks. There was already a huge line of worn out hopefuls. Day three was another carbon copy, though with a tremendous difference: there finally was a boat! But we realized all too soon that it was not to be for us. No, our ship had not come in. All the waiting had been in vain. I felt like Madame Butterfly.

On each of these three days, I had noticed a beautiful blonde standing at the deep curve opposite from us. I had seen her previously on local advertisements of her upcoming singing performances. This local celebrity was just another sufferer, but when it became clear that the boat was not for us she attempted to resolve our plight. She addressed the captain in English. I joined to give her some reinforcement. Together we tried to make him realize the proportions of the profound international crisis. She pleaded with balled fists and clenched teeth. I took on an entreating, cajoling and beseeching stance. All the captain would do was cross and uncross his arms, emphasizing his authority by rocking back and forth from heel to toe. His arrogance reminded me of another uniformed potential lifesaver at the US consulate. All of this led to a frustration of tragic magnitude. The disappointment that at long last a ship had come in, yet was not to be ours, was too drastic. It made me lose my composure. Both of us spoke from the heart, because we were painfully aware that we, two young women—though strangers to each other—where pleading on behalf of the entire "maybe-ship-load". But all to no avail.

Once again the neat lines dissolved into a mass of worried, hungry people who had nowhere to turn. The crowd automatically dispersed into small groups. Everyone was questioning the stranger next to him: "Now what? What now?" We were seized by the terrible fear that there was no way out, when, at this very moment, suddenly and literally from out of the blue a *Messerschmitt* was diving downward into our group of civilians, machine gunning us without mercy. We were their only target. The hellish screeching of this flying monster intensified the horror. Did he handpick us for a private inferno? With shattering noise this evil devil kept aiming at us from a short range. Children were whimpering, women crying. I was afraid to breathe, look or listen.

Vati, who was no soldier, ordered all of us to get face down on the ground, cradle our heads in our arms and remain motionless. I felt as though I was going to be executed. I had to accept that my young life would come to a sudden bloody end.

At last, it stopped. Breathlessness! Stillness!—Combined with panic of the next attack. I realized that in the shadow of death, one seems to be immune to physical pain. Therefore, I ventured to check and was overwhelmed with joy that my limbs were intact and there was no blood. As I was about to leap up, I was compelled to freeze and shout: "There they are coming back for us, aiming to mow us down!" The agony of angst had overcome me again. The nightmare made my heart pound. The strafing seemed to rip the earth under me. I lay flat and still, not daring to breathe. I was prepared to die.

They left, then came back in rapid succession, each time diving while machine-gunning us. This was it! I shall never come out of this ordeal alive! I remained motionless and transfixed, awaiting Judgement Day.

Chapter 8

The airborne devil vanished to turn to more monstrous activities. It was when Vati deemed it proper, and only then, that we fled the perilous wide-open space. The narrowness of Lange Straat offered protection against another slaughter attempt. Survivors' euphoria overcame us when we were surrounded by the safety of the main street again.

Vati was the hero of this horror-filled morning. Everyone thanked him for the guidance and praised him for being calm. The grateful group was dispersed while three individuals clung to us. We started toward the foodless restaurant, anxious to share our nightmarish adventure with our mates. Suddenly, to our disbelief, there they were, coming towards us, eyes bulging with ironclad determination. They seemed to be in a trance, totally unaware of our presence.

Mutti yelled, "What's going on, Whitebeard?" He kept walking, as Mutti pleaded, "Don't expose yourselves to the murderers!" Remaining in step with him, she hysterically sputtered parts of the ordeal we had just encountered. Transfixed, they continued their stoic march.

Frantically, I begged them to stop, "You warned me of a Nazi air-raid while I was awestruck by the beauty of my first ocean view. Your fear is reality now. A German plane looms ahead to attack you just as it did us." Spellbound, the silent caravan strode on. Protecting them from horror was impossible. Their minds were dead set.

We entered the restaurant in shock after seeing the almost psychotic daze that had enveloped the "Whitebeard people". The chairs now looked most welcoming. We delighted in the familiar setting as we were attempting to regroup with three people, a married couple and the husband's brother. The wife noticed the paintings. I told her about my dining experience evoked by them and shared my amazement that fear had halted my hunger. This prompted Vati to plan a scavenger trip. However, since the brothers knew the territory they advised against it.

Looking at the sea, Vati asked, "Does anyone know how to fish? Besides being the largest passenger port, Ostend also possesses the most important fisheries. Let's try our luck with the fruits of the sea!" Because of the danger there was a flat "No!" from the brothers. After rest and discussion, we decided to flee on foot to France. "But then we'll have to start out near the docks again!" Mutti objected.

"Not quite," they answered, "We'll walk in that direction, but then we must turn left and cut across the wharf by the hotels where there are shelters. We have no choice!"

It was against our hearts, but we had to leave. Vati took the fine pigskin suitcase and I lifted mine while I bade goodbye to Max Lieberman. When we were on the front step of Lange Straat, I too felt Mutti's fear of going back to the perilous zone. In fact, I was petrified. Wanting to make certain, I asked a passerby if the wharf could be avoided. We were relieved when he directed us to the opposite way past Monaco Plaza, the Kursaal, the Lido and the Albert promenade into the Zeedijk.

"Our beautiful seaside promenade," he sighed. "If the quay should prove dangerous, you could escape into Koningspark, our lovely royal park. I will take that route soon also."

I thanked him for sparing us from danger as I went off into a daydream about the luxury of these appealing places. While passing elegant structures, I felt embittered that my youth was marred by such ugliness. C'est la guerre! or, That's war! I said to myself to justify my frustration.

Once we reached the outskirts of the city, we followed a flow of people wheeling carts of every description loaded with precious belongings. To our right were spectacular dunes and creamy-yellow beaches, and beyond, the azure sea. Admiring how wonderful the world was, I tried to make the weight of my suitcase more bearable by switching hands often. I felt I was cursed as I followed the weary, silent people. Wherever there was a path, street, road, or highway, we snailed along, and when our energy permitted, we walked faster.

Suddenly, we were shaken out of our somnambulism by the wailing of the air-raid siren. "Oh no, not again!" I uttered. Once more we were in a wide-open space between a path, the dunes, the ocean, and the sky. Fear numbed me, but fast action was required. Everyone was desperately looking for shelter when Vati discovered an isolated villa. Clutching my suitcase, I ran with all my force. Fear made me selfish. I did not have enough air to warn my parents. Upon hearing the thunder-like roaring in the distance, a wild stampeding urge gripped me.

The once proud villa was the perfect shelter. Though it was deep and black, I felt safe. When I heard sounds in the dark, most of my anxiety subsided. To shut out the far away noise, I focused on the soft near-by voices and was amazed to see a group of mostly older people. They taught me to stand under the strongest pillars because those would remain standing if the villa was hit. Though none of these elders could have been of much help, I felt more confident having them around. One couple led me to a secure spot. While waiting out the attack, they looked at me fondly. Both seemed rural, refined, honest, and good. They could pass as non-Jewish Germans of pre-Hitler time, reminding me of the wonderful Grimberg family who babysat me in Cologne.

Finally, the monotone "siren of relief" signaled that we were out of immediate danger. Everyone was as anxious to leave the shelter, as they had been to flock in at the onset of the howling. The nice couple, who in my mind I called "Mama and Papa," gently held me back and inquired whether I would stay for the night.

"I hadn't thought about it yet."

"Look, Fräulein," they said softly, "We've spent two nights here already and know it is safe."

"Great, I shall tell my parents!"

I was a flower girl at the wedding of my baby-sitter's sister, my oasis! Walter, their brother, my *"anti-Semite-protector."* (1st row, left). The offspring are still very much in my life.
(2nd young lady from right), my beloved baby-sitter Thea (since age four).

I found them and the three others at the entrance of the villa. Dusk was setting in as I reflected on what had been my longest day ever. Yet, I found relief in the glorious prospect of sleeping in a real bed, in a villa, overlooking the ocean, in the company of the sweet older couple. I tried to remember how long it had been since I saw a mattress. The repetition of trotting between wharf and restaurant made it hard to establish how many nights we had spent on chairs.

I slept deliciously well and awoke to the distant rumblings of war intermingled with the eternally peaceful rhythm of the sea. Even people who had always lived in this serene place had not dared to stay. As a result of the wonderful rest, everyone was energetic as we took in the invigorating aroma of fresh coffee. Notwithstanding the far away man-created thunder, we felt early morning tranquility when Mama served brew and biscuits. Over the cozy meal it was decided that Vati and the threesome would go to look for bread.

While clearing the dishes, Mama recounted how much anti-Semitism they had felt in their small Bavarian hometown near Bad Kissingen. "Well, of course," I retorted, "National Socialism was born there."

Mama continued, "Would you believe that the early Nazi elements, the infamous S.A. men, took Papa and the few other male Jews to scrub the sidewalks with toothbrushes. Then they smeared 'JUDE' on the newly cleaned surface and forced them to erase it under their mocking laughter. This went on for weeks."

Caressing his faintly smiling face, she exclaimed, "Oh my poor Papa!"

"May I share some of my experiences?" I asked.

"By all means!" they insisted.

"Though Cologne was known to be the least anti-Semitic city in the entire Reich, I did have my share. Particularly during the first five years of my life and then again shortly before we left. A large group of children, mostly boys bigger than me, ran after me with a hate-rhyme, *'Hep! Hep! Hep! Jew! Jew! Jew! Your nose we'll stick in a water ladle, and when you're dead, we'll bury you in an egg box!'*

In my immediate community I was the object of much scorn. However, downtown I was most admired and the focus of attention."

With pride, Mutti added, "I made Fanni beautiful clothes and the most prominent photographer had her magnificent portraits on display at all times." She continued sadly, "Still, every day was heartbreaking when my child stepped out looking like a Renoir and was subjected to abuse, persecution, and at times even physical harm."

" . . . And the parents?" Mama asked.

"These ex-Communists-turned Nazis just snickered and slammed the door in my face," Mutti answered.

"But still," I interrupted, "one cannot generalize." I told Mama about a family with many red-haired daughters and two sons who lived only two blocks from this hell. "I found love and even admiration there. The younger son, Walter, my hero, once witnessed my plight when he took me for a sleigh ride. He fought off my bullies. As a result, I was able to enjoy the winter wonderland for many days.

When Mutti had stepped out of earshot to talk to Papa, I said to Mama, "I was not quite five when I started Catholic elementary school on the right bank of the Rhine River in an area called Mülheim. The teacher, Herr Bodewig, was really sadistic, but only with me. For instance, in math we used little sticks to calculate. Before I did anything, he would yell at me, causing me to drop them. I was punished by him forcing me to outstretch my palms to be hit with a bamboo stick in front of all my classmates. Math was never without fear, shame, sobs, and tears. In fact, there is one part too shameful for me to reveal.

Despite math class, I was very popular at that Pestalozzi School with students and other teachers. One of them, Herr Spang, developed a fondness for me and everyone soon called me 'Mr. Spang's darling.' Also, I had a standing invitation for luscious meals at the principal's villa. I especially enjoyed the warm friendship of his wife and their three daughters. My parents demonstrated the same loving interest toward their girls, especially the eldest, Lucy. She visited us almost daily on her long way back from university.

On Sundays, we took the youngest, Steffi, who was a bit older than me, in our horse and buggy, enjoying picnics and rural Biergardens together. Oh, those were fun-filled days!"

"The daily torments by Bodewig blocked my concentration," I continued, "Luckily, as I progressed, my beloved principal took charge of all subjects except math, which was still given by Bodewig. The principal's constant praise made me forget past humiliations and I was able to rise to the top of the class. Attempting to spare me the emotional contrast, Mutti transferred me to a Protestant school. Although I resented this move at first, the school proved to be adequate and the visits with the principal's family continued."

"Later, a ghastly, insidious change in attitude evolved." Startled by my emotional voice I tried to compose myself, "The principal encouraged me to see Steffi and friends in their garden just as I had done before. Knowing that Steffi was waiting, I rushed to get my homework done. By this time, there were only colorful flowers, no friends. Feeling a sense of loss, I began to wonder. Later on, I detected that this lovely place was filled with BDMs. This Nazi group had attracted all my former friends."

With pathos I continued, "One cannot imagine the tremendous pressure exerted upon young children to belong. Only a few leaders of the Brownshirts were of academic background, but all had much malice in their souls. Each morning, the non-members would be cross-examined about their resistance to join. They had to stand up while being questioned. Everyday, fewer girls would get up until I was the only one left. Foolish as it was, I felt compelled to rise. 'Sit down!' they commanded, mocking my obvious incompatibility."

"The Nazi parents were thrilled to have their children included, while the non-Nazis made their children become members for fear of repercussions. I could now understand why my friend Steffi and her circle had also joined the ranks. Adult Germans were subjected to the same method, although most of them needed no coaxing. Reprisals were severe even in 'mild' Cologne. In the early thirties, Jews and anti-Nazi Aryans alike were submitted to the same arrests and brutality. Most of them would succumb to the bestial treatment in the cellars of the 'Braun Haus,' the S.A. headquarters. Their ashes would be sent to their families with a phony sick note and a letter of condolence neatly attached. A fee was charged for this macabre delivery."

I added, "Living around the block from Pestalozzi School gave me the exasperating opportunity to see Herr Bodewig swagger in his brown S.A. leader uniform."

"Only four years ago, I was forced to leave school altogether. There was just one Jewish school in Cologne, right in the urban center. Despite the long tram ride and the inconvenience, it was the right move, for I was happy at the Lütow School. At last, I felt free amidst Jewish teachers and students. Our instructor was yet another beloved principal, Mr. Kahn."

"My last personal anti-Semitic experience in Cologne happened only two years ago, shortly before our departure. When I walked along the Mülheim freight depot station, a pack of boys ran after me, chanting the same Jew hating rhyme of my childhood. They threw stones at me, causing blood to run down my head. Since it was Saturday afternoon, nobody was around. Isolated and shocked by the gang-attack, I was shaken with tremendous terror and anger. With my heart pounding, I raced desperately around the corner toward the entrance of the freight station where they were not admitted."

"Then we drove her to the police station," Mutti added. "She had head wounds and her pretty clothes were bloodstained. The policemen were sympathetic but powerless since we Jews had no civil rights."

I concluded by telling the final tale of rejection in Cologne. "Lucy, our marvelous, blonde friend, happened to walk past us, avoiding eye-contact. She was hanging on the arm of a high-ranking S.A. officer. Even though they had not been talking, at the moment they passed by us she burst out into a nervous loud laugh for no apparent reason. She must have been so embarrassed for shunning us. I had felt as though I was repugnant and everyone had an aversion to me, though I had been so popular. It was as though the world had turned against me." I could still feel the sadness and pain of rejection.

In the silence that had followed my long-winded story, Papa suggested, touching Mama's shoulder, "How could this have all gotten so out of hand? What seduced and bewitched the intelligent Germans? Why should a child have to experience such feelings of banishment? For heaven's sake, how could all of this have taken place so quickly?"

"Fear was spreading," Mama answered.

"But why? What was the catalyst?" Papa investigated.

"I can only relate what I learned in school. After the Great War, the terms of the Allies were harsh and oppressive. The entire population felt that they were treated unfairly. Anti-Semitism always fed on two premises: the story that the Jews killed Jesus and the envy of them being over-achievers in banking, commerce, music, and the performing arts. Put some fuel on their vulnerability as a minority, and you have a raging bonfire! Each occurring evil, frustration and any negativism will fan it into an inferno. Along came Adolf Hitler, the savior, the substitute Kaiser, but even better, being of the people, for the people. He was a born orator and used his gift exceedingly well. Here was a mass seducer with conviction. A suppressed nation turned into suppressors. Anyone not swept into the Nazi paradise was swept away forever. There was no turning back."

"By now," Papa said, "only very few would have liked to reverse it for these reasons: humiliation to Teutonic pride, reduction of territory, loss of military power, poverty caused by inflation, and mass bankruptcies. Out of these German ashes arose 'Phoenix Hitler'."

It was quite unusual for Mutti to stand on the sidelines. Now she took a step further by pointing out, "Any opposition to the Nazis was stopped on the spot by terror and oppression. Friends of Jews were treated as Jews. Justice was absent. So was political dissent, because all other parties were prohibited. Everything that did not flow with the Nazi stream was eliminated by violence. All of this made it possible for Hitler to invade other countries."

"As we are now being attacked," Mama quickly interjected.

Mutti acknowledged, "Yes, the persecution of the Jews, as seen in Poland, could be executed without any interference. Eventually, this could lead to the conquest of Europe and the establishment of a German Empire. The primitive radicalism of the Nazis with its apparent strength, and the appeal to unify in order to rebuild a lost nation, had an overwhelming influence on every individual German. The Nazi doctrine was drummed into them until it engulfed the entire population. On top of that, businesses, such as Vati's, were flourishing."

"Oh my God! Vati! He and the others have been gone so long!" I exclaimed. "It has been hours since we started discussing our Nazi experiences." I felt a dismal foreboding mounting to great impatience. At this moment, I felt all my love for him and longed to see him instantly. I felt guilty for having been so deeply involved in the conversation that I forgot about him. Yet, there were still so many things that had remained untold.

The marvelous smell of freshly ground coffee yanked me out of my thoughts. Mama led me to a room filled wall to wall with books. This reminded me of my Catholic principal's study, where I spent many a carefree hour. "We refugees haven't seen any décor like this in seven years." Mama remarked as she served coffee on borrowed Sèvres cups in a borrowed villa on borrowed time.

"How wonderfully serene peace time must be!" I sighed. "If not for the explosions in the distance and my anxiety for Vati, it would feel just like it." I closed my eyes to inhale the fragrance. My lips and taste buds were intoxicated by the rich flavor and the warmth was stimulating. Even more so than Liebermann's fruits, because this was delicious reality!

Suddenly, everyone stood up. It was Vati. Was this disheveled, forlorn, and pitiful man really my Vati? He staggered to the chair, threw himself down, placed his head on the marble table and sobbed. I patted his silky hair as I leaned over him wordlessly offering my precious cup. By the time Mama had replaced mine, I asked in a whisper, "But Vati, where is my Rock of Gibraltar?"

At last he opened up, "Even . . . even . . . worse than the wharf bombing"

"Are the other three on their way?" we asked hesitantly.

"No!" He kept shaking his head, unable to stop. Images of the recent experience must have been repeating themselves as he searched for words. After a long pause, we heard his exhausted voice, "Frightening sounds of the air-raids, the confusion, and the panic!" Finally he was able to form sentences, "It was a blood curdling nightmare. Two Nazi flyers were droning low over our heads. And, in the truest sense of Stuka, they did just that! Whom did these air-devils battle? Us Civilians! We crawled under a large poplar, the only cover. Everyone was running in different directions. A family shared my refuge. There were three little ones. Imagine, that's who the the Stukas were after, machine gunning all of us as we huddled together, pressing against the ground, shielding ourselves in our folded arms. The tree caught fire and so did the hair of the children. Their screams were frantic. We had to– –"

The mournful wailing of the siren followed by the screeching of dipping planes interrupted Vati. We gasped. I ran down into the shelter followed by Mama and Papa. Wide-eyed moaning people poured into the cellar. My parents appeared last. Petrified, strangers and the five of us flocked under the strongest pillar in the darkness. We all prayed that no physical harm would come to us. Safe as it seemed down there, everyone was scared and breathlessly waited for the relief siren. We sat motionless and silent for the longest time, when our prayers were finally answered.

After the last stragglers left, Mutti turned to us in great excitement, "We've got to run! We can't stay here any longer! Next time, the enemy planes will come to bombard us. This seems to be a combat zone."

"Besides, there's no food here," Vati added quickly.

Mama and Papa looked at each other with frightened eyes. Mama said shyly, "But we thought we were more sheltered here in the villa than on the open road."

"This is all right for a few days. Then, we'll be sitting ducks like on the train, only dead ones! We are living on black coffee only. Who knows how long this will last." Vati chimed in.

"So, let's pack and run!" Mutti commanded.

When Mama finally gathered their things, Mutti snapped, "I thought you felt so safe here! Why bother packing?"

"Did you intend to leave us behind?" Papa asked with a quivering voice. I echoed his question for I had grown very fond of them. They felt like the grandparents I had never had.

"We are leaving you where and how we found you, where you feel so protected!" Mutti retorted.

"Please, don't be angry with us!" they begged.

The more they persisted, the more Mutti resisted. Vati, embarrassed by the emotionally charged atmosphere, apologetically pointed out that Mutti had a certain instinct, a sort of sixth sense. Mama cried as Papa held her in his arms and I joined in to console this sweet old couple. When they disappeared for a short while, Vati and I tried to negotiate with Mutti.

They came back with an apparently precious package. Mama first unwrapped the paper and then carefully unfolded a cheesecloth. Its contents smelled heavenly. Like magic from Mama's kitchen, a magnificent roast was revealed. "We'll share this," she smiled benevolently through shimmering tears. All our worries turned into sheer joy. Upon smelling and tasting the first bite, my chest expanded. Concentrating on the flavor, I closed my eyes. I even smacked my lips and let out a joyous sound. To have abandoned all my composure made me blush, but everyone smiled and Mama gloated with delight.

"What a culinary delight," I exclaimed.

"You would have enjoyed anything, hungry as you were," Mama said humbly.

Though we were not very religious, we had previously kept a kosher home and I had never eaten pork before. I knew it would not be the last time that I tasted it, and I was already trying to analyze whether I enjoyed it so much because of its flavor or simply because I was starving.

When I helped Mama in the huge kitchen, she asked, "What was so dreadful and unspeakable that your teacher did to you, my child?"

I was completely taken aback that this shy lady would address such a touchy topic. But I could not tell her, or anyone else, about that. I had never dared to reveal it to my parents. In order to prevent repercussions, I had suppressed my anguish. It remained my secret, causing tremendous torment for the rest of my life.

In a way, I had been right to keep it to myself. With the boys who had thrown stones at me, I had been able to prove their deeds with my bleeding wounds. But in this case, it would be a little Jewish girl's accusation against a mighty Nazi officer. An accusation so big, so embarrassing, that I could not tell a word of it. How in the world could I possibly describe it?

There was a desk on the podium. Bodewig and I were behind it, the entire class in front. His huge knobby fingers aimed for the most delicate feminine part of my little body. Terrified, I tried to tear myself from him, but each time I pulled away he would jerk me sideways against his leg again. It became a silent, shameful tug of war until I was powerless and he succeeded. I was burning to scream, but was paralyzed, frightened and humiliated. It will haunt me forever. I could not find words to describe this horrible episode so full of shock, shame, and seething wrath accompanied by terror.

I could, however, relate the emotional ordeal and inner turmoil that usually followed. "When the weather permitted, we went outside and formed a circle. Playing with my peers, especially my close friend Johanna Zanders, made me momentarily forget my plight. Sometimes, I got so carried away by our games in the sunny, fresh air, that I could feel happy again. Bodewig seized precisely this moment. Darting out from nowhere, he slapped me across the face so hard that his devil's hand left a red imprint. I did not always manage to suppress my tears. Since then, whenever I feel elated and someone upsets me, I am reminded of those slaps of Bodewig." I studied her compassionate expression wondering whether this true story had convinced her even though I had omitted the main event.

Mutti, followed by a pleading Vati and a distraught Papa, burst into the kitchen. "Los, los,los" she commanded. "We must leave this cozy nest immediately. It was too good to be true anyway!"

Amazed, we inquired in unison, "But why so suddenly?"

"Let's pack and take off! No questions asked!" She snapped, adding, "I can feel it! Something terrible is going to happen here!"

"But to be under the hostile sky without food and shelter?" Mama pleaded.

"No buts! Los, los, los!" She shouted imperiously. Softening her tone somewhat, she turned to Vati, "Don't you know after all these years that I have a sixth sense?"

"Like the black American in Antwerp." I added.

Without hesitation, Vati, looking at Mutti admiringly, turned to the elderly couple and stated, "Yes, my wife is gifted with extremely fine sensory perceptions. One must blindly follow her whether it seems to make sense or not. So we'd better leave right now!"

With much sadness, we left the wonderful villa that had served us so well.

Chapter 9

"On the road again, on the road again!" has been the opening of many a song or poem throughout the centuries. What came to my mind while walking was the lone carpenter experiencing the world. As a child I had watched these individuals pass by sporting their black velvet outfits complete with bellbottoms, flap-hats, brass buttons, coins, and one earring. They were looking for adventure-just as I had initially done before leaving Antwerp. With these thoughts in mind we blended right into this exodus of strangers with only one aim in common: to run for our lives. Taking one last long look at the villa I began marching like a good "infantry man."

The early morning sky was blue as could be, but the beauty was marred by the sound of doom: the dreaded crescendo of the devils' engines. The closer the deadly droning, the stronger became the pain in my stomach. There! They were near and flying low! The four of us gave Mutti looks of contempt: God, we were on the open road with no place to hide! Only splendid dunes to our right and nothing but sand to our left. Panic made me feel as though I was turning into an embryo in desperate need of a sheltering womb. There was none. Frightened, I rammed against one of the dunes and dug my nails into it while literally holding my breath, not daring to look upward. The planes passed and I sank to my knees in relief and gratitude.

A second later I heard a sharp whistle followed by a violent explosion from the direction we had come from. "Look, the house is gone!"; Papa shouted with a cracked voice. "'Our' beautiful villa wiped out in one single blast", I managed to mumble.

Gape-mouthed we all stared at Mutti with overwhelming admiration and gratitude. Vati praised her: "Didn't I tell you about my Sofiechen's keen instinct?" Mutti, the heroine of the day, screamed: "We all would have suffocated underneath the debris of that wonderfully 'safe' shelter. A death more torturous than that by sudden machine gun fire!"

When Vati could finally take his eyes off Mutti, he explained: "These German 'Stukas' were no doubt purging their deadly cargo on us in favor of a refueling trip to Germany for more killing missions."

With great relief, we stepped up our pace, pausing only briefly to shift our ever heavier belongings. We could not really take a rest, being so engulfed in that human tidal wave of fleeing people. I tried to make the best of each peaceful moment during the march that had already lasted for hours. There was no overhead droning— only occasional deep sounds of cannons. To the right, there was the beautiful ocean with its invigorating air. Splendid sunshine was bursting out of the clear sky (despite all its negative connotations: war was never boring nor lonely for me). Considering the immensity of the steadily moving crowd, it was fairly quiet for everyone was deeply immersed in thoughts. It took some effort to direct my thoughts to more pleasant topics. The sun was so warm, that I could shed my second sweater—which meant more to carry—but it felt good nonetheless. The surrounding natural beauty strengthened my will to live.

When I looked to my left, I could not believe my eyes: In a fox hole there was a young "Tommy" looking like a heroic statue. Apparently, his flat helmet had been blown off his head. It revealed a fine profile and a fresh hair cut, his stiff fingers braced against the trench wall. However, this vision was not cast in bronze. Here was a real monument of young flesh, petrified into that pose of bravery forever. A picture so dramatic, I shall never forget. Petrified, I was neither able to utter any sound nor to stop walking. I only managed to tug Vati's sleeve and point with my chin to the tragic sight. Vati left out a deep sigh while his eyes moistened.

I was torn from my morbid thoughts, when Mutti frantically grasped my arm and shrieked: "Watch out, watch out!" There, directly in my path, lay a dead French soldier. My toes were about to touch him. Cringing with sympathy and horror I broke my stride abruptly to pay my last respects before making a large half circle around him.

Soon the path got narrower and the ocean was obstructed by an industrial site, a fishery. Men, ant-like, were lugging heavy cases. Despite the apparent weight, they were full of smiles. Vati also ran into the shed and soon returned triumphantly with a load. We were all eager to check the booty. It was full of tins of oil sardines! Vati was as proud of himself as though he had caught them himself. For all the fright of the Nazi planes and the numbness I had felt after seeing the dead warriors I had forgotten all about food. In anticipation of a gourmet feast I yearned for the sardines desperately. Mama and Papa seemed to feel the same way. Mama threw up her hands in delight and exclaimed: "This could not have come at a more needy moment! There are only some nibbles of the roast left to go around amongst the five of us!" Only Mutti was of a different opinion: "Bring this right back', she commanded: you are pilfering and plundering. "In such a hopeless situation you are looking for honesty and decency?! All of us demanded. Vati asked: "So what are we going to do for food? Bakers stopped making bread. Grocers and butchers fled just like we did." For once, Mutti was speechless and kept the sardines.

When Vati was about to open the first tin my keen ear alerted me to the droning of aircraft. My heart felt as though it were pierced, my body shivered. I was in panic. Hungry as I was, the sight and smell of the sardines could not entice me any longer. The survival instinct had priority over any other drive. I took flight to the nearest bunker. Everyone was fleeing, only Vati remained. He positioned himself on the highest dune, consumed the sardines with gusto and looked to the sky like a spectator anticipating an aerial show. I yelled: "Vati! Vati", but having no alternative, we left him behind and scampered to the shelter.

Strangers were commenting on him: "Did you see the man eating on top of the hill?" asked one. A second answered: "I wish I had his cool!" Yet another said: "It's downright stupid!" Mutti finished with: "Dumb and frivolous!" I enthusiastically and defensively exclaimed: "What bravura!"

For a brief time we heard the whining of air-craft and the constant staccato of guns. In order to divert my mind from fear I asked the people next to me: "Where are we really going from here?" They replied in French: "Vers Coxide, vers Coxide!"[1]

That is almost at the end of the Belgian coast, isn't it? Are we now in Middlekerk or Niewport?

"Somewhere in West Flanders," they answered.

After the relief siren everyone hastened to get into the fresh air. I hurried up the steps to catch an anxious glance at Vati's dune. As soon as my eyes had adjusted to the bright light I saw him perched atop the hill, right where I had left him.

Upon getting closer I detected an ecstatic smile on his face. When we were in hearing distance he joyously exclaimed in a boyish manner: "What a fight! What a fight! I would not want to have missed it for anything in the world!" Playfully I asked: "the sardines or the battle?"

"The duel between the *Messerschmitt* and the *Spitfire*!" Curious to comprehend his motive for jeopardizing his life, the crowd approached him. Bewildered, they questioned him: "Were you not afraid?" "It was restricted to air combat alone," he answered defensively. "Shrapnel or a plane crash could have been fatal." blurted the bystanders.

"The airmen above have so much life ahead of them. I am already a middle-aged man of forty-three," was his calm retort. "I thought you love your daughter so much!" Mutti reproached him. He gave me an endearing glance and confirmed: " . . . and how!"

He continued to rave: "I have just witnessed that the Nazis are not invincible. They just give off that impression. We are all aware of their air superiority. Nevertheless, this Spitfire acted as though the opposite were true. He did not dodge from the German strike. Quite the contrary! He must have believed in the old adage: 'A good attack is the best defense'. Did he rip into the Messerschmitt! The technical geniuses Professors Messerschmitt and Hinkle who created this unique battle bomber and the Luftwaffe darling General Steinhoff would have been stunned at the speed and aggression of this heroic adversary."

---

[1] "To Coxide". Coxide is a resort town on the Belgian coast.

"The Messerschmitt was left with a smoking tail and a strange, screeching sound from its engine. It tried to get away from the Spitfire, which chased it over there." Pointing to a barn he continued: "You see the electric wire there. They almost touched it! I am positive the Messerschmitt will have to make a forced landing." Having said that, he finally slid off the dune.

Our small group merged once again with the immense, tragic exodus of weary people. Despite an almost overwhelming desire to lie down and sleep we continued. My share of sardine tins made walking even more burdensome. Vati's leather case and the new acquisition of food caused his load to be almost unbearable. But he managed to explain with some enthusiasm: "Look, there are more farm houses! Probably we'll soon see clusters of homes and a town."

After many kilometers, his prediction became reality: we discovered a train station. Inside was a turmoil of people seeking even the most meager shelter for the night. The cordiality of the station master compelled me to risk a foolish question: "Are there any trains running?" His lips curled into a semi-smile. I pressed on: "Would I get the same response if I were to ask for a hotel?" Glancing at my four companions fleetingly, he answered: "I have the very best in town, just for you. Come, I'll show you!" He lead us to a quaint gate which opened to a small cubicle with a mountain of clean wood shavings. "It is yours for tonight, just for you!" He emphasized again. Graciously, I accepted. When I heard the shed being locked from outside, I became worried: What risk had I exposed myself to? But I was too exhausted to pay much attention to all the "what ifs" that crossed my mind.

Vati beckoned: "Do you want to eat?"

"No, no, thanks, my sleep has priority!" I called. "Don't worry about a thing, my child," he reassured me, "We are going to stay with our backs against the plywood." I slipped into deep sleep. I reveled in the best dreams with tempting visions of food and promised myself to think of the wonderful wood shavings if I ever should have trouble falling asleep.

When I rose, the door was ajar. My parents and Mama and Papa were indeed still in front of it. Weariness was imprinted on their face. Whereas I felt selfish and guilty, they were delighted to see me so well rested. In the waiting room I could at last, at long last, rejoice in eating the delicious sardines. Always tasty, they now seemed to be a gift from heaven. Nothing but sardines, nonetheless a great breakfast! Someone approached us with an offer: "I'll exchange chocolate bars, some even with nuts, for several of your tins." After a private conference, the trade was done. Desert was heavenly!

Vati asked Mutti: "Did I say or just think that the tins offered possibilities such as this one when you wanted to reject them?" Mutti turned her head: "Does that deserve an answer?"

"If only we could barter some bars and tins for bread!" Vati sighed and added with an air of renunciation: "I suffered enough looking for food."

Having relieved my hunger pangs, my thoughts turned to the weight we would have to carry: "If only we had wheels!" On the road, I solicited for anything rollable, knocking at every door, but to no avail! With the last house went our hope. Again, the walk seemed endless. When I read a Flemish sign *Kooksijde* I realized that we had reached the original destination.

Hordes of people jammed the highway. Some were heading west toward the coastal resort town of *La Panne*, but most turned south. The hesitance of so many created a bottleneck. Mutti and I clung to our belongings for dear life. Luckily we managed to remain together as the moving masses jostled us around. The hassling continued for a while before we noticed that Mama and Papa had vanished. I turned around and called for them. I continued my futile attempts to locate them until the crowd became so tight that it was impossible to move. Vati exclaimed with moist eyes: "Oh, these poor little old people!" I bit my lips and sobbed, much to my surprise. "What a shame I didn't tell them how happy they had made me in our brief time together!"

The backdrop had now evolved into a lush country-side carpeted with green rows of already ripened vegetables and fertile fields dotted with farm houses. I did not leave one of these untouched by my inquiry.

One of these houses was empty. It was nine o'clock, when day light would slowly give way to the night. Along with the three of us, many refugees were scrambling into this place, which was totally void of its occupants and possessions. In utter fatigue, humanity was strewn about. Lightening myself of our heavy belongings created a sense of relaxation. All enhanced by a hearty dinner of *les sardines en huile* followed by *du chocolat aux noisettes* and some conversation.

There was a lone older lady. She was extremely busy writing. I admired her determination to record the encompassing drama for posterity rather than engaging in the talk of present day hardships. At this point, I committed myself to emulating her expression for the next generation and those to follow to eternity must have the awareness of the devastation and earth shattering events which occurred. Yes, I must survive, even if with rage. I must! I must! . . . so I can leave a legacy of so many tragedies, caused by just one man, then by one nation . . . !

The following morning, I woke to the background of soft conversation. Lazily, my eyes adjusted to the beckoning daylight.

Amazed at the threesome smiling down on me, I thrust my torso to an upright position. I saw the brothers and the wife embrace Vati as though he were their sibling also, while ecstatically shouting almost in unison: "So we miraculously escaped the flying devils!"

"Look at what we subjected ourselves to for just a few slices of bread . . . and all in vain! Vati nodded with moist eyes and sighed: "Oh, God, what we went through! Ja, ja!" "We had to react like Hitler's war itself 'the Blitz'" (lightning). Spontaneously we ran in opposite directions dictated by our own instincts," the brother philosophized with great excitement. "Look at the price they extracted from me!" The husband exclaimed as he demonstrated his newly acquired limp. "Yes, he became a civilian war casualty right after the panic forced us to separate. His leg was hit by shrapnel as we were dashing for cover. We had to come to a dead halt, thus exposing ourselves fully," lamented the wife and added with a grateful look at Vati: "After all, it was you who taught us to prostrate ourselves in the face of danger. My poor darling was laying there bleeding and unconscious. It was downright frightful!"

"When the turmoil subsided we felt like three war buddies—the wounded one in they center—clutching on to each other", the brother continued: "As soon as it was feasible, we desperately searched for an infirmary. It was under duress and suffering that we finally found one." The husband concluded: "My leg was patched up with quite a few sutures. The pain created this": he demonstrated his walk while managing a forced smile in the face of excruciating pain.

"That's all anyone of us needs right now!" I interjected and warned: "For God knows how many miserable kilometers lie ahead for us on foot into France!"

In fascination I watched as the lady continued recording her impressions on endless sheets of paper. Since I could not create eye contact, insight told me not disturb her, although I was very much tempted to. After I finally had washed and even applied some lipstick, I wanted to complete my hygiene with a manicure, as I watched her. The wife and her brother-in-law wanted me to work on their nails, and many others followed. I tried her first, but was unable to do anyone else. "No sorry, I can't be a professional manicurist", I said facetiously and added: "in any case, my ambitions lie in other directions such as acting, dancing, singing and writing . . ." I sighed wistfully while looking straight at the industrious woman, but to no avail.

After quite a while, with the sound of cannon-fire less threatening, we were given the signal to get on the road again. Although sleeping on the hard floor was nothing like the luxury of the villa nor the soft wood shaving I still had misgivings about dragging myself onto the open highway.

Once more we blended into the unknown masses. Here the world unfolded in front of us—a universe in every hue of green, lovely enough to be embraced rather than be feared. There was such natural richness of the scenery's picturesque character surrounding us as though it came straight from the Grimm Brothers' fairy-tales. Now and then we encountered the most stately farm houses. Some were so stunning that they reminded me of a gentleman's acres. I asked Vati: "do you recall the 'Litz Estate' of your client? I'll be forever grateful to you for taking me on a surprise ride on your wagon with your great-looking, strong horses, Fritz and Lisa, and literally transporting me from an ordinary day at home into a magical world. Though this is Flanders, Belgium, and that gentleman's farm was in Germany, do they not have wondrous similarities?" Unfortunately, Vati's usual exuberant personality had dwindled during this flight into a "Ja, ja!" accompanied by moist eyes. Of course, this came particularly into play when emotions ran high.

"Even the plentiful twittering of the abundant variety of birds is reminiscent of that childhood day gone by. This large family treated me like a princess. They lifted me up to admire their adorable ponies, graceful colts and many other animals, I had never seen before. At the coffee hour they spoiled me with delectable pastries while we were seated on heavy, ornate oak furniture in their ancient palatial mansion." Sad nodding was Vati's answer.

I pointed out that there was still the delightful salty sea breeze. Since he lacked the sense of smell, I described its invigorating fresh aroma, just like you would provide a blind person with an explanation of the vistas. The pleasurable surroundings lent me a new vitality. Thus I kept on talking to my parents and the trio while lugging my valise and walking. Incessantly I continued enumerating our major advantages even under such dire circumstances: "Firstly, we are not alone, only Jews against Nazis, but we have the great military Allies! Second, our escape route is on easily traversable flat land. Thirdly, also the weather has been exceptionally wonderful and dry. It might have been cold and rainy. Fourthly, even the landscape is cooperating with its natural beauty. We could have been plagued by offensive industrial areas."

Unfortunately, my observations were suddenly shattered by the agonizing siren followed almost immediately by—yes!—the droning of Nazi planes. In panic, I raced for shelter assuming my group closely behind me. Once settled in the security of the bunker, I became frighteningly and painfully aware of being alone and shouted: "Mutti! Vati!"—again and again!—each time more frantically. Sure, there were strangers everywhere but the response

I desperately longed for never came. I was overcome with excruciating horror. Now, I had a most urgent and compelling additional reason for a swift end to the air attack. Oh, my God, what am I to do?! Where and how would I begin to seek my parents?! If only I will be able to recall each step before the all-clear-signal goes off. I remained transfixed on all that had happened after I had presented our four advantages. Endlessly, the super ego dictated the same questions: What did you see, do or pass after the onset of the alarm? Filled with angst and desperation, I continued the self inquisition. The answer did not vary from: Everything looked beautiful! My mind encountered a blank. Right here the light was dim and my chances of finding them, extremely slim. Wait, wait! Think! Be strong! Defeat "it" before "it" defeats you! was commanded in rapid succession.

Running back and forth like a caged ferocious tiger, dying a thousand deaths, as my spirit was ordered to conjure a solution to my self-imposed questions: All right, everything was beautiful! Wasn't there anything that wasn't quite as lovely or something that was even more outstanding than the rest? There, at last, the longed for "all clear" monotone sound! My heart was beating fast from over-anxiousness, I dashed up two steps in a stride. Maybe the fresh air will help to clarify the situation, I consoled myself.

As so many other times before, there was the need to adjust to the atmosphere outside. I was tempted to ask: Was there a man—carrying a leather suit-case—? That would apply to everyone in this crowd. Should I stay or should I run, and if so, where to begin? My inner interrogator commanded again: What did you see after the last word of your monologue? I steadfastly answered: Nothing but green beauty. Again the last question from the shelter: Wasn't there anything special or impressive? Wait, wait! Let me think! Yes, yes, as I was finishing the comparison with the industrial site I was fascinated by a tree. It was big and lopsided, and this very crookedness made it unique. It stood out from the rest. Wait, wait, when I was a small child, what did Vati tell me to do if I was lost in a crowd?—"Always return to the spot where we were together last!" Then this is my cue! Yes it was the twisted tree!" I thought jubilantly.

Anxiously threading back against the tremendous stream of people I almost questioned: Did you see a strangely bent tree? "Ridiculous, nobody would have noticed, I scolded myself. I prayed to God, begging him to find my parents and end my ordeal. Somehow, my anxiousness was shrinking from a new ray of hope. This was reinforced by: —it could be worse—there might have been a bottleneck such as at Coxide which caused us to lose "Mama" and "Papa". There was some optimism, yes, even faith, although all odds were against me. I had to boldly thrust my way back through the oncoming crowd. It felt morbid to regress and to resist the forceful forward flow. How exhausting! Apologizing was so fatiguing that I did it less frequently and finally omitted it altogether.

"There! At last! At long last! There was my beacon! The tree!—and beneath it—by God's will—my parents! My whole being burst forth in Händel's Messiah's "Hallelujah! Hallelujah!!""

"With renewed energy we proceeded from the lone tree where we had reunited. Again we mingled into the mass march with many weary kilometers and anguishing experiences left behind. It was almost ten o'clock at night. Daylight was ending. Other concerns gave way to the thought of finding refuge for the night. We followed the flow of lost souls which continued unabatedly. Fortunately, shelter loomed just ahead. It was a nondescript and decrepit barn. We were blessed with its presence. Speechlessly we entered and shortly the pleasure of sleep took us into another more pleasant realm.

As day broke, while still in twilight slumber, the precious aroma of brewed coffee delighted my whole being. Upon opening my eyes, I was startled in a most curious and agreeable way, when an enameled cup, billowing with steam awakened my senses. It was held by a gray suited, neatly cuff-linked arm. No matter the source, it was welcomed with great joy, but after a first, careful sip, my glance wandered upward. When I recognized his familiar face, I shouted: "David, David! What a pleasant . . ." Considering the unfortunate and drab circumstances, my initial enthusiasm was muted. His stoic attitude and mood seemed to concur with our present plight. He presented a most forlorn and dejected figure in a haze of dust.

While drinking my coffee, I attempted to encourage him by reminding him: "You were the one who was so greatly excited in Antwerp and enticed everyone to study English with me. It was your idea! You boosted me and set a shining example by becoming my very first student! I could afford some clothes with my 'English' money. Of course, nobody can really become as elegant as you are. My lessons were successful. I wish to thank you for this—and for this also!" With a grateful smile I held up the blue cup. David just nodded politely.

At this moment, two gentlemen who looked like bankers, approached him. The elder pressed him: "Let's go! We have a very trying and dreary trip ahead of us! I'm David's father and this is my others son", he explained and continued urgently: "You must forgive us. Their mother vanished in the crowd. Now we have only one hope of finding her: at the wharf in Ostende. All this plodding into France will soon prove fruitless anyway. My wife will be in Ostende!" He seemed to want to convince himself by continuing: "She must be there!—either waiting for us or ready to embark on a boat to England. It is our only hope! She could not stand any of this! Many times she repeated: "For me, it's either England—or death!"

"Oh, I remember her now! She told me the same but included the US when we met at the *Korte Heerenthals Straat Restaurant* in Antwerp on the night of the Passover Seder. Most mommies were crying at their first feast away from home, but she wept the most. That's where I met David. Of course, I understand your concern and hurry, Mr. Mellon!" When hearing his name, a faint smile briefly lit up his face. I shook hands with him, the younger son and especially with David, wishing them luck for their reunion.

Thanks to David's coffee we had an early start. Getting on the main road we were thinking about the three men. Vati broke the silence by saying: "Mr. Mellon was probably right about all of this trudging into France being useless. How lucky we were to have found each other so quickly!" He said with a loving glance in my direction.

Suddenly, I observed the strangest sight coming from the East: A lone French soldier!—

"Let's ask him! Let's ask him, what's actually going on. Here we are in the middle of the war without knowing the military strategies. Let's ask him! He's our only source of information! Who can speak French?" Everyone seemed to demand.

"My daughter!" Vati proudly exclaimed.

" . . . but, . . . but . . . . !" Before I could explain that I had not quite finished my French studies due to the invasion everyone was urging me: "Go ahead! Go ahead! Ask him! Ask him!"

I felt terribly nervous and embarrassed as though it were a command performance. "Monsieur", I finally addressed this rather mature man in French uniform. Self-consciously I struggled with the question in a language I was barely conversant in. Attempting my debut, especially under these circumstances, became superfluous now.

He defensively exclaimed in beautiful Parisian French I had never personally encountered: "Don't look at me that way! I'm no deserter! It's sheer folly to fight the victorious Germans!" I quickly translated into Yiddish. Now, understanding the situation he pressed on: "Oh you are *des Juifs*, running from them also?! They are cunning masters of deceit, who outnumber all of us Allies in everything; quality and quantity, encircling us everywhere. Not only did they invade these parts at their natural borders, the *Ardennes*, but very insidiously created a "belly attack" by overflowing the highways from *Echternach* leading to *Luxembourg* over *Junglinster*. I'm sorry to admit that the swiftly advancing German troops were met by hardly any resistance." "Well", he apologized, "we were not prepared."

It seemed, that unlike his dead comrade, the people did not circumvent this live one. Behind me, a large crowd had gathered, everyone first anxiously nagging, then commanding me: "What is he saying, tell us, tell us quickly!"

I did not want to interrupt his descriptive flow of events, while being thrilled to understand his artful distinctive language. It

contrasted with the terrible happenings. Some of the men became
so impatient that they showed visible anger at me. Vati tried to
calm them down, but his kind way did not help. Mutti thundered
at them in no uncertain terms to stop it.

"An Allied force landed", he continued, "and pounced upon
convoys at *Grevenmacher*." Once more, as though asking my
forgiveness, he added: "What could they do, what could we do in
the face of the spectacular superiority of the sophisticated enemy?!
We were defenseless lacking all commodities of arms." His face
grew more somber when he said in a low voice: "None of our
heroes ever made it back to their base in England."

It felt that this was the right moment to gently stop him and
interpret for the impatient crowd. After my Yiddish relay of his
account we empathized with Mr. Mellon (who had questioned
whether the walk into France was worth the effort).

After my interpretation, the soldier set forth: "Forty-five thousand
persons from that area fled into France with the slogan: 'We don't
want to lose our soul!' General Busch penetrated into France thus
encircling all of us Allies. I had learned that the Germans had prepared
for this quite in advance. In fact, the whole stretch of the Southern
Eifel, leading directly into Luxembourg, including the *Maginot Line*
had been prepared for the invasion since the 1930s. How ironic that
the Tommies were singing the song by the Irish composer, Captain
Jimmy Kennedy: 'We're gonna hang out our washing at the Siegfried
Line'. Reality was just the opposite: A sinister place for both English
and French. With the Nazi's bold moves, we Allied military felt like
worms. All these places such as *Prüm, Bitburg* (with the famous Pils
beer brewery) are part of a whole line of bunker and arsenal called
'*Katzenkopf*'. All of these were under close scrutiny of Hitler himself
in 1938 and again 1939 by General von Runstedt. As you can see, we
are lost!

The magnitude of Nazi conquest is just too overwhelming for
us Allies; we, the unprepared ones. I'd better be on my way! Sooner
or later the *Boches* will catch up with me, I know it.[2]

---

[2]   Boches: derogatory French term for Germans

They will be coming up like weeds, anywhere and everywhere, above all, when least expected. Notwithstanding this sad and shameful report, it felt good to talk again after days and nights of silence since the Nazis cut me and my company off. Let's wish each other the very best! Please, tell this to all of them, Mademoiselle!"

With these words he gave me a firm handshake and honored the crowd, including myself, with a military salute and went off, soon disappearing in the civilian march towards Paris. Before I translated the last portion of his report I expressed what I felt from the bottom of my heart: "Let's hope he'll make it without any intervention from the Boches!"

After the Frenchman had left we automatically and obediently joined the desperate, pathetic exodus. Scattered among those on foot, every conceivable form of wheels was put to use: horse drawn carts, baby carriages, farm vehicles, wheel barrows, ice-cream carts and, as though to accentuate our anxiety, even a hearse drawn by black horses. How I yearned for any such means for lightening our burden! The wish became more obsessive with each step under our heavy load.

As we were about to turn the corner westward, Mutti screamed with all her might: "Let's hold on to each other!"— fearing that the clogged artery would again separate us. Panic was written onto almost every face. For it was not only "Mama" and "Papa", Mrs. Mellon or I who had gotten lost during mergers. These were by no means isolated cases, but had happened to untold others. Steadfastly we were clinging together with the commitment to remain that way even in the event of an air attack. My heart was pounding as we were making the perilous turn. There was no crooked tree nor any other landmark this time. The havoc of humans made this corner a bedlam. Fear was compounded by the sporadic distant pandemonium getting closer with each step. Why in the world would we go any further and approach the threat?! I asked myself—and answered: Just because everyone is following the other one, and the next one. Never shall I get caught up in such deadly masses!

I renewed my promise to myself and prayed for two things: not to lose each other and no Stuka nor Messerschmitt to suddenly drop out of the sky . . . I felt scared and downtrodden.

To our immense relief we successfully maneuvered around the corner. The grim feeling subsided because we remained linked together. As though in compensation there was a vision of such peaceful beauty. It could have created an *art naif*. The straight canal and the road evenly lined with poplar trees on each side imparted a most serene picture of perfect symmetry.

The resigned, wretched refugees poured onto both sides of the road, oblivious to the simple, yet striking beauty. Although we were overburdened, the placid scenery never seemed monotonous and even added to maintaining a pleasant attitude.

Continuing along the canal, we passed heavily laden barges being drawn by individuals with long harnesses of heavy rope. I had only seen this previously in a film about the Bolshevist boatmen forcing the Tzarist elite in their elegant evening clothes to pull similar crafts accompanied by the rhythm of the song: "Pull hard! Pull hard!" That was exactly what these peasants were doing right now, as we were just following the crowd.

"This must be France! This must be France! The way I imagined a French village to be!" I exclaimed.

It sure is! It sure is!" Was affirmed by my walking neighbors.

I was fascinated by the characteristic very narrow double side-walk and the typical weather-worn window shudders. Frenchmen wearing their berets were sitting at small tables enjoying green drinks. If the patrons' faces had not been shadowed by such somberness this rustic village would have imparted a peace time atmosphere. The entire main street was clustered with bistros and cafés. I stepped into each one asking three questions: "May we order *Chartreuse*?

"No, we're out of them!" was the snappy answer.

"Can we barter bread for sardines or chocolates?"

A full throated mocking laugh was the reply.

Now, my last question. This one was difficult to formulate—not knowing the French word for "wheels" I itemized: "Wheelbarrow, stroller or cart?" I was so embarrassed for soliciting in such poor language that I found myself holding my foot in my hand.

There must be a better way. Although there was the denial of the liquor, I continued to ask in the other cafés and bistros, but I omitted the bread question. For the third one, I wracked my brain and came up with one word: "rouler" (to roll). My question thus turned out to be: "Est-ce que vous avez quelque chose à rouler?"

Relentlessly, I dragged from door to door with my inquiry until it became a tragic outcry of utter despair. The night started to close in on us and we had no idea where to find shelter. Like sheep we followed the others into a huge hay loft.

A mature, big, strong man came charging like an angry bull. His French roared rapidly in no uncertain terms for all of us to leave.

Someone from the crowd approached me and demanded that I tell this wild man to contain himself. All at once I realized that the stranger was Mr. Rinsky, my most difficult, lemon sucking student. Under the circumstances there was no chance to express my enormous amazement.

"Talk to him! Talk to him! Calm him down!" The changed Mr. Rinsky commanded.

"Our host" was seized by fury and shouted at all of us collectively. Watching his rage, Mr. Rinksy threw disdainful looks at me, as he mumbled in disgust: "Ach, why in the world can't you talk French as you speak English?! Now, that it is of such dire importance!"

At this moment, a brave, middle-aged woman approached the raving manic who threatened us with a pitchfork. She was pathos personified, when with a hand gesture of begging, she said almost in a whisper under tears: "Monsieur, s'il vous plaît . . . !" His answer: . . .—he kicked her, he actually physically kicked her!

None of the men challenged his inhumane behavior. How dare this monster boot a woman, and one of such small and frail stature? Nobody defied his despicable action, nor even risked to move. The horror and disbelief of what had just come to pass left everyone in shock.

After this, there was total silence. I took a deep breath—and from afar I cried: "Monsieur, vous ne regrettez pas, si nous restons ici pour une nuit, une nuit!" [3] Many of the men then resounded: "Une nuit! Une nuit!" until it became a chorus.

Like a miracle, the maniac disappeared. Everyone brought my family as well as the abused lady the most hay.

Since things had simmered down and most of the people had fallen asleep, I was curious about the "new" Mr. Rinsky and went over to him. As it turned out, he was quite unapproachable. Not only his look had changed since I had last seen him (so pitifully sitting on his big, brown suitcase at the Antwerp station), but what was even more drastic, I found a different person from the resigned, sad, lemon biting, broken man. He turned out to be downright nasty, not even giving me the opportunity to express my astonishment of our chance meeting. He also ignored my inquiry about his wife Trudy in the U.S.A.

When I returned to my parents and our haybed, I shrugged which told them everything. I was delighted that they understood. Gratefully, I flopped down on my straw-stack wondering about Mr. Rinsky. Maybe it's the present lack of lemons, I thought jokingly. The change of personality must have deep psychological roots such as feeling alone and abandoned.

Exhausted even more from the constant French question for anything to roll than from the actual lugging itself, I drifted into the land of dreams.

---

[3]   Sir, you won´t regret it if we stay here for just one night

Chapter 10

"Get up! Get up! Wash yourself!" There's water and nobody is in line." Mutti was as triumphant as though she had made a great discovery. "Get up! Get up! Wash yourself!" Her voice urged me, barely penetrating my wonderful world of dreams. I had to rearrange my thoughts to form the simple question: "Is it morning already?" "Oh, no, you slept soundly for a couple of hours and since nobody is using the water at the moment we better rush and get there—so that we can have clean feet at least!" she commanded.

"And for this you tore me out of my precious, deep sleep which for me is like a rare jewel?" I asked reproachfully.

"So is water these days! Let's seize the moment!"

"Only to someone with a sanitary addiction like you, Mutti." I dared to object. Like a somnambulist I was dragged outdoors to the large spout. Pointing out to her that they weren't even dirty, I obediently washed them with the ice-cold water.

When I returned to my hay bed I was miserable. My feet were fresh, but freezing. This, and my anger at Mutti, combined with the bad situation kept me awake the entire night. I was the only soul who was desperately and vainly seeking sleep. During the restless night my animosity turned into hate. I questioned my own ambivalence about the fine line between love and hate. I tried to modify my negative thoughts by remembering how much I loved my parents and how anxiously I had searched for them when I had lost them. But I was not able to extinguish my strong and dark sentiments throughout these endless, lonely, nocturnal hours, lying among those many snoring strangers.

The Islam obliges its followers to bathe their feet and genitals at least once a day. It's not a bad idea at all! I agreed trying to push my resentment aside. Yet, it reappeared:—but not under such arduous circumstances! It was absolutely heartless of Mutti! Then again, as though trying to force a pain to subside, I compared the Moslem law with one of ours: never to partake of food without cleaning your hands.

I was thrilled when day broke, because I no longer had to lie there. Mutti still believed that she had done me a great favor pointing out when we were leaving: "You see the long line at the faucet?"

Since we were not on the main road everyone dispersed in order to get there. It felt great not to be in the caravan—if only briefly. The three of us traversed the village again. There were some simple, small homes with white picket fences surrounding small gardens. Of course, I knocked at each of them. There was no answer. One door opened, though, and an elderly Frenchman of slight build appeared. In reply to my "rolling" question he said: *"Un moment, s'il vous plaît!"* After ten minutes he emerged beamingly holding up one steaming egg in each hand, a very touching gesture. I had not even seen any since I had left Antwerp. It must have been a sacrifice on his part when he chivalrously said: *"Pour vous, Mademoiselle!"* He apologized for not having a third one. Maybe this was compensation for the lack of the requested equipment. As we were devouring the tasty and (for the first time in weeks) hot food I said: "One just cannot generalize. We could have assumed by the madman's uncouth behavior that all Frenchmen were equally evil. But here, in the same village, we found the opposite in character and appearance."

Soon we arrived at the continuation of the café-tavern row—or was it the next village? I again took up the double burden of lugging and begging in the hope to barter food for a rolling device.

In one bistro the barmaid beckoned a jovial farmer. I explained our request. We needed to trade the huge cumbersome, pig-leather suitcase for two plain burlap potato sacks. At first, there was compassionate surprise in his Gallic eyes. Quickly though, he recognized the irony and realized his good fortune due to our need. He politely asked whether he could take our heavy Pullman in his green wagon drawn by a broad-chested white horse into the neighboring place. What a comfortable suggestion!

Aside from my small valise we gave him everything, the most important belongings which were the contents of the big satchel plus the sardines and chocolates. I kept some of the latter in my little case. He was swift about loading. In view of the fact that we had envisioned another weary day of dragging we felt relief—but mixed with uneasiness. Could we trust his honesty? There was no alternative!

Our situation would have been aggravated by the walking crowd. It seemed that here in France was a density of a moving mob. It crossed my mind that he might take us on the wagon also. I was astonished that there was nothing forthcoming from Mutti. Not daring to push my luck, I omitted the question. He spurred his proud, snowy steed, and with that he was off, lost in the crowd as did the first military Frenchman. We were to meet at a corner which he described. Vati carried my valise and I felt relieved to just walk. While doing so, I was still apprehensive and abhorred the fact that the man had not offered us a ride on the empty carriage next to our suitcase. The whole deal was peculiar, but urgent! Aloud I said: "Can you imagine how wonderful peace time would be, to amble along without cumbersome baggage or frightening noises!" These constantly loomed threateningly in the distance.

We arrived at the designated place. Glad to have encountered the depicted shingle of yet another white horse: *"Au Cheval Blanc"* named appropriately enough. But in reality there was no such mare nor the green wagon. In fact, the place was shut down.

Vati bit his lower lip and uttered on word: "Oh weh!" Mutti demanded reproachfully: "Now what?!" I ran into the adjacent café—fortunately it was open—asking for the fellow with the white steed. In my nervousness, however, my French did not turn out very coherent. They misunderstood and added to the confusion by repeating with a crescendo—as though I were deaf—that the "White Horse" is next door, but closed. More people meddled into my cause getting louder and louder as though wanting to make matters worse by choosing not to understand. Had I become paranoid to think that there was a conspiracy against me? With upheld arms, the gesture of resignation, I ran out, my parents at my heels wanting me to interpret. Rushing around the corner I knocked at the adjoining house on the small side street.

Now that we were without our belongings we were seized by an empty, naked feeling plus the fear of being without any food. As I was calling at the door, I felt my original uneasiness turn into angst, the dread of loss until I was on the verge of panic. Evidently, it must have caused my banging to be more persistent. At last, the entrance was reluctantly opened by a mother with two teenage sons.

With utmost control I inquired about the owner of a green wagon pulled by a white horse. As I was doing so, Mutti seemed to have been struck with hysteria. She was alternately wringing her hands or running her flat palms over her head muttering: "Oh weh, Oh weh!" Even though she accused us of having been frivolous to trust the man, she looked so pathetic in her suffering that my heart went out to her. She was looking desperately at the street trying to spot the white horse.

The physical load of the heavy baggage had been bad enough, but being without it was emotionally unbearable. In the best French I could muster I related the upsetting event, when—I could not believe my eyes—there he was on top of his green wagon spurring his horse just as he had done when we saw him last. He made the animal run as speedily as the walking crowd would allow. *"Monsieur! Monsieur!"* I yelled with all my might. As I was shouting, I waved my arms vigorously like a flag ship sailor and raced toward the "White Horse" tavern. All this commotion forced him to have brief eye contact with me. He continued into the direction where we had first met him.

All eyes followed mine. *"C'est lui, c'est lui!"*[4] I cried. The boys quickly brought out their bicycles and followed the evasive man. Had we been deceived or would we see him with our precious belongings and food?

Fortunately and finally we came face to face with the friendly, yet fleeing fellow, escorted by the teenagers, who were heroes in

---

[4] That's him!

our eyes. He dared to grin and handed us two burlap bags. For the last time, Mutti unlocked the still elegant leather satchel. Vati transferred our belongings, sardines and chocolates into the potato sacks with the sad feeling of "adieu". "This is the story of our lives", Vati pointed out: „the genuine pig leather suitcase of what we were, and the old, ragged burlap sacks of what we have become— ja, ja!" He handed the boys sardines and chocolates, priceless gifts these days, caressing the suitcase one last time.

At first, Vati did not seem to realize nor mind the awkward weight on his back. When he saw my compassionate grimace, he was the one to console me: "Ah, I am used to this type of hard labor from way back. When I first arrived in Germany from Poland—my destination had been America—I decided to stay and work in Köln and work I did arduously! Until I made it in my own flourishing steel business. So don't worry!"

We distracted ourselves by speculating on the intention of the grinning Frenchman: "Did he want to eschew us? Was he cunning and crafty or did it really take him that long to look for the sacks?" I questioned. "But why in the world would he pass the 'White Horse' tavern? It will remain a mystery forever!"

Again we were among the density of the marching mob alongside the picturesque canal. I felt so sorry for Vati walking with these poor bundles just like the eternal wandering Jew. I was even more compassionate for the man in front of us pulling an oversized handcart with assorted freight and five children. They made me think of Mitzi and her family. I wondered how they were surviving. The cart puller paused briefly, so did we. As he looked into our direction he took notice of Mutti. Seizing this rather friendly moment, I conferred quickly with my parents. Then I suggested to the short, dark bearded father: "Why not put our forces together?" He was more than pleased using the Yiddish saying: "Sure, two men towing are better than one, just as two heads thinking are better than one."

I thought triumphantly: "Finally, finally, we made it! We got something that rolls!" For the moment we were content. We had our belongings, *quelque chose à rouler,* friendly company, idyllic scenery and fine weather. But seeing Vati like an ox dragging the big harness on his shoulder distressed me. When our eyes met, he comforted me again: "Don't look like a cocker spaniel! Remember what I told you about my working!" He pointed to the strap and cart: "This preceded the Mercedes, the tractors and the heavy Büssing truck. Ja, ja and all that for nothing!"

But what did I see down there? The barges on the canal were drawn by women only! Oh, further down was one lone woman towing a smaller one single-handedly. Incredible! How differently I had imagined the fashionable French female! There was nobody who could tell me whether women were doing this now because of the war or whether this tedious job had always been their lot. Vati pointed to the woman at the canal saying: "Calm down, it's not quite as bad as it may appear."

At least for me there were a few fine hours of just walking without the valise. It would have been a relief had it not been for the war noises getting closer. There was an exchange of twenty frightened eyes. The five children seemed to have been trained to accept any catastrophe silently. They huddled together in the cart as if to seek solace in each other. The bigger ones were protecting the smaller ones like miniature mother hens. The sounds were of a most terrifying basso. There were again horrified glances among the ten of us. As the bedlam approached the children clutched even tighter.

Not again, for heaven's sake, not again will the dreaded shelling threaten our lives! From afar we could see an orange-yellow-gray-black horizon. How heart wrenching to leave this beautiful, deceptively peaceful world forever! Here, on the open road, it could happen to anyone. Once more, I was seized by dark terror. Nothing can compare to the dread of approaching flying enemies.

Everyone around us looked somber, deeply depressed, exhausted, troubled, and petrified to be here on this exposed highway. The fear of an ensuing stampede and the absolute certainty of confronting death in case of an attack was agonizing.

"I do not want to go through the experience of those hellish seconds ever again!" I surprised myself by almost screaming.

Indeed, there they were, the dreaded sirens! Mutti was the first to shout: "Off the road! Off the road!" "But there is a ditch along the highway!" the two men protested. "Let's just get away from the canal and the street! At the shallowest spot, we'll unload everything, getting the empty cart onto the grass. Away, away from here to avoid being crushed by the human landslide! In case of a strafing attack, we'll be helpless, unable to fend for ourselves. Let's get out of this chain gang at once!" Mutti ordered firmly.

"There is logic in her words. Her ideas are plausible", we all agreed.

The toughest part was splitting the crowd so that the cart could pass horizontally. Vast pastures lay in front of us. Of course, pulling the big handcart through the rather coarse turf was difficult for the two men.

"Look, look, there's a pathway just fit for our purpose!" I shouted. Vati and the young father pulled hard to reach the dirt road. Alas, before arriving, there they were: the dreaded air-vandals! Unmistakably and unavoidably the buzzing was approaching. By now the ground was dotted with refugees who had followed our footsteps. Instinctively, we dashed for cover underneath the cart.

"Let us be as lucky as we were last time!" I cried out loud. It is punishment enough to suffer the excruciating suspense: will the planes with the black double cross zoom out of the sky to machine gun us? Will they release their murderous cargo or—please, please, let it be this way again—fly overhead as they did last time. Knots were forming in my throat and stomach as the inevitable moment was upon us and the roar sounded as though it came straight from above the cart. We all lay breathlessly. The poor little ones did not dare to blink for fear that it might interfere with the enemy's moves. It was no conscious effort, but the terror literally forced us to choke ourselves. I continued to pray: Please, please, spare us the bombs and gunning!

We were lying there still and motionless for what seemed like an eternity. Planes are supposed to be so fast, but it was a long, slow process as the deep, ferocious, rolling hum became less and less audible. Finally, finally the much desired "out of danger" monotone siren went off! My prayers had been answered! The planes had passed just as they had done before.

"Children, let's get out of here! And children, we can breathe freely and naturally. So take many deep, deep breaths!" I exclaimed with huge relief. It was adorable and amusing to see all of them inhale together as though they were in dancing class. At the same moment we heard a tremendous blast. The dice had been cast for over there where in all likelihood people were dying, while we were safe for the moment. I remembered the last blowout when "Papa" saw the beautiful villa explode in a second. As I was pondering I realized that by now more people were pulling their carts over the rough but lush grass, I praised Mutti for her foresight: "Again you were a pace-setter with your great ideas and determination!"

When we were finally ready to continue our walk towards the dirt path Mutti turned around exclaiming: "Wait a minute! What are we doing? We are just walking aimlessly! We came here to avoid a stampede in case of an air attack. Now we don't even know which direction we are taking!" "Beautiful little face, do you need a compass like Columbus?" the father of five questioned in jest much to Mutti's annoyance.

Suddenly, he stood before us: the self-appointed elder who had served us rather well at the empty house. He was big and strong and had a mane of white hair. A toga and staff would have completed the image of the biblical Moses. This impression was emphasized when he spread his arms as though to bless "his flock". Instead he pointed in his far-reaching voice that further up the pasture there were wooden, empty, former army barracks. "Look, we all deserve a rest. We would have a roof over our heads for tonight without searching," he addressed those who would listen to him. I was one of them.

We did not have to walk far. In the midst of the rolling green there was indeed a huge wooden barrack. Rather new, plain tables and benches were the only furnishings. It reminded me of the place where our steel workers used to take their lunch, coffee-or beer breaks. The barrack was spacious and smelled fresh. Mutti, practical as always, advised: "Let's pick which tables will serve us as tonight's beds." While everyone got settled she left.

I was grateful for everything that resembled peacetime—such as the *Chartreuse* in the bistro. I was now enjoying to see the children play outside. "This is the first healthy, normal activity they have engaged in since we left Antwerp," their painfully shy and quiet mother finally uttered. When Mutti returned she seemed aggravated and said in a disappointed voice: "There is absolutely no water, none!"

"Well, beautiful, little face," the young father said teasingly in Yiddish: "Did you expect to find Robert Taylor here also?" Mutti could dignify so trite a remark with a haughty gesture and a disgruntled German: "Ach!" This time I would have more than welcomed even ice cold water since it was still late afternoon. Therefore, I went to look for it myself. Instead, I found another teenage girl, who said in beautiful French: "No, there is no W.C." "No Winston Churchill, our best friend?" I asked facetiously since each second without danger made me euphoric. She seemed to appreciate this little joke and joyously explained that she had not laughed since she had left Paris. She related her unfortunate decision to visit her refugee aunt in Liège, Belgium, thus getting caught up—needlessly, for her, a Parisian Jew—in this mammoth turmoil.

I would have tortured myself if it had happened to me I thought to myself but to her I continued my comic remarks: "No wonder our Allies lost, if they were stationed where there was no W.C." Her laughter reminded me of the foodless restaurant in Ostend where we had been in great danger also. "It seems to be a human defense." I reflected and told her this and many other experiences. She complimented my French so that I made more progress in that elegant language with her than I did since taking it up. "It is the first time I'm simply conversing without being under enormous stress, immediate fear and humiliation." I explained. It is great to have an exchange of opinions with one's peer," she answered with glee.

"When you are smiling you look like I had imagined a Gaelic girl to appear—quite unlike the boat-women we saw." I flattered her in all honesty. As we continued to indulge in this verbal fun, the sun set, showing off her last, still colorful glitter like an aging beauty. Our banter was like an oasis enhanced by my amazement as to how, precisely at this moment, the French language had just come to me. Yes, now my thoughts automatically were French. Thus I conquered the secret key to the knowledge of any tongue. In the newly acquired speech and in softer tones—some people were "bedding" on the tables—we continued: "I am so pleased that our conversation made both of us forget the agonizing fear of bombardments. We are actually in dire danger right at this moment." I was sorry to point out. "This sole barrack, surrounded by nothing but pastures, is highly visible, which is in favor of the enemy. Besides, they may assume that it is still occupied by the Allied soldiers. The more reason for the Nazis to throw their deadly cargo on us. I'm so terribly frightened of that ghastly feeling—to be startled by the shrill whistles announcing our eventual death by Stukas or Messerschmitts from above at any time."

"Even more scary are the concentration camps and dreadful killings directed solely against us Jews for merely being Jewish. The unspeakable acts the Nazis perpetrated in Poland! What's more, your greatest terror is of a temporary nature. Once they'll occupy, there might be occasional bombings, but we'll be living or dying in constant panic, and that for God knows how long?" she theorized most logically and sadly.

"Isn't it bad for us teenage girls in the spring of both, the season and our lives, to be comparing our fears of Nazi-imposed methods of deaths?" I questioned. We bade each other "Bonne Nuit!" in order to spend the night or whatever was left of it on the wooden tables.

Once I had arrived at mine I was careful not to disturb those around me. In the darkness I drew close to Mutti, the only one still awake. Though the dialogue with the French girl had turned out alarming, I again felt good about myself based upon mastering her beautiful language. The next morning, she came running toward me apologizing: "I felt so terrible to have filled you with black thoughts just so shortly before bedtime that I could not sleep." I assured her: "No, *au contraire*, the triumph of possessing this new gift—French—was more powerful than the worrisome predictions. Consequently and amazingly, I slept soundly, if briefly." We were both looking to execute our elementary necessities. In the process we were shocked and ashamed at what we discovered. We came to the conclusion: "Look, how low humanity can sink!" Men and women were managing to serve their most primitive needs side by side forming cubicles but minus the wall separations. We were so appalled at this scene that we ran further until we each found a tree. "What a dreadful life! I'd rather be constipated." I sighed afterwards and complained: "There is no water to wash our hands at least." "Why don't you put on some lipstick?" La Parisienne asked. "What, on an unwashed face?" I was startled. "It'll make you feel better!" she insisted. It was against my nature but I acquiesced. "Doesn't it put you in a better frame of mind?" She questioned and remarked: "Even in this mess you look so sweet!" "So do you and what's more, you are!" As I was about to embrace her . . . oh, no! . . . the humming, oh, that dreadful humming . . . I threw myself down onto the dew-moist grass and pulled her with me. Oh, no, not again! My chest was bursting with fear! Oh, no, I thought in horror, not being able to utter a sound, while they flew overhead. During these petrifying moments, my mind played tricks on me coming up with a dangerous analogy: There was a hissing cobra in the grass, near me! Cobra, that's what the boys called me at Principal Emil Kahn's class. It was a school secret. The girls didn't know and the boys wouldn't tell. Was it because I had all the bright answers at my fingertips and was so anxious to reveal them announcing this with a wiggling serpentine arm? It still baffled me.

What a relief that my own thoughts had me hypnotized thus desensitizing my terror of the flying black crossed devils. Now, the buzzing was moving away. One last handshake, a warm glance to my *Leidensgenossin*[5] and off I was, dashing in the opposite direction to my worried parents.

Now that we finally got wheels it was hard to drag them over the grass. We were weaving in and out of dirt roads. Meanwhile,

---

[5]   A German noun meaning "buddy in suffering"

the war noises were no longer just a distant rumbling but an ever-increasing man made iron thunder. I still could not help wondering why all these adults were herding towards the threat. I wanted to stop them especially in the face of the increase of enemy planes. Inner turmoil was driving me out of my mind. When I looked around, I realized that I was no exception. Excruciating fear was on every face.

Quite abruptly and without any provocation to everyone's amazement—even the five cherubs opened their little mouths in surprise—Mutti ordered firmly: "Halt! I want out, out of here! We must leave instantly! We'll perish if we'll continue this endless walk!"

"But where do you want to go?" Vati asked rather timidly.

"Where we set out to be, in Dunkerque! Into a city! Into a hotel, where we can wash up!" Mutti yelled hysterically. "Sure, the Grand Hotel, the Ritz, the Excelsior or The Savoy are no doubt waiting for you. Which one will it be, Madame?" was the father's mocking question. "No, no, I've got to do this! Nobody dare to stop me!" Mutti asserted herself. "But Sofiechen, Sofiechen!" Vati pleaded. "Mutti, think about it! Think of what we went through about quelque chose à rouler, just think about it!" I besought her. "I dare any of you to stop me!" she protested resolutely while swiftly trying to detach one of her additional bundles off the cart handle. In the process, the impact threw her backwards onto the ground. This appeared so tragicomic that I was embarrassed for her sake.

"Get these sacks!" she commanded and emphasized: "Off the cart! Off the cart!" "How can you be like this to all of us?" Vati and I entreated her. "You were just as upset about leaving the villa with or without these two old people. Remember, what happened shortly afterwards?" she pressed her point. "By any chance", Vati asked, "are you obsessed with that sixth sense, that mysterious instinct of yours again?" "Do you feel like that blind, black man again who 'felt the earthquake coming in his bones'?" I demanded. "Yes the inner warning is creeping up within me just as it did at the villa," she admitted. She was so convincing and strong-willed that we had no choice but to follow her.

The young family was flabbergasted. To the father it seemed to have been such a blow that he screamed at her: "Beautiful little face, what do you think you are doing?" For the first time throughout the difficult "hike", I saw his good-natured smile turn into hot, red anger. Ashamed of Mutti's action, I shrugged: "Sorry, I can't help it!" I warmly pressed his hand with both of mine.

I left with an awful feeling, which was strongly accentuated, when I heard: "Beautiful little face, what are you doing?" As we went further we still could hear: "Beautiful little face! Beautiful little face!" Parting, leaving, again pulling our bundles, we heard softer lamenting of "beautiful little face!" It faded out into a dramatic echo resounding over the vast green pastures—.

Slowly, we dragged ourselves along the bumpy trail. We both eyed Mutti. Mutti stared at us. She asked in an aggressive yet defensive way: "What was I to do?" With that we silently continued until we reached the canal again. I was the one to break our hushed trudging by saying: "Now there are just the three of us, all by ourselves, yet surrounded once more by that dense crowd, composed of individuals who are dense in their heads as well," when the ever-increasing noise of heavy war machines hit our ears.

Vati's answer was his sad: "Ja, ja!" as he glanced over to Mutti this time somewhat sullenly and reproachfully, which she ignored. I could not help to point out: "Look, how that mob of people is marching toward the waves of danger—and so are we!"

We finally reached *Dunkirk* "Church by the Dunes" under the frightening sounds of shelling. "Other than the weather, everything appeared so grim as though we were lured into a deadly trap," I heard myself whine. The town itself was to the right of the canal road. We stopped and had a serious private conference. Vati said: "It is hopeless to waste our physical strength on a lost cause. We must regain it by rest. Two of us have to look for a place to sleep in order to gather our forces for a return. Now, that we were actually close to a city, there must be rooms. After much pro and con, it was decided that Vati and I venture into *Dunkirk*.

It was one of those very rare moments, when I saw Mutti embrace Vati, tearfully just whispering one word: "Jakob!" Then she hugged me wordlessly and sobbed as though this might be the last time, since we could easily lose each other. Tears were running down her hollow cheeks: "Don't forsake me! Don't abandon me!" When Vati and I took off, we turned around to wave to her, to one little pathetic figure amongst that desperate exodus underneath a poplar tree guarding burlap bags—. Vati and I walked until we found *la Grand'Place*, so characteristic for most European cities. In the middle of it stood a statue of Jean Bart, a French naval hero. This was a ghost town! We were astonished! Never had I seen a main square so totally evacuated. There was no living soul to approach. It was frightening to realize that we were the only two people here. The soundless, normally certainly charming carillons were just threatening towers.

We left the plaza and went toward the tall, but shattered port cranes. Arriving at the wharf we realized in shock that the shipyard had turned into a ship-graveyard. It looked as though these still proud majestic huge vessels had been invaded by ghouls leaving them with still burning fires as though they were open wounds, to smolder slowly until they would perish. The oil tanks were aflame. The smoke-filled scene was a ghastly sight. Again, we found ourselves all alone directly witnessing such devastation. We decided to hurry back to Mutti. Here it was easy to rush. I remarked to Vati: "Either there is total emptiness or we are squeezed amongst hordes. A loving glance and a sad: "Ja, ja!" was the answer and he added: "Our odyssey must stop now, because they will catch up with us. What you kept asking, mein Kind, why walk toward the danger, is easy to answer: because the further West, the further away from the Nazis we will be and the better our chances of fleeing them. Judging by what the French soldier told us about them encircling the Allies and hearing the heavy artillery it seems that they almost succeeded in closing their fire ring. We were in the remaining gap. Then, as an afterthought: "We should have returned right after that encounter with the military man. But you experienced firsthand how it felt to go against the current."

"Yes, these were precisely the words of my dear German friends and business associates whose hearts were definitely dead set against the Nazi mania who sighed: 'Ach Jakob, one cannot go against the tide', when they had reached the conclusion, after fighting for so long, that they were in a no-win situation. Ja, ja, it is human nature to go with the stream, even if you are fully aware that you are wrong, dead wrong. Verstehst, mein Kind?" He studied my face to discern whether I fully and truly understood. We spotted Mutti at the edge of the canal. She looked so wretched and pitiful. I sensed the relief she must have felt on seeing us. She embraced both of us simultaneously and sobbed, totally out of character: "My dearest ones, my two dearest ones in the whole wide world!"

As we were telling her our ghost story, some eavesdropping refugees exclaimed: "Great, let's go there! That's perfect, our multi-presence surely will 'de-ghost' and populate Dunkirk's *Grand' Place*!" No sooner said, all of us were on our way. After a while people were all around the square. Their presence actually enhanced the plaza, so different from when we first had seen it. After the stronger ones made a fast forced entry, we were able to go freely into one of the bistros. Only a few days before it must have been a charming place. Underneath the dust, there were highly polished mahogany tables, benches and captain's chairs. I felt solace to be amidst the many strangers.

We tried to figure out how to make our "beds". The high gloss on the benches looked good, but made the wood slippery. We tried to improvise with the captain's chairs, when—suddenly, oh God!—it was as though all the devils straight from hell were unleashing their wrath in unyielding fury. Did their rage come to haunt me? Now there was this new fright that took my breath away: that horrific shrill whistle cutting the air on its earthbound way. It was ready now to strike us with sudden death. I cried and wept out loud. Mutti cradled me in her arms like a baby and during the brief intervals whispered: "See, I'm protecting you from that terrible danger!" I thought how she could possibly shield me sideways if death was zooming in from above? But it was grand of her that just before I should perish, I did have a mother, when, indeed, I needed her the most. It was reassuring that for once, she had not been the "queen". This was just the right time, because the secure feeling would at least make me die in peace.

Planes were screeching overhead. The suspense of waiting for death was unbearable. There, again, there it was: the cutting, screeching, shriek-whistle straight above our heads. I tried to hypnotize myself like I had done before in utter danger—but this outdid it all. My thoughts were sober, but solemn, about how ironic it would be, that the very sky that would bring my torturous death, my own mirage, clad all in white, would wind up in those same heavens afterwards.

The agony continued throughout the night. Enemy planes were zeroing in constantly from the air. Oh, those Stuka dive-bombers with their terrible screams and the culminating fear of the air-cutting whistle. Each piercing sound could mean my last breath, the last minute of life. It felt as though the world above had been ripped open. Look, listen, it would yell internally when in a flash the rapidly increasing crescendo of the whistling would burst into shattering pandemonium all around us. It was a hair raising suffering of a thousand deaths. Some religious Jews would yell out: "Shma Israel!" a last ritual outcry. Except for some human eerie wailing noises of angst, no other words were heard. To be in the midst of so many was the only comfort, though no words, gestures, not even glances were exchanged. Each individual crawled completely into himself enduring bravely his own pain. The panic paralyzed all of us into breathless silence and petrified immobility.

If I live, I renewed my vow, but with the afterthought, that if anyone here survives, I would never be the recipient of such torment again. All the while the Teutonic fury was relentlessly lashing out upon us.

After quite some time, there suddenly was stillness in the air. This was interrupted by sounds of coughing, as smoke came curling in everywhere. Suffocation forced us out into the cold early morning. The sight was hellish. The main square of Dunkirk was a true inferno. Every house was ablaze and miraculously "ours" had just started catching fire from the neighboring one. Now what? We sank onto our sacks in the middle of the plaza, forlorn, shivering from fear and chill. The sky looked like an ominous painting in orange, red, yellow, a deep black and gray.

Though we were exhausted and without any roof, I felt relieved at being saved from the flying Nazis—for now. We were literally sitting it out until day would break. What will the sunrise bring us?

In a daze we saw a whole city perish in front of our eyes! It lit up the dawn. To think that only hours ago, this was downtown Dunkirk, presently looking like a curse of a biblical image. God only knows, what had happened and was still occurring in the flames right now. No firemen were at hand. Like a miracle, also straight out of the Hebrew Bible, was that we and the other shadows of humanity, strewn about the non-burning part of the place, were alive. Stunned by the striking victorious Germans, we decided to be on our way eastward as soon as light would come. "Yes, Mr. Mellon was right. This whole odyssey West was a mistake and completely in vain." Vati broke our bewilderment, not taking his eyes of the thousands of flaming tongues and nodding ever so sadly: "Ja, ja!"

At long last, day broke. We left the burning square only to be accompanied by the dreadful humming from above. I could only internalize a prayer: "Oh, God, let this past night have been the culmination of your punishment and—thanks for having let us survive this nocturnal ordeal."

Chapter 11

We were not the only ones to have made the decision for a retreat East. In fact, most of the refugees did, but this time, not in the chain gang manner. Everyone rolled, dragged or carried their stuff through meadows and pathways individually. We did not quite know the reason. Did the columns of people attract the enemy planes? Was there a temporary regulation by the Allied High Command to have us refugees off the main roads because we were congesting them, thus interfering with their military plans? We could only guess.

We were staying overnight whenever and wherever there was a roof overhead. The sardines and chocolates were devoured whenever and wherever it was feasible. Worryingly, Vati said: "If we don't find any bread soon, we won't even have our precious cans anymore. Now it is no longer a question to fill our stomachs, but prolonging our stock. The only positive result of this," he sighed deeply, "there will be less weight to lug." This was the end of his monologue and all conversation. We felt grumpy.

We passed the village of Malo. Then in the next village of Bray just prior to crossing the old cobbled main street, we stopped short, looking at each other big eyed and stern faced . . . for . . . we heard German men's voices. Every so often the command like phrase "Auf nach Dunkirchen," "on to Dunkirk" was audible. Villagers were in front of their houses and a number of them were lining the corner of the tavern. Lo and behold, a small corps of German soldiers was approaching this, our intersection. They seemed exhausted too, and minus their usual swagger, which seemed to have rendered them more harmless, for the moment. Even though they were not in their customary top notch fit condition, my heart was beating faster. It was quite a shock to have come at an unexpected moment face to face with the enemy.

Simultaneously, I saw a Frenchman leave the bar and join a marching Nazi as though he was a glorious liberator and offer him: "Deutscher Soldat, Kaffee, Wein, Wasser?" When he declined, the traitor kept up with him in order to continue his insistence. This insolent one then tried unsuccessfully, sweetly smiling, to tempt the other soldiers with these goodies. I was enraged to view such high treason unfold right before my eyes. This indicated that they were here to stay in France. Otherwise, this Frenchman would not dare to show his sympathetic inclination so brazenly to these cunning invaders, fearlessly before all his fellow countrymen. With my anger having built, I wanted to explode! To counteract that strong feeling, I thought, he should have some intention to shake venom into the coffee, wine, and water. To regain my dead seriousness, I felt that to be in the shadow of a Nazi, nowadays, means to be in the shadow of death, if not right now, then later on.

Though we dragged ourselves for the first time without stampeding crowds, it seemed not quite unending as our westbound trek.

Then, the first wonderful whiff of a fresh sea breeze revived us. There once more, the splendid dunes were beckoning. The side of a larger one offered some shelter. All this beauty was possibly deceptive war area, but we were starved and weary with miasma of ominous threats surrounding us.

This cold dawn had turned into another sunny, magnificent day. It was beautiful and frightening at the same time: the dunes, the majestic ocean, the treacherous blue sky out of which the Stukas or Messerschmitt could screech at any given moment, and just the three of us . . . or were we . . . ? Did my fatigue cause me to hear voices? I stopped chewing the chocolate in order to sharpen my senses. No, I did not go mad. My parents froze with a swift exchange of frightened glances. Our hearts and motions were suspended. Once more, this total paralysis and suspense of the looming menace, this time merely feet away, was too much to bear.

Shudders went through my entire being, now, after having seen German soldiers firsthand. I felt my eyes, ears, and body incline in the direction of whispers. Suddenly, my muscles relaxed. A faint smile must have flashed because my parents appeared just a trifle less tense. I found that these soft-spoken words were incongruous with the harshness of German. Only the English language would reveal that certain mellowness so dear to me. I indeed spotted two live Tommies to our immense relief. It was like a brief cessation of immediate danger. We came quickly though to the sad realization that we were in great danger. When Vati urged excitedly, "We are in the fire line! The Nazis there, the Tommies here, and we are between these forces, just fit to be military targets in the combat zone. Let's be done with our elementary and alimentary necessities and get out of here speedily! Before we do, ask the Tommies for bread!"

"I feel embarrassed to make such a request," I objected.

"Ja, Ja, mine Kind, in addition to the obvious, this war does ugly things to us. So ask them for bread. Let's eat and run inland! Go ahead, go ahead!" He kept encouraging me.

Very much contre coeur, I had to push myself to go over there and ask them. This was the very first time I approached any Englishman in his own language, having made my debut with an American at the U.S. Consulate and then with the black U.S. fighter Ralph, both in Antwerp.

Not knowing the hour, I moved toward them with: "Good day, gentlemen! My parents and I were agreeably surprised by your presence!"

"Better us than the Jerries!" the two Tommies exclaimed.

I made a fast mental note that Jerries must mean the Germans. As to answer my curiosity without any question (as did their French counterpart), they said: "We are 'whiting'. We are anxiously 'whiting' in this twelve kilometer stretch between Dunkirk and La Panne in order to get another crack at the Jerries. The French say, "Sauve qui peut". We call it "everyone for himself". The "D" of Dunkirk stands for death trap and destruction. Some 'dai' we'll become 'faimes' for being part of the most heroically and hazardously rescued troops in history, that is, if these 'maikshift' liberators of yachts, boats, ships or anything that's 'navigaible' will ever show up, and if we survive. If not it'll be a "Masada" of mass suicide rather than to be 'enslived', yes, even as prisoners of war by the relentless and remorseless Nazi murderers. We are 'whiting' 'paitently for 'dais' to be mopped up off of these shores.

I was aghast at this information and at the strange way they put it, "to be mopped up."

"May I ask you now an embarrassing question, gentlemen? Namely, do you have any bread?" I finally popped this simple, yet for me so difficult, question.

Up to this point the conversation went fine linguistically. As of now, though, they did not seem to understand me. I thought there were just a couple of them, when they yelled, ironically "Tom! Jerry!"

Two more Tommies appeared in their flat helmets. The first ones asked me to repeat my question. Here I felt relieved that I finally got it over with . . . ! Again I had to make the same inquiry. The four of them looked at each other and shrugged. The first ones then called, "Jaimes and Jaike!"

Promptly James and Jake appeared from behind the third dune. Who knows how many were hiding in pairs behind each dune? Again I had to withstand that feeling of humiliation to make the primitive demand, "Do you have any bread to spare?"

Jake hit a high note: "Oh, she means breaddd . . . breaddd . . . !"

Instead of being content, my embarrassment was threefold: the original nature of the request from the well known English teacher in Antwerp was not understood and I might have taught so wrong to so many. I got the long awaited, but negative answer: a mocking laugh like the bar maid's in the village which we came to pass again just today.

"Bread, food and drinks?" They asked in jest and exclaimed, "Bread, what's that?! We haven't seen any of it since 'dais!'"

I apologized, thanked them anyway and wished them "good luck" to get to the other side of the Channel safely as I bade them "farewell", especially to Jake, the only one who did understand me.

When I returned to my parents' big dune, we rushed to consume the sardines and started to watch the quantity wane. It was good to fill our stomachs with chocolates!

How panic-evoking that there was just the sky, the ocean, the dunes and the three of us. Vati said, "No wonder we are reduced to a trio of loners now. How in the world did the other refugees know that this beach stretch could be ripe to become a death trap at any given moment? Let's sift through the sand as fast as possible!" In anxious silence we did just that. Hurray, we made it! We made it without any close enemy aerial interference.

Breathlessly, we seemed to have reached Belgium. We were in a Belgian coastal village at that, stumbling upon a place of beer, laughter and good times. As I was always the avant-guard, I opened the door to the smoke-filled tavern and again—lo and behold— German soldiers—were clanking their full glasses of foaming beer. As they were lifting their mugs, zealously and with fervor, they yelled out: "Sieg Heil!" (Their insidiously catchy ancient Roman imitation greeting.) This was accompanied by outstretched arm and flat palm and by clinking their booted heels enthusiastically and vigorously together.

I was audacious enough to enter just the same. When they stopped their Nazi rituals in order to gape at me, I felt high-spirited and was amazed at the absence of my own fear.

When they started singing: "Lore, Lore, Lore, schön sind die Mädchen von siebzehn, achtzehn Jahr" (Beautiful are the girls of seventeen, eighteen years!) which they stole from the old U.S. Battle Hymn of the Republic—sung to welcome me, I felt triumphant.

When they came running toward us with three mugs filled with frothy beer, offering one to each of us, I felt victorious.

But when we were hesitant in accepting it, I turned into a shy, little girl.

They were insistent not unlike the treasonous Frenchman.

When they referred to the beer as liquid bread, I could no longer resist after the bread quest, semi starvation and thirst. I could not be a proud hero and throw it into their faces based upon so many reasons. While this was going through my mind, I lifted my mug and downed the lush, strengthening foam in one single gulp. Promptly, another stein was set in front of each of us.

Of course, Germans are known to drown their sorrows in beer. Drinking when they are winning for celebration; drinking when they are losing for consolation.

I had long forgotten that there was the existence of enjoyment. To the victor the spoils, I thought.

"You see, we are not such bad fellows!" they claimed, "Why were you running away from us?" they asked.

I brought the focus on the danger of the shelling effect and was most sincere about it because, "It frightens me to death!" I exclaimed, being careful to put the accent of each word on the last syllable to give my German a French touch. Whereas Mutti rolled her r's "au naturel" since she was born in Poland; and for the same reason Vati had a slight foreign accent. Everyone believed him to be Dutch and he would not dare to deny it. It's far better to be a Hollander than Polish-Jewish. One could not sink any lower than that.

"You speak German exceedingly well", said platinum blond Franz.

"Oh, I'm studying modern philology." I answered as casually as I possibly could.

"No one, but no one can speak German like this from studying modern philology", objected reddish blond Karl Heinz as he was mimicking me, which I resented. Careful, careful, a red light was flashing "Achtung" (watch out!) in my mind.

"Your comrade plays piano very well," I remarked. With this I went over to the handsome pure Aryan military man. He had glanced over at me as he was playing the old happy tunes to cheer up everybody, including himself. Nevertheless, there was a melancholy look about him as every so often he seemed to sigh deeply. He was the picture perfect German image of Goebbel's propaganda, but his beautiful blue eyes had a warm mellow look as opposed to the steel cold fanatic ones depicted on Nazi posters.

He was about to ask me whether I could play the piano also, when another "liquid bread" was set in front of me, its frothy foam beckoning me. I felt ashamed that of all people, a Feldwebel German sergeant made me feel like a woman each time his deutsche blue eyes gazed, sensually, deeply into my Jewish ones. In order to break that spell, I remarked: "You are managing very well with a piano that is definitely out of tune."

His well-shaped lips repeated, "Yes, it's definitely out of tune!" but in his eyes I read a different phrase entirely. "If you would care to sing, I would love to accompany you at the piano or anywhere, if that were only feasible," he suggested without taking his dreamy eyes off of me, as he was going through some international music sheets. That's when I took notice of his heavy typical German hands, including the wrists. This was the French method of detecting German spies.

"Ah, Heimat (from home) pieces", he exclaimed with glee. Gallantly, he got up for me to sit at the piano. The enemies were listening as though waiting to hear a great soloist. I quickly glanced at my parents who stayed at the sidelines, but no silent message was forthcoming. This time, it was my turn for an internal "Oh, veh!" This was based upon the fact that my playing was mediocre, but mostly because of this particular audience. The war must have made me look older, I thought, good for me at this point! Yes, I better play the keyboard, so I would be forced to read the music instead of tremendously enjoying his exciting stare. Our confronting German soldiers certainly took an unexpected turn, which we never, ever could have imagined. While leafing through the German songs, ironically, my glance fell upon "Freut Euch des Lebens!" (Enjoy life). I rushed through it at my first school recital so I was very familiar with the piece. That caused me some relief, but when the happy words "Enjoy life, while you still can!" came rolling out of so many German throats forming quite a thunderous resonance, I was overwhelmed with ambiguity: I was tempted to sing along, but, of course, would not dare. I had sung this song since my earliest childhood. It accompanied so many early memories. My anti-Semitics' protector, Walter, first taught it to me. He might be one of them. Yet this whole family that babysat for me was so dear to me. Nevertheless, I felt like a traitor. How was I so different from the treacherous Frenchman? He offered physical comfort to them with coffee, wine or water, and I provided them with spiritual pleasure, I scolded myself. There was an inner consolation however: "circumstantial!"

I could not help noticing that underneath that German Feldwebel uniform and apparent gaiety was a frightened boy. The music, the beer and above all the nuance of flirtatiousness created an intimate ambiance notwithstanding my parents' watchful eyes, the people and the noise surrounding us. Again, he made me feel like a woman.

When his last glissando of "in der Heimat, da gibt's ein Wiedersehen" (At home, there'll be a W.) still echoed in this seemingly cozy atmosphere, he seemed to restrain himself from taking my hand, and he said in a controlled voice: "I know this is going to be the very last night of my life. I know, that you are the very last girl I'll ever talk to. In the morning it's going to be: "Auf zum Kampf!"

"Need I say I'm impressed," I uttered with hidden bitterness, remembering the statue of flesh who was the poor, fallen Tommy. Therefore," he continued, "I'm not going to sleep. I want to be fully aware that this is my very last night on this earth. I want to celebrate it . . . ," he paused and then almost whispered: " . . . and share it with you!"

My big frightened eyes must have caused him to explain: "No, no, I just want to talk to you, while your parents use my room, the best in the house. Should you ever get tired of my conversation, you are free to join them. After all, I'm not a Barbarian!"

"You sure don't look like one," I retorted and asked: "May I explain all of this to them?"

"Better yet," he answered as he was getting off the piano stool, "I myself shall present this to them."

"Before you do," I held him back, "may I know what makes you so sure, that dead set about your predestination?"

"I feel it deep inside here!" He pointed to his German heart underneath the gray green uniform.

"You feel it in your bones?" I questioned and thought: ah, another one like the big, black, blind man the first Negro I ever talked to in Antwerp, and my own mother who could foretell doom. I related the story of the American Negro fighter and his predictions to him, curious what his reaction to a black man would be. Yet when I compared the soft Southern talk of North America to jazz, I was agreeably surprised when he sat down at the piano and asked with a caressing glance, "like this?" as he played the "September Song". When the last tone faded, he said sadly: "Though it's springtime, I feel that my lifetime bell is tolling midnight of the last day in December. I feel I shall perish. With these words he grew very melancholy. After recapturing his composure, he walked over to my parents, introducing himself as Feldwebel Günther von und zu Schnell, clicking his heels noisily together. But at least he did not stretch out his arm and palm in the Hitler salute; I felt relief. It was quite incongruous for him being just a Nazi sergeant yet emanating from so lofty a heritage. To me this meant that he wanted to fight our Allies and die for Hitler by his own merits rather than his descendance. He, indeed, was very blue blooded, as I thought the "von" was not enough. Yet there was the "zu", probably meaning that his present domicile was on his ancestral estate. Everyone in Germany was amazed that many of the aristocracy was also swept into the Hitler madness. My parents cast a suspicious glance at him, which suddenly turned my opinion into doubt about his alleged nobility introduction. Especially now without anyone to witness this when most of the German soldiers had cleared out to get their sleep for many, indeed their last in order to get on to the battle to kill whatever poor young Tommy was left waiting on the beaches.

I wondered whether platinum Franz or reddish blond Karl Heinz had any inkling whatsoever about us being Jews. Most of the refugees were, but Belgian, Dutch and Luxemburg Gentiles took to flight from the Swastika also if they were opposed and feared the Nazis. At any rate, it must have been plausible to these soldiers that anyone fleeing the Nazis was not in their corner.

No, I consoled myself, they were beyond suspicion, for they would not have been this nice, and certainly, they would not have poured us that many mugs of beer in such a friendly manner. Yet, had they have been aware of us being Jews, they would not have touched us, probably thrown us out of the tavern in a verbally abusive way. These were regular soldiers and none of the feared SS nor Feldgendarmerie last but not least, the ruthless Gestapo. The Nazis are a highly organized hierarchy. Without any command from the top of any of these four dreaded Nazi authorities, they would not have arrested nor harmed us physically at least not here in the West.

When my parents finally answered his suggestion for him ceding his room to them for my company in the tavern (so to speak), they thanked him politely but firmly and steadfastly replied: "It's either the three of us in your room or the three of us will spend the rest of the night in this tavern."

He obviously felt embarrassed and explained that by my "company" strictly chatting was meant, since this was to be the last night of his life.

After we spent a pleasant hour of an apparent peacetime foursome we saw to it that he did most of the talking, so not to betray ourselves, he handed us the key to room A1. My parents were watching reluctantly when he kept shaking and shaking my hand until I unlocked his grip.

We hadn't seen or walked thickly carpeted steps for a very long time each held by a gleaming brass bar. The room was like out of a fairy tale. I guess any quarters would have seemed splendid to us after not having slept in a real genuine bed since weeks on end. Of course, nothing but the best for a Feldwebel. The bed was spacious enough for the three of us. In order to escape Mutti's elbows, I placed myself next to Vati, who whispered: "This was really nice of him anyway. Whether he is blue blooded or not, it's such a shame that he is a Nazi. After all, he was raving about the new 'World Order,' and what a shame! What a shame!" We two women chimed in, "such a seemingly fine person fell under Goebbel's propaganda spell as did alas, and amazingly, even the zenith of the German population . . ." and with that we drifted into a luxurious dreamland, being in the midst of High Society.

We were so exhausted from our walk from France into Belgium that we didn't realize that there was adjacent to our great bedroom the sublime elegance of the luxury of a long forgotten real, genuine bathroom beckoning us. My parents were done really fast by having prearranged with Mutti taking a bath and Vati using the bidet. I was tempted to linger in the tub after my parents had left for the downstairs tavern, where I was to meet them. When my toilette was done, I liked what reflected in the mirror: a smiling, young bronzed, healthy looking image, my very first seashore tan. I grabbed my little valise to rush down the soft stairs, lo and behold, there on the steps was Feldwebel Günther von und zu—begging me for a kiss, just one kiss. Again, he fervently swore that I would be the very last girl he would ever kiss on earth. Had he just been a German and not a Nazi praising the "New World Order," he certainly would not have been hard to take, very attractive and seemingly nice as he was. His half parted lips and soft blue eyes were torridly begging me for this last kiss, to send him on his way to kill "my Allies." Just this thought and his words of the great "New World Order" would make me feel a far worse traitor, would I concede, than the Frenchman with his kind offer of drinks. This made me ever so unyielding and yes, fanatic about my refusal. I had to admit to myself that it felt great to have a good looking Nazi at my feet, but felt instant relief for my parents' sheer appearance. He left fuming from the great disappointment. Of course how in the world under these circumstances could I even wish him "Good luck!?" Well, I thought to myself, that's what the "New World Order" enthusiasm did for you and not I! Still, I felt sorry for him as a mere human, but proud of myself as a Jew as a young female. Besides, according to the Nazi law I was within its limit. There was a severe penalty for "Rassenschande" (disgrace of the race) if any erotic dealings were forthcoming between Aryans and Jews. I remember the dreadful humiliations the Christian girls and the Jews had to endure in addition to the severe penalty. I saw them being dragged through the streets with a sign on their chest "I'm a pig" and worse, being spat on and lynched. I congratulated myself for my fanaticism, though generally I disliked this characteristic as did Erasmus from Rotterdam.

After taking a deep breath, I joined my parents for a quite tasty, if unusual breakfast of sardines with beer after a paradise night and an eventful, sort of romantic morning.

Peu a peu, it quieted down here considerably after the last soldiers had left. Now, our steps led eastward with Antwerp as our destination. It was most amazing that even though the Nazi cloud was immediately and undeniably hovering over us, thus placing our future at stake, we felt better walking toward something we knew. On the way back we recognized some landmarks. When I saw the beautiful, crooked tree that was responsible for uniting me with my parents yes, indeed, that was the time I was forcibly walking against the stream of the exodus yes, that was very hard, almost impossible as Vati and I agreed in smoldering Dunkirk; I had to run over to the poplar to touch its trunk gratefully. I was so thrilled at that moment for finding them underneath the tree and at this very instant for seeing them smiling amusedly. I had forgotten what a happy expression looked like on their faces. Vati's mind must have reverted to the French soldier, when he remembered: "The French soldier said that the whole bunker line in the Southern Eifel mountains just North of Luxemburg was called 'Katzenkopf.' The same word in Yiddish means a forgetful head."

"C'mon, Vati," I was joking, "who knows whether cats do have forgetful heads?" You are certainly aware of my having a "Katzenkopf," Vati continued falteringly. I am truly ashamed of the fact that I completely forgot that I have the key to this lovely villa at the shore, which my banker stockbroker, Mr. Weinstock of Antwerp, has entrusted to me.

"But Vati, how could you just have forgotten a matter of such great importance," I reprimanded him, but stopped myself, because he seemed to feel terribly guilty without any further reproaches.

"What, that stockbroker who sold you those ill-fated shares of "Tanganyka"? We had lost about everything, you barely could smuggle out of Germany."

"Please, not that again, Sofiechen!" he pleaded with her.

When I felt our good mood being destroyed at this young sunny day, I wanted to desperately reestablish it by questioning Vati factitiously: "O.k., Mr. Katzenkopf, what about the key?"

"Oh, at least we don't have to worry about a roof over our heads on the way back," he answered sheepishly.

While we were walking this time not in the tightly spaced hordes of people, Mutti every so often got back at Vati, needling him about the "Tanganyka" shares.

"Mutti," I tried to refrain her from an eventual crescendo of her anger, "you are right, but just think of it: the Nazis are hunting us, we are escaping them. During this process, we were haunted by constant depressing financial straits. But look Mutti, throughout our great escape now, we lived without any money worries for the first time since we became refugees!" I completely forgot about this pecuniary curse, a constant companion of an illegal alien. Now, that you mentioned the "Tanganykas" we were reminded of this sad by product, which I never knew before we got to Antwerp. "Therefore, Mutti, let's be thrilled that we are alive and celebrate every moment."

"You are so right, Fannichen," they both agreed and we came to the conclusion that it was a fact that we hardly needed any money throughout this flight. Vati pointed out: "We were fending for our bare, naked needs. That's when money no longer is the first priority."

"How interesting, how very interesting!" I'm glad I acquired this awareness early in life," I concluded and we continued our walk in silence probably each philosophizing to our respective selves.

After endless hours of marching we finally arrived at Middlekerk. We looked anxiously for the villa lined main road paralleling the quay. It felt great that the first time since leaving Antwerp, Vati could make use of a key to a pretty villa at that! It was not quite as stately as the one we stayed at with the sweet old people, the one that went up in one single blast after Mutti made us leave it. This one was also quite inviting.

"Well, at least we're getting something like a token in return for the lost 'Tanganykas'," Mutti mumbled while looking around and sizing up the charming contents. "Look at all the marine frescos! Oh, and over there are the oils portraying Mrs. Weinstock. Even here, she does not take off her sunglasses, probably being ashamed for forming the main part of a ménage a trois." It dawned on me that they had always been a threesome, but I did not quite know what to make of it.

The seascapes depicting the wild foaming open ocean are of a dramatic beauty," Vati honestly exclaimed, but mainly in order to get on neutral ground, while all of us collapsed on the very comfy sofa, chair, and I on the divan making believe to be Goya's "Naked Maja" or Josephine Buonaparte.

"Don't those well chiseled figurines on the marble table remind you a bit of what we used to have only a couple of years ago? Yes, all of this for our money." Mutti was half teasing and spoke half in anger, while relishing this sudden repose. I also could delight in this marvelous relaxation. Again, sleeping was my immediate priority. I felt now exactly as I did prior to the heavenly night on the wood shavings at the small station.

How I yearned for the sporadic heavy artillery to stop as well as for Mutti's light one about these Eastern African shares to stop. I reminded her that two years ago, when I needed it the most, through precisely her scene about this, my wonderful friendship with Lili was created. At this moment we heard a gentle ring at the front door. I reluctantly slid off the divan. As I approached, we could hear several voices, and a female called: "Hallo! Hallo!"

When I opened, four people were standing before me. I took it upon myself to invite them in, while I explained our situation that we were not the owners and said: "Well these days all refugees are regarded as kinsmen!" (Thinking to myself: how big of me!) There was a vivacious, charming Mrs. Friedman with her nondescript, little husband, her friendly younger sister, Rachel, and a tall bony brother, Yossel.

We all seemed to like Mrs. Friedman's bubbly personality. She related her recent flight experiences in such a delightfully funny way, that she sent mixed messages to our psyches. We did not know whether to laugh or cry. Throughout her stories, I could not stop watching her dancing eyes; neither could her brother take her enormous, haunting ones off of me. I felt their penetration even though my attention was completely absorbed by his sister.

Then there was the interruption of the front door being unlocked. Enter Mr. and Mrs. Weinstock, the latter wearing sunglasses, followed by a tall, nice looking gentleman, then Mr. Weinstock jr., with his beautiful, blonde fiancée.

"What a coincidence and what joy to see you here at this particular time!" Mr. Weinstock exclaimed, running up to Vati embracing him in the French manner.

"Of course," Mutti muttered under her breath sarcastically, again her mind dwelling on the East African shares.

I felt relief that she did not mention them to Mr. Weinstock, outspoken as she is.

He did not pay any attention to the other people. Calling Vati aside, he informed him that he would stay here only until tomorrow. They have a deal to get smuggled into Spain with lots of money and high risks involved, in view of the dangerous fact that there will be several borders to be crossed. Of course, both ladies, being tall and blonde, and everyone speaking accent free native French would be most helpful for Jewish concealment. The use of their bedrooms would be to our discretion. All this was related to us by Vati just before we fell asleep in the cozy, elegant living room.

There was no food. Instead, Mr. Weinstock made all of us gather around the large, oval table. He brought out a crystal set, and poured out liquor from the decanter and filled exactly one dozen of the glasses up to the rim motioning to all of us to partake. Upon lifting his, he made a special "Broche" blessing in Hebrew praising the Lord that all of us were spared the perils thus far. He set forth in Jewish German creating his own prayers for life in freedom, and that none of his family would be caught on their long, precarious, illegal journey. "Amen!" we finished in a chorus with bowed heads. When Yossel tried to meet my eyes, I responded with a neutral but friendly nod, then doing so with each of the other ten persons, who felt like family for the moment. Most of the men downed the schnapps with a delighted sound of "Aaah!", while the women were grimacing, sipping it. This one drink had a good, warm, strengthening effect upon us.

Mr. Weinstock led all of us into the back and offered seats on the various lounge chairs, which had been carried out to the veranda. From here, we could smell and yes, even see the ocean. Having been brought by Mr. Weinstock's benedictions into a spiritual frame of mind, I remarked: "It seems that heaven is compensating Hitler's invasion with the spring of the century!" I closed my eyes, relishing this luxury, of which I was deprived for so long. Now, it seems that more and more people are losing their true station in life, except the ones that yell, "Heil Hitler!"

Suddenly, there was a whiff of fresh hot coffee right underneath my nose a déjà-vu scene. When I opened my eyes, there was not a cuff-linked arm handing it to me, but a bare, very lean, long fingered one. The steam and aroma were emanating into the air. It produced the same pleasant feeling I had with David's cup. Savouring the wonderful brew, I thanked Yossel profusely but felt guilty that he must have deprived himself and his family of this treat. This war makes one really self-centered. I thought and then had to smile to myself that these days, a hot cup of coffee seemed to have replaced a bouquet of roses as an appreciation to a young girl. "I like to watch your million dollar smile!" he said.

"Here, smile some more!" With this friendly command, he offered me some de Beukelaar's cookies.

"What a treat!" I exclaimed, "this is the first variation of my long standing diet of sardines and chocolate! Maybe we can offer those to you?" I asked. There was no answer. He seemed to be too busy enjoying my "million dollar smile" as much as I did the coffee.

At this instant, the Weinstocks and the others came out to the veranda. They took leave of everybody. Mr. Weinstock again embraced Vati like a long lost brother. He asked whether Vati knew anything about Mr. London. Vati shook his head negatively with his sad expression.

"Let's not worry about that fellow! He'll joke, charm and pay his way out of any situation. Who knows what's going to happen to us? Give my love to Antwerp and to . . ." He could talk no more for he was all choked up. It was even a secret to us, where they would proceed with their very light luggage, because nowadays, there was no chance of transportation, not even for the rich. We waved to them with our best wishes for a safe not all too tough journey into the unknown. There was tremendous fear and worry on each of their five faces.

Shortly thereafter, we heard people knocking and children's voices. When I opened the door, I could not get over my amazement: the five children and their parents were standing in front of me, all smiles to see me again. The little ones looked so strange. I bade them welcome and invited them in, asking, "What became of you? What happened to your hair, children?" I inquired while being taken aback. My concern made them ashamed. I regretted that my questioning made them stand with downcast eyes.

"Beautiful, little face! Beautiful, little face!" their father greeted Mutti, walking straight up to her without any further ado. "I'll tell you what happened right after you left," he volunteered. "I got so angry at you, oy, was I ever so furious when you left so abruptly," emphasizing this with squinted eyes, clenched teeth and fists, the latter shaking menacingly at Mutti! "I felt like an animal with rabies. Then this fury turned into tremendous fear! For once more, we went through the same horrendous experience as we all did together," he now stepped up his tale in an ever increasing excited staccato: "Sirens . . . bombing . . . crawling underneath the cart, but then . . . not one but many whistles . . . thus many bombs close by . . . strafing . . . fire on top of us . . . screaming all around us like on a battlefield . . . especially the children . . . I crawled out on one end . . . my wife on the other . . . both coughing from smoke . . . pulling out the children hastily . . . fire spread from our bundles on top of the cart so rapidly, their hair started to burn . . ." . . . his voice cracked. With this, sobbingly, he sank down on a chair, burying his head on his arms on top of the table just as did Vati when he returned without the threesome to the first villa. He remained in this position for quite some time. When he finally lifted his head, he looked at Mutti, but this time in his original kind way, asking rather himself: " . . . but beautiful, little face, how could I possibly be angry at a lady prophet?"

Vati and I looked at each other. Mutti proudly threw her head backwards enjoying all this admiration from that family and her own. Vati just gloated over her, nodding approvingly: "Yes, yes, my Sofiechen has that certain instinct, that sixth sense. Vati attempted to embrace her, but as usual, he was rejected. This time the reason, however, was the presence of too many onlookers, which obviously embarrassed her. He concealed this awkwardness by continuing to rave about the previous time she saved us with her high-spirited, abrupt manner, from the blast of the villa just after we obediently followed her command.

"I wish I had inherited her vision!" I lamented and proceeded to tell everyone about the big, black American fighter Ralph's prediction about "the very soon upcoming terrible earthquake that will make the world a hostile and ugly place to live or rather to die in."

Each time, when the sporadic heavy artillery got closer, I saw Yossel and his sisters cringe. "I know exactly how you are feeling." I tried to console them: "I too became terribly scared, when I heard the shrill whistle of the bombs cutting the air sharply just preceding the horror-filled seconds of the breathtaking suspense of the life or death verdict. Yes, it's the suspense, that awful suspense of the inevitable explosion, that drives me out of my mind from inner terror. Musically, a very deep sound is so much more dramatic and fear inspiring than a high pitch."

There was no answer. I knew first hand how these siblings were suffering.

After quite some time, when there was a pause of the pondering "iron thunder", Yossel said: "I heard every word you were saying and we were grateful for your attempt to comfort us. It helped to get my mind off the immediate threat by your interesting philosophizing. I really appreciated that," he nodded approvingly.

Shortly thereafter, the villa was divided into various sleeping quarters with the three of us in the master bedroom as Vati pointed out: "We must gather strength for the fatigue that lies ahead of us."

Very unlike myself, I was the first one to be on the veranda. Yossel again surprised me with a delicious hot cup of coffee.

Savoring each sip and delighting in the seaside surroundings, I felt as though I were in the lap of luxury on this sunny morning. "Imagine, Yossel," I said, "this is what life in California must be, but without bombings, artillery nor Nazis!" I sighed wistfully. "Do you suppose Californians appreciate their good fortune?"

"If and when there will be an open world why don't you go there and find out for yourself?" he suggested and added rather timidly: "You are surely beautiful enough and if you are talented—" now, the others joined us.

The young father looked around and exclaimed: "This is the life!"

"Yes, but unfortunately we must leave it!" Vati said . . . and so we did as a large family of nine adults and five children.

"Remember the Tommy on the beach had suggested that it's safer to walk toward inland away from the shore, where the war action is taking place?" Vati remembered.

"Oh, God, oh God!" I could not help myself yelling out upon spotting the half charred cart. Mutti, open-mouthed, put both of her palms to the sides of her head as she always did in utter amazement or dread.

" . . . But it works!" the father bragged good-naturedly with his easy smile.

We looked at him and his family with great compassion and said: "What you must have gone through and I patted each of the five children, concealing my strange feeling as though touching straw instead of hair.

Then our grateful glance wandered to Mutti. Before we could utter anything, the young father said: "Thanks to you, beautiful, little face, you avoided it all!"

Our group finally started our trudge toward the East. We passed so many déjà-vu places, landmarks and events. It was like a repeat performance.

Chapter 12

After many hours of marching, we were now somewhere between the dangerous coastline and a wooded area. There was one of these 'landlordless' houses where refugees just entered, to look for the most meager of shelters. Probably, it must have previously been a plain pension. Each family took a small room on the various floors.

I flopped on a barren bed standing next to me, because I felt more fatigued then ever before. Even the smell of sardines, of which, amazingly, I never tired, would not deter me from my precious sleep.

"Come downstairs, come downstairs," mainly Mutti and other voices awoke me from my deep slumber. At this moment, I heard the dreadful, constant artillery nearby. I didn't even realize, nor did I care who half carried, half pulled me. In the dark, we were all on our feet, crowding into a narrow circle, which filled the entire room.

As I was wedged between my parents, every so often, the roaring cannon-thundering dared to wake me. It was then that I thought of James, Jake, Tom, and Jerry, and yes, even Franz, Karl-Heinz, and especially the frightened Günther.

"You are actually sleeping while standing! I never knew this to be physically possible! So I'm discovering this through my only child," I heard Mutti say as though she were far away.

The blustering ceaseless pandemonium of artillery raged on relentlessly. *The Totentanz La Danse Macabre,*" by Franz Liszt, I thought briefly, and without trying, continued this strange somnolent pattern throughout the war-torn night.

Suddenly, there were some weak singular cannon sounds, when Vati remarked, "This is the last futile resistance of our poor Allies."

Then, there was total silence outside, when Vati sighed, "Yes, once more, Hitler's Wehrmacht and Luftwaffe conquered all-including our souls."

Now I was being dragged upstairs to bed like a rag doll. Thereafter, it felt heavenly to be horizontal and hear my parents whisper to each other. But now, instead of guns, I heard Mrs. Friedman from above, implacably filling the now silent night with talks about "La Panne, La Panne!" Between my dozing on and off, that last Belgian coastline city was mentioned over and over again: how food, drink, and comfort could have been available there. How outrageous, I thought. Doesn't she know that there is only a twelve-kilometer stretch between Dunkirk and La Panne?

How strange, that if one likes somebody; the most annoying behavior can be forgiven. How I would have resented another person awakening me sporadically under such dire circumstances with reproaches to her husband, which I found amusing. Again, I fell asleep with a smile, during the dark hours.

Wakening, I felt superbly strong, and rushed as though there was a whip over me. Curious about the latest development, I dashed downstairs. Everyone seemed delighted to see me as though they had been waiting anxiously. My gaze went from one face to another. After suspenseful silence, the young father exclaimed, while clapping his lifted palms, "Now, we are liberated," emphasizing this with a crooked sarcastic smile.

"*Ja, ja,*" Vati said with moist eyes, "it was like a whole night of giving birth to a monster."

From the next room, Yossel was waving and beckoning me, disappearing a moment, and then returning with steaming coffee in a chipped cup. He invited me to come to the next room. Aha, I thought, he wants to be alone with me. I was eager to enjoy it though, while still hot, so he didn't have to motion me a second time.

"Oh Yossel, Yossel," I started the hit song that I first heard at the 'Dancing' in Antwerp last year, which seemed ages ago, "thank you, oh, thank you."

He observed me sharply as I felt my eyes rolling with delight.

"But now, I want something from you," he said, being anxious for me to finish sipping so my head would be clear. After a short while he led me to the kitchen window, and pointed, "Look, just look!"

As I downed my last gulp, my heart started to beat faster. My breath grew panic laden and heavy: Underneath an almost impressionist setting created by the beautiful trees, incongruous with these peaceful surroundings, there he was, a mere few meters away, sitting arrogant and tall on his WH (license plate for—*Wehrmachts Heer*) motorcycle with an empty side-car, so typical of a German vehicle. I scanned the insignia on the front corners of his collar. I felt immense relief not to detect the flower-like one of the Gestapo nor the sharp double SS, who in battle also wore the gray-green uniform as opposed to the usual fear inspiring black one. But I never saw that breast plate before in Germany, when the Wehrmacht was parading past my balcony. In front of him there was a map in cellophane attached to a long chain around his neck.

"I don't like that breast shield. Any pagan imitation of the ancient Romans seems as dangerous to me as the salute of '*Heil Hitler!*' itself," I remarked to Yossel and lamented, "He is just sitting there as if he is waiting for his prey."

"Yes, and we were impatiently waiting for Mademoiselle, to finally, after such an eventful night, rise so you would approach him. We cannot stay here indefinitely. Besides, he might grow suspicious by our lack of communication." Yossel advised and warned, "You see, farther down in the woods there are surely many more of them."

I turned to Vati and looked deep into his eyes. I felt mine becoming moist when I repeated his words on the way back from the flaming Dunkirk harbor to the canal where Mutti was waiting in utter despair. "Our odyssey must stop, because they will catch up with us! Ja, ja, Vati, so they did."

I suddenly found myself in a high stress situation to confront the adversary. After all, there was no comparison with the beer delivering soldiers in the bistro or with the small troop marching through the narrow street of a French village. This lieutenant seemed to be here on official business and to all appearances, would stay. It must be better, that the first move should be forthcoming from us, but how to conceal that we are Jews? I was pondering, and demanded, "why me?"

"Need you ask?" was Yossel's simple question, and he added, "If I were to enumerate all the reasons for you to be the prime choice, you would jump to conclusions. Therefore, I can only point out that you have all the prerequisites for this task."

All the others, including my parents, crowded into the kitchen, entreating me to go ahead with this mission.

"But my German is just, well, too German!" was my last objection.

Since my parents agreed, I braced myself, going to the front door, where I was standing for quite some time, gathering courage and rehearsing to end each word with the accent on the last syllable.

"Do I wave a white rag? Do I raise my arms?" I was stalling.

They did not have a ready answer. Instead they just looked at each other and again collectively pleaded with me to proceed.

My heart was beating fast. Other parts of my body seemed to be pulsating as well at the mere touch of the door-handle. Again, I practiced to be as neutral as I possibly could: not too friendly, not too restrained, not open the door too fast, or too hesitantly. Neutral, neutral is the key word.

The moment of truth and confrontation had come when I passed the threshold of protection. The instant he spotted me, he gave me the military salute. I responded with a distinguished nod accompanied with "Guten Morgen!" (Not forgetting to put the accent on the 'en'). I was more at ease when I heard no "Heil Hitler!" Very politely, he beckoned me as he said admiringly, "Oh, you speak German?"

"Well, I'm studying philology." I lied somewhat sheepishly.

I had to control myself, when he offered me *de Beukelaar* cookies, the same ones Yossel had on hand the first day. Yosssel and this apparent distinguished lieutenant acquired them the same way as Vati did the sardines. Only for us it was plundering, and for them, requisitioning.

"Please, do taste them, they are very good," he suggested.

Well, what could I dare to utter, I know, I am very familiar with them, since they are from Antwerp. I passed the plant at Lange Kievit Straat on the way to my poor relatives many times when we were chased by the Belgian police, because we were illegal aliens, because of you! Instead, I tried to enjoy and praise them.

His German, as he questioned me, was I not rather uncomfortable with the invasion, contained aristocratic inflections.

Neutral, remember, neutral, commanded my inner voice.

"Well, what can I say, Herr Oberleutenant?"

"Oberleutenant Wolfgang Schimmel," he introduced himself. Another white horse, I thought, but stated that I had already two favorite Wolfgangs: Goethe and Mozart.

He was impressed. Now that I seemed to have found common ground with him, and he appeared accessible, I asked whether I could call the others.

When he agreed, I dashed inside the house and put everyone at ease by rapidly telling them the details, and above all, explaining my observation: "Look, how cleverly they go about their conquest sending as *avant guard la crème de la crème*, at least here in the west, as opposed to other despot conquerors throughout history having their scouts be the most savage, raping and violating swine on earth." I reassured them truthfully that they could approach him without any apprehension as long as he was mistaking us for regular Belgians. "Therefore, don't talk, just listen, please!" I urged as a last precaution prior to them venturing out.

When he saw the children, he motioned for them to come closer as he was waving the familiar box of cookies. The Pied Piper of Hamelin, flashed through my mind. When they were hesitant, he stated, exactly as did his comrade Gunther von und zu, "Do not be afraid children. We are no barbarians."

Eventually my whole group joined Oberleutnant Schimmel. The entire situation presented the strangest picture. Hopefully unbeknownst to him, he was talking in a friendly manner to a bunch of Jews. Again, I had to contain myself, when he offered the identical sardines that had sustained us throughout our flight.

After the initial small talk, he became more solemn. Starting out softly and slowly with a few well-known Nazi praises, he crescendoed into a full blown fervent Hitler speech not unlike the Führer himself. It began with the question, "Isn't it going to be wonderful that all of Europe will be united under the New Order of the 1000 year old Reich, led by the greatest genius and the most magnificent human being that ever lived?"

At this point, tears of enthusiasm were welling up. This reminded me of my English teacher in Cologne, when she also raved in glowing terms about Hitler. So did our cleaning woman thereupon relating to us, when the masses chanted in front of the Dom Hotel, "Ach, Führer, sei so nett, tret doch an das Fensterbrett! Be so kind and show yourself at the window!"

Now nobody dared to look at the other one for fear of self-betrayal by a mocking facial expression.

"The New Order must be considered as the Bible of modern times," he set forth, "how very fortunate we are to live in this era!" He continued in measured sentences. His endless monologue about the wondrous deeds of Adolf Hitler seemed to have been prepared in advance. How could anyone who appeared so educated be so blinded by this AustrioCzech guttersnipe, I asked myself. Instantly, I answered in silent thoughts that this happened with the great industrialists and aristocracy just as well. The more he glorified and worshipped the Führer, the lower he sank in my eyes, with each eulogy about Hitler, starting with the Autobahn, the economic wonders, down to the eugenics. He was driven by fanaticism empowered and crazed by this Nazi passion. In true Hitler fashion, he finished softly, still fervently, "I wish my father could have seen the new Germany." He fell short of banging his right fist into his left palm. I was seized by a desperate urge to leave. This was reinforced when I saw the gray-green uniformed men springing out of the woods, just as Yossel had warned earlier. Of course, they wanted to talk to his younger sister and me.

Once inside we were all busy packing and thinking. Vati consoled us collectively by saying, "Look, it could have been worse. He could have asked us all kinds of questions instead of his Hitler ranting and raving."

Rachel was the only one who was giggling when she referred to her 'romance' with a German.

Rapidly, we were on our southeast hike.

"Does everyone realize that this is our first march under the feared official German occupation?" Vati asked.

"Yes, this is our debut under the New Order of the 1000 year old Reich." I sighed as we started our way to the famous lace city of Brugge.

After hours at a steady pace, Vati again consoled us, "Soon, very soon, we'll be in Brugge."

The skin of my heel started to get red and felt very irritated, getting more painful by the minute. It felt great to, at last, spot the clean peaceful outskirts of the city. When there was a pause in our walk, I looked and discovered a huge blister. I removed my shoe in order to seek relief.

I was so charmed by *Bruges* (French), a mini *Venice*, with so many dainty bridges surrounded by sprawling lush lawns and gabled houses. This medieval beauty made me forget my physical pain and my walking on one bare foot. Since this created lameness, I tried to go completely barefoot, alternating with Yossel carrying me. Because of his being so tall, it felt strange to be that high above the ground. Also, he was so thin that I feared he would collapse underneath my weight. I hated to admit even to myself that I was actually scared. What? Me? Afraid now after all the danger I was exposed to? But I could not help it, even though the entire picture did strike me as very funny. This caused me to laugh hysterically. I wanted to yell, "Stop! Pause! Bathroom!" My own mirth prevented me. It was as though I was tickled by a thousand fingers, which in turn trickled some warm drops down Yossel's spine. It was his gallantry by continuing to carry me as though nothing had happened, which amused me even more. By now the giggling was uncontrollable. This 'merriment-distress' reminded me of the foodless restaurant in Ostend. It took utmost exertion on my sphincter to avoid further embarrassment. Already I anticipated with great apprehension the transfer from high up here onto the ground.

In the interim, however, since I got even a better view from the top, I enjoyed and admired this fairy tale town. How picturesque to behold the reflection of the narrow pointed houses in the canals, contrasting with our lives, it truly had such peaceful beauty with a calming effect upon one's spirit. Enhanced by the absence of the gray-green uniforms was the presence of women sitting in front of these lovely houses with busy fingers and many little bobbins to create the world-renowned lace. I asked them for an infirmary. They did not understand French. That's when I detected that real Belgians couldn't even talk to each other, yet I, a foreigner, was able to. It was evident when I posed the same question in Flemish, I got the right directions.

The First Aid Station was housed in a fresh wooden barrack not unlike the one where I met La Parisienne. A young medical man was directly on hand. I was ashamed to ask in such urgency for a bathroom. What double relief, when I spotted one. The doctor was very pleasant, but the strong ether odor offensive. It reminded me of when we visited Lucy, the principal's beautiful daughter, at the hospital, and the same smell made me pass out. This time I had to control my mind not to lose consciousness, now I saw the wounded, the bandaged, and the blood. Then there were lots of colorful dots—I was on a white-sheeted cot, just as I was when I was ten years old, with Lucy, at the hospital. Two weeks later she walked past us with her SA officer, ignoring us with a nervous fake laugh.

Now, I awoke. My parents, the medical man, and a doctor were looking down at me. I felt as though I returned from the beyond, but there was release from the terrible, black, inner panic just before the fainting kaleidoscope in my eyes. It seemed this morning I could not make these little fears subside. The huge painful blister had to be removed. I hoped I would not faint a second time during this procedure and the effect the smell still had upon me. I got carte blanche treatment. The medical man saw to this. I auto-hypnotized myself by dancing the French Can-Can, this time in my imagination, hearing the happy music of the Cologne born Parisian Jacques Offenbach. It worked and I walked out of there, glad that Yossel lost his job of carrying me. The medical man accompanied me outside. When we reached the end of the street, I looked back in gratitude and the man in white was actually waving. Of course, I responded with a good feeling for a fine treatment.

It was a long way from Brugge to Ghent on foot. I felt like a new person and quite capable of another march, especially one without enemy planes, bombs, artillery, or blisters. Now and then a German convoy truck would pass by. The soldiers started chanting to me "*Lore, schöne Mädchen gibt es überall.*" (Everywhere there are beautiful girls), which melody they stole from the old U.S. "Battle Hymn of the Republic." I threw them a scornful look.

"Better be careful. Remember: neutral, be neutral," I was warned by Yossel.

Ghent was another cozy medieval beauty. But this atmosphere was quickly dispelled when at this *Grand' Place*, the Swastika unfurled from the most impressive looking buildings.

"Of course," I suddenly remembered, "this is the capital of East Flandres. That's why we see the gray-greens crawling and busying themselves like ants. Look at the many WH trucks!" I pointed out.

"Yes, so Fannichen, ask them whether they are driving to Antwerp."

"But Vati, how ironic to go with the ones we fled so desperately."

"Yes, mein Kind, that's what life is under the Nazis, full of irony, intrigue, and deceit."

Again, everyone spurred me on and pleaded with me to approach them. More returning people were filling the square. Everybody was carrying all that was left of their belongings on their backs and heads. It was fatigue, weariness, and hunger that drove them to such despair that they would do anything to return.

Soon, a large group of strangers were around us. Nobody dared to get near the front of the truck, where the Germans were sitting. When they sized up the situation that I was spokeswoman, they joined in with their persuasions. This was worse than with Lieutenant Schimmel. I was able to observe him clearly for quite some time and my mind checked him out as aristocratic-looking.

Besides, I had no request from him, but I had no idea what these Germans were like. I took a deep breath and with lots of courage I quickly rehearsed once more, to put the accent on the last syllable and to not forget keeping the h's silent to formulate the hitchhike question: "Guten Morgen!"

I briefly greeted the two soldiers, "Oh pardon, I did not mean to startle you," I apologized.

"*Guten Morgen!*" they replied as they jumped to their feet as though I was Oberleutnant Schimmel. Before I could ask anything, they politely showed me to their front cab, asking whether I would like to go to Antwerp.

"Oh, would I? Would I! So do they," I quipped gratefully pointing to the large group.

One of them ran to the rear, rolled up the canvas, and opened the back of the WH truck.

"*Ja 'woll', Fräulein,* we'll take as many as can fit in there provided you'll sit in front with us," they suggested.

"*Ja 'woll', ja 'woll',*" I mimicked them.

All of the Jews climbed up. Among the group was a newly wed couple. They were sitting so romantically. She was cuddled by him with her blonde hair flying in the wind.

The soldiers were simple working type people just like Vati's favorite employees. They might as well have been Karl Hafka or Toni Bruckner, our chauffeur. He even drove us privately to Bad Ems on the weekends when Vati was in Belgium, smuggling our money there. I called our driver affectionately "Tünnemännchen".

Back here, they were even helping the women and children up, especially Mutti, after they recognized her by our facial similarity.

"Be seated here right at our and your schöne daughter's back. There is less draft," they advised, and one winked.

Both helped me get into the cab.

"What a beautiful medieval ville, I mean Stadt," I said, pretending to correct my French into German.

These two regular seemingly married guys, their wedding bands revealing this, agreed. Well, who could or would not? What a shame, they were my enemies.

We were driving through scenery that looked as though it were on canvas. No wonder so many world renowned artists hailed from here: Rubens and his students Van Dyck and the brothers Van Eyck, famous for their painting, 'The Altar' of the Ghent cathedral St. Baro, just to name a few. Would it have been Wolfgang or Günther sitting next to me, I would have mentioned it.

At the moment, I felt great, with the breeze tousling my hair while admiring these scenic live 'tableaux', and this time on wheels.

The soldier next to me asked, "How do you feel to be approaching your 'Heimat'?"

I replied, "Of course, fine," thinking, if he knew that Antwerp was not really my home but rather Cologne. Therefore, I volunteered to answer once more, this time enthusiastically. Besides, I did not fake too much. Though not knowing, what sooner or later would happen to us, I was glad that this was the end of our three week long odyssey.

At long last we arrived at the side of the Antwerp station, the Queen Astrid Square, where we had lived in various rooms.

The Germans brought us 'home' safely, for which we thanked them. Again, they helped the women and children off the WH-truck. We refugees bade each other a tired but heart-felt goodbye.

This time the three of us took the trolley.

It felt heavenly to finally be back at the apartment. That's when we realized in the rush and excitement after our wrong decision to flee the Swastika, that we had never locked our residence nor cleared anything from the last breakfast. The old beautiful sugar bowl with the big pink rose, one of the very few items from Cologne that linked me with my early childhood, was standing on the table. I took this for an omen, symbol and hope, that our lives might become sweet after all.

Chapter 13

A new era of the world and my own personal life came into being.

My parents were exhausted and so satisfied to at last use their own bed. They insisted that I follow suit, but I could not help feeling exuberant and too curious to rest. In fact, my drive to see for myself what Antwerp was like under German occupation was just too strong to resist. The moment of truth had come, the moment to witness history first hand, however sad. I could and would not miss it for anything. It was amazing that there was total absence of sleepiness. I had to take advantage of this fact—and off I went into my dubious future.

For three weeks I had not marched the long haul into downtown, but what was this by comparison to my recent past? Breathlessly, I arrived at the Keyserlei. Secretly, I wished for this many times during the "Flucht" (flight).

The Karnot Straat had less merchandise but here, "my corner" was more mobbed than ever. There was a big change though: the "paper boys' corner" was devoid of them. Thus no more press releases! Soon that too will be Nazi controlled.

Otherwise, there was the agreeable clanking of cups and glasses. Also the sound waves of a thousand voices in French, Flemish and mostly German emanated from the busy sidewalk cafés. Actually the "Century," "de Londres," the other, outdoor and indoor bistros, plus restaurants, were populated now by Nazi high ranking officers nonchalantly sitting there with their glossy leather boots. Orange lapels, matching the outer leg stripes and bands surrounding their good-looking military hats, almost fashionably contrasting their green-grays, imparted them a quasi operetta look of Cálmán or

Franz Léhàr. Nevertheless they were fear inspiring, as they seemed arrogantly to enjoy the gaping passers-by, their mochas, filters and snifters of cognac. Often bursting out laughing in groups or individuals sizing up the pleasant scenery of their newest territory conquered, visibly pleased with themselves. Although in another country they appeared to feel very much at ease as if they were in their own habitat. I felt angry about this and so deprived, that I could not even afford to sit at a terrace table. My little business of teaching English came to an abrupt end. Again, I was thus plagued by my economic present and future. I lessened my anxiety by walking my favorite blocks.

At a small table was a lone General. As I passed by, he scrutinized me with bold intensity, causing his monocle to drop.

Underneath the one-eyed glass, laced by a black ribbon, was a "Studentenschmiss" (scar by fencing, on purpose without facial protection, was a great Heidelberg student honor). First, I was amused by his theatrical appearance. He was the actor Conrad Veidt's mostly spy film characters personified. He played these roles with such savvy and glee, possibly for he too, being Jewish, was driven out of Berlin by the Nazis.

Then, his glance made me feel like a woman again. But when this resulted in the drop of the monocle, the child in me burst out laughing aloud, a pleasant change from the financial worries. I wanted to emphasize these agreeable feelings by attempting to make a momentary surface comparison of masses: the worst forlorn drudging on, the one I could leave today at long last to this elegant leisurely strolling one in which midst I found myself right now. All the fears, distrusts and sufferings of my so recent experiences, frightful mortal dangers and difficulties were painfully engraved on my mind. I realized my humor made them milder. Did I fool myself? Life is so strange! The worst had happened, but didn't feel like it. After all a satrap and many others of Hitler's victors flattered and amused me by admiring glances. General "Conrad Veidt's" monocle prompted me to laugh, and from this we ran away going through so much in the process?

I finally was longing to end this extended adventure and go to the flat where I would sleep in our bed for the first time since "eternity," starting with the onset of our odyssey. To think it was still the same day when the German WH-truck brought us safely from Ghent home to Antwerp!

The following morning, the first sound to penetrate my ears was Mutti's voice arguing with Vati about the foxes from her sister Pauline in Canada. It seemed so long ago, when she insisted that for our hard earned and then smuggled money for Canadian immigration purposes, we should get Canadian foxes, since all immigration plans went astray.

We decided one morning that I go to the Antwerp customs authorities to find out about the "import." It was the first breakfast in three weeks minus the sardines. Vati must have gone out of his way to have found rolls at the baker's—who had returned as did we—and two eggs, which he generously gave to Mutti and myself. He probably had searched for them at many an "Egg'n'Cheese Shop," where he also bought a bit of butter, we ceded to Mutti since she loved it so much.

I marched a very long way to the quay which was even further than City Hall, where we went so often and met Mitzi two years ago, still wondering about her fate. I finally got there—but to my dismay ten minutes too late so that I had to repeat the story the next day at an earlier hour, but I was an experienced fast walker by now. They handed me a petition for the German Kommandatur. On my way back, I stopped at the Place de Meir. There was an enormous long and wide line reminiscent of the U.S. Consulate and the failed Ostend boat ride escape. It seemed endless hours until my turn arrived. After the long wait, I was directed to a different office to get the release of the foxes.

On the third day, I went to an impressive confiscated building. After dutifully presenting the form and repeating the fox story so many times to each of the various uniformed secretaries, I finally was shown into a most elegantly furnished office. Hitler's dead stern eyes with frowning brows stared right into mine. They frightened me to death even though they were only of bronze by Arno Breker.

"Mademoiselle seems to be a connoisseur of fine art and sculpture?" I was startled by such a sudden interjection, and this time lo and behold—if I were a monocle wearer, it would drop straight out of my eye from astonishment . . . if it was not "General Conrad Veidt" who posed the question. He continued: "Oh, Mademoiselle, you mystified me before with your alluring flair and style. You appear well, well," he seemed carefully to probe for the right choice of words, "so fresh and vital. Am I being tactless?" he interrupted his easy flow of compliments.

"No sir, just gallant," I answered while I unfolded and submitted the paper, which began to show signs of having been over-handled.

He adjusted the monocle deeper into his eye. For the first time, I saw him with a grim expression. I grew nervous, when he exclaimed, "From Canada!" I realized that I had to prevent at all cost his finding out that I was Jewish. Totally unprepared, in case I would be questioned how such an unusual request came about, I had to think fast. I remembered the William Penn saga, vaguely, from when I studied English—so I could avoid the immigration story of Canada. Should I be asked, my answer would undoubtedly be that the foxes were a payment for a loan to my uncle from my parents. Yes, I figured instead of land (later Pennsylvania) from the English king to William Penn, it would be foxes. Unaware that I was smiling caused by making up the loan-Penn-fox tale, he changed his serious expression into one of a broad grin, when he offered me a cigarette and a liqueur. The Nazi satraps were known to initially use this procedure before pushing the button for the torturers, but I knew I had nothing to fear, especially now with my alibi and his obvious interest in me. I accepted the smoke in order to establish good rapport with him. He was amused when it made me cough. He liked to observe me sipping the confiscated French cointreau.

"I would like very much to see you again. Shall we have dinner tomorrow at the Century around 8 p.m.?" He glanced over the custom's fox-paper again, and with one sweeping motion signed the release, still waiting for my reply.

Relieved that my Penn-fox story was not needed, but anxious about what I let myself in for. How would I possibly get out of this one? I was glad the phone was ringing. Berlin was calling. At first he seemed worried too, but then he babbled, as he fixed his glance at me. I've got to use this telephone time to my advantage, feeling embarrassed under his unblinking stare. It was now, that I realized that "Hitler" was looking on all along. At this very moment, I was compelled to dash out, come what may, while motioning to "Conrad" that I would call as I waved the fox release and was nodding gratefully while making my exit. Upon leaving the building, acting like Mata Hari, and even more so, when some Jewish familiar faces saw me come out rather satisfied from Nazi Headquarters with the swastika unfurling over me, I winced

The furs were an enormous financial disappointment. Mutti's idea was a good one after all, but they were of a pitifully poor quality. Hailing from Canada, we expected the finest, full-bodied, glossy, perfect, silvery, bushy specimen of foxes. To our dismay, they looked more like rats and undernourished ones at that. These were skinny, dull reddish, ragged, shabby ones with mangy tails.

From a friend of Mutti's hometown, Czestochowa, a furrier with the strange name of Chmurra, who adapted the habit of yelling, warning: "ASH! ASH! All will be ASH!" came the best offer. We received a rather small amount to hold us over for a while without being forced to sell any of the jewelry at once.

Now, I was back at the starting point, being most desperate to earn money. David had developed the idea of the lessons at our first Passover away from home. Of course, my little flourishing "business" of teaching English was out. I absolutely dreaded the prospect of supporting myself now that German was in. I answered ads that required bi- or multi-lingual skills, only to discover they were German firms. When I had to fill out the column "nationality": "Polish," I was rejected—although I passed the tests with flying colors, since it was easy for me. I truly would have loved these jobs and gladly awakened early.

Back at the apartment, I was happy even to wash dishes and pots after the good hot meals Mutti prepared. One day, as I was doing so, our bell rang. When I opened, a very tall, skinny, young man stood before me: Yossel, who had gone to great lengths locating us. He cringed, when he saw me scrubbing big pots. I chuckled to myself remembering the scene with me being on top of his shoulders on the way to the infirmary.

"After you finish those, would you not need a break? So let me take you downtown—or . . ." he looked at his watch, correcting himself "better still to Brussels since it's early enough."

Briefly I recalled my Belgian girlfriends' warning about going there alone with a man. Nevertheless, I felt I could use some pleasure. I even dared to ignore Mutti's refusal by shaking her head negatively behind his back. I accepted, for once contradicting her.

It was only a thirty-five minute ride in the streamlined, electric, blue train. It looked and felt ultra-modern. Brussel's main Boulevard Adolphe Max was just as busy as de Keyserlei. So was the Rue Neuve, the narrow shopping street. Men with cameras took candid photos of each passerby as in Antwerp. It was such fun to redeem and pay for them three days later at the cigar shop, if one liked them. I doubted whether they would please me since we were such an unlikely pair, with me half his size. Even less so, this afternoon, he started calling me "Shirley Temple," because of my height, short skirt and curls. Whereas some people and I thought they made me look more French and particularly like that typical Parisian film vedette Viviane Romance.

We went to the matinée of "La Gaîtée." It was all gilded and red plushy. I enjoyed the variety show enormously, and the star Tomala, a young beautiful, exotic looking petite, did a wonderful rendition of a catchy song, I never heard before. It had instant appeal:

> "Tu m'apprendras, dis, tu m'apprendras, dis,
> comment l'amour fait naître des merveilles.
> Tu m'apprendras, dis,
> Les mots calins, qu'on murmure a l'oreille.
> Quand je suis pres de toi,
> Je voudrais parfois
> Lire au fond de tes yeux
> Tout-ce-que tu veux.

Tu m'apprendras, dis!"
I loved the tune but the lyrics I found absolutely enchanting:
"You'll teach me, won't you,
How love gives birth to miracles.
You'll teach me, won't you
To whisper caressing words into the ear.
When I'm close to you,
I would like sometimes to read
At the bottom of your eyes
Everything you desire.
You'll teach me, won't you?"

Sadly, I could not reciprocate his romantic sparks. Instead of looking at the stage, Yossel made me the center of his attention while I was totally enthralled with the performance. Why was he not someone I could share these emotions with? I scolded myself. My consolation was, that I would not have experienced this wonderful afternoon altogether, were it not for Yossel. I had not been at any kind of function since I was a child. When I was big enough to appreciate it, Jews were forbidden. Then throughout our two Belgian lean years, we had neither the economic nor emotional means to delight in anything. So I was certainly grateful for this treat. Many such days followed. I made it absolutely clear to Yossel that our friendship had to stay just that: platonic

When I did not see him, I walked on de Keyserlei in order to find work or business. There I met a few students who kept up with the English, I had taught. Others wanted me to give their children piano lessons and I did. There were some that showed me various ads of merchandising including a position for anthracite coal to be sold far in advance for winter deliveries. After I applied, meetings were held for the proper pitch. Also I went to various stores to offer the assorted other wares. For my soul, it was dreadfully unrewarding, full of rejections. That's when I regretfully dreamt of the tri-lingual stenographer's jobs in the German firms—how well suited I would be for them. I sort of welcomed Yossel as compensation for all my tribulations.

I felt that the anthracite had possibilities and was proud to be the only girl. I actually enjoyed the orientation, giving up all the others in favor of the coal. My industrious footwork got me to sell tons. My commissions made my parents and me elated.

On the way to my new piano students and coal sales contacts, I ran into more former pupils. Each time, it was a pleasure, even more so when they were nice looking brothers. It was fun to walk up and down de Keyserlei and Pelikaan Straat in their midst and then to enjoy their company at a sidewalk café, such luxury, without the risk of Antwerp society's gossip against my reputation for there were two men.

Between business calls I visited my girlfriends on the Pelikaan Straat: Lili at her restaurant and Rosalie at the jewelry shop. They acted, each separately, as though walking a tight rope—surrounded by German soldiers and officers, creating a real boom in Jewish business. These entrepreneurs, including my peers, understood and talked German or at least Yiddish, which was Southern German and used by the Nazis from the South. There was hardly any difference between the two languages.

I continued plugging the coal, but after a while, we vendors learned that it could not be delivered. Thereafter, the company made the absurd request that all commissions must be returned.

"What?! All that footwork, sales pitch, time and energy for nothing?" I asked in dismay, at the grim prospect of having to return my hard earned money. At this, our last meeting, after much discussion, it was decided we salespeople keep our respective commissions, come what may. That's all I needed, I thought, to be a defendant in court, even if collectively.

I wanted so much to have a normal job, but found it hopeless when still answering ads. I was more than willing to even discipline myself toward getting an early daily start. Since amongst the other languages German was my forté, I encountered the same rejection and resistance due to my Polish ancestry.

I went to Pelikaan Straat and de Keyserlei in search of some economic future. "Fanni!" was spoken by a male voice. If it was not Sasha Horowitz! Almost two years ago at the identical spot, our former "newscast corner" I heard my name being called twice by the same person. That's when Mutti and I met that wonderful family. Now, it was Sasha by himself.

Our conversation about our respective recent experiences flowed easily. When it came to my present financial worries, he invited me to Kipdorpvest for the following day at four p.m., my favorite hour.

I was both curious and hopeful, scurrying by the main avenue. Since my return from the "Flucht" I had not been North of the Quellin Straat, where I studied my pet subjects: French and the international stage dances including belly dancing. The whole street gave me a fond feeling. Yes, Sasha emphasized going by the Frankrijklei. I cast a scornful look to my left, for it was there where we stood for days on end in the long lines in vain. This was the result of the "beloved" Roosevelt and his administration creating new immigration laws to bar us from entering the U.S. by strict quota regulations, previously non-existent in American history, turning a blind eye to Hitler's cause to have us perish.

In the next little quaint street I stood in front of an imposing black, wrought iron entrance. After ringing the big bell, I waited in anticipation. Clad in my custom-made Cologne pure linen dress, which I saved for business occasions, I felt self-confident about my first impression—enhanced by my ocean-tan face and dark curls against the stark white outfit.

Though not really pretty, a very charming lady, in her forties opened the Baroque gate. As she smiled beneath her mascaraed eyes, she introduced herself as Mrs. Diemenstein and ushered me in most graciously.

It seemed as though I entered a place of an artistic fairy tale, not knowing where to look first: the magnificent originals of the great Flemish masters appeared as though they were done by the genial hands of Peter Paul Rubens, Jacob Jordaens or Otto Venius. Here also were housed the most important collections of impressionist and expressionist paintings. Awed, I took notice of the white baby grand with the gigantic bouquet of fresh cut long stemmed red roses held in a huge oddly shaped vase as well as the green felt-lined tables surrounded by men and a few smaller ones where smartly dressed women were playing bridge.

Only one familiar face, Sasha's came towards me. He led me to his, the largest table, where he introduced me around. Everyone treated me with such respect. Quite different from my experience of late, offering the various merchandise or begging for quelque chose à rouler. Yet I was the same person, under other circumstances, of course. I never saw Antwerp men to be such gentlemen and rising dutifully as I was presented to them. I nodded and smiled, nodded and smiled, until I tried to ease down on a chair which looked like that of the "La Gaîtée" theater. While doing so, I was interrupted by even more introductions and mutual greetings.

When at last I started to feel the plush of my chair underneath me, still waving and winking to the many new acquaintances, I heard a resonant, marvelous male voice from the other side asking: "So, and how is your Mr. Father?" (A very polite way in many European countries.)

When I turned to my left, I had to catch my breath answering: "Oh, my . . . my Mr. Father . . . I mean my father is doing fine, thank you."

At first, my face must have flashed fire red, then turned pale. I struggled to regain my composure. It was Mr. London! Vati's and Mr. Weinstock's friend. When Vati had pointed him out to me only once, while surrounded by a group of men, I had an immediate crush on him.

When I belly danced in my class, I fantasized performing for Dr. Koenigsmann and Mr. London.

I'm super delighted! I almost exclaimed. The fact was that I was totally thrilled to have finally and suddenly come face to face with Mr. London.

This encounter caused me to feel like a woman for the third time in my life, but now, it was unbearable! I felt my sensuality being aroused and something new, strange and wonderful stirred within me. It bothered me though that we had no eye contact, because steadfastly he looked at his fanned out cards as he was addressing me, even though passing when his turn came. I was ashamed of my feelings, especially since he was more than twice my age. He did not take his beautiful soft warm hazel gaze off his darned cards. I detected a beauty mark underneath his eye—just like Pola Negri's. It enhanced his looks. His graying temples added a finishing touch to his well-shaped head covered by a fullness of slightly wavy hair.

As I did often in the past, when I was embarrassed, I just rattled on about our "Flucht" experiences and, above all, our mutual acquaintance, Mr. Weinstock.

"Yes, he wondered about you," I ventured to say and even quoted him: "That fellow will get out of any situation."

He laughed so fetchingly without sharing it with me. I could not stand it! "Did he?" he asked with his glance still on the cards. "So, tell me Mademoiselle, what are you doing these days?" still with maddening concentration on the "fan" in his hand.

I never knew before what it meant to desire a man until this moment. I finally answered: "Well, I would not give German lessons. That would benefit those with Nazi 'ideology" and conviction. Though suited for the German private firms they threw me out as soon as they learned about my nationality, prior to knowing my religion yet!"

"Why don't we meet for breakfast tomorrow, say, at the "Londres,'" he suggested.

The prospect absolutely elated me twofold: about seeing him so soon, and with business in mind. Anticipation consumed me, feeling like a school-girl which I should've been, were it not for us having to leave Cologne.

With high expectation, I arrived on schedule at the "Londres." For the first time I saw the inside of this renowned hotel/restaurant. There was subtle elegance. Artistically, fresh fruits were displayed. I took a deep breath upon spotting Mr. "Londres" (London in French).

This time, I had his complete attention—but emotionally I was far from satisfied. Alas, his eyes did not meet mine, as so many men tried lately, but over the most tempting breakfast he came straight to the point. I was most content, though, with the real purpose of this meeting.

"I understand you have a good head on your shoulders and enjoy doing business—despite your young age. Therefore, I appoint you, Miss Cukier, as my courtier!"—courtier and—courtesan I wished wistfully. "I shall give you on consignment, cut stones and ready-made diamond jewelry—some of which you may wear. I am waiving the usual collateral, signature and any other type of security. I know your Mr. Father and trust your honest face. Besides, as you saw, I'm a gambler. In addition, you are free to work for any other diamond dealer. I want you to be successful—and you will be, for you are young, willing and I understand, ambitious."

After the waiter poured our second cup of coffee out of an ornate silver pot, he asked with an irresistible smile: "So when do you want to start?"

"Right after this wonderful breakfast, Mr. Boss!" I beamed and lifted the fine china cup, a far cry from the chipped ones I held only weeks ago, as though to toast the bargain. Besides my yearning for him, I liked him as a person and associate, which formed a nice relationship.

We left and I was proud to walk with him, the all too short distance, to the diamond center. It seemed as though every passer-by greeted him with great reverence.

In the back of the Diamond Bourse, right near the "Passover" restaurant was the little, almost square Hovenier Straat. It was black with people of the diamond trade. The minute we stopped there, I found myself in a reversed harem. A group of men were flocking around us the same way as when I first saw him as he was pointed out to me by Vati, then introductions followed. With his winning smile and great aplomb he withdrew, wishing me all the luck in the world.

I hated to see him leave for numerous reasons. Although I did not fail to seize this opportunity by extending my hands. Trying to hide my initial embarrassment, I exaggerated finger motions, to show off the sample ring he gave me.

"What fanciful, long fingers!" Some said admiringly, "What nice, tapered, red nails!" Others flattered.

I was shocked at my sudden boldness, when I objected: "No, Gentlemen, never mind the shape of my hands! Take notice of the beautiful oval sapphire surrounded by lupe clear diamonds. Aren't they exceptionally big for this type of setting? And the price is only bfrs.75,000!"

They looked interested. For a moment I thought I did not ask enough.

"How about bfrs.60,000?" One of them offered.

Well I knew I had to bring to Mr. London bfrs.50,000. Anything exceeding this figure was my profit.

"Gentlemen, I believe in compromise! For bfrs.70,000 it's yours!" I suggested.

He was thinking . . . This Arabian souk reminded me of Mutti and Mr. Bialystok, when I met Rosalie.

"No, bfrs.65,000 and not a centime more, Mademoiselle!" This pale-faced man offered.

"Sold!" I copied the auctioneers and was more than thrilled to have made my first sale with a gain of a whopping bfrs.15,000 (ca.$300) in just a few minutes.

"I could use a cup of coffee!" My happy client exclaimed. "Let's go around the corner to the Vesting Straat Café!"

We entered a lively, busy, noisy place. A blond man with very dark eyes served the espresso. "Paleface" introduced him to me as the owner's brother, Moishe. As he served "Paleface" and me, he looked so admiringly at me. I asked myself, why couldn't Mr. London give me such a glance? The thought angered me. I might have shown it, so that I almost was about to apologize to Moishe: No, no my annoyance isn't directed against you, sorry!—but I wound up being polite and friendly, since I was in a great mood, even more so after I saw Belgian francs in bundles of thousands being piled up in front of me. I stripped off the beautiful ring reluctantly.

"Do you know, Mademoiselle, why you made such a quick sale?" My first customer asked and answered himself: "because you really believe in your merchandise! I can tell. Therefore, you should only sell what you would like to own yourself," he advised.

I thanked him, bade him good-bye and on my way out, waved to Moishe, who did not take his eyes off me—busy as he was.

Right at the exit of the Café, an old man looked scornfully at me and, in contrast to my high spirits mumbled: "Why don't you go home and help your mother, or better yet: get married and work in your own kitchen!"

I was mad at him not only for what he dared to say but also for spoiling my merry state of mind. I proceeded back to hover on Hovenier Straat, anyway, trying to find other potential buyers, Mr. London introduced to me, to get lucky once more. I did not see any of them. I was amazed that contrary to my recent "black diamond" business in the genuine diamond trade, there was a grey-haired willowy lady dressed from head to toe in navy. Her face radiated kindness and congeniality, and a much younger woman who was also a courtier. The charm of this thirty year old was on a parallel with the gallery owner, Mrs. Diemenstein. She exuded that undefinable "je ne sais quoi" without being really pretty, and was dressed in excellent taste. The stylishly classic avant-guard Deanna Durbin hat completed her ultra-fashionable outfit. That I was not the only woman in this world of men—being exposed so publicly—truly pleased me. Especially, each of these ladies appeared refined and distinguished. The older one smiled invitingly, while the younger one was busy with a transaction as I had just been.

When I approached the grey-haired woman in navy, she was most receptive; so was the colleague, upon her return. The first told me that she was a widow and took over her husband's trade. The other, Mutti's name sake, Sofie, did not know whether or not she was a widow. Her husband was in the infamous concentration camp of Dachau, founded in 1937. There was no way of really finding out the truth. Whereupon she grimaced her perfectly made up face, put both hands on her stomach and excused herself.

"Poor Sofie!" lamented Mrs. Steiner compassionately. "Whenever she talks about her husband's shaky whereabouts, she gets her gastritis. Therefore, most of the times this job is an emotional and good financial healer—and you, Mademoiselle?" Mrs. Steiner inquired.

I told them simply that through Mr. London I got this position.

"Oh, Mademoiselle, how fortunate you are to be his protégé! Isn't he the most attractive man you ever saw with that fetching smile of his, Sofie?" she tried to distract the latter from her pain.

Sofie nodded and added: "He's so well known and liked for his big heart and wit and is one of the rare people who is in a perpetual good mood. Yes, you are lucky, indeed, Mademoiselle," Sofie confirmed still grimacing and holding her flat abdomen. I felt great empathy for this young woman. As a child, when Mutti was all too strict and Mr. Bodewig treated me all too shabbily and abusively, I was plagued by belly-aches. That's when I laid my stomach across a chair. How little I must have been then, because my feet were dangling—not reaching the floor yet.

"This is a good and respectable profession." They both praised my new trade. At this moment tall Mrs. Steiner approached a man. He ran by, nodding his head negatively.

"Upon first glance it does not look that honorable, to be frank." I objected and told them about when, almost two years ago, the Belgian police were chasing us, and the only place we could lose them from off our heels—so to speak—was the underworld on the ill reputed Statie Straat. "The same female action and male reaction occurred, I'm sorry to say, Mrs. Steiner."

"But look at the difference in merchandise being offered. They understand this diamond business, and they also know us and will get acquainted with you. Especially as Mr. London's courtier, you will even be held in high esteem. We are very well aware of Antwerp's ethics."

With this I said good-bye and left my newly found territory to report to Mr. London.

Again, fast-paced and with great anticipation I went to Kiepdorpvest. There was nobody I would have rather shared our good news with than Mr. London. Also I was proud of my first success desiring to please him.

This time, Mr. Diemenstein opened the door, introducing himself. I fantasized hearing a thousand balalaikas; that's how White Russian-Jewish he seemed to me. He had an ethnic, interesting face and as I noticed right away, an eye for the ladies. Upon entering, his palatial place, it was just as appealing as when I saw it first, perhaps even more intriguing because Mrs. Diemenstein was negotiating a sale of a magnificent oil painting. It looked so real with its impressionist clouds—how many commas this great artist must have used—to make it appear at first glance so sunny and happy but in the back forebodingly, there was a dark threat—just as our lives at the moment—but in the meantime, let's enjoy each good minute—I thought—when I saw Mr. London approaching me and asking: "So how did you make out?"

I told him briefly, but would have loved to giggle with him about "Paleface" and Moishe, but I revealed my anger towards the old man.

"Rest assured, we modern men are just beginning to think differently!" he tried to convince me, while ushering me into a big cloak room where I handed him the bundles of thousands of francs while he asked: "Did you enjoy your work?"

"Very much so!" was my enthusiastic reply, "especially selling an article, I really like"

He pulled out of his vest pocket a similar ring. This time, it was an emerald surrounded by diamonds.

"Yes, it appeals to me; it appears daintier then the other one." I remarked.

"Therefore, I'm going to give you several other precious pieces." He suggested. After he had given me some selling pointers on each lovely item, I returned to the apartment sharing the good news with my parents.

When I got home, Yossel was waiting with them. I related my fortunate business present and future to the three of them. Vati not only gloated over the fact that I had found my commercial niche but that my dealings took place with his favorite bourse person. At the end I turned to Yossel adding: "Well, sorry, 'Shirley Temple' can't see you any more in view of her being busy."

"You take everything so seriously! I know you are angry at my having referred to you as 'Shirley Temple,' because in my opinion that skirt was too short. That was all. Also you forgot, I'm in this business—a bit longer than you. As a diamond cleaver I know that our trade closes on Friday afternoons, the Sabbath, and reopens on Monday mornings," he pointed out with some bitterness.

"Yes," I agreed, "it's mostly in Jewish hands," and added—as though doing him a favor: "All right, I'm free this weekend,"—quietly wishing I would not be the next one, though Mr. London's private behavior toward me was not very promising. I would not give up hope in my yearning for him. Also, I thought to myself, if the relationship with Yossel would not be severed abruptly without any particular reason, it would be less harsh.

When we met, he suggested a walk to the Brilschans. "No, not those threatening-looking, nightmarish fortification towers!"

"Then let's go in the direction of the Schelde River and pass the 'Groen Plaats,' Grote Markt,' and the Brabo Fountain?" he asked.

"What, there I went almost daily for months on end!" I told him how I had met Mitzi there with her children and was still wondering where she was. "No, I don't want to seem difficult, but I don't wish to be reminded of such a depressing past when finally, now, for the first time I'm almost happy in this city,—no wait!" I paused recalling the initial weeks when Mutti and I lived a most pleasant tourist life style at the Hotel Locarno.

"Very well," Yossel answered, "we are right near it, so let's have a filter there."

"Most delighted!" After we were served on the lovely terrace, which I fondly remembered, I said: "When I started telling you my sad stories of being a refugee prior to meeting you, I'm talking 1939 and pre-war, how we were chased! There is a direct connection between those two places. When I said, unjustly, the police woke and picked us up at dawn with ready handcuffs—even though I ran earlier—to prevent this calamity, begging for an extension at City Hall. Indeed, I did receive the most desired visa prolongation. Nevertheless, the Belgian police took us anyway. When finally after endless hours the chief arrived at the precinct, he told us just the same that we had to return to Germany, imagine! I'm still very bitter about this."

"Would it help, if I were to take you to a movie? There are hardly any American films around any more, just some French ones, but mostly German."

At the "Scala," adjacent to the hotel with the same name, where Mutti and I stayed—after our pleasant sojourn at the Locarno—the Scala Hotel was another bad, noisy refugee memory—we saw "Paramatta" or the German version of "To New Harbors" with a Swedish actress Zarah Leander. I liked her and the movie. Though not a blonde, she was to substitute the Nazi loss of Marlene Dietrich, who absolutely did not want any part of the Nazis. Commendingly so, for she was a non-Jewish true Berliner from a Prussian officers' family at that. Zarah Leander sang with that deep voice of hers—which was also mine—portraying a British cabaret singer—the following saucy song in German, which translated:

"They call me Miss Vane, the very popular 'Yes Sir!' The not so popular with aunts and uncles 'No Sir!' Because they are thinking, that I might meet their well-protected nephews at the casino or at the canopy bed and seduce them with thousands of cunning wiles to do something they don't know yet. Yes, Sir! Yes, Sir! That's how I am and shall remain from head to toe, Yes Sir!"

When we were sitting in one of the smaller terraces later, called "Hilversum," I wanted to discuss this interesting film with Yossel, saying: "Really, this movie taught me a lot: first about man's betrayal: he added a zero to her check, and left her to worry about the prospect of being arraigned for grand larceny. Now, her mood changed literally to a melodiously haunting tune, in a melancholy minor key. I actually jotted the lyrics down in shorthand, Yossel!" I tried to emulate her:

"I'm standing in the rain and waiting for you.
At every corner I'm thinking of you.
The hand on the steeple clock moves from stroke to stroke,
Alas, where are you, my love
Have you forgotten me?
I'm standing in the rain and waiting for you!"

"I could more than sympathize with her. I know how it feels though being innocent, to be persecuted by the law. That's why I refused to accept your suggestion of going to those places to remind me of my lot," I emphasized again. "Wasn't he a terrible coward not to have come forward with the truth? She was forced into prison for him. Wasn't it fortunate for her that it was in Australia, the British penal colony, where men could choose their wives while incarcerated? This glamorous star became the spouse of a much younger farmer, thus a complete turnabout for her. This most likely would have happened to us, would we have received a visa to the U.S., Canada or any other country, where I tried so hard in vain to go. We would be safe but it would have altered our entire future nonetheless, wouldn't it, Yossel?"

"Yes, but we don't know whether for the better or worse." He finally answered.

"Our lifestyles changed drastically, since Germany, plus we are living in these uncertain times." I reflected, and wondered: "Relating to the plot it might have been a true one—does it mean that the Australian descendants of today came from hard-boiled criminals?"

He shook his head and rolled his eyes as though to a child that is asking too many questions and inquired: "Would you be angry again, if I wish to know how many Shirley Temple questions will you be posing?"

"Yes, I would be!" I said, while I was mischievously thinking, that after this remark and with my lively projection of the film, which he did not share with me, I could ease out of the relationship.

Were it not for this, I might have had a pleasant enough Saturday. Somehow he had put my upbeat feeling down, not unlike the old man. I consoled myself with the multi-dimensional challenge that lay ahead of me in the diamond business.

Chapter 14

I was not as lucky every day as I was on the first one, but each Friday I did manage to make a good sale. Things became more stable as my business life spilled over into my social realm. Work days were so much more interesting than weekends. When it was very cloudy, the diamond industry came to a virtual standstill. If the light did not shine at a certain angle, even the best-trained eye couldn't determine the exact quality of the gems.

Sofie, Mrs. Steiner and I met every day at our favorite hangout, the Vesting Straat Café, in spite of the fact that the old fellow still hadn't forgiven me for being a professional woman rather than staying home and working in the kitchen. The three of us were always joined by diamantaires. Men usually flirted with me, and I flirted back, ever so coyly. I enjoyed Moishe's attention, the lively atmosphere and the heated conversations we had.

All of this fed my ego and made me glow. One afternoon, Sofie beckoned me to the ladies' room. She gave me the impression she had something important to tell me, but as it turned out, her sense of style was bothered. "You're wearing far too much rouge," she said. "We must get rid of it."

I protested. "No, Sofie, it's not make-up, it's my natural complexion. Maybe it's genetic. When my parents and I used to go out in Cologne, we were sometimes ashamed of our faces. My father always said we looked like farmers visiting the big city. There's nothing we can do about it."

"Yes there is!" she said, and magically produced a beautiful red leather compact. She unzipped it and powdered my face affectionately with a cloud-like puff.

Every sunny Sunday at a different resort. Age 14.

"Oh, how right you are, Sofie!" I approved, looking at myself in the mirror. Suddenly I felt a twinge of sadness when I thought, why couldn't the other Sofie, Mutti, ever do anything for me in such a loving way? But the thought was quickly dispelled when we returned to our seats, where we commanded much attention.

When I got home that evening, Vati was exuberant. "You'll never ever guess who I ran into on *de Keyserlei*!" Vati exclaimed with delight.

"Please, Vati," I begged, "no games."

"I met an old friend of mine. And would you believe, this time it's a German!" he announced, his big green eyes beaming.

"A German?" I inquired in disbelief. "And that's something you're happy to report about?"

"Yes," he said cheerfully. "I ran into Hans Griez from Bad Godesberg."

"Hans was your best friend and a great business associate right to the bitter end," I nodded understandingly. I recalled: "The last time we saw him, we sat together with his wife Nellie and his sister in their cozy flat on Brunnen Allee in Bad Godesberg." Their apartment consisted mainly of bookcases filled with good literature. "One day they cried with us over coffee, when we came to tell them in dismay that every café, restaurant and hotel in the entire resort we loved so much—their hometown—was displaying signs stating: 'Jews and dogs forbidden!' How could it be that the very establishments where we had dined and danced regularly now wouldn't even serve us a simple glass of water?"

The mood changed. For the first time since our *Flucht*, Vati's eyes moistened with tears and he said sadly, "*Ja, ja, mein Kind.*"

"But let's delight in the happy moments we're enjoying now," I pressed. "Tell us about your friend Hans!"

Vati began, "Imagine, he knew that we would seek refuge in Antwerp. He also knew that although Antwerp is a cosmopolitan city, it's also a small town, which means it's very likely to meet one another unexpectedly. It was a wonderful reunion! And we're going to do business together again, just like we used to do back when I was in the steel and metal industry. I'll be providing his family with furs, textiles and other consumer goods for their own use. In other words, now that he is the main executive of the very company that made me rich in the past"—here he finally paused and interjected a sad "*Ja, ja*", being fully cognizant of the fact that he was no longer prosperous—"I'll be his personal shopper to leave him more time."

Mutti listened to all this and answered apprehensively, "Yes, I like Hans, and Nellie, too, and even his sister, but they are still Germans, even if they are not Nazis. And it's true he's here with a purchasing company, as opposed to being on any military or official mission. But I still don't like this arrangement. Remember: Our daughter was not accepted in spite of her high qualifications, even at private companies like Hans' firm! Germans are Germans. If you had any sense you would deal with our own people, just as Fanni is doing," Mutti said reproachfully.

And indeed, things were finally going well for me, especially my business life. My right index finger actually felt sore from counting currency in the way I had been taught, by peeling just the upper right corners of the bills, for speed. One evening, as I turned the key to unlock the door to our house, I had to smile about this minor pain, thinking how many people in the world would love to have a "finger ache" from counting money. When I entered, I couldn't believe my eyes: My beautiful chrome bike from Cologne, with the thick red wheels, my parents' gift to me on my twelfth birthday, stood proudly in the hallway. I dashed up the flight of stairs on the double. Yossel was there, anxiously awaiting my arrival.

"Tell me, tell me!" I was bursting with curiosity.

Vati related this story: "Hans Griez is such a wonderful person. On his own initiative he went to Mülheim specifically to ask the Jungs, whether I might have overlooked any of our possessions in the tremendous rush to leave town. Since the Jungs own the bicycle store, it would have been easy for them to pretend this was their merchandise if the Nazi tax enforcers had come—new as it looked. So they were going to keep it indefinitely until it could be claimed on our behalf. They were amazed that someone came for it so soon, Hans told me. So, now you know, *mein Kind*. At least you have your beloved bike back."

My answer was a silent, grateful embrace.

Yossel proposed we celebrate with an evening out on the town. My mind was set against his suggestion, because I wanted to share these nostalgic moments and my present financial success with my parents.

The following day, I rode my beautiful bicycle into traffic. We were the subject of much admiration, dispelling quickly my initial apprehension about not having used it for years. Also, it saved me a lot of time. I could safely park it behind the restaurant, as Moishe was always agreeable to any favor.

Later, I was most anxious to arrive at the gallery. Mrs. Diemenstein was rather amazed at my new acquisition. Friendly but impatient, I wheeled it quickly past her and into the cloakroom.

I didn't realize how fast I had been riding, because my chest was still heaving when Mr. London entered. Glowing, I looked from my favorite object to my favorite person. He seemed not to notice my two-wheeler, but his warm, beautiful, soft eyes locked into mine. It was so sudden, a wonderful and unexpected surprise—just as meeting him for the first time had been, right after the *Flucht*, and at this very same place—intensifying my breathlessness, causing hundreds of fountains to gush into wild streams within me. Even standing at a distance of several feet away from him, I was overjoyed by an intoxicated sensuality. I loved it—and him. I had for the first time entered the realm of such overwhelmingly impetuous emotions.

The silent, spellbinding magic was broken by the unwelcome entrance of one of his associates—we called them his "fans" because they seemed to respect and admire him so—seeking a diamond consultation. Only when I waved goodbye did he notice my bike, and accompanied me for the first time to the exit. He suggested that instead of me returning to the gallery after work, we could meet at my "hangout."

That evening, at the end of my business hours, he appeared as agreed. It seemed that nearly everyone in the Vesting Straat Café was to meet him there. I found this interesting and amusing, and was even quite proud when he favored me above the cluster of people vying for his attention. Moishe's dark eyes darted from Mr. London to me to the ever-demanding patrons and waiters. I felt exalted walking with this popular man, nodding to Moishe, the on-looking acquaintances and new friends.

"I'm starved. I waited to have dinner with you," he remarked tenderly, looking at me in a way I had been craving for throughout the entire summer. He led me across the street to Prager's.

Upon entering the restaurant, the most incongruous picture unfolded before my eyes: The majority of diners were Nazi military personnel, talking their loud, rough German. *"Zum Donnerwetter nochmal!"* ("Damn it!") could be heard everywhere, although they obviously were enjoying the strictly kosher food. The remaining guests were diamond entrepreneurs and other lofty Jewish clientele. But the oddest paradox of all was seeing Nazis being served by the long-bearded, black-behatted Orthodox Jew Mr. Prager himself, along with his daughter and Shmendrik, the awkward waiter. Mr. London, being a great joker, was amused when I expressed my fear, not said in total jest, that Shmendrik might spill the tempting but steaming *kreplach* into any of the gray-green laps. I truly was alarmed for his sake.

Feeling most uncomfortable at the interest we were receiving from the officers, I was afraid to talk above a whisper, not wanting to risk speaking English or my accent-free German. Mr. London seemed to find it entertaining that I chose neutral Flemish, a language we had never used before. We felt like children trying to behave under the watchful eyes of strict adults.

Shmendrik served us gefilte fish, and when he recognized me from the other nearby restaurant, he asked, "So, how did you make out with your English classes?"

In view of the men in uniform, my answer was, "Shhh!" I was glad he understood.

"I made an appointment with my dentist," Monsieur London said unexpectedly. "Not for myself. I took the liberty of arranging it for you, because you were on the run for three weeks."

Viewing my dingy teeth in the mirror of the red etui Sofie had so generously given me, I asked coquettishly, "Is this your polite way of telling me they need cleaning desperately?"

He nodded affirmatively but flirtatiously.

After the scrumptious meal, we walked to *van Eycklei* and entered one of the stately private buildings. Like most professionals, this dentist combined his office and living quarters. His home-like waiting room looked like a king's anti-chamber with its invitingly graceful Victorian furniture. We chose the most enticing leather-upholstered, S-curved settee, and sat down facing each other. Now, unlike before in the cloakroom, I was in very close proximity to him. Again, his beautiful eyes sank into mine. They were like deep wells, inviting and beckoning me to submerge myself in them.

A Bach fugue filled the air. It enhanced the tender passion and intimate feeling. I was consumed. When he took my hand into his and his lips brushed against mine, I did not resist.

He gave me his first, all too brief kiss, and another one and another one—then looked probingly into my eyes—my lids got heavy. I wanted more and more, longer and longer. His ardent embrace set me aflame, whirling on a carousel, ascending into heaven, into paradise. I wanted to stay and enjoy this luscious sensation forever—but then I vaguely heard a man clearing his throat. From someplace far away, someone said, "Bonsoir, Monsieur London!"

I felt both terribly embarrassed and annoyed to be torn out of another world so suddenly and entirely. Yet I managed to whisper dreamily, "I never thought a dentist's waiting room—however elegant—could be so romantic."

"—and sensuous," Mr. London added.

The next day I arrived downtown with sparkling teeth and still starry-eyed. Near the spot we had dubbed "newscast corner," where the paper boys had previously hawked their wares, there was a large crowd looking at the wall, reading. I followed their astonished eyes and was aghast to see a tri-lingual *Bekanntmachung,* or public notice. Though it was only a white flyer printed with black words and glued quite simply to the wall of the Excelsior Hotel, it had Nazi power behind it, for it bore the miniature fancy emblem with the swastika and the eagle. It said:

"Forbidden for Jews to withdraw any money from their accounts without permission by the proper authorities. Signed, Alexander von Falkenhausen."

Although this regulation had no bearing on my personal life, I did worry about my business, which I loved so much. After we left Cologne, where Vati's dealings had been with the Deutsche Bank for as long as I could remember, we had no bank account in Belgium. Everything was illegal for us, even before the occupation. We were not even supposed to be living here at all.

"They are starting with us! They are just starting!" Mr. London said to all of us. At the gallery, it was like Tisha B'av, the day of mourning the loss of Jerusalem's temple. The green felt tables were empty. Even the most fervent card players had lost their desire to deal. Everyone was crowding around Mr. London. It made me feel very important when he, upon seeing me, excused himself to meet me in the cloakroom—much to everyone's annoyance. After a brief but heart-felt exchange of niceties, he consoled me by saying, "It's very sad for each individual in the trade, but we'll overcome this obstacle. One must always turn tragedy into triumph."

"That's exactly my motto!" I exclaimed, and added, "but in this case, I wonder how?"

He half sat, half leaned against a stool. He pulled me into his arms, and between tender little kisses to my burning face he called me his "little kitten" in Yiddish, whispering, "For you, *Kätzele meins*, it's definitely an advantage. Actually you'll have two professions: the courtier job you are performing so well, plus as of now, I am appointing you as my exclusive money courier. You and your bike, which will mean even more to you from now on."

On a happy impulse, I stood on my tip-toes and gave him a lingering, wonderful kiss—quite a departure from my usual inhibited behavior. This seemed to thrill him. With an adoring smile, he shook his handsome head like a duck emerging from a pristine pond, as though trying to jolt himself into another frame of mind. "Judging from your enthusiasm," he said, "I take it I have your acceptance and you are willing to begin?" Not waiting for my reply, he produced, like magic, the usual neatly folded diamond packet and opened it carefully. It concealed a superb and huge single stone.

"I would like you to take this to Mr. Lipshutz, my biggest competitor, who has rarely left his house on Albert Park since the invasion. You need not tell him that I own this diamond. If asked, just give him the names of various people you know, including Sasha's and mine. I am offering Mr. Lipshutz a most favorable price. I am sure it is an offer no one could resist. Then return with the money, which need not be counted. You'll receive ten percent in addition to your usual brokerage fee."

Upon re-entering the gallery, Mr. London announced beamingly, "We don't need any banks." He gestured to me and said, "*Voilà*, this is our money institution."

The men in the group looked at each other, baffled.

After Mr. London explained my new role in the diamond trade, they were all smiles, especially after he told them he would start this deal right away, with the strange and elusive Mr. Lipshutz.

On a sunny day I cycled downtown along the busy *Pelikaanstraat*, down *Simonsstraat* and *Mercatorstraat*, then turned right into the beautiful *Belgielei* before finally arriving on *Mechelse Steenweg*, where I searched for the exact address. Before finding the house I encountered a platoon of German soldiers, marching and singing a song I had never heard before. It must have been new: "*. . . denn wir fahren gegen Engeland, ahoi!*" (for we're on our way to England, ahoy!). What? I thought to myself, now they also want to occupy England, which has been our only hope? This song surely made it sound as though they definitely would.

"*Aufhören!*" the officer shouted for them to stop singing. Then he commanded them to look to the left. "*Augen links!*"

What a sense of humor! I reflected scornfully as so many blue eyes collectively fell upon me and my bike, which I parked in front of a huge white lacquered door and rang the big shiny brass bell. A maid opened. After mentioning names that might be familiar to Mr. Lipshutz, I was ushered into a handsome room furnished entirely in leather and oak, designed for a gentleman's comfort.

A tall, somber-looking, mature man entered. I introduced myself and the sparkling stone to him. He anxiously went to the French door and studied it with his loupe, measured it and looked at it again, and again, asking the price. I was prepared for the ensuing "souk" tactic. He thought and figured, took his magnifying glass out of his vest pocket and scrutinized it again, this time more nervously. More bargaining took place, until we were on common ground. Then, in a dry tone, he said, "*Mazel* and *Brache!*" I repeated the Hebrew phrase for "luck and blessings," more cheerily than he had, and shook hands with him, which is the traditional Jewish way of consummating an important business deal. He left briefly and reappeared with a sizable bundle of Belgian francs, neatly stacked in thousands. "You needn't count it," he said.

"I know, Mr. Lipshutz. But may I bother you for something to wrap it in?" I asked.

Only reluctantly and without a smile did he hand some wrapping paper to me. He was a strange fellow, all right. After attempting as best I could to secure the precious package without any cords or a rubber band, I just left with a cool nod.

Despite the buyer's unfriendliness, I got onto my bike feeling victorious.

Everything I was doing was illegal. To start with: Living in this country—then, any type of work or business—and now this "couriership," which probably was too. Since the job I was performing hadn't existed before I began doing it, there was no law explicitly forbidding it.

And yet at the same time, I loved my unlawful life. My dual business was pleasurable and the income, substantial. I was advised by both Sofie and Simon—no longer was he "Mr. London" to me—to dress accordingly, especially with the Jewish holidays and the autumn approaching.

I visited a well-known custom-tailor couple and had several wonderful, figure-flattering styles designed, along with an elegant coat trimmed with blue fox. While they were taking my measurements, I listened to their suave American records. Hearing the voice of Morton Downey instantly made me want to be with Simon.

My whimsically stylish hats were created by the eldest daughter of our former neighbors, the Hungarian family. Her millinery salon was located on *Lange Herentalsstraat*, where we had found the studio in which we had hidden from the Belgian police. What a difference in my life then and now! Currently I was blessed with the greatest gifts: I was in love, full of energy, exuberant, chic and high-spirited, always in an upbeat mood. In short, I was happy—but I was also a bit scared of my own elation.

In the presence of Simon I felt pampered in every way. The lyrics of many love songs expressed my sentiments exactly. He made me sparkle like the diamonds I was selling and wearing. His kisses made me tingle, but would I surrender? No!—I was thrilled I hadn't been asked, for I valued my virginity. Aside from the fact that it was a "commercial asset," to me it was also sacred.

One afternoon we saw a film called "The Blue Fox," a musical comedy starring Zarah Leander. I told Simon about my own farce involving the "Canadian silver foxes" and we had our own private giggle. "Soon you too will be wearing a blue fox—but not a mangy one." More laughter. The film was a bubbling delight. It contained a song that was to become a hit in occupied Europe, *"Kann denn Liebe Sünde sein?"*:

> "Can making love be sinful?
> Should it be kept secret when lovers kiss,
> And when they lose themselves in happiness?
> I shall never regret what happened and what I did for love.
> Can making love really be sinful?
> And if it were—I wouldn't care!
> That's why love exists!
> I'd rather live sinfully than live without love!"

Simon was enchanted by my rendition of this catchy tune, pulling me gently toward him as he said, "You are the perfect girl to be kissed—and only kissed, and no more." He looked deeply and promisingly into my eyes, as though making a vow. In silence, I gratefully accepted and kissed him with abandon, for I felt free.

The evenings were still balmy as he accompanied me home after another great kosher dinner at Prager's. There was total black-out because of the "enemy" planes, the British. By law, shades had to be placed tightly against the windows so no light could get out. It was the perfect setup for romance while walking through the darkened streets of the city.

My parents were very excited about my financial success. It was theirs, too. After all, there was enough money to support all of us. Nonetheless, Mutti objected to my personal relationship with Simon and to Vati's business relationship with Hans. She wanted to curtail both.

We pointed out to her how delighted Vati was to renew his old friendship. Rather than living like an old retiree at the age of forty-four, he was enjoying his small-scale commercial dealings. They brought him in contact with the local Jewish business community. "Just look at the moral effect this has had on him," I pleaded.

"What, how dare you mention morals, being the mistress of a man closer to my age than to your own?" she cried.

She made me feel ashamed. In one verbal swoop she perverted the wonderful life I was living into something ugly. I was crushed.

"Don't you see how happy each of us has become?" I protested.

"Yes, happy," she mocked. "He is working with a German and you are romancing an old man!"

Vati and I looked at each other, shaking our heads in disbelief.

That night I slept badly and was glad to get up early the next day. I joined Vati in the kitchen, relieved that Mutti was still asleep. While pouring coffee, Vati said, "Oh, *mein Kind*, continue being happy. At the moment you have every reason to be. Many a young girl would be elated to be courted by that 'old man,'" he laughed.

Still, I couldn't help feeling hurt by Mutti's outburst, and answered, "She has been treating me nicely since I became the main breadwinner. It was quite a shock that she suddenly turned against me, being all gloom and doom just when I was on top of the world."

"Don't let it worry you, *Fannichen*. She just has a morbid and secret longing for suffering and martyrdom," he consoled me, and urged me to carry on in the pursuit of my business and happiness. We embraced.

On the way downtown, all kinds of thoughts crossed my mind. In most families where there is one very strict parent, especially in Germany, it's generally the father who is feared, while a sweet bond is formed between the mother and her children. In my case, the opposite was true. Mutti seemed intent on mistreating me. Although I felt terrible remorse about doubting her love, nonetheless I ventured to ask myself, deep down, whether she really and truly meant well for me.

When I arrived at *Hovenierstraat* I ran into Sasha. I could sense something was wrong.

"Sasha, tell me what's happening?"

I had never seen him so troubled. In a lowered voice he said, "We have just received news that our cousin, Manny Stern from Cologne, and his Dutch wife—you were at their wedding;

you referred to him as 'the jaded Charles Boyer'—both . . . ." Taking a deep breath, he continued: "Both of them were found dead. They chose to commit suicide rather than live under German occupation."

"I'm so sorry," I exclaimed, "and so shocked! She was so lively. I can't imagine her being dead. I can envision him clearly before me, dictating countless letters to embassies and consulates. If only they had received a positive response, they would still be alive today," I reflected.

"Yes, and in fact it happened in the same apartment, on *Lange Leemstraat*, in the big, new building where you typed them. And there's more: Remember the newsreels we saw at the cinema about the maneuvers involving the German Navy, and how the British feared the Nazis would invade their country? It seems Hitler has abandoned that idea. Instead he sent enormous *Luftwaffe* formations to assault Great Britain with a continuous, six-week air raid, culminating these last three days. Thousands of Londoners lost their homes, were killed or injured."

"How awful! I know what it feels like to have that kind of terror overhead. I lived through it first-hand, for I was in Dunkirk. The poor, poor Londoners!" I erupted in hostility, remembering how I had cringed at the lyrics of the song I had heard a few days earlier. "That song, that foreboding song I heard on *Mechelse Steenweg* just recently," I told him. "A company of Nazi soldiers were singing as I cycled past them. The lyrics predicted an assault on England!"

During the time Vati was away in Cologne, Sasha had often referred to himself as my "substitute papa." Now he reminded me very much of my own father, with his sad nod, which was quite unusual for Sasha, a man I knew to be full of optimism, humor and laughter, and boyish mischief. I had always liked that about him, right from the start.

He changed the subject back to his wife's cousin, Manny Stern of Cologne. "It was such a shocking, sad discovery. The first indirect, civilian casualty of the Nazis in Antwerp. You and he both came from Cologne and had the same opportunities to become part of the local Jewish community. But you managed to assimilate, while

Manny and the other refugees stayed among themselves. You were able to find happiness here, but many others weren't. Is it just because you're young and beautiful?" he wondered.

"It's because I have a hunger for life and even adventure," I said. "I want to meet people, to learn more about the world that is closed off to us now . . ."

"That's it!" he agreed, "you immediately began studying our two languages. By the way, we missed you when you postponed your visits to us," he added.

"You truly brought me a lot of *Mazel* and *Brache*, for which I cannot begin to thank you." We shook hands and I went to visit my two girlfriends and find out how they were coping with the highly stressful situation of having their enemies as their prime customers. As I was about to enter Mr. Bialystok's jewelry store, two women stopped me. They knew my name. I noticed they were profoundly upset and recognized them as Yossel's two sisters. Mrs. Friedman grabbed my arm in great urgency, exclaiming, "Thank goodness we ran into you! You are our only hope! They snatched Yossel from his apartment on some kind of currency charge. After interrogating him, they sent him to a concentration camp. We don't even know where."

"Oh my God!" were the only words I was able to utter. Before I could ask, "Why me?"—the same question I had posed to Yossel the morning of the occupation—Mrs. Friedman pleaded, "You have connections with Nazis in high places!"

"Me? Connections with Nazis in high places?" I asked in astonishment.

"Yes, you have been seen leaving one of their offices," she said.

Then it dawned on me: The foxes and "Conrad Veidt." It was obviously a misunderstanding—but how could I possibly relate to her such a trite and comical story at a dreadful time like this? Still overcome with outrage about Yossel's arrest, I selfishly worried about my own skin, mostly about being a currency courier. I wanted to help them and free Yossel if I could, but by returning to "Conrad's gilded cage"? What a risk for me!—my mind was reeling.

I said, "I must give the matter some serious thought." I already felt as though I were in their clutches, the same feeling I had had with "General Conrad." I barely managed to tear myself away from them and their despair, and decided to forego visiting my friends.

Naturally, I was drawn to the gallery. As soon as it was feasible, I related my encounter to Simon. "I understand your wanting to give them some hope and encouragement, but you can't possibly be considering actually returning to 'Conrad Veidt'," he said. "That would be your present and future downfall. Just think of all the repercussions you would expose yourself to. Someday the Allies will liberate us, and then you would be considered a collaborator, although in your heart, you had fulfilled a noble deed. So, *Kätzele meins*, don't you dare try to be a heroine by playing with fire! Leave it to me. I have my connections. There are bold specialists for such dangerous missions. Tell the Friedmans that endeavors are being undertaken on their brother's behalf, but make it very clear to them, definitely not by yourself!"

We also discussed Manny from Cologne, whom he did not know. Still, a painful grimace appeared on his charming face. "Death is so final, not to be sought, not even as a last resort. Some miracle is always apt to happen in the last minute of utter agony. Remember this, *Kätzele meins*!"

As to the England invasion, he consoled me that the Royal Air Force had enough planes now, and the *Luftwaffe* attacks would literally be an aerial boomerang into Germany.

Concerning my illegal business, I reiterated what I had mentioned numerous times before, that my life itself was illegal. As always his love, faith and sheltering comfort made me feel like a different person by the time I left the gallery. When I reluctantly said goodbye, many dark clouds had been lifted.

Upon meeting Mrs. Friedman and Rachel, I said what I had been instructed to tell them. They were just as grateful as though I had carried out this dangerous task myself, asking me what the redemption fee would be. They implied a rather large sum would be at my disposal.

"No, no, my source refused any monetary gain. Sheer idealism is its own reward," I told them.

Tears of gratefulness welled up in their eyes. In her extroverted manner, Mrs. Friedman grabbed my hand and kissed it. She was too choked up to verbally express her thanks.

Soon it was Friday again, my lucky day. It never failed, each week: No matter how hard I tried to make a sale from Monday to Thursday, I did not succeed. But Fridays were different. I was chatting with Mrs. Steiner and Sofie when "Paleface," my very first customer, approached me.

He could not help noticing the splendid, opulent diamond bracelet, bordered on each side with sapphires, that I wore on my wrist. Since it was nearing the Sabbath, the Vesting Straat Café was less busy than usual. We found a quiet corner. "Paleface" took out his loupe, stuck it firmly in his eye and let the exquisite piece of jewelry slowly glide over his fingers as he studied each graduating stone. Moishe kept winking and nodding approvingly while polishing glasses. My cheeks were burning, but this time it was from business excitement, not passion. My asking price was vast, but my souk technique was practiced! "Paleface" did a lot of pondering and figuring. We finally agreed upon a sum. Another *"Mazel-Brache"* handshake followed. My client excused himself while I unzipped my etui to tone down my glow.

Upon his return, "Paleface" handed me a bulky bundle wrapped in a Nazi newspaper. He unlocked the safety latch of the bracelet and removed it from my wrist. Seizing the sizable amount of Belgian francs uncounted, I swung onto my bike so I would make it to the gallery before closing time.

Simon was in the cloakroom, just about to finish a deal. Coincidentally, it was for the same amount I had received for the bracelet. I gave him the nondescript packet, which he in turn passed on to his Chassidic customer, who stroked his beard and *payes*, apparently feeling quite uncomfortable in my (female) presence. The Nazi-newspaper-wrapped package was not even opened, let alone counted, neither by me, nor Simon, nor the Orthodox client.

After the latter left, I exclaimed that I had never encountered so many honest, trusting people who consummated such high-stake business agreements without any contract nor signature, only on one's word and a handshake.

"Yes, we are rather proud of our tradition," he explained. "And it's actually a very sound business relationship. We have our own arbitration board rather than a regular court of law. Any merchant or broker who did not comply would be blacklisted! Nobody would have any dealings with anyone whose name appeared negatively on the bulletin board of the Diamond Exchange or Diamond Bourse—at least not until his name had been cleared. It's possible he might even be spurned from the trade forever. Most of these rare felonies are not even committed willfully, but result from misunderstandings or misplacements of merchandise. And that's when the only unfairness in our trade occurs: when someone has been cheated. He in turn is also no longer trusted, for he might consider taking vengeful action against others."

Then he pressed me to his fervent heart. I felt myself burning like a flame. His pre-Sabbath kisses made me fly high, like Marc Chagall's sensuous lovers framed with Jewish overtones.

The wonderful summer, my favorite season of the year, slowly started chilling into autumn. Ironically, under the occupation, my lifestyle had become more exciting. However, thoughts that soon a cold, withered world would present itself created inner fear and doom. In order to dispel this feeling, I substituted the waning summer joy with pleasures of fashion, and spent even more time at the gallery. Although playing cards or any other game is a waste of time in my eyes, I felt regal just sitting alongside Simon amidst the atmosphere of his elegant, cozy hangout. It held a strong appeal that was enhanced by a charming social circle.

One day, Simon said, "I'm on a winning streak and I would like to share my proceeds with you—but only if I win. If I lose, the loss is all mine." Everyone laughed, including myself. He won, and handed me a huge bundle of Belgian francs, saying, "May these be well spent on your beauty!"

My blue fox-trimmed coat was almost ready when I came for the third fitting. Through the magic of paper-thin gramophone records, Morton Downey was still singing, "When I Take My Sugar to Tea." And as the last strains of "Dancing in the Dark" faded out, my sessions with the designer couple were over.

The coat and matching hat met with everyone's approval, but were quite incongruous with my bicycle mission. This time, the usual folded parchment contained many carats of loupe-clear, blue-white, loose diamonds that I was to offer Mr. Lipshutz.

There were no swaggering, singing troops when I arrived at *Mechelse Steenweg*. After I dutifully presented the precious little package, the valuable contents of the pale azure wrapper were the subject of much scrutiny. Now I became privy to another diamond tradition, "*le cachet,*" consisting of my quoting Simon's price plus my commission. If rejected by the client, a counter offer would be secreted within the packet. The client then applies a personalized marking across the flap, thus creating a primitive yet effective tamper-proof seal. This is what Mr. Lipshutz did. It was my first unsuccessful Friday, though I still retained high hopes for the *cachet.*

As always, my weekend with Simon was delightful and ever so romantic. On Sunday, he offered to buy some fine pastries and beautiful flowers and visit my parents. "I haven't seen your father . . ."

"My MISTER father," I giggled, reminding him of the necessary courtesy.

He winked and continued, " . . . for quite some time, and I have never had the pleasure of meeting your 'MRS. Mother,'" he kidded.

It occurred to me that this fact was probably precisely the reason why our relationship was such an enormously enjoyable one.

Simon inquired anxiously, "Why do I detect a sudden and drastic change in you, *Kätzele meins?*"

"Mutti can be quite abrasive and strict in her mores, specifically when our concepts of male relationships clash," I retorted bitterly.

"May I find this out for myself?" he asked.

On our way there, I ruminated: Would I have regrets about this meeting? Here was my last chance to retract from the anticipated visit, as I unlocked the door to the house. There was no response to my tapping at the door of the flat. We used my key, only to find no one home.

Never had I been alone with any man—much less with one whom I cherished so profoundly—face to face in such a private situation. Even though Simon had told me that he had two different dwellings, I truly appreciated the fact that he never suggested we go there. And the cloakroom of the gallery was no longer conducive to passionate kissing, as it was beginning to serve its original purpose, now that the weather was turning cooler.

I called, "Mutti! Vati!" There was no reply. Suddenly I found myself in what I thought to be a situation of peril. The last of the sunshine announced the arrival of twilight. I clutched the big, colorful bouquet as though creating a protective fortification around me, to shield me from an opponent. But no, Simon was no adversary! It was merely the shame-based tyranny of naiveté and inhibitions that befell me. I asked myself why this was so. My answer came rapidly: That darned teacher Bodewig! He had indeed scarred me. But I wouldn't let anything spoil this exciting moment, which was building up momentum as we stood gazing at each other in the all-too-disturbing but exalting silence. I was still holding the bouquet like a child bride walking down the aisle totally unsure of herself. But she was in a far better position. I was underneath that Sword of Damocles; it was forever over my head; I clung fiercely to that holy, almighty virginity. As a result, I felt extremely vexed, forlorn, embarrassed and weak.

At last, he broke the unbearable stillness by stammering breathlessly, "Roses are most becoming to you. You and a bouquet of flowers, you and your bicycle, you and diamonds—it's you, you, you!" He bent down to kiss me.

I felt this to be a most delicious discovery. But when he cupped my chin in his hand and tried to lift my head to look deep into my eyes, my embarrassment was overwhelming. This gesture brought to my mind the most disturbing flashes of Bodewig, who had tried to force me to look into his face. At the time, I resisted so firmly and strongly that my hated teacher gave up the struggle— but alas, only the struggle to lift my chin, not the struggle to lift my dress.

Simon must have sensed my inner battle. He gently took the flowers out of my arms to place them in a vase. This gave me some time to stall and muse. Seeing the tender way he handled the flowers only made me desire him all over again, knowing full well the next blossom would be me. Yet here I was, the coquettish, flirtatious and worldly courtier-courier of the biggest diamantaires, hiding behind a veil of prudery. No one but Simon, who was witnessing this, would believe my taboo. I was simultaneously thrilled and ashamed when he approached me, ever so slowly unbuttoning my coat, his eyes not letting go of mine as he gallantly removed it and whispered again, "A girl like you should only be kissed, nothing less—and nothing more!"

That statement once again made my world look rosy. I was able to allow myself some abandon, relishing his compliments and exulting in his kisses covering my face. When he pressed his soft, yearning lips against mine, I felt bewitched. My stored emotions for him started to find release, whirling in supreme delight. The last thing I saw before closing my eyes was the beauty spot on his left cheek. The alleged bubbles of my outward personality must have entered my entire being.

Like a conquistador, his tongue prevailed against the fortress of my teeth, searching for and meeting my own. Together they were like happy dolphins, emerging caressingly from the sea, and my shame and inhibition subsided. Instead I was overcome with anticipation of electrifying frenzy. His magnificent nearness drew me to the sweetest, all-consuming passion.

Swiftly he placed the chairs tête-à-tête, as in the waiting room. Our rapturous longing for each other continued in this intoxicating fashion, creating scenes of ecstasy and aesthetics, like a beautiful Rodin sculpture come to life, flowing from one sensuous, chiseled pose to another. Only ours were *puris naturalibus*. I wanted these superb embraces in those artfully changing poses—a visual experience—and those exploring caresses to last forever! Had my parents entered at that moment, I would have been incapable of escaping this mesmerizing rapture. Again I was ascending—this time on wings—into heaven, into paradise! It was like the refrain of a love song.

Shortly after he left, my parents appeared. I was grateful for the perfect timing. During the short, dreamy interim between Simon's departure and my parents' arrival, I arranged the pastry and flowers on the table. My heart seemed as full as the vase. I recalled times when we had had nothing but sardines, and relished again my current happiness.

"Look how beautifully our child has set the table," Vati exclaimed approvingly. "How colorful and appetizing everything looks!"

Nothing was forthcoming from Mutti but an arrogant, haughty nod; I was not sure whether she liked or disliked it. Even though I felt so fulfilled, having just heard the most endearing words, I longed for Mutti to express them also. But I hardly dared dream she would someday be able to do so, and I felt relief on the other hand that her criticism about the "old man" at least remained unspoken.

Instead she began prying, prodding and probing about the lovely items on the table. In this case, it was far better to conceal the truth. Being a poor liar, I had to think fast: "Why, I'm earning enough to set aside for bad times—which surely will come sooner or later—and then some. Certainly I can buy a few flowers for you, Mutti."

"But such a stunning bouquet?" she questioned, looking at them and then suspiciously at me.

"Oh, *Sofiechen*, let her be. Just enjoy it and be grateful!" Vati objected.

Quickly, I changed the subject without even mentioning Simon. "Tomorrow the first item on my agenda is a very important one. I have to bring this cachet," I said, removing it from my purse to show it to my parents, "to Mr. Lipshutz. If the deal goes through, just think how much money I'll be making with my ten percent plus the brokerage fee. So let's drink to that!" I brought out a bottle of schnapps and three sterling tumblers.

Mutti still stared at me skeptically. Although I felt she was being unkind to me, I hated to admit her cleverness, or her special sixth sense—which was an additional cause of Vati's profound admiration for her. Now, he was enthusing over me and my business deal, saying, "You see, that's our child!" He lifted his glass and toasted, "May there be many more such wonderful get-togethers!"

"How much better off we are now than we were at Mr. Weinstock's villa," I said, recalling a similar occasion toward the end of the *Flucht,* "when we sat together with Yossel and his sisters. Poor Yossel—may he be saved!" I raised my glass.

"*Omein!*" my parents prayed.

Mutti, a great maven of fine jewelry for as along as I can remember, tried on the various pieces of merchandise I had with me and admired herself in the mirror. This, the schnapps, the pastry, and the sight and scent of the roses did wonders for her. It turned out to be a joyous family evening. What marvelous eight hours I had spent today, I thought, hiding the precious pieces primitively but securely in the blue fox pockets of my coat, since I was not planning to wear the elegant garment. Tomorrow I would be conducting courier and not courtier business. We retired late and happily.

Once in bed, I recounted in my mind the eventful, magnificent day, evening and night. My feelings stirred anew. As I drifted off to sleep, I felt enormous satisfaction about the charming reunion with my parents—compliments of Simon's delicious pastries and lovely bouquet—with me being the most desired flower—of someone so—exciting—so—

Chapter 15

"*Aufmachen! Aufmachen!* (Open, open!)" Thundering knocking was heard. Out of a deep sleep, I gasped, jolting upright in bed.

"*Aufmachen! Sofort!* (At once!)" With great urgency, accompanied by even more violent banging on the door.

"Oh, my God!" Moaning, we darted out of bed.

Pandemonium outside! Vati opened the window and calmed them by calling, "Moment!" he cried. Biting his lower lip, his face gripped with terror. "It's one of those big, dreaded WH cars," he managed to utter breathlessly on his way down to reluctantly bring up the uniformed men.

Two soldiers entered with the *"Heil Hitler!"* salute. God, what a frightful sight: Nazi military, the look of war in the privacy of our apartment.

I scanned their collars for any panic-evoking insignia. Finding none, I felt some relief to be dealing with the regular *Wehrmacht*.

"We are here to search the entire contents of this apartment," they announced in a sober official voice. Whereupon both walked into our bedroom. One of them started "working" on his knees from the bottom drawer of the commode. Removing everything, he methodically examined each item and sheet of paper, handing some of them to his comrade.

Oh, for heaven's sake! The *cachet*! They'll confiscate it and torture me to find out to whom it belonged. Simon, Mr. Lipshutz and so many others would be implicated and what about me? I eased out of the bedroom while they were engrossed in seeking and piling up. I grabbed my purse, dashed into the bathroom and with shivering hands, tucked it firmly into my bra. The parchment corners scratched my skin, which upset me terribly. I looked for something soft to wrap the packet in, wanting to avoid any movements that might reveal my secret. In the kitchen I found a rag—too big and bulky. Dread of discovery added to my nervousness. Any old, thin kerchief might do. At last I was able to slip the concealed diamonds into my bosom. I hid my handbag underneath the sink behind a curtain skirt. Feeling much better about the rearrangement, I returned voluntarily to the bedroom. The soldiers were too busy combing through everything to notice my brief absence. Hopefully, they would not enter the kitchen.

The kneeling one felt he had made a great find. For a moment, he was excited about fulfilling his goal, exclaiming to the other one: "Ah, shorthand! Oh, oh, German stenography!" My tension slackened when I saw him smile. Relaxed, but deeply disappointed, he read out loud:

> *Hast du die Lippen mir wund geküsst,*
> *So küsse sie wieder heil*
> *Und wenn du bis Abend nicht fertig bist*
> *So hat es auch keine Eil.*
> (You have made my lips sore with your kissing,
> Now kiss them to be healed
> If you're not done when night comes
> Don't rush, my dear, I'll kiss and hold you tight.)

It was a joke on them. Had I planned this humiliation, it could not have turned out more vengeful. Also, how apropos Heine's poem was to yesterday!

Mutti cringed as they unfolded each clean, wonderfully scented linen piece, which she had boiled and hand-washed. We felt proud of how impeccable the stacks of sheets and towels were—wrapped in red satin ribbons. Unable to make up their minds if we were filthy or the world's imperialistic financiers, the Nazis surely could not say: "Those dirty Jews!"

I shuddered when they moved into the kitchen. They opened the curtain skirt underneath the sink. Finally, they did find my handbag.

"How careless of you to place a fine genuine leather purse in such an unlikely spot!" He mockingly reproached me, while making a triple "t" sound with his tongue, shaking his head. He opened and turned it upside down so all the contents spilled onto the wooden table. My eye fell on a sheet of paper. Oh no, I thought with the greatest of restraint! I had so nicely tucked away the merchandise into my fox pocket, totally forgetting the list. How could I have been so foolish as to endanger my profession, so to speak. I used it everyday, crossing out anything I had sold and adding new pieces that Simon had given me. Whenever it got untidy, I made up a fresh one, which I had just completed. The polite beast rattled off my tally with glee: "One broach: two pearls, 1 carat diamond, one 18 carat ring: center cluster diamonds. One watch consisting of diamond hearts! And so forth. I was furious at myself and at him, the only male that knew steno—and yet so well!

After the rich haul of papers was meticulously piled into their briefcase, the good "stenographer" clicked his heels with the proper Nazi sound and Hitler salute, taking leave of Mutti only. My heart stood still when he ordered Vati and myself to come with them. Oh, my God—the two of us were under arrest. Was this to be the end? We bade Mutti "bye" and once on the street, we were led into the back of the big WH car. "What now?" I pressed Vati softly for an answer, both of us in utter terror.

I had to be inventive. Quickly, quickly! Think, think! Certainly, these two will bring us to their chief just as did the Belgian policemen in Berchem. I recalled a Russian word that was in a play Vati performed as a Polish youth. *Slédovatel* (inquisitor), I mumbled. Vati understood, looked at me, nodded with moist eyes, grabbing my hand and holding it tight as though it was the last time, nodding again, sighing deeply. Their boss would deal with us. How was I to explain that list? I would have consulted Vati in Yiddish, but the "stenographer" would likely have understood, especially since the helper was driving. He took my daily, pleasant route downtown. By car it should have been a brief ride, but it seemed long and slow, as though to my own funeral. My sad thoughts bade farewell forever to Kerk Straat, farewell to Karnot Straat, farewell to my second home, where at long last I had found great happiness. Gazing from the car into the sunny day, already feeling imprisoned in the automobile, I wondered if I would ever see daylight again. If I leave you, my beloved streets, I'll leave my life as well. *Adieu* my familiar streets that I pounded every day with so much hope and energy which ultimately led me to good fortune. If I do not perish, I'll return, oh, yes, return, I vowed with passion and tears, feeling a poisonous mixture of pain and wrath caused by so much injustice. Every so often I would turn to Vati. Looking at him, I saw my emotions reflected in his eyes, which appeared even larger and greener. Wordlessly, we nodded to each other in such despair, curious and petrified, speculating where they would take us and what would happen.

They stopped in front of the Excelsior Hotel, just a few steps from our former "news corner". Since Antwerp's busiest spot had a wide sidewalk, when we were taken from the car by the soldiers, rows of onlookers formed rapidly on either side. I was extremely embarrassed. Poised for a rendezvous with destiny, torture or death, we entered the luxurious establishment. We were ushered through plush passages. Even though a heavy cloud of anguish hung over me, I was amazed that the Excelsior and my favorite, the Century, were connected inside, both requisitioned.

Despite the broad and thickly-carpeted hallways, as I marched down the long corridors, flanked by my captors, I felt as if led to the gallows. Instead of using a stark waiting room, we were motioned to sit on petit point armchairs, the décor of the place left unchanged. While remaining there for the longest time, bouts of anxiety befell me whenever I remembered the list and the hidden *cachet*. The ticking and chimes of the grandfather clock heightened the tension.

Vati beckoned me. I jumped up and when I bent my ear to his whispering lips, I heard an excellent suggestion, a story he had just made up. Vati had relieved my heart in the nick of time, because now the moment of truth arrived in the form of the "helper-driver", who brought us into an exquisite suite. The French Baccarat mirror showed

the reflection of a most appealing man. The "helper" was carefully
fussing around him, arranging everything on a huge desk inlaid with
mother of pearl, joyfully executing orders with: "*Jawohl, Herr
Hauptmann!*" Beneath the Bohemian chandelier, he was studying our
case, his officer's hat at a jaunty angle. Without looking up, he
motioned with his upturned palm for us to take a seat.

Timidly and fearfully we sat down, bravely facing our fate.
Finally, *Herr Hauptmann* seemed ready for us. He took off his hat,
revealing a shock of blond hair. His eyes still fixed on our file, he
spread out its contents on the majestic desk and slid the large-
winged chair under him. When I looked at our chart upside down, I
became even more frightened, amazed to detect my mini business
card, printed for my English teaching. This seemed all so long ago.

Now he fired one loaded question after another, tricking and
tripping his victims with his arsenal. This interrogation in the
truest sense of the word attacked alternately Vati and me. Vati was
hit hard, which caused him utter dismay. Though thorough, *Herr
Hauptmann* went easier on me. His voice, demeanor, gestures and
looks were most authoritative. In his late thirties, highly skilled as
a legal combatant, he sensed my innocence. Nevertheless, I shrank
when he picked up my list. He studied it while shaking his head
sarcastically with raised eyebrows: "Very impressive, most impressive,
indeed!" he said, reciting some of the big items.

Darn! I thought. How accurately the "stenographer" transcribed
everything!

"What about it?" *Herr Hauptmann* pressed with a most earnest
expression which made him appear arrogant and the epitome of
Nazi efficiency. "I repeat," he said, slowly and clearly: "I want an
explanation of this!" Holding my inventory up high, he asked:
"Are you getting my drift?"

"Yes, *Herr Hauptmann*. This is a sort of safeguard, for the future,
from my fiancé."

"Where is he now, this fiancé of yours?"

"He emigrated to Palestine," was my brief answer, knowing
full well that responding as curtly as possible to questions from a
prosecuting official—and a Nazi one at that—was best.

Boss Vati, giving orders from bottom of wagon to part of his crew loading daily 20 tons of scrap iron—

—while Mutti on bike with me standing. 1935 Cologne, Schanzenstr.

"How did he obtain so many jewels?"

"He inherited them after his mother's death."

"Where and when?"

"In Vienna . . . 1937!"

"That's a tall tale!" he exclaimed, tapping the fingers of his left hand with the pencil in his right, from one end to the other, creating a steady little rhythm that scared me. He emphasized it by making stern, inquisitive eye contact with me. His expression took on a deadly seriousness.

The Captain had found himself a fertile field for shaping stress situations. This was stark reality void of hope. Chances were, we might never get out of this trap. Anxiously, I thought things over, wondering if I should say something, anything, such as sorry, there is nothing else I could add; or should I just stay locked in this heart-thumping situation, and if so, how long could I bear it? I decided on the latter. A strange stillness had fallen over the room, interrupted only by the ticking of the ornate French clock. It must have been made by the court horologist of Louis XIV. I tried to mask the suspense with this thought. But the heavy silence grew thicker, until I could stand it now longer. Then he began hurling other questions at Vati. "How did you know Hermann Rauter?"

"He worked as my apprentice-stockboy."

"Why did you give him this?" He attacked Vati, holding up my tiny card.

Though confused, Vati managed acceptable responses, which angered the Captain, whose relentless questioning descended from nasty to downright diabolical. In a way, I was relieved that he abandoned my list in favor of tormenting Vati about Hermann Rauter. Every so often he demanded answers from me, praising my intelligence as being superior to Vati's. Ideas started to brew in my mind as to why we had been brought here in the first place. The matter seemed to relate strictly to our ironyard stockboy. I recalled this youngest of Vati's working crew. I remembered him well; not only because he was so small, but also appeared naïve and frail. One Saturday afternoon when the business was closed and Vati and the main staff had left, some of the other workers tortured him. They did terrible things to him. One was stringing him to the *Fallbirne* by his feet and letting him dangle there without his pants, high up in the air, head down, for quite some time, continually raising and lowering the wrecking ball, all to their amusement, as an eyewitness told Vati. He never reported back to work. I felt sorry for him. He had helped me with my little side-trade for the do-it-yourselfers. While I was busy with homework for the Commercial School—my presence preventing any metal theft—he had loaded the profile iron onto the scale and then the buyers' vehicles. As a German soldier, here, in Antwerp, he seemed to be in trouble.

I was angry at Vati. His giving Hermann my card had caused this endless interrogation and terror. At times, the Captain, his clear eyes narrowing, lashed into Vati, reminding me of a painting by Paul de Voos, one of the Flemish greats: "The Fight between Cock and Peacock." It was as though the cock attacked the peacock while the frightened female, whom I saw as myself, looked on helplessly.

The whole situation became grim until—until I could no longer trust my eyes—in the French Baccarat mirror, where I first saw his reflection, totally out of character, there was now a friendly, smiling, handsome Hauptmann. I picked up meaningful stares and remained motionless, even though all kinds of feelings stirred within me. I was completely mollified. It was as though the glacial ice had softened and melted into a fresh, new dew, dripping from the sudden warmth. I was stupefied by this instant change of behavior. Was he also an actor, in addition to being a top-notch prosecutor? It felt great! Now, I had power over him and with this, to my intense delight, he had given up his controlling position, and gladly done so! This was revealed by his relaxed facial expression and easy tone of voice—hitherto unheard. The mirror conveyed one final, intimate message. Satisfied, he strode to his opulent desk, saying quietly, "The questioning is over. Your are free to leave!"

"Thank you, thank you!" I said emotionally as we made our exit back into life. The Captain was right behind me. Upon arriving earlier, in my fear, I had not even noticed the short stairway. Before

I was gliding down the steps, he exclaimed, most charmingly, "I would love to see you again, but never, ever here!" As I proceeded to move down, he continued, "But never, ever under these circumstances!"

I turned around and looked up at this blond god who had decided to allow me to live. He was beaming as much as I. Containing myself not to wave at him, I nodded instead, accompanied by my best smile.

The late afternoon felt fresh, liberty sweeter than ever. As we were passing our former newsstand, I delighted in my happiness and wanted to embrace Vati. This was the first time I ever remembered his not being receptive. I knew he felt guilty about the incident that might have turned out lethal for both of us. I did not want to ask about Hermann and my card. After all, he had suffered enough interrogations. "I shall dash to the gallery at once, Vati," I said.

"I'll run home to Mutti. She must be terribly worried," he mumbled, still choked up.

The joy of release put a spring in my step, even though I kept wondering about Vati's connection with his former stockboy. When I finally arrived at Kiepdorp Vest, Mrs. Diemenstein opened the door. She seemed thrilled to see me. So were all of the others. I was amazed to find Mutti next to Simon. Everyone jumped off their seats to gather around me. Anxiously, they wanted to hear what had happened after our arrest. I accommodated them with a step-by-step chronicle. Mutti, smart as usual, had grabbed the unfound jewelry out of my coat pocket and taken it to Simon; thus meeting him on her own, under such dire circumstances.

From then on, our lives continued on a pleasant course. Business went on as usual. So did my romance. But Mutti occasionally nagged Vati about my card. With moist eyes, he admitted his mistake, when Mutti reminded us that the torture was not the main reason for his quitting. His father did not want his son to work for a "Jew boss" any longer. Yes, now it dawned on us that this was true. The knowledge was even worse for poor Vati.

One noon, with Mrs. Steiner on my "post", a newcomer to our trade, who seemed distraught, approached us. We had recently noticed this very young, blond, abnormally tall man named Norman. With his pure Aryan looks, it was amazing, even to us, that he was Jewish. He only had eyes for Sofie, who was quite a few years his senior. His long legs carried him toward us. With great agitation, he told us: "When I brought the antacid for Sofie, she did not answer. I kept knocking. Positive she was inside, I yelled: 'Sofie, if you don't open, I'll break down the door!' Finally, I heard her faint, plaintive voice: 'Go away. Just leave!' When I repeated my threat, she appeared at last. Doubled up due to her bellyache, her eyes bloodshot from crying, she crawled into bed. While handing her a glass of water for the medicine, she, in turn, gave me a frightful-looking package with a lot of swastika rubber stamps and an official letter. I was aghast reading it." He continued with visible effort: "It said something like this: 'You'll find, enclosed with this mail, a packet containing the remains of your husband, who died of unknown causes. Sign the receipt and pay five hundred Belgian francs (ten dollars). Heil Hitler! Signed,'—I believe—'SS Sturmführer Siegfried Schmitz.'"

"Imagine having loved a person, having lived with him for many years and all that's left is a small package of ashes—and after unbelievable torture, actually having succumbed to such torment!" He paused. His moving Adam's apple told the rest.

We were shocked and speechless. Mrs. Steiner pulled herself together and immediately offered to go with him to look after Sofie. I minded "the store" making a good sale, even though I could not get Norman's story out of my mind. After quite some time, the slender Sofie arrived, flanked by Mrs. Steiner and Norman, wearing sunglasses on this gray day. Her pale face shaded by a Deanna Durbin hat, she forced herself with all of her will power to be among people.

Needing the lift of his company and Prager's food, I looked forward to meeting Simon. As soon as I arrived I told him about Sofie's fate. When I had finished, he took my hands, kissed them, then held them tightly as he gazed into my eyes, saying, "Most of the time you seem so happy. I did not want to spoil that mood for anything in the world. Now that this shattering story has surfaced, it's not quite that hard to report the following: Remember when you left 'General Conrad Veidt' to play 'Mata Hari' in order to rescue a young man because his sisters implored you to do so, thinking you were a real big-shot with that important Nazi office?"

"Yes, of course. But you insisted upon taking charge yourself," I recollected.

"Exactly. But before I could start, imagine, Mrs. Friedman, his older sister, even offered to pay you for this dangerous mission. May I tell you now?" He braced himself. "Only days after she had entreated you to save her brother—she, too, received the same package as Sofie, accompanied by such a letter."

"No, no! Not Yossel!" I cried out. In my mind, I saw his ghostly image—this tall, lean, gaunt, good person standing before me. I felt my chest cave in from pain and horror. In a frenzy, all of our meetings flashed in front of me, and now everything turned to ASHES! Just as the furrier, Mr. Chmurra, had predicted. I could only sit there mournfully until I was forced to regain my composure as two German officers marched in to dine.

In an effort to console me, Simon pointed out: "Only think of the bright side. You charmed even *Herr Hauptmann*; for whether one is innocent or not, they keep you and that's how one winds up after unspeakable suffering. Remember, once more, how lucky you and your father have been!" Taking hold of my hands again, he added: "I'm deeply moved by your compassion for this human being. Had I had the slightest idea you knew him personally, I never would have told you about his dreadful fate. I just assumed he was as faceless to you as Sofie's husband, and each was to me, which is horrific enough! You never told me!"

This was the time to relate some memories of Yossel. Now, I was able to explain to him: "Yes, on the way to the Excelsior, when we were in the WH military car, I had envisioned this Nazi horror upon me, bidding 'good-bye' to all the streets I passed—*adieu!*— to life, to you and everything."

I felt his sympathy and delight in me as he kissed my fingers, murmuring most affectionately: "*Kätzele meins!*" while the Nazi officers were looking on.

Since that lovely "flower and pastry" Sunday, we had learned coincidentally that my parents made it their habit to have their outings then. So, at first, I went most reluctantly to our apartment with Simon, but then those romantic hours filled my life with even more excitement. Simon stuck to his word, so I could keep my morals: my virginity. Our delectable embraces still reminded me of great sculptures by Rodin.

On one such afternoon, when we had almost arrived at the house, my parents turned the corner. I was totally taken aback and never had felt more ashamed in front of them. They seemed very happy—even Mutti. It occurred to me that they must have had an enjoyable time as they did—I imagined—upon conceiving me. Both of them—especially Mutti—must have felt ill at ease also, so that she blushed and rattled on that they had been invited to a *Landsmann* from her city of Chestochowa. She continued with a red face, that there is this good-looking man with the strange name—not unlike her furrier-countryman of Wojdeslavski. He is married to a young, tiny blonde. They have an eleven-year-old son. She set forth, driven by embarrassment, even giggling: "*La petite* has this huge typical matriarch mom, Mrs. Schwartz, who is living with them. She is supposed to be a fine cook and great housekeeper."

"So let's see what Frau Schwartz 'baked up' for our Sunday coffee hour, Sofiechen!" Vati said, with a loving glance at Mutti. Everyone was relieved that he had extricated all of us so graciously from this collective uneasiness.

As for me, the entire day was ruined by my shame and worry about the parental encounter. I was terribly concerned that repercussions might ensue from Mutti on Monday. No matter how much Simon tried to soothe me, it was to no avail. I was agreeably surprised that Mutti, most discreetly, did not mention our "chance meeting." She just raved over the nice Kaffee Klatsch they had had, Frau Schwartz' culinary delights and her son-in-law's fine, interesting features. A good, attentive listener, I learned that most worrying is, fortunately, pointless.

However, a bit later, another shock troubled us profoundly, something bound to alter our pleasant lifestyle. It was a Nazi paper requesting us to *stellen* within forty-eight hours, at six a.m. at the small Berchem train station. We were devastated.

With this despised "invitation," I ran, in great dismay, to the gallery. My head was spinning. I realized this would be the end of my business and my entire world.

When I arrived at Diemenstein's, and they saw me this way, everyone stopped their games to gather around and share in my disaster. My eyes scanned the beauty of the gallery I loved so much, not only for its visual enchantment but for all the rapture, success, and warmth it had offered me. As in the past, Simon beckoned me to the *vestiaire* (cloakroom). Again, he half-sat, half-stood at the stool, taking me in his arms, whispering: "There is a way out: I have a second apartment I do not use. It is near the Mechelse Steenweg where you closed that nice business deal with Mr. Lipschutz." I nodded sadly, knowing full well that I would no longer be able to do so.

"You and your parents will have to hide there. I definitely don't want you to become Nazi prisoners. Is that clear? I'm dead set against it! Is that understood?" he exclaimed emphatically.

I agreed wholeheartedly and told him about the promise to myself when I was facing the deadliest of dangers at the Flucht, having briefly lost my parents—that I would never, ever find myself in such a calamity again. He pressed me closer and sighed with relief: "As long as we understand each other. I'll have a car pick up your necessities, since your quartier is furnished. For forty-eight hours, you may still have access to your dwelling. That's when it's moving time, but we must act fast!" he urged.

The four of us met at the apartment. It was our last time in the place where we resided the longest and survived so much in Belgium. My English classes had flourished here. I had even written the book, devising my own fast, yet thorough method. Then the invasion killed it! Now, I had found all this happiness with Simon at last, and in one Nazi swoop it ended—gone—it seemed—forever.

With heavy hearts and *contre-coeur*, we started packing, when almost simultaneously, the warning siren of an air raid went off. If only the Allies above could help us instantly, was my wistful thought. Also, at this very second, there was a hard knock at the door. We cringed. Had the Nazis come to fetch us prematurely? Simon answered while we hid in the bedroom. It was a civil guard complaining that lights were seeping through the sides of our blackout shades. Naturally throughout an air raid, we had to be in total darkness, but in our rush to get our things together we had forgotten that law for the moment. We lost working time to just wait it out. Unlike the *Flucht*, "the enemies" were our friends, since they flew to Germany without dropping bombs here in Belgium. Thus my deadly fear during our three-week escape was eliminated. Simon did not waste one precious minute to softly kiss and embrace me. The presence of my parents made me feel most uncomfortable. Even though they could not see anything, I feared his touch on my dress would make some kind of noise, however faint. This was the first time I was not enthralled with his secret advances, though his spontaneity amused me even now, and I reflected that were it not for him, I would be engulfed in total gloom.

Simon's apartment consisted of two spacious rooms. It looked, indeed, "unlived" in. There was no time to wonder why he needed two flats. Even though his other one was downtown, I never knew its precise location. Possibly, I did not care, because I was glad that he never offered to take me there.

Life in this flat would be such a stark difference from the lively, at times glamorous lifestyle among the many human contacts, which fascinated me, since I am a "people person." It seemed that Simon's love alone could not fill the void of the business deals and my outside world.

The forty-eight hours passed. We did not *stellen* or give ourselves up. Although our needs were met, especially as Simon brought us the wonderful Prager food at the end of the day, a strange feeling of human deprivation came upon us. It must have been "cabin fever." The four of us spent a very quiet New Year's Eve, going into a tough new decade at the clandestine apartment. We realized our desolate situation. I asked myself why everything seemed so bittersweet and why I could and did not feel any happier. After all, there was love, warmth, family, conversation, great food and wine.

On the second day of the year, 1941, in the late afternoon, my parents went to visit the Wojdeslavskis as they did so often during that time. Shortly thereafter Simon arrived as he had each night before going back downtown to his dwelling. I used the extra time to tidy up the place. He was thrilled to find me alone. Suddenly, amidst his caresses, he held me firmly, explaining: "Look, sooner or later, they'll get all of us Jews."

"Everyone is of the stubborn opinion that this misery is directed just against us refugees," I said.

"Now listen, my dear, beloved, adorable refugee, *Kätzele meins*. When such a time arrives, and it will, I intend to go to Southern France and wait it out. How safe it will be, no one knows. There might be danger on the long train trip. Also, the Nazis might change their minds and negotiate with the traitor Pétain, for them to occupy the region. Another possibility is that they might delegate the Jewish persecution to their allies, the Italians, who are right there at the most beautiful border in the entire world, the French-Italian Riviera. Danger lurks everywhere for us, so we just can't wait." He paused for an extended time, continuing: "And I want to do this with you. We often worry about people's gossip and my being more than twice your age. Hold your head up high, give me your hand, and together, we'll walk underneath palm trees and flowers, in high hopes of a final Nazi crush, as the French say over the BBC: '*Nous allons les écraser, nous les aurons, les Boches!*'" After we had a little fun imitating them together passionately, he clasped me tighter still. With a strange, enigmatic stare I had never seen before, looking straight ahead as though there was a crowd, he announced: "I would be proud for you to be my wife!"

At this emotionally charged, suspenseful moment, my parents returned from their visit. Mutti's face was flushed, as though she had some happy news, and suddenly declared: "We are getting ready to *stellen* ourselves, the day after tomorrow! I'm all excited about our departure and so is Mrs. Schwartz. She was the only member of their family who received that same order for the second transport!"

I tried to halt this madness by pointing out: "They'll punish us on the spot because we were not obedient over a week ago, when we were supposed to report.'"

She was so fanatically enthusiastic she didn't even hear me; instead, she went on raving: "Mrs. Schwartz, too, is all worked up about this! I can't live anymore without an identity and worrying if they'll come to get us. If we step forward, ourselves, it won't be as bad as if they catch us hiding illegally."

"But Mutti! Don't you see the pointlessness and danger in this? Especially since we have such a comfy place in which to 'disappear' and Simon has taken all the precautions with food, so no one will bother us here."

"No buts! There are no two ways about this! We're giving ourselves up!" She was as preposterous now as when she insisted we leave the villa, which then went up in one blast. I felt so powerless and looked for help from the two men. Vati, as during most of his life with Mutti only, was slavishly submissive.

I fervently hoped for Simon to ask Mutti and Vati for my hand in marriage, officially, the old-fashioned way. Since this was such a perfect moment to do so, I looked at him with pleading eyes. Obviously, he was extremely upset and so was I. But as he failed to say anything, I felt hurt for the first time in our relationship. What a let-down! This led me to assume he had planned our escape to France without the formality of a wedding. Would it be too aggressive on my part to suggest anything on so delicate a matter?

Visibly agitated about Mutti's sudden and most determined decision, he finally asked—although not what I had hoped for: "What about the holy promise to yourself of never getting caught again among the hunted masses? I assure you this is far worse than the Flucht. Now it's directed strictly against Jews. Did we not have an understanding for none of you to ever become Nazi prisoners?" He then motioned for me to come into the next room and said: "In time—and I'm talking short term—we would go to the 'Unoccupied' together, with you as my wife. Sorry, but I can't afford to take your parents, also—not only for financial reasons. My main objection is the warning you gave me about Mutti and men who are interested in you." Ever since I had received this cursed German order, I had not seen that sensuous irresistible glint in his eyes, until now, when he continued: "I'm referring to our first Sunday visit to your parents with the flowers and pastry. You were right! Therefore, I did not mention the most important item: marriage. Don't you think I sense how she would ridicule us about this and our age difference? No man could stand such a blow. As you told me, she is not even interested in the ' Unoccupied' just as she was not anxious to immigrate to the US, even if feasible. However, to an unknown destination, determined by the Nazis, she would venture. Does that make sense? As I mentioned, there might be perils on the way to Southern France. But if you *stellen* yourself now, you're in immediate danger. Does that make any sense?" he questioned again, with a faltering voice—totally out of character—for I felt his heart was screaming out to me.

But I said and did nothing.

"I dare you not to go!" he exploded.

"I dare you to tell Mutti about the marriage proposal!" I finally managed.

"She is so tough and difficult. That's why I want to take only you. Not just because I'd have to support all of us there—without any income." He sighed: "It's beyond me how anyone this competent in business can be as indecisive as you are in the most human relationship. If you do go, don't think for one moment I'll accompany you to the Berchem train station to deliver my *Kätzele* like a lamb to the Nazi slaughter. I could not bear it!" Now his voice cracked as he murmured: "No one will ever love you as I do." With this, he turned around and left, just like that.

I let it happen. Did Mutti, as always, bewitch me? I felt like a coward, as when at long last, the lady officer at the U.S. consulate was about to issue the much-sought-after visa for me alone, because of my German birth, but not for my parents on account of their Polish origins. I had the American dream on a string, at age sixteen: maybe Hollywood? While here in Belgium, I was without any human rights, even prior to the Nazi occupation. This time I had Simon, the love of my life, with the promise of the wonderful atmosphere, the Eden of the world versus a somber fate; once more I chose hell over paradise. Did I want to please, and thus obtain, Mutti's love with the price of my very life? I asked myself.

On the way out, I heard Simon say, quite angrily, to Mutti: "If Mrs. Schwartz is that excited to deliver herself to the Nazis, and she is supposed to be so smart, I bet, with my gambler's instinct, that she wouldn't even be there!" The door slammed downstairs. It was Simon, walking out on me, and rightly so. Paralyzed, I could not do anything.

"Let him be angry, the old man!" Mutti exclaimed.

She would stop at nothing, I thought.

"Oh Sofiechen, don't you see the child is suffering?" Vati tried to intervene.

With Mutti's strong opposition, Vati's sanction and Simon gone, I felt I had no one, so I continued my flow of thoughts. I was furious with Mrs. Schwartz, even though I had never met her, for she made my life just that: *schwarz* (black). Mutti seemed so impressed with that whole family, especially this matriarch, who persuaded, influenced and convinced her to surrender. Actually, this was more likely to happen to impressionable me rather than Mutti. I was doubting her, as I did in the past. She must have felt that having given life to me entitled her to total domination, which promised a shabby existence at best.

There was no way out except to have the courage to rebel and stay by myself right here, in Simon's *pied-a-terre*. The Nazi occupation had been too good to be true. In the last few months, I had lived in an ambience of quasi-opulence with the wonderful spell of romance, great passion, and, yes, frenzy. I did have the notion that sooner or later this wonderful lifestyle had to come to an abrupt end.

Needless to say, I slept badly, swamped in nightmares. Then I was up until dawn, thinking and brooding.

The following day, our last one in Antwerp, I kept making final attempts to change Mutti's mind—presenting the real worry about our failure to *stellen* ourselves on the original date. Then I painted a picture of absolute drudgery: wallowing in misery and completely losing control of our lives. Rarely did emotions and logic fit so well. There was a total lack of communication and understanding. She, as always, was on a pedestal up there and I was down at her feet, beseeching this arrogant, unyielding and defiant woman to save our lives, including her own. Again, I had to resign myself, my very being, my unfulfilled longing, my desire and lust for life. Everything was lost! She started packing a few items we had just brought from our flat into Simon's. Throughout the day I was still deluding myself she would come to her senses, but to no avail. She went on to stuff the suitcase and even threw some of my clothes in. Would she have asked me to do so, she knew that there would be more fighting and nagging.

Once more, I felt paralyzed when Simon arrived with and for our "last supper," leaving some for the sad, unknown road. His facial expression hinted strongly that he was extremely upset. To boot, Mutti demanded, presumptuously, for him to ship the rest of the items we had just brought here, plus the ones from our flat. I was disgruntled and disheartened. A profound hopelessness invaded my innermost consciousness.

Simon and I had never seen each other in such a deep, negative, emotional state. Contrary to his usual upbeat personality, his face was most serious, his words sparse though spoken in a modulated voice. This was a major disaster. I felt anger at each of us: obviously against Mutti, toward Vati for his acquiescence to her, at Simon's not mentioning his proposal to them right now, but especially my own lack of guts not bursting out: Yes, I accept your marriage offer and yes, we'll see the sunset at the Riviera together! This time it was *my* heart screaming, but I did not listen. It was a sad repeat of the scene at the U.S. Consulate: I could not explain the reason why I chose my parents over freedom. Wrapped in sorrow and enveloped in misery, there was a silent, crushing, excruciating and difficult "bye" when Simon left. I felt he would not come to see me off, just as he had said. I absolutely did not want to let go, desiring desperately to hold on to him and my "rage for living." It was a great relief that my insomnia of the previous night was generously compensated by a sound sleep from sheer mental exhaustion and deep depression. Therefore, contrary to my nature, I was able to get up in the wee dark hours when the moment of truth arrived. Hardly able to bridle my fear, disappointment and anger, I could barely restrain my tears.

It was wickedly cold at the beginning of the day, the new year, the new decade with a frightening future, when we rushed out into the dense fog to deliver ourselves into the hands of the mighty enemy—an act I considered irrational. The starless world loomed enormously sad and empty. Again, I knew destiny had put me to the test. It was as though fate stalked me, to destroy and make me an outlaw. Neither my poor heart nor mind could grasp that from now on, my days would descend into an abyss, my wonderful recent past never to return. This defeat contrasted with my early blossoming—I shall never see again his desirous glance sink into my eyes, longing for his eager lips to kiss me when he drew me close, after I got on my toes. He had set me afire, in sweet rapture, and driven me mad with lust and love.

My frustrations, fury and hurt could scream out into the quiet, icy morning. Who is going to console me in my grief? I felt abandoned. He'll always represent a sort of haunting nostalgia. Having become part of me, how will I ever forget him? Was last night the final time I saw him? I now realized that I suffered from Nazi and lover's sorrow. Such desolation, such wretchedness! Bye, my second home, Antwerp, my Simon, my diamonds, my pampered universe!

Immersed in thought, I didn't realize that the small Berchem station—this suburb was also one of the many places we had lived and where I had enjoyed the success of my English classes—now stood before me. Quite early for this "event," we climbed up the steps with our meager belongings. In front of each car entrance of the long train was planted a Nazi gendarme in steel helmet, machine gun pointed at us. I cast Mutti a most poisonous look, and under my breath, with gritting teeth, I managed to mumble: "So, is this what Mrs. Schwartz and you had been looking forward to?"

On approaching THEM, a few things startled me: THEY were the most miserably mean-looking beasts. Also, THEY were built differently than the ones I had encountered since the occupation. None of THEM was young. All of THEM looked squat, with breast shields on THEIR murderous chests.

I had viewed myself as a healthy, young, vibrant, sophisticated, popular mortal being; however, in the presence of THESE swine with their deadly hardware aimed for killing and THEIR total non-involvement with any normal feelings, I was instantly metamorphosed by THEIR attitude into a lowly, sub-human creature called "Jew."

While at first I was foaming with intense rage, suddenly a mournful somberness befell me.

Chapter 16

Upon getting inside the train, I visualized it as a cage, out of which there was no escape. The cars had divisions instead of compartments. Except for four persons, it was still empty. Oddly enough, in one such section was a counterpart of our family, only the parents were quite aged and their daughter was about a decade older than I. She, too, was dressed fashionably. We both wore wide-brimmed felt hats. She was attractive and even pretty were it not for the gap between her front teeth. She introduced herself, in beautiful French, as Betti Fass. At a nearby seat was the back of a broad shouldered man, looking out of the window, although there was nothing to be seen. When he turned around, we recognized each other—only being nodding acquaintances from *Hovenier Straat* and the *Vesting Straat Café*. We had even exchanged a few words before. He was a dentist, although, being a refugee also, he was without a license.

"But you look so 'Aryan'!" I exclaimed to the deportee, "blue eyes, blond, straight hair, at least 1,80m (6 feet) tall. You are a single, unattached man, with lots of flexibility at any given time. So, why in the world would you turn yourself in?" I questioned, curiously. "I'm so weary of hiding and this illegal life and being chased like a criminal."

Mutti met my eyes, briefly but piercingly and nodded affirmatively, as though to say, you see, as always, I was right again! Being *Leidensgenossen* I felt free and compelled to air my fears: "Since *they* didn't check us outside the train, *they'll* probably march in here, later, and verify, at least, our name when *they'll* find out that we didn't 'stellen' ourselves with the very first transport."

"*They'll* be so glad for any Jew caught and won't be particular," they unanimously consoled me. "I'm truly very upset to be here because it was my humble way of fighting by not obeying. It goes so deeply against my grain." There, I got it off my chest!

It was a one-woman war. They felt that they could not live like murderers on the run, in order to hide from the true criminals. More victims entered the train. I was amazed how many 'Aryan' looking blondes were amongst them. Surely, whatever I had said to Mr. Abbühl, the dentist, held true with them. Anger welled up in me just as it did against myself, Mutti, Vati, and Simon, each for a different reason, resulting in leaving. All seats of our car were occupied by now. Whistles pierced through the sullen dawn. I despised the entire scene and quite especially when these ugly, stocky, uniformed evildoers appeared, wearing *their* fear-inspiring helmets for *their* great warrior mission—US!

There was a hush throughout the train. Even though I expected *them*, my heart was pounding as strongly as it did when we were strafed. The words of "La Parisienne" at the barracks in France echoed: "To be a prisoner of the Nazis is far more frightening to me than the temporary air attacks." I wondered what her fate had been since our hygienic experience, beneath our respective trees. Under what dire circumstances would the morning's functions occur, I asked myself, when this nasty looking, hideous brute stood before me. I dutifully submitted my white *carte d'identité*. The thug's glance brushed over my face, for comparison with the photo on my document. *He* registered my name on *his* list—and with this simple act, I now had become, officially, one of the threatened masses, instead of being the elegant, successful, beloved courtier-courier Cukier. Again I threw Mutti a venomous stare, while the Nazi *Feldgendarm* checked her and Vati's Ids to file them among the same list of victims.

Two brothers arrived, breathlessly, as though they were missing the most important event of their careers. Though it was obvious that they were siblings, the younger one was attractive, which could not have been stated about the elder. The soldiers did not take kindly to them. I had been prepared to be ruffled, verbally by *them*, the same way, because of the belated "stellen" date, but I felt relief when *they* either didn't notice or—my most recent acquaintances'consolation had been justified. At least, I could deduct one worry.

The feeling of tension cut through the interior train sections as the Nazi roughnecks were checking out its live contents. Now the stark reality of the whistles interrupted the otherwise peaceful dawn. Instantly, the train was set in motion, and with it, our unknown destiny. "Will I ever see Antwerp again—or Simon?" became the irregular rhythm of one, two—one, two, three accompanied by more high-pitched sounds and big puffs of steam, billowing into the grey emptiness. After daybreak, some hopeful rays, daringly, tried to peak through the drab and fateful morning. The rocking of the train, by now having reached its full speed, seemed to have lulled our jarred nerves. I observed the sun fighting a one-woman war with the clouds—reminiscent of my own fight here on board. It emerged, though, giving a lift to the entire landscape we passed—and quite especially to my spirit. Sitting across was an "Aryan" looking blonde. Her dreamy eyes were moist. Our glances met when she shook her head up and down as if to say: "alas!" For an answer, I mimicked her sad movement expressing: Yes, we are all in the same boat—train—with an equally dismal future.

I was the first to break the silence with a soft voice, by stating in a consolatory way, "It needn't be all that bad!"

"What makes you think so?" she probed.

"Of late, things I worried about, never came to pass," giving her as an example my last, serious concern about our Nazi notice for the very first transport in December 1940: "Yet you witnessed that they made nothing of our late 'stellen' right now, in January of 1941", I pointed out. She nodded with a sigh.

Sitting next to her was a lady with an unusually beautiful profile. Wait a minute, I thought, I know this distinctive face and tall, unapproachable carriage. Even though she was squeezed between the blonde and the window, she was intimidating. I asked, inquisitively, "Aren't you Erika from Erfurt? I met you at the New Year's Eve party 1938/39 at the Hungarian family, in whose house we lived."

"Yes, I remember you and your singing, dancing and keyboard talents," she confirmed dryly. Just as she had acted two years ago, again, I got the feeling that she desired to withdraw into her own shell.

I was enormously glad that my natural inner poise was strengthening, as the train was passing the pleasant sights of the Belgian scenery. From the signs of the various provinces, towns, and villages, I speculated that we were traveling Northeast, direction Germany; a frightening thought! Denial allowed me to escape that dark spell as I tried to spread some comfort among my fellow deportees. This helped to subdue my own fears, made me feel social and, yes, noble. I talked to the Holzer brothers. The younger one revealed that he was amazed that *they* picked him for he was married to a German and what's more, they had a baby. People within ear shot frowned. Suddenly brakes were screeching—the train was stopping. During this procedure, I read the sign "Limburg." I knew there was a Dutch and a Belgian Limburg. I rooted for it to be Belgian, for various reasons: It would still be under the auspices of *General von Falkenhausen*, thus military, which was far better than all other Nazi authorities. The capital of Dutch Limburg is Maastricht, which is much closer to Germany.

Now there was a lot of commotion. Train doors were jarred open. The steel-helmeted Nazis were seen and heard with *their*: "*Los, los, los! Raus!*" Again, with *their* machine guns, playing the great warriors against women and children. There were whistles, screams and commands and the barking of *their* German shepherds as frightened people were herded out and placed in rows at a small station. They obediently stood there, about one hundred men, women, and children of all ages. My "nobility" was destroyed by the sight of the horrified faces and the crying, screaming children. I went over to Mutti, looked squarely into her fine face and asked: "Do you see Mrs. Schwartz anywhere?"

The uniformed bullies returned with *their* dogs and machine guns. Even *their* whistles sounded harsh. Doors were slammed— more shrill sounds. Then, that irregular rhythm again, when the train started puffing away. Now, its tempo stayed at a slow pace.

After what must have been a very short distance, it stopped again, with the ensuing pandemonium, shrieks, barking, more "*Los, los! Raus! Raus!*" For the third time, there was the same procedure, but now *they* entered our section and yelled out some names.

Among others, I saw the blonde getting up, nervously, as did Erika, after being called. I remembered how upset she had been at that pleasant party over the loss of her husband who had been "liquidated". Once more, doors slamming, dogs and men barking. There were now one hundred and twenty-three people standing outside the train. I counted them! This station looked larger. It was called *Bilzen*. The neat rows of people were left in those strange places: *St. Truiden*, *Tongeren* and *Bilzen*. Mrs. Schwartz was nowhere in sight. How clever Simon had been!

Upon *their* return, there was once more *their* predictable Nazi system. Now the train dragged at its slowest speed. There was no longer any sunshine, and my good spirits left. I stayed close to my parents. Was it for me to protect them, or for them to shelter me, the now anguished child, from so much evil? My heart was pounding uncontrollably. Then—just a few meters further—it was our turn, yes now *they* came for us—. This small stop was called *Hoeselt*. So this was it! A village named Hoeselt. A repeat performance: "Off the train!" (We were the very last ones)—the final nasty commands, accompanied by whistles and the tumult created by "inhumanes" and animals.

At last we got off under *their* watchful eyes. The three of us were forming one of the rows ordered by *their* rough roaring. Once outside, I looked around and thought: This village looks innocent enough. Even more so when the bedlam faded in the cold, as *they* climbed into the emptied coaches. With much shatter, whistles, barking and yelling the outer doors were shut with the *Feldgendarmerie* inside. What tremendously good news! Would *they* return to haunt us—or who was to come for us? They couldn't be worse than the ones that had just unloaded us here, as though we were goods.

The trip ended as it had started: frigid, grey, and scary. It was, however, accompanied by welcome facts: we heard the engine chug the brutes into the distance. What a relief for now. Also, just getting off the train after sitting for hours on end and walking those few steps in the invigorating air gave us a little life. But soon the waiting seemed endless, especially since we did not know whom to expect, and panic started building up within us. After some time had elapsed it began to snow. Small hailstones tapped upon the smartly curved brim of my elegant hat. It got bitterly cold. A rough North wind took our breath away. Even it was hostile. On the inside, my heart cried in terror. My anger screamed out in silence: what in heaven's name did I need this for?

Then finally, yet suddenly, from out of the drabness, a tall man emerged. He was all dressed up with hat, tie and scarf, approaching our miserable, freezing group purposefully. Our anxiety was alleviated when he most dramatically and compassionately addressed all of us in Flemish. Kind words sprang from his sensuous mouth, when he introduced himself: "I am your Burgemeester (Mayor) René Nartus, of Hoeselt. Please follow me!"

We had high hopes. The mayor's relaxed manner caused us to relinquish the Nazi enforced rows. Trailing after him made us feel more like tourists. We found ourselves on a typical country main street. At first it was residential, becoming lined with shops and then a corner tavern, creating the center. This was called *Dorpsstraat* (Village Street). To our right, there was the *Dorpsplein* (Village Plaza). A steepled church and a quite impressive monastery greeted us; but the quaint view was marred by a barrack that looked temporary and incongruous with the square. It was reminiscent of the wooden structure where I had met the Parisian girl somewhere in Northern France. The mayor led the way to the wooden shag. It was clean and above all, warm. It had briefly served the Belgian Army, the mayor explained. I was glad it was odorless, and that there was a brand new kettle filled with aromatic pea soup. Betti Fass and I got in line to ladle it into our bowls, feeling elated about the caloric and human warmth and, above all, the complete absence of Nazis. First things first; we sat down on the benches next to our parents and devoured the piping hot, amazingly tasty soup. Then we worried about where and how to spend the night. We all agreed that in here it was at least warm. The congenial mayor shared the hot potage also. He sat across from us. He was a pleasant, handsome man with soft green eyes revealing reverie plus just the right touch of rogue. He was apologetic about the lack of sleeping provisions, for they could not have been met at such short notice. "Why don't both of you come to my office, across from the beer warehouse which bears my name. Let's say tomorrow afternoon," he suggested in Flemish bidding bye to the group repeating: "Make the best of the bedless night!"

It was amazing how many men rapidly fell asleep on the hard tables, just as had happened in France; the other analogy being that I talked in French with Betti. We chatted until after midnight when we realized that we were disturbing too many would-be sleepers. Always having pad and pen at hand, I reported everything matter-of-factly to Simon, addressed to the gallery.

The next awareness was a whiff of fresh coffee awakening me. I found myself with my head buried into my folded arms on the board, the notebook next to me. The brew was a déjà-vu scene, at an even worse situation with David, my first student, and poor, poor Yossel. This time it was the dentist. As he handed me the old cup he said demeaningly:" You know, this is really not good for you! Just think of the consequences to your beautiful, snow-white teeth!" His remark reminded me of the beginning of my romance with Simon, in the Victorian dentist's waiting room, which urged me even more to continue the letter to him.

As in the past, whenever I was in a bad spot, somehow it was never boring, for there was plenty socializing until it was time to leave for the appointment with the mayor.

On top of the hill was an old, interesting white house. We entered. To the left was the mayor's office. It was spacious and comfy, but having seen the ultimate in luxury and elegance of late, my taste had grown selective. Yet, needless to say, I felt at ease here as opposed to "Conrad Veidt's" and certainly the *Hauptmann*'s super plush surroundings. After some niceties, the mayor got to the point about sleeping accommodation. "I shall do absolutely everything in my power, to match each expelled family with a

Hoeselt gezin (family)", he assured Betti and me. Then, with an
excusatory, warm glance at me, he said to Betti: "I've even got my
own sister in mind for you and your aging parents." Then he
explained to me: "Sorry, I do have several sisters but this one is the
only one who did not take the vow to be a nun. However, I shall
contact a young couple with a baby today. They do have a large
spare room for a family. I have the distressing duty, though", he
paused and his well-shaped features took on a somber expression,
"to inform you that housing requires permission granted only by
the *Feldkommandantur* of the Province of Limburg." He gave me
an official paper for our group of 120 Jews to be submitted to the
Feldkommandantur 681, Kamer 333, 3de Verdiep. So it came about
that I was our spokeswoman.

From then on, each day brought me closer to the confrontation
with the highest Nazi boss of the entire province. My anxiety
heightened and culminated in a morning of absolute dread. I tried
to console myself remembering previous experiences with Nazi
high-brass such as "Conrad Veidt" or the "blond god-interrogator",
but could not achieve a calming effect, for I realized that a
Kommandant including the entire *Kommandatur* was top Nazi
territory. I rehearsed a favorable visualization *ad nauseam* but did
not succeed in pacifying myself. Every minor matter accelerated
my nervousness. Other than having gone across the Rhine river to
the Jewish Lützow School and later to the Commercial College by
tram I had never traveled alone. Thus, even the thought of opening
the tricky handle on an old-fashioned rural train, or, for the first
time since my arrival here, wearing my most elegant outfit had me
on edge. As my parents accompanied me to the station, others
eagerly sought my assistance to absolutely ascertain housing
permission for each of our 120 souls.

Upon my arrival in Hasselt, the capital of Belgian Limburg,
fellow passengers had opened the compartment door. The town
would have been charming, if I could have visited it under other
circumstances. It was not hard to find the feared *Feldkommandantur
681*. The flying Swastika proclaimed it. I took a deep breath and a
lot of heart to enter the most beautiful building, confiscated by

them. I was glad there was not as long a line as in front of the Antwerp one when I had tried to obtain the foxes. It was evident now, that the regrouping had been done so that the Nazi efficiency machine was well oiled.

Once I arrived at the third floor on foot (a sign on the elevator clearly specified: "forbidden for Dogs and Jews") a young female secretary without make-up showed me arrogantly to the bench in front of room 333: "Jewish Affairs" only after I had indicated that I had been sent here by the Mayor of Hoeselt.

Every so often, thunderous yelling *à la militaire* was clearly audible from the inner sanctum. My earlier apprehension flared up again, so much so that I felt like running to the bathroom. But, better not! I controlled myself. As at previous high-ranking Nazi experiences, the waiting increased the unbearable angst.

When at last the door flung open, a man, all shriveled up from terror, exited from this horror chamber which I was to enter. He was so shaken, that he left the door ajar. Seizing the moment, I knocked and fearfully ventured in, shutting the door with my right while waving the mayor's paper with my left. I felt the thickly carpeted floor as I uttered shiveringly from afar, "Pardon, *Herr Kommandant*—!"

"How dare you be so insolent!" His grueling growling was upon me. Yet, lo and behold, I noticed that he was wearing a monocle also! Lo and behold, it dropped out, but not from flirting like "Conrad Veidt" but from roaring, "Out of here Jewess! Out of here!"

Because of my fear his yelling was distorted. Though looking my elegant best, I was the object of his fury. It caused his face to turn crimson, when he thundered: "*Zum Donnerwetter nochmal, raus, raus!*"

Amazingly, at this time of utter stress, even though still plagued by my anxieties, I was able to focus on the extremely nasty Nazi official, bravely taking another step toward him requesting, "Would you please—."

"Are you deaf, Jewess, out with you, out with you! I don't want any Jews here in my office. Judenrein! (Clear, clean of Jews)!"

His anti-Semitic verbal abuse was accompanied by a sinister expression on his wrinkled, ugly face, which could not quite manage to conceal amazement. Despite my terror, I had to be resolute in my purpose. Not concentrating on the anti-Jewish phrasing, I inched up to this wild beast, petrified, with chattering teeth, I pleaded, feeling like a sycophant, "*Bitte, Herr Feldkommandant,* I need your permission." "Jews have nothing to need, want nor choose!" he spat, looking at me as though I was the most repugnant creature on earth.

Upon getting closer, his vile words finally registered in my mind. Terrified and humiliated, I still took one step and another forward with, "But, please, *Herr Kommandant.*" Though banging both fists on the desk, he still could not quite hide his astonishment at my bravura, so much so that he finally stopped himself in the midst of yet another anti-Semitic rant as I was now standing in front of him, frightened, as though I was facing a lion fresh out of his cage. I stated my case rapidly and briefly, at long last submitting the mayor's paper. He stared at me icily and meanly while reluctantly getting his fountain pen to quickly scribble something on my sheet; then threw it in my direction with a hostile look.

Desperately wanting to get out of that Nazi jungle, I did not press my luck. Before I could say: "Danke!" his unbelievable shouting started all over again with: "*Jetzt aber raus, raus, schnell, schnell! Los, los, los!*" This was accompanied by another Jew insult, which my mind and ears refused to record. As I was turning the door handle, his verbal cannon was still firing at me.

Back in Hoeselt, I was congratulated by all the Jewish Antwerp expellees upon my success in obtaining housing permission. For once, even Mutti openly showed her delight. The day after my return from Hasselt, we were promptly given the room; so were all of the deported Jews in Hoeselt. I was like a Joan of Arc in the eyes of my "subjects" and even in those of the mayor. It made me feel like a real heroine for conquering my own fears and achieving my goal in such a risky mission.

Sharing sleeping accommodation with my parents was neither new nor strange to me. It sure beats spending the night with my head on the table.

We had been under the impression that the village was small, but it spilled over to its outskirts where we found the slender, blonde Yvonne Maenen. Her big, rough-looking husband was actually gentle, especially with their sweet baby boy.

At the center of the large room, which was designated to us, stood a very tall statue of Jesus with stretched out arms so as to give his benediction. Though not of our religion, I thought it would be nice if some of his blessings came our way. "Our quarter" consisted of this bedroom and the use of their downstairs. Mutti took to the baby and the baby to her. She made him take his first steps and persisted until she succeeded in having him walk amid the great applause of his young parents. This was one side I did not know about my mother. Vati was elated and could not take his eyes off his wife happily guiding the little boy. Neither did I, but based on another reason: agreeable amazement and a comforting reflection crediting her for having been an affectionate Mom after all during my earliest time of life.

We took our daily long "hike" to the barrack. Mutti found a youngish admirer and spent her afternoons playing chess with him. Mutti's face was flushed with the excitement of the company and the game. Did her "sixth sense" surface again when she was so dead set to come here, that she would feel content in Hoeselt of all places? Vati socialized sometimes and as for me, I suggested that Betti needed for her English exactly what was necessary for my French: practical conversation. "Why don't we walk in the crisp winter wonderland for two hours: the first one we'll talk English only, with corrections, if you so desire, and the second we do the same with French," I suggested. We did exactly that, strolling even beyond the mayor's office where the Dorpstraat curved to the right. It was as though a live picture postcard was unfolding in front of us: the white slopes were covered with happy, colorfully dressed children having fun with sleds, their multi-colored scarves flying against the stark background of the snow. Topping this lovely sight, there was no Nazi anywhere.

On the first Sunday, it seemed as if all the young men came to visit and look me over. Of course, I thought, they never saw a

Jewish girl before. The afternoon turned out to be very lively and amusing in the innocent-looking village of Hoeselt, Limburg. During the week, our rather pleasant activities continued. The mayor had seen to it that—as he had promised—each refugee was settled with locals. The barrack continued to serve varied social and even religious purposes. Everybody was overjoyed that the anticipated nightmare turned out so mildly, yet crowned with the absence of the feared gray-green uniforms; a relief which can never be overemphasized. Jews were shown in films as rats and described as vermin in the anti-Semitic paper "Der Stürmer" by the murderous Julius Streicher. No matter what THEIR individual appearance, in my eyes THEY were the deadly, green plague and not to see THEM "crawl around" was a great, welcome relief from the Nazi pest.

The church bell was heralding in our second, very chilly Sunday. On our way "downtown" we saw some people in the far distance, walking toward us. On coming closer we noticed a redhead and another woman carrying a baby. Alongside them was something shiny and large, glistening whenever the pale winter sun succeeded in glaring out from behind the clouds. In the center was a tall, broad-shouldered man. He resembled Simon—my heart stood still—it WAS Simon! My exhilaration caused me to leap for joy. Wordlessly, I turned from my parents and approached the small group with running steps until I melted in his embrace. When I was finally able to catch my breath, I cried enthusiastically—as I had done once before at the gallery's cloakroom: "My favorite person, Simon, with my pet object, my bike!" He looked splendidly well and oh, so very appealing! Again I realized that I had very special feelings for him. It was a wonderful sensation when he took my arm and squeezed my hand as he introduced the young redhead and the other woman, carrying a baby, as Frau Holzer. She must have been the German, non-Jewish wife of the younger brother who had been bullied for their lateness. Everyone made a great fuss over the tiny girl, especially Mutti. More amazement from Vati and me, when she asked the mother whether she might hold the infant.

Since we were still close to our abode the four of us went into our narrow patio kitchen and sat around the stove telling our respective adventures. Simon was visibly happy that our lot did not turn out as badly as he had dreaded. "Are the Nazis off on Sundays?" Simon asked with a broad grin. Filled with amusement, we laughed: "No, we are blessed with the good luck that the last we saw of the green pestilence was when they left us off here."

"This makes Hoeselt a great place. The other enormous relief was when I learned from your letter that you are in Belgium. Thank you for informing me so promptly", Simon stated.

While I related to him that I wrote it in order to overcome the first confusing, bedless night in the barrack, my parents prepared lunch with Prager's goodies, which Simon had brought along with the bike. "Do you remember Moishe of the Vesting Straat Café, the one that stared at you incessantly, no matter how busy?" Simon asked with one of his beguiling smiles, and continued: "Well, he arranged for himself and others to go to Havana, Cuba."

"What! That terrible story! There were casualties! They wouldn't even allow the two half-Jewish sibling on land after that long sea journey, even though their father was right there waiting for them. What upsets me about the Americans in addition to their tight Polish and German quotas, was that this entire human boatload was ordered back by the U.S. Coast Guard. Off the Florida shore, the good German, yes German, Captain Gustav Schröder was cruising ever so slowly, but no, they were forced to return. Imagine, they could not make this single exception! After all, there were no riff-raff on board but mostly families, professionals and businessmen." I kept rattling on about the tragic ship with the name of the U.S. city, "St. Louis". This really was the "St. Louis Blues", I thought, knowing that no one would understand the musical allusion, whereas they did recall the facts of the wretched story. "You really are feeling very strongly about it, of course, every Jew does, but you in particular!"

"Yes, when I first came to Antwerp, I met the sister of someone I knew from Köln, who was on this ill-fated vessel. Later on, I even saw a photo of all the passengers on board. He was at the very center of the large picture. I felt as though I was a quasi eyewitness. He had never been heard of again." I finished.

"Moishe is street smart. He is getting a number of people together, mostly men of some means. As for myself, I still prefer Southern France."

"At the moment it is not the worst here," Vati said. "Look, we are not in hiding and although officially under the auspices of the Nazis there are no Germans here—as you noticed yourself. Hiding takes a lot out of you. It's called 'hiding' but one must have a lot of guts, a strong heart and plenty of money."

"What an enormous risk to travel to another part of the world by sea with the uncertainty whether or not they will allow you to enter a country." Mutti mentioned.

"Yes, and there are rumors that even in the unoccupied Vichy France or Switzerland you are not free. When things get too hot for me in Antwerp, I would still choose the 'Unoccupied' just for myself," and with regretful yet profound eye contact, he continued: "but I could never bear the responsibility if something were to happen to anyone going with me, on my account, ever since I heard that the unoccupied countries intern refugees. Since this bad news, I no longer visualize the most beautiful spot on earth, the French Riviera, under palm trees with white villas and colorful flowers, surrounded by the azure Mediterranean as Eden. Right now, it's just the most likely place I would choose to wait out Hitler's end," he explained.

His ardent, though brief, kisses created such breathless momentum that joy oozed out of me. My heart joined forces with my tingling body in this sensuous encounter. A minimum of contact was able to bring about a peak experience and oh, such ecstasy. Even more astonishing was the fact that this sweet happening inadvertently came about with my parents' present in the kitchen. Though we forced ourselves to veil our feelings when they were about, surely they were aware of our romance. It was frustrating to act like children hiding evil, but this was by far better than being snarled at in utter mockery by Mutti. Where could we really go on this sunny, but very cold Sunday? What I had seen so far of this village that might lend itself to our situation where the white slopes. In my imagination they had turned into lush green lawns, where I saw myself with Simon under blossoming trees delighting in our special brand of love-making feeding my inner fire and restless heart. At this instant I felt like a Stradivari being tuned. Again, I was spellbound in a world all of our own. This was one of our private moments, when, for emphasis, he touched my knee under the table, as my parents were busy doing my usual job—clearing the dishes. I was pleasantly surprised that they at least granted me this little opportunity to be with him. He was even bold enough to steal another kiss or two. In these instances, I was overcome with euphoria. Alas, they were suddenly and rudely interrupted by Mutti saying: "Mr. London, would I be presumptuous in counting on you to collect the rest of our belongings at the apartment and to send us the items peu à peu?" The idyll was shattered.

This time, Simon seemed even more embarrassed than I was for he exclaimed: "Yes, Vichy, here I come! Yes wishy washy, Vichy, old Marchéal Petain, here I come and trust you, but how can I?" Then, turning to my parents to counteract his self-consciousness, he warned: "But there lurks danger by the Vichy government, if Petain could betray his own Frenchmen who held him in such high esteem, how can we little Jews rely upon him? Well, as you refugees used to say, 'wait and drink tea'—I'll have their Vichy water; their tasteless club soda, and eat their equally flavorless Vichyssoise, their cold borscht, which until this Vichy government was the only tribute to that city. Mutti was baffled but Vati understood and had a good laugh at Simon's humor.

Simon continued on the subject, "but Southern France, Switzerland, Sweden and Russia are the only places not yet occupied by the Nazis", laughing again, he asked Vati, "So what should I pick? Russia and Sweden are always far colder than it is today, or the 'Unoccupied'?" Then he sighed as he turned to me with one of his charming glances, "Yes, the world could have been our playground, but we can't get beyond that shadow of war and persecution!" I was agreeably surprised that he finally confessed this much in front of my parents. How glad I was that Mutti gave her mouth a brief rest.

Now, Simon got serious again as he uttered, with an edge to his voice, "How will we know when the last dice of Vichy will be cast—so to speak in my gambler's language, but it's still the only place in Europe where Robert Taylor can be seen."

Robert Taylor! My thoughts went to my cousin Maurice. The resemblance. I had completely forgotten my poor relatives in Antwerp, so caught up had I been in my rapture during the last months. Unexpectedly, Simon tapped the table with his flat palm: "Now to business!" "Is there any now, here?" I asked timidly, yet anxiously. "Indeed there is!" He answered with glee taking out a marvelous diamond brooch and a ring similar to my first sale, and symbolic of my initial business success. "Look, this is your collateral with the compliments of Mr. Gerstel. Remember the one that was always,"—and in a choir we exclaimed, "who was always geshochten." An obviously rich diamond dealer who liked to refer to himself as "being slaughtered", chronically broke.

"This fine piece alone," pointing at the beautiful pin, "is of such great value as to cover the amounts you earned, which you could loan him for a 'Shylock's' interest. Here your money is probably hidden in some strange place or you have to carry it around with you at all times and pray that honesty prevails. Have your money work for you! Frankly, if he never pays you back, this is worth far more than the principal you would lend him. So it is completely free of risk and you will continue to make a nice living." The offer appealed even to my skeptical Mutti. "Aren't you thrilled, Kätz—?" He caught himself, "well, aren't you? You don't look it!"

How well he sensed my feelings! Normally I would have been delighted, but I grew quite sad at the thought that he might have come here mainly for business. But there wasn't anything in it for him. There possibly could not be any reason but to help his sporadically broke associate as well as me.

I had lent money to Mr. Gerstel in the past through Simon's intervention and had fared quite well. After all these deliberations, I exclaimed: "*Masel und Bracha*!" extending my hand. He could hardly let go—even beneath Mutti's critical eye. My parents rushed upstairs to bring down all my earnings. Before they did, Simon put my monthly bfrs. 25,000 (ca. $500), quite a respectable sum, on the table. "In the future, Mr. Gerstel will be mailing this to you directly."

The minute my parents left, he drew me close, sweeping me into his arms, and finally we could let go of our unbridled desire in one ardent kiss. But all too soon they returned with the cash. After the business deal was consummated, Simon looked at his watch and advised, "We'd better break up this lovely meeting. Aren't reunions a most rewarding experience?"

Though my parents were walking next to us, they did not notice that Simon took my gloved hand and put it into his overcoat pocket. Ever so slowly he removed my glove. It was more as though he were undressing my hand. With his fingers he caressed mine. I felt my heart jump! I looked up teasingly at his handsome profile. His sensuous lips spelled invitation, desire and passion. So did his eyes. What a lovely, soul-elevating sensation! Nevertheless, I was painfully aware that oh so very shortly, all of this would come to an abrupt end. This fragment of romance would have to sustain me for many sleepless nights to come. I knew that it would allow me to indulge in my most erotic fantasies. I knew that, alas, in reality, my delights of any kind were only ephemeral. With wonderful feelings, alas, accompanied by sad thoughts, we approached the barrack.

Upon entering, the redhead, Frau Holzer, and her husband carrying their baby, approached us—as did almost all the people. Simon's humor, enthusiasm and flamboyance attracted everyone. A distinguished looking man in a bowler seemed to know Simon and said with a shrug: "Well, here I am in this quaint village and things are fine. Even though I am not a refugee and they didn't deport me, I stepped forward of my own free will.

"Your own free will?" Simon and our small group asked in unison with indignation and amazement. "Well, I'm a philosopher. When my student," he pointed to a nondescript, but intellectual-looking young man, "depicted this place, I decided to move here.

Sooner or later they will find all of us, so it might as well be here and now." Accompanied by his charming laugh Simon gave this macabre analogy: "If sooner or later we all have to die, does this necessitate our going to the cemetery to bury ourselves before our time has come?" The philosopher was speechless. So was the whole group.

After a while, the redhead broke the silence when she turned to me saying: "Mr. London is certainly the most intelligent and attractive man I have ever met. You are very fortunate."

"And so, too, is Mr. London because everything he told us about you on the train is true. Maybe you could visit me sometime. I have a spacious apartment, located right in the diamond center, in the middle of Pelikaan Straat. I would love to have you!" Mrs. Holzer concluded with a warm glance.

Her cordial invitation left quite an impression on me. Now it was time for "farewell". The four of us left for the train, followed by the three and a half of the Holzer family, the redhead with her relatives, a very tall, good-looking couple, the Franks, who seemed to have been made for each other. We were nearing the same rails where the last German *Feldgendarmerie* had delivered us like merchandise. When we all got to the stop of Hoeselt, everyone got quiet and pensive. Only Mutti reminded Simon to collect everything and send it here. I was embarrassed at her request, especially since such a menial task was out of his character.

When we heard the approaching train, everyone became anxious. Simon took my hand and kissed it while his gaze betrayed his thoughts quite like the song in the operetta: "Victoria and her Hussar": "I kiss your little hand, Madame, and dream it were your lips." The moment of truth had come when the slowly moving train came to a screeching halt. After our respective loved ones were on board and the door was shut, the sad waving and choking-up started. It was as though I didn't want to let go of him as the locomotive chugged off, I was compelled to run and wave alongside the train. I did not realize that Mr. Holzer was to my left, but his long, muscular legs carried him further still to get some last glimpses of his wife and baby. His eyes were filled with tears.

Upon my return, Mutti shook her head in reproach over my little manoeuver. When the last whistle faded, I felt such emptiness. My heart was definitely missing something, someone. It was reminiscent of when I last saw Dr. Königsmann. The train had taken along all my *joie de vivre*, my feelings of happiness, my enthusiasm, my curiosity, my sense of protection and belonging. I felt abandoned.

Upon the return, the gawking young villagers talked to me, thereby helping me to ease the pain of farewell.

The following morning, we all washed up. Mutti's towel was soaked. Since her "germ idiosyncrasy" forbade her to hang it next to ours, she, frustrated, looked for a spot. I could not believe my eyes, when she finally spread it on top of the outstretched, fine hands of the large Jesus sculpture.

"But Mutti," I protested, "you cannot do that!" Vati just shook his head in disbelief. "But Mutti," I pleaded again, "this is their faith, and here in the village people are more religious than in big cities. It would be terrible if they were to see this!"

"It would be terrible," Mutti mimicked me, "if they were to peek in, but since we rent it's unlikely they will." "But we might lose the room and privileges altogether!" was my concern. Well, after a few days of coolness from the Maenens, we were somewhat dismayed when told to look for other lodgings. Though clearly Mutti's fault, it was up to me to pursue appropriate contacts.

Straight across from the barrack—the Hoeselt "downtown"— was a butcher shop. A huge, vintage door formed its entrance. In front was a fresh-water well complete with pump. Never before had I seen anything like this. I asked myself: Why not try the place which holds the most appeal? Plus, there will always be food at a butcher's.

When entering the tall, wide gate, the inside reminded me of the U.S. Consulate in Antwerp. But fortunately, here I was ushered in by a white-clad, very friendly couple. The charming face of the stout Madame Molenaer lit up. Of all renting experiences since we had left Köln, this was by far the easiest. I was shown into a huge country kitchen facing a backyard. As I entered, there was another first for me, a rainwater hand pump instead of a sink. Across from it was a long, white, scrubbed wooden picnic-type table with chairs. Most importantly, straight ahead, proudly stood a round black stove and more chairs; a cozy sight in this wintery weather. Back through the mini driveway, one flight up, there were a few bedrooms. Madame Molenaer was kind enough to let me choose.

Obtaining the two rooms would require to see the mayor first. I did just that and permission was granted instantly. Once our primitive, yet typically rural domicile was established, things went smoothly. Mr. Molenaer's good-looking brother was his partner. At times he visited us and imitated Charlie Chaplin accurately. Occasionally, Vati was asked to assist them, which must have been difficult for his gentle soul. The result was staggering, though: we got the freshest, finest meat. Nobody else was quite that fortunate. Now and then people came to pump "our" rainwater in the kitchen. Not everyone had such convenient wells—for cleaning purposes directly inside and for consumption in front of the building— others had to walk far to fetch their buckets. I congratulated myself on my choice.

A wave of "hausfrau" ambition came over me. Daily, I scoured the huge white and black tile floor and the large table until it looked like a new wooden cooking spoon. Maybe work helped me through these bitter times when I yearned for my childhood, the characteristic Cologne taverns called "Kölsche Kneipe" where beer was served with "rievkooche," the typical potato pancakes. The waiters were referred to as "Köbes" (dialect for Jakob). Mutti had always been impressed with the scrubbed tavern tables and therefore I thought it might please her. As I performed this menial work, which I amazingly did not mind at all, again, country boys sat idly by—gawking and talking.

One evening the Molenaers invited us to the one bistro in the village. We were the only non-locals there. Besides, it appeared that many Jews were not "bar people" but through Vati's masculine business in Köln, we were. The slightly protruding teeth of the friendly bar-owner as well as her humor reminded me of Lili. She introduced us to the sole Hoeselt physician and various friends of the mayor. Soon we knew all prominents of the village.

The Molenaers kept the place immaculate. This included the outhouse, which was conveniently located across from the kitchen, in the corner of the backyard. In favor of pleasant smells, they had created a draft. Unfortunately, this caused an abdominal cold for me. The pain persisted and I was ashamed to see the young physician and just sat around the black stove and kept studying my languages to ease the constant ache. If there had been a lady doctor or had my pain been in another area, I most certainly would have sought professional help. Since it did not diminish, Mutti was worried and went to the young doctor to explain the symptoms. The pain subsided somewhat after I took the prescribed frequent camomile vapor baths. The rest of the cold days were spent in front of the hot stove, brooding about the past and rooting for the future.

Chapter 17

Always having been curious about the cloister across the street, back of the barracks, I dared to enter one day. After being interviewed by the director—a monk in his long, brown habit—I agreed not to discuss religion or politics once inside the premises. The nuns made a big fuss over me. Though the sisters were not young, they were lively, involved, interesting and personable. They enjoyed singing along while I played the piano, as they turned the sheet music. They taught me their reweaving technique on Vati's silk shirts. I felt I was living a life of virginal purity—except when I went to the Mayor's office and he tried to kiss me. I eased out of that situation, but since he was such a handsome man, I felt rather flattered.

Mutti nagged me about household items which could not be replaced during the war and were needed now that we had set up "house." She urged me to go to Antwerp. I also wanted to do more business with Mr. Gerstel. Last but not least, I was anxious to see Simon. He was not one for writing, so there was absolutely no contact between us at the moment.

The mayor informed me that travel to Antwerp again required the permission of *Feldkommandant 681*, *Kamer 333* in Hasselt. A most depressing and frightening case of dèja-vu—but now I knew what to expect from the Nazi beast. So be it! A repeat performance, as on the previous trip, for housing. Indeed, it was a shouting, humiliating encore of my first *Kommandant* "visit." But at least, once more, I strode beneath the unfurling swastika triumphantly and felt relief to be on the return trip from Hasselt to Hoeselt with the prospect of getting to Antwerp. Nonetheless, this was accompanied by sadness to the rhyme of Heinrich Heine's "Lorelei": "*Ich weiß nicht, was soll es bedeuten, dass ich so traurig bin.*" ("I don't know the significance of my being so sad.") The chance to see Simon, Antwerp and maybe even the relatives should have brought me great joy. Instead, I was rather melancholy.

Mutti, a daily barrack visitor, knew when Frau Holzer would see her husband. It was decided I would return and stay with her. That suited me fine, since I liked Erna and the apartment was centrally located. I did not tell Simon about the upcoming trip, as I wanted to surprise him.

In the meantime, I frequented the convent daily, then just crossed the square to be home. The Molenaers' children were always there when I got back. Lizy and Jani wanted to know so much about my life. Both sisters absorbed everything I told them. When little Joske was pulled away by his mom for his nap, he shrugged her off without taking his big, clear, inquisitive eyes off me. Lizy seemed so fascinated that I noticed her emulating me.

The day of my departure arrived. Each time I dealt with the railroad in Hoeselt, there was so much excitement that I hadn't noticed the small waiting room with benches around the walls. Maybe it had been closed the other times. My parents warned me that I should never place my handbag in back of me, especially when carrying cash, as now. This money was intended to be put to good use with Mr. Gerstel. I was glad to see Mrs. Holzer and her baby girl again. Mutti harped on her list of new cleaning rags, kitchen towels and utensils—everything very practical—to be sent by Simon. What an embarrassing, weary and boring task!

There was plenty of room in the coach. Mr. Holzer ran alongside as long as he could manage, repeating "Take good care of each other!" as his eyes moistened and he could no longer catch his breath. For a long time, Erna Holzer remained earnest and taciturn. When looking at her sleeping baby and then at me, she melted into a state of contentment. I liked the way she gazed at me, full of kindness and admiration. Her sweetness compensated for her bad skin. Instead of the formal Mrs. Holzer she wanted me to call her Erna—very rare unless you were one's peer. The train ride was pleasant, passing fields and wooded areas but nothing as impressive as western Belgium I'd admired even while subjected to real terror.

As we approached *Berchem* station, my nervousness quickened with each second, not only because this was the very point of our departure under the Nazi bullies who were to seal our fate, but from anticipation. I took in all the curious glimpses of the *Mercator*, *Simonstraat* and at last *Pelikaanstraat* as the train carefully rolled into Antwerp station, which was a terminal for all incoming trains. I hadn't noticed this before.

Outside, we stood in front of the majestic old entrance. The late afternoon sun cast a golden hue over this city of Rubens and diamonds. We crossed the street to my favorite corner, where on my first day I'd heard the paper war of the various voices. We were fleeing the swastika then, but this symbol of hate caught up with us.

Once again, I walked the familiar streets where I had experienced much anguish and poverty—then happiness and comfort—and now sadness mixed with anxiety. Upon passing the short block to *Vestingstraat*, my heart was pounding, when a strange feeling came over me. I peeked into this well-known street and was filled with melancholy and nostalgia: Prager's was no longer there. Neither was the *Vestingstraat Café* nor Mr. Bialistok's jewelry store. "Such somber changes," I murmured to Erna. Just before *Café Riga*, she unlocked one of the few private apartment houses that impressed me. "Your husband had to leave a sweet woman like you and an adorable baby and all of this!" I mumbled. Maybe my statement was indelicate. She just went on to proudly show me the guest room. It had been rare of late that I had slept in a bed all by myself in a bedroom all alone. "Like a queen!" I exclaimed. It was as being in a castle, even though it was just a nice flat, however roomy.

This was the first time I ever fed a baby. I marveled as her eyes got larger with each mouthful. After she was put into her crib, Erna wanted to shampoo my hair. She did it with such sincere warmth that I felt a soothing satisfaction. When I glanced into the mirror with my wet hair, I was pleasantly surprised to see how well I looked. Erna noticed this and said approvingly, "You see!" There was even a tile bathroom like the one we'd left in Köln. It felt great to take a real bath, totally submerged, then rinse off with a regular shower as opposed to the bucketsful Mutti poured. Whenever she did that, I felt uneasy somehow, hearing noises. But Mutti, the notorious worrier, reassured me that it was just a cat. Now I was enjoying a luxury I hadn't had since Simon's apartment.

A pleasant aroma filled the air. Erna was preparing two large cauliflower heads with eggs, butter, flour and nutmeg. All smiles when she saw me coming toward the kitchen, she sheepishly said, "My husband told me I could make a feast out of cauliflower."

"Having any produce at all is a banquet now," I remarked elatedly since I was starved. "He's right about this food!" I complimented her after the tasty meal.

Erna sensed I was restless to accomplish everything during the short time allotted by the miserable *Feldkommandant*. I told her my plans on the train. She related that when the visitors left Hoeselt on our first Sunday there, Mr. London appeared despondent throughout the return trip, hardly talking to anyone, which was totally out of his character.

This had me concerned. Nothing had stayed the same since I'd left this charming city. The buildings looked just as they had, as did the familiar streets I loved. But it was no longer that cozy, lively town with all my personal landmarks—my Antwerp. "I bet there might be a change in the gallery, too. It could even be closed, of course." I looked at my watch. "Anyway, it's past their opening hours. So I'll kill two birds with one stone—visit Mr. Gerstel to find out about business, and contact Simon, who according to your story is transformed."

"Unfortunately, I must agree with you on all counts," she nodded. "Yes, as for Mr. Gerstel, the night is still young and only a pleasant fifteen-minute walk from here, and good for your digestion." She laughed and added warmly: "I shall wait up for you with a nightcap of sour milk, and you'll feed my curiosity with news." By now, my hair was dry and since it's easily manageable, I got dressed. Erna accompanied me to the door with well wishes.

As a city dweller, I found it invigorating to walk the busy streets again. Physically, I felt great and refreshed in the evening breeze, but emotionally it was a different story entirely: especially when I saw that the *Café Riga*, where all the political debates had taken place, had also shut down. How I missed Lili and Rosalie! After this sad realization, I made a turnabout toward *de Keyserlei*. After a few months not having seen the "gray green pest"—except in Hasselt—it was upsetting to be aware of their presence disgracing this lovely main avenue. I made a left, passing the *Quellin School*, where I'd learned so much—the French language, international stage dancing—and where I'd performed my first belly dance while dreaming about Dr. Königsmann and Mr. London. I smiled inwardly.

Close to the hustle-bustle of center city, at the edge of its park, there was a fine, quiet section. In the first pristine street, called Maria-Theresialei, one of three named after international feminine royalty, I found the nice architecture matching Gerstel's address as given by Simon in Hoeselt. Even this lovely *Stadspark* where I had spent time with Maurice and his burly friend during the Belgian police threat—amazingly—was in the shape of a diamond! Was this a coincidence?! It contained more contoured bodies of blue water than greenery. Each facet was named after a great old national master: Rubenslei, Van Eycklei and Quinten Matsijslei. To the right of the diamond point, I entered their well-furnished home.

Mr. Gerstel looked at me as though seeing a ghost, jumping off his seat, exclaiming: "You are not allowed to leave your village! My God! THEY will punish you! I guess you know that!"

I showed him the permit signed by both the mayor and the *Feldkommandant*. With hand on heart and a deep sigh, he walked up to greet me cordially, introducing his children and attractive wife, who dwarfed him. She offered me cauliflower, but I accepted the Jewish desert of stewed, dried fruits instead, making further arrangements with her husband. He informed me, though, that our dealings wouldn't go on much longer, for he was seriously considering—like most of the last money people still in Antwerp—following *Moishe to Cuba*. They were hoping for a far better and safer solution than the doomed "St.Louis" after I had raised that question.

"Why in the world did a smart girl like you ever let yourself get lured into the Nazi claws so early in their game? Your first priority must be to escape your Nazi cage. I know from Mr. London that you will say there are no Germans in your village, it isn't all that bad. Yes, not yet. But I'll bet you didn't realize there are well over 3000 Jews within the Belgian province of Limburg!"

I was amazed and speechless, indeed.

"You see? You are astonished. There are 123 in Hoeselt and another 123 in neighboring Bilzen—a total of 246 adults, plus 21 children, in these two villages alone. That's a darned good reason for the Nazis and a most distressing one for you, the intended victims. We don't know yet victims for what, in which way nor where. But to gather 3000 Jews so perilously close to the German border must have a deadly aim. Sorry to alarm you, but your young life is at stake!" He shook my hands pleadingly: "Don't let anything happen to you or you parents!"

In a lower voice, he continued: "Mr. London had his reliable sources do a thorough study and was terribly upset. He is no longer the same lively, passionate, witty man we all knew and loved. His mind is dead set upon the 'Unoccupied.' It's entirely too close to the Nazis, in my opinion."

Suddenly, he interrupted his thoughts and said: "If you want to stay with us, we do have a guest room, and would love to have you! Tomorrow afternoon, I'll invite Mr. London so we can all have tea together."

"Thank you so much for your kind offer. But may I accept this another time, when it becomes a necessity? For now, I live with Mrs. Holzer."

"I'll give Mr. London the address and he'll see you there instead. The gallery has remained solely for art's sake and not a meeting place, so you can't see him there. I don't know his schedule, but I'm sure he'll drop everything for you," he said, smiling for the first time during the visit. He then handed me a smart-looking ruby-diamond pin as further collateral in exchange for the actual interest I had received in Hoeselt. As long as the going is good, one must strike, because no one knows when the next money will come in. Another "*Mazel and Bracha*" not only about the deal but also concerning our future. After this I went on my way alongside the park on the lovely van Eycklei, then past the monument of the Spanish Conquistadores. I made a left into *Plantinlei* and stopped at the big, white lacquered door to surprise the *Horowitzes*.

Upon entering the apartment, I was shocked to find it looking barren. The cute items were gone—and so was Sasha. Mary read my questioning stare and asked: "Were you aware that, back in the thirties, before you lived here, Nazi reporters infiltrated the diamond centers? Of course, their purpose was to create anti-Semitic, derisive propaganda to be spread in the German press. In an effort to avoid this, some brave Jews attacked them and destroyed their tell-tale cameras. Sasha was about to join in, but the Nazis fled first. German informers acquired their addresses, and now that they are the occupying forces, the Gestapo hunted them including Sasha. Even though he never took part. He was forced to flee to Paris, where it is just as dangerous as here, but no one knows him, nor is he persecuted in France," explained Mary, of whom I was so very fond, sadly.

"How long has he been there?" I asked anxiously.

"It's been six long weeks," she kept nodding dolefully. "We are about to leave illegally for Paris, or better still, for the 'Unoccupied' and join him there." Mary, forever smiling with that lovely, florid complexion, had to force one now.

I gave her a long, profound hug and both of us gazed mournfully at each other. I kissed the boys and with that, I was on my way back to Erna.

"How nice of you to wait up for me, Erna!"

"My pleasure. I will even enhance it with some refreshing sour milk and bread," she smiled while fetching the nightcap.

I was about to share my innermost thoughts with her instead of Rosalie and Lili. Neither of us wanted to retire, not just yet. I had some apprehension of waiting for and seeing Simon. I did not rest and became more nervous as the meeting grew closer. I wanted to cut the night as short as possible. I hardly dared the comparison, but the fear I felt now was a miniature version of that which I had with the *Feldkommandant*. I finally worked up the courage to express this to Erna.

"It would have been awful for me were it not for Mr. Gerstel, who shared my opinion that there'd been a definite change in Mr. London," Erna explained after I laid bare my strange, uneasy sensation. "That's the reason those negative feelings are creeping up on you—not knowing what to expect from him."

"This may be so," I agreed half-heartedly.

"Make yourself at home," she said the following morning, giving precise instructions as to where I could find everything and informing me that she stayed out with her baby each afternoon.

Because Mr. Gerstel had not specified the hour at which Simon would come, I was terribly on edge. Usually my days passed swiftly; today seemed as endless as that hot, sunny Sunday my cousins went swimming and I had to stay home because I was a hunted refugee. I tried to follow Vati's early advice: Each minute must be productive! I was too agitated to concentrate on making lists. As in Hasselt, on the bench prior to seeing the roaring Feldkommandant, nature was constantly calling upon me, but I always hurried for fear of missing Simon. Also, I hastened from mirror to mirror, forcing a plastic, pleasant smile, scrutinizing my image. My youthful face did indeed amazingly reflect a wholesome glow.

Finally, at long last, the bell rang. I stopped in my tracks, for there he stood before me. He had come upstairs. This suddenness made my heart pound rapidly. Yet I was beaming. The familiar, charming smile was absent from his handsome face. Instead there was his certain sideways, imperceptible grin which, up to now, was used only as a non-verbal reprimand on rare occasions—such as my being very late. Even this smirk was fetching now, though I did not know what to make of it. I threw my arms around his neck. He coldly removed them, accompanied by a painful, stern expression.

This is rejection at its ultimate! Too proud to say this out loud, I ushered him into the dining room and offered him tea or ersatz coffee-chicory. He declined. I folded my hands on the large square tabletop like a schoolgirl waiting to hear her grades, only slightly less shaken than in Hasselt.

Without looking at me after clearing his throat, without any further ado nor small talk, he got to the point: "You are certainly the most beautiful and exciting girl I have ever met. I truly did not want to get involved with someone that much my junior. I suffered plenty from close friends, constantly being reprimanded and receiving numerous anonymous letters. I never told you this, because I didn't want to upset you."

As he was talking, I was overwhelmed by a paralyzing passivity. I thought: Could this romance be ending as it started? Even though this time he did not hold the fan of cards in front of him to avoid eye contact, as he had the first time I came face to face with him at the gallery. Now, he chose his words carefully, stating: "You have such exaggerated love for your parents, so much devotion—the closeness amongst the three of you compensates for the lack of harmony—so there is no place for a fourth person in your lives. I feel I cannot belong and that you can never belong to me—completely!" Then with a sarcastic, nervous laugh to himself, a gesture I perceived for the first time, he continued: "You certainly perfected the art of chastity. At first it was a challenge, but then it became a tough task for me, especially looking at this remarkable, memorable, mobile face of yours. You lit my days with your warmth and energy. In fact, it turned my life around. I relished the moments of joy!"

I felt only shame, despair and utter amazement in the light of such profound change. The more determination he displayed in ending our romance, the more I slid on a losing streak. The exuberance I usually had for Simon now turned into foreboding intuition. This was confirmed by his attitude and action. He did not sound dry nor cold, always talking with pathos, but his strange monologue was surely soul-chilling. Where was my much-lauded, beguiling, enchanting flamboyance? Instead, I was feeling sorry for myself, especially when he continued: "It was unrequited passion—during these tumultuous times. Only I was to blame, I should have known better, but I am human and was caught up in the rapture." All this he said without ever raising his eyes to look at me.

How dare he call it unrequited passion, when he is the one who turned out to be the ingrate and I was just as aflame for him as he was for me in the past. So totally stunned was I by his behavior that I could not voice the words. I could only manage in the bewildered, first rejection of a young girl, to ask: "and this is the emotional aftermath?"

"Yes. I have no other choice but to confront the truth. Everything that's good and beautiful is unattainable for us, because we have to hide in the shadows of 'our world' because there is barbed wire around it. But nevertheless, we created a beautiful illusion."

I gritted my teeth.

Without looking at me once, he set forth slowly and in measured tone, at first repeating: "Truly, I did not want to get involved with your youth nor detract from the deference you have for your parents, but I sensed how you felt about me and oh, too soon I realized it was a mutual . . . well, almost diabolic attraction only to be compared with that of Heloise and Abélard. It was a volcanic eruption tumbling into an emotional frenzy. So gripped was I that I allowed my very existence to be intoxicated into the splendor of the prelude to our romance. Such was your amazing appeal. Besides, I really liked you as a wonderful, young, smart human being right from the start. Yes, the very first time you came into the gallery, I liked you a lot, maybe too much. I allowed it to get out of hand. God, you are lovely, and oh, so beautiful!"

"Oh, am I now?" I asked sarcastically, while thinking he was magical, but no longer mine. There was a vain inner search for sympathetic emotion from him, but nothing was forthcoming. I felt like a tormented tragic character out of a Goethe scene. It was like a symphony playing Mozart's "Requiem" to the end of my world. I was devastated.

At last, his gaze was upon me. But it was void of love. My melancholy emotions were stirred even more so. What about our wonderful madness of near fulfillment, I asked myself, but did not dare these thoughts aloud. Was it pride or outrage that caused my inertia? I questioned myself. As slowly as he spoke, that's how slowly my emotional downward slide descended into the abyss of despair. What an anxiety-ridden prospect! What a cruel, miserable experience for my poor young heart! Such humiliation! What a blow to my ego! And what a great loss! In the throes of deep emotion, I heard his voice become low-pitched and husky: "There is only one light flashing in my mind: how to get out of this Nazi trap before they really start taking inventory for their racial cleansing." Such grim grief! I had no courage to ask him so many "ifs", mainly about walking together underneath palm trees; in the 'Unoccupied' would I have given him an undaunted "Yes!" then. But I did not ask. I could not ask! The complex drama being played out seemed to have ended now, as the key player got up to leave the suffering heroine behind with "has been" and "has been had"-"might have been" syndromes.

This witty man had turned into a morose one, I observed to myself as we went—probably our last walk together ever!—through the corridor. In silence and in a mist of tristesse and yes, anger, I had to let go of him. When he reached for the door handle, I was near tears, especially when I did not hear his sweet "*Kätzele mines!*"—so very dear to me! How I missed him referring to me like this. Instead he exclaimed with a shrug: "Such is the nature of the beast!" and the eternal present cliché in French: "*Oui, oui, c'est la guerre!*" and with this he was off! Just like that. I could not believe it! I expected him to return; not to leave me with my choked down indignity. No, he won't come back. This was it! My ego, my heart—I myself was hurt, deeply wounded. Tears of self-pity and anger started welling in my eyes. I wanted to release my stifled, repressed pain when I heard the key turn and the baby cooing. I intended to save face, but Erna knew instinctively that my rendezvous with Simon had gone astray.

"I don't want to pry, but if you are willing to share your heartache of the afternoon with me or need a shoulder to cry on, just think about it. I'll be in the kitchen feeding the baby and preparing whatever I have for our supper. I shall be most attentive, should you so desire. I won't be a bit insulted if you decide otherwise," she suggested.

Since I could no longer bear my agony in solitude and I am an extrovert by nature, I decided to relate Simon's monologue and actions.

"Both ways on the train, I was definitely under the impression that he liked you and was very much in love with you. His conduct and words of today confirm this." When I looked at her in amazement, she answered my inquisitive eyes: "All these obstacles! The war with its Jewish persecution, the separation caused by it, the age difference, plus your high regard for your parents, possibly all his reverence for your chastity. These many barriers resulted in his determination for a clean break, so no one could get hurt."

"But Erna—how can you say this?" I objected vehemently. "Am I not offended to the very core? First he worms himself into my heart and then he breaks it! I trusted and loved him. Surely, there was this tremendous change within him—"

"—most likely caused by the severity of this painful break-up—" Erna quickly interjected.

"Hence, my feelings of foreboding, anxiety and nervousness. Imagine. They were so grave, I likened them to those prior to confronting the Kommandant. What irony to have suffered through the trip to Hasselt, in order to endure even more here in Antwerp, were it not for the one consolation of my business deal with Gerstel," I lamented, adding: "I'm so glad I can pour my heart out to you. Even though I haven't known you for a long time, I feel through your genuine kindness as though we are friends from way back. It's so easy to talk to you, Erna."

"In these hard times, one generally gets closer to one another; all kinds of relationships grow much more rapidly," was Erna's opinion as she continued her consolatory pep talk: "In both cases with the Kommandant and Simon your ego was deeply hurt by rejection. As for Mr. London, precisely because of his love, strong attraction and, yes, infatuation, he would not dare as much as to shake your hand, because that would spark the entire romantic relationship anew. He is smart and also human enough to know you would never leave your parents behind; and his mind is definitely set upon going to the 'Unoccupied.' Naturally, the separation from Antwerp to Hoeselt facilitated his decision for a complete split."

"This only shifts my anger from Simon to Mutti," I mumbled.

"But as you admit," Erna objected, "Antwerp is no longer the same city you had left. It is not at all the way it was! Neither would you have been able to continue your nice lifestyle."

"You do make me feel better, Erna. There is a lot of logic in your words. For this, I wish to thank you!" When I went over to embrace her, she was most responsive.

"I feel so claustrophobic from having been indoors the entire day. I should visit my relatives in *Borgerhout*. I cannot recall the last time I saw them." After the discussion, the walk in the evening breeze was refreshing, even on the wrong side of the tracks, the *Lange Kievit Straat*. It was a rather long way to **Borgerhout**. Now, the offensive smell of the candle factory heralded this poor suburb. As at numerous times in the past, I crossed the quaint street. Still I could not come to terms with myself, much less find any balm to ease my tormented soul.

"They don't live here anymore!"—a woman yelled out her window in Flemish. I had started to feel better, but now, I could no longer dampen my rage. Because of self-talk and self-hate my mind had lost track of why I was there. My legs had simply carried me, so this Flemish information startled me. My anger was compounded when I realized that I'd passed the relatives' new abode in the Lange Kievit Straat quite a while ago.

I turned on my heels to where I had come from, hoping this brisk hike might help me out of my black mood. But then I realized no ordinary consolation would help my crushed spirit recapture the innate optimism which had always helped me overcome any obstacle. There was an inner hate and self-pity monologue: "Why did he do this to me? So suddenly! Just like that! He stopped loving me, just like that! I stopped being his *Kätzele*! Just like that, he walked out of my life forever! With this, I reached Provintiestraat. Now it was not all that far to the other end of the Lange Kievit Straat. It was astonishing. In this poor Jewish section, I noticed little difference. There were still the grocers and shoemakers. When

I peeked to the left, in passing Leuwerickstraat, the hub of Jewish life, there was hardly any change.

I hadn't felt such torment since the day our business in Köln had been aryanized. I cried in front of the buyers, who also had tears in their eyes at this sight of a teenager in the depths of misery. But this was even worse, for with Simon, I was singled out, as opposed to Aryanization, which was against all Jews. Though each Jewish person was hit hard, it was not so personal and intimate as my case with Simon.

I had finally arrived. At least now my relatives lived only minutes from Erna, so I could stay a while with them. I rang the bell. Frima, my cold Prima let me in, acting cooler than ever or should I say as usual? I entered their poor apartment. It was downright depressing, befitting my present mood, especially with Maurice's absence.

"Your uncle is in a very bad way, at the hospital. We spent the entire afternoon there. Now Maurice is with him. His 'baker's cough' had gotten very severe," my aunt explained.

"Poor little Uncle Manuel. He is such a frail person!" was my honest compassionate remark. Yet Frima gave me one of her proud, hostile glances. End of conversation. I felt most uncomfortable, except that little Sara smiled. But there was such sadness in her huge, blue eyes. Her dark, long, thick lashes threw shadows on the high cheekbones in the dim light. I saw tears rolling down her hollow cheeks. Her thick, blonde, curly hair was parted in the center. It gave her a halo look. My eyes were fixed on her. How did Simon refer to my face? Yes, a remarkable, memorable one. Hers was truly so. Unable to take my eyes off such beauty, the more I studied it, the more I realized Simon's words would fit hers. Yet, it resembled her father's, Vati's half-brother. I thought of his tough life, work by night, sleep by day and coughing forever!

"I hope that devil cough leaves him be!" With these words, I got up, wanting to hug gorgeous Sara but felt awkward about the other two and just threw her a kiss. There was relief when she offered to take me downstairs. Before leaving her, I kissed her haunting face and held my little, sweet cousin tight, saying: "As all the children in *Borgerhout* call you 'little Marlene Dietrich' you are even more beautiful. May your father enjoy seeing you grow up!" With this, I pressed her to my heart.

As I went the few steps through the underpass, a train puffed in and sounded its whistle as I reached the corner where I saw Dr. Königsmann for the very last time. Everything was so mournful!

Again, Erna was waiting up for me. Over a cup of mixed coffee and chicory, I related tonight's frustrations and informed her about staying on for another day to comply with Mutti's demand to secure the assorted towels. Though brand new and unavailable now in stores, I regarded them as rags. I considered visiting my uncle, but without the bike, I had no idea how to get to the hospital, since it was very far and the way complicated. I had to leave Antwerp the following day.

Tomorrow came and I went straight to *Groenvinckstraat*, our last apartment. On *Carnotstraat*, the many stores offered little display, a sign of scant merchandise. No, Antwerp was definitely not the same for a number of reasons and of course, the most poignant for me: there was no Simon. Without him, the whole city seemed empty.

I was overcome by a strange feeling as I stood in front of 79 *Groenvinckstraat*, for instead of turning my key, I had to buzz. The mother of the two little girls opened the door as she had done the very first time to show us the flat. She was surprised, yet elated, to see me. After telling her briefly about our entire Nazi-village-story, she did hand me a bunch of "rags," stating that she had not seen Simon.

Since the quartier was not occupied, she must have guessed my desire to see it one last time. "Feel free to browse around. Maybe some more of these were left there."

I went up the familiar steps. I was seized by nostalgia upon entering and found it exactly the way it had been, my entire being seemed to rush into one colossal tear drop, but then when I saw the overstuffed chair, all my pent-up melancholy emotions came flowing out of me uncontrollably. Past images of comfort were unfolding so lively in front of me: When I was receiving my students, one after another, like a doctor his patients; when during my free time, I wrote the book of my own English teaching method—according to the various pronunciations of each English vowel accompanied by grammar—then when, for the first time, I sat erotically on a man's lap. It was Simon's.

Chapter 18

Still in profound despair, my heart remembered happier times before the Nazi invasion, when I had hastened to my students via varied routes. Now, I was returning downtown, possibly my last passing through Kerkstraat. A bittersweet feeling came over me as I recalled the more recent past, rushing through this long street with great expectations of happiness, business and joie de vivre.

The best I could hope for now was to find my cousin Maurice, despite anticipating his justified reproaches for failing to keep in touch. Deep in thought, I became startlingly aware of the "practical bundle" for Mutti only after entering Erna's apartment. Disappointingly, there was no message from Maurice, so I stayed indoors. Perhaps, subconsciously, I yearned to see my cousin because he was the only relative and friend left in Antwerp to whom I could relate. Conceivably, I considered him consolation for the loss of Simon at this moment of sadness.

Being, in essence, a Nazi prisoner, I was concerned about leaving for my village on the last permitted day. My intention was to take the next morning's train, which necessitated a stopover in the dreaded city of Hasselt. One comfort was not having to report to the tirading Kommandant there. It would simply be an unemotional transfer.

I was so appreciative of Erna's existence. During our exchange of opinions I again expressed my gratitude for the speed with which our warm relationship had developed. Weary from past events and the waiting for Maurice had drained me to the point of exhaustion.

Several light but urgent knocks at the door were fortunately accompanied by Erna's sweet voice. "So sorry to wake you this early but there's a visitor who insists on seeing you."

Although I had slept soundly, getting up took enormous effort. Additionally, terrible cramps induced by my emotions, which should not have arrived until later in the month, were tormenting me now. This seemed to be compounded by my recurrent abdominal infection. When normally blessed with good health, even minor discomforts become magnified.

Drowsiness befell me and I had to summon all my inner strength to finally crawl from bed. Doubled up with aches, I quickly brushed my hair and most reluctantly concealed my nightwear with a warm coat.

When I opened the door, a woman I had never seen before, was standing in the teaming rain. Holding my cramped abdomen and crouched in pain, I was embarrassed to have to face this complete stranger in such a sad state. "Your relatives sent me! Here's the address of the cemetery." She announced dryly. By the time I grasped the paper, the torrential rain had rendered it illegible. I was baffled, yet had a foreboding hunch about poor, sick Uncle Manuel.

"Be there in one hour for the funeral of your Uncle Manuel! The family said not to disappoint them," she proclaimed, delivering the message as a command.

I countered with "I'm so very sorry, I didn't even know he had passed on and I've no idea where the cemetery is located. In any case, I've just got up feeling awfully sick and I'm far too ill to move. It took a gigantic effort simply for me to walk downstairs." I wanted her to convey these words to my aunt and cousins.

She shrugged her broad shoulders and with an abrupt "suit yourself!" off she went.

To climb each step was an arduous task for me, especially when this was accompanied by my feelings of helplessness and guilt about being unable to attend my poor uncle, who was being laid to rest at last to find peace from his accursed cough. Instead of my usual dashing upstairs two at a time, I was now barely able to hang onto the balustrade with my shivering hands. My physical and psychological condition was causing me to shake so uncontrollably that I had to lean all of my weight on the rails to save myself from collapsing. After what seemed like an eternity, I felt redeemed when I finally dragged myself into the still-warm bed.

Erna came running, with her burping baby over her diapered shoulder and covered me gently with her free hand, while assuring me that she would return as soon as her little girl was settled. At that moment I felt she was dealing with two infants.

She soon returned with a cup of hot tea and propped up the pillows in back of me. Miserable as I was, Erna still managed to make me feel like a queen. "Do you know how much I wished Mutti would treat me just a little bit like this?" I said wistfully, while being soothed with each hot gulp.

"What! She doesn't? Her one and only child and a precious little flower like you, no?" She asked in amazement.

Again I was surprised that I had confided my innermost feelings to her, but already she had taken on the mantle of an old-time friend. "Especially when I expressed my desire to leave for the U.S. some day after the world is free." I answered. "Hollywood no doubt, where you would fit in quite easily?" she suggested playfully.

"I would be happy if I could wind up in Paterson, New Jersey where my Uncle Maxie lives" was my response, as the brew continued to work its wonders. "Apropos Mutti, who claimed the following: 'who's going to have time to bring demoiselle hot tea? Wasn't your cousin Ida's letter most descriptive, the first English one you could read fully without the help of a dictionary. She gets up at dawn, rushes to her job, hurries through her entire day's work then hastens home to fall exhausted asleep to get ready for more of the same each following day. And this is in Canada, which is supposed to be less stressful than the U.S.!'—so each time I craved hot tea," I set forth "her command for auto-service was upon me: 'You want to go to America? Then help yourself the American way!'"

With Erna's leaving the room, my glum ruminating about my uncle's funeral, the trauma with Simon, compounded by the rustling of the incessant rain, soon made me fall into a deep slumber. I despised myself for turning daytime into night—and yet another mournful thought for Uncle Manuel, whose job had forced him to live this way each day of his miserable life, flowed into my consciousness.

When I awoke, I asked myself "Is this the dark dawn? Then it's the day I must leave Antwerp." Quickly though, I realized that this was the dusk prior to my official Nazi-designated departure time. I felt grateful that I still had this extra day and through resting I had regained much of my strength and health and even my natural happiness, which had been absent for the couple of days since I had seen Simon for the last time. Feeling like a recuperated patient, I had to nod sadly to myself when I thought what a heavy price my emotions extolled from me in exchange for the happiness lasting less than half a year.

After my morning toilette was completed—this time in the evening—I remembered today's funeral and was overwhelmed by guilt for my non-attendance. Fortunately, I felt like a different person from earlier in the day. Totally refreshed, I ran into the kitchen and embraced Erna, who beamed upon seeing me so much better. I expressed my gratitude for her pampering when it was most needed and added, "At least I now feel able to observe the relatives' 'Shiva'—(mourning)".

"Had I not seen for myself how much you were suffering this morning and the contrast with your appearance now, I would never have believed it, but for the fact, of course, that I trust you. Will your relatives understand though?" was her sincere concern.

This had crossed my mind, but for various reasons I felt compelled to go to their house to mourn for the deceased and to sweeten the lives of the bereaved—the real purpose of the 'Shiva'—especially for little Sara and her brother.

After another delicious cauliflower dinner, I left. While running down the stairway as usual, Erna giggled: "—not at all like before,"—adding, "Be prepared for some 'flak' from the family!"

I needed courage to ring the bell, but truly, I was in luck, for it was Maurice—the one I really wanted to see—who opened the door. We faced each other breathlessly and speechlessly. He looked like a very young, gaunt Robert Taylor. His present harrowness made his beautiful blue-green eyes appear even more smouldering and expressive.

With my favorite cousin Maurice on my break form
commercial college. Spring 1937 Antwerp.

"My heartfelt sympathy. I'm so sorry . . . I wasn't . . ." I
stammered.

"Say no more, my beloved cousin. Shhh . . ."—as he did a few
years ago—he gently sealed my babbling lips with a kiss, which was
surprisingly wonderful. Then and now the flow of my blood stopped—
streaming in the opposite direction, because the embrace was not at
all cousinly. I didn't expect nor deserve this, not even from Maurice.
My fondest memories of him during our initial refugee chase, including
the Belgian Police hunt in Berchem, were revived. He truly sweetened
my 'Shiva' of the mourning about the loss of my roots. At this moment,

he was easing my current pain also. Thankful to walk up, with him, being held at the waist and gazed upon with love, I actually congratulated myself that coincidentally, I was able to shed my grief over Simon at the threshold of real sorrow. Besides the nice, unanticipated sensation Maurice aroused in me, there was doubtless a touch of a teen's vengeance against Simon.

The fact that we entered the apartment together made me feel far less awkward. Beautiful Sara jumped up to greet and hug me, pouring out her little heart. I approached Frima and my aunt cautiously, to hold them briefly. It was the empty chair upon which my uncle used to sit and cough, that made me cry too. Only then did I notice that there were a few friends present. The only one I recognized was the woman from this morning in the downpour.

The rain had cleared the air, so it felt invigorating when Maurice walked me slowly to my place. At first, he was taciturn, but then seemed to take heart when he said, with some pathos in his voice "I've always loved you, ever since your first Belgian visit when we were children and Sara but a tiny baby." "Yes. I remember. Your mom was so weary holding her because we were late" I interjected. "But then your second trip took place during your Commercial College break" he continued, "and my heart stood still when you descended the train, like an angel, a queen, a Hollywood star— alas, that was but a short stay." he reminisced, suddenly full of energy, passion and desire, like Chopin's "Scherzo" in B-minor.

"I sensed the way you felt about me," I confessed, "when my left foot hurt so much from walking because there was no car and the way you removed my blue velvet slipper and took care of me. It both embarrassed and pleased me."

"Only it was the reverse" he smiled sadly "you were the princess and I the poor 'Cinderello.' How thrilled I was" he exclaimed "when you finally came to settle down here after your father's various money-smuggling visits to us. How I wished he would have brought you along. Once, I was even brave enough to ask—'Uncle Jakob, why doesn't your daughter accompany you, so I could teach her French?'" he said this in his fluent American English, as though he was emulating Cesar Romero.

"Then" he continued: "when your refugee drama unfolded, I often felt like your rescuer during your hardships. I hate to admit how strong it made my ego. I'm fully aware of the extent of my Aunt Sofie's control over your spirit, but I'm surprised that she didn't exercise her usual power over you concerning Mr. London" he dished out cautiously.

"Oh. So you know of that brief episode in my life?" I questioned, glad that there was the blackout to spare my blushes.

"Hmm. Mr. London and his courtier-courier was the juicy gossip of the town—a sort of verbal dessert after Hitler's success stories," he pointed out.

"Oh, my reputation!" I exclaimed, half-joking.

"Well, prior to the war, a rich Belgian Jewish girl in a similar situation would have been carefully packaged and shipped to America to some relative or finishing school. I'm serious." he stressed, then added "Many a time I had to defend you. Besides, it made it easier on you because despite his charm and comfortable lifestyle, he wasn't known as a womanizer but rather as a popular businessman's man and advisor" he said, trying to console me.

When we arrived at my apartment, in order to prolong my time with Maurice, we kept on ambling on the now-quiet and darkened Pelikaanstraat. "Putting this aside, my dear cousin, your presence creates sensations I don't want to feel, but remember, I always cherished and loved you and I will forever" vowed Maurice. His voice took on a dead, austere tone when he said, in just above a whisper "I have the strangest feeling that this will be our last walk together."

"Why in the world do you utter such an awful ominous thought?" I shrieked.

"Right now, you're all but a Nazi prisoner—Aunt Sofie's will again. With any luck at all, you must get out of that net and fight in order to stay out! Do anything to prevent being caught again," he warned. "We here in Belgium are more fortunate than any other Nazi-occupied country," he explained, "because it's far better to live under the German military control of Alexander von Falkenhausen, who is the supreme authority to head the Belgian and Northern French territories. It would be disastrous if King

Leopold's mother, Queen Elisabeth, wasn't spokeswoman to plead on behalf of us Belgian Jews. She pointed out to 'Alexander the Great'—one blue-blooded 'friend' to another—how much riches and knowledge Belgian Jews had brought to this small kingdom since her husband, King Albert, had allowed them to settle here. In ancient times, when the Netherlands and Belgium were still one country, they flourished here also, until Martin Luther came from Wittenberg in Eastern Germany to spread anti-Semitism. Thus, for centuries, between Martin Luther and King Albert of modern times, this country was 'Judenrein' (clean of Jews). "Because of this" he continued "our numbers in Belgium are tiny and since von Falkenhausen isn't a fervent Nazi—another enormous advantage for us—he's given his holy promise to Her Majesty to leave the few of us be, but there's nobody, but nobody in the entire world to defend the many German and Austrian refugees. The Nazis are really after you and should you, by some miracle, succeed in getting out of the village for good, promise me you'll live in Brussels. As much as I would love to have you here, I know Antwerp is too dangerous. It's very anti-Semitic because of the old jealousies, especially with the diamond business having been so concentrated in Jewish hands. This made it easy for troublemakers to stir-up Jew-business envy and on top of this, the Gestapo has a stronghold on this town. Only 35 minutes from here by the blue electric train" he went on "the one million inhabitants of Brussels have a very different temperament and attitude from that of the Flemish. One of my teachers claimed that the name 'Belgians' derived from the 'Belgaes', a former belligerent, Gallic people of Northern France and Belgium. In Brussels, Jews are primarily in leather and bag-manufacturing. A far cry from the diamond prosperity—and it's spread out discreetly all over the city. Consequently, there's none of that violent Antwerp coveting in the Capital. Also because of its size, it's good to submerge, if need be." Maurice at last finished his long-winded, honest, most interesting speech and advice.

"You make it sound as though there's a contract out for me to be killed, or else a death sentence!" I said, unable to conceal my astonishment. "I tell it as it is," he emphasized. "That's exactly it!"

Grabbing my arm, he said somberly "Now, let's take these last steps together, one by one, ever so slowly."

When he started walking in measured paces, I interrupted his solemn mood by exclaiming "My premonition differs from yours completely. From now on, I shall follow my own instincts and not those of Mutti or anybody else. I'll shake myself loose of this and already I'm feeling that I shall survive, no matter what the Nazis have in store for us. I will survive!" I cried, "I'm not going to be caught up with them again, even though I must admit the village wasn't bad, but no matter what, I'll survive. That's going to be my battle cry. I'll live to show you so!"

"Omein, from your lips to God's ears" he answered in a grim voice, then lowered it as he murmured "Our last embrace."

As I found myself in his arms, I thought, he's still insisting on his outrageous, aggravating theory—though his kiss again made my blood stop for an instant and its flow changed from anger to a wonderful warm and genuine feeling.

He unlocked the house door for me and in the dim light I could see his marvellous penetrating eyes piercing right through my heart and soul. He took my hand; held it for a while; squeezed it as though to leave an imprint on it, felt my knuckles and then he reluctantly allowed the very points of my finger nails to ebb away from his touch. All the while he evidently was impressing upon me that this was the end, the absolute finale—with my perishing—the inevitable finale.

Chapter 19

On the following day—my last Antwerp "permission" stay, again, from the train I saw Pelikaan, Simons and Mercatorstraats all bathed in sunshine as though the downpour had washed away all the sins of the city. Once past Berchem, the irregular buildup of the locomotive's rhythm of 1, 2, 1, 2, 3 had settled in. My thoughts whirled in all directions. In the brief time of my sojourn, there were also four key players: Erna, a fabulous hostess, friend and confidante; Mr. Gerstel, a successful deal for me, with him being most cordial; Maurice, strange but sincere, sympathetic and most uplifting; Simon, ha . . . just like that I stopped being his Kätz . . . enough! I pushed these laments aside with the lyrics of an American hit, Lili used to sing in her husky, Negro-like, soothing voice, "Tonight I mustn't think of him. Music, Maestro, please!" My chant was the sun-drenched woods, fields and farmhouses. Their serene sight, the tempo of the train and last, but not least, two comforting thoughts arose: one Simon was NOT a womanizer, therefore candid with me, and two his very last words: 'Oui, c'est las guerre!' Truly, it was the war, with its Jewish persecution which had changed him—in everyone's opinion, including my own—that ultimately altered his feelings for me.

Nevertheless, I could not help thinking at this very moment—also being alone on the train—like Tolstoy's "Anna Karenina", after Vronsky had rejected her—I felt abandoned. I must let go of this! I commanded myself. But now, the immediate and imminent future was, above all, Mutti. What about her? What a worry! I may never reveal my life's fiascos. Not now, nor ever! It would be followed by her never ending 'I told you so . . . you see this happens if you don't listen to your smart Mutti! It serves you right!'

Could I tell Vati though? It would be of great solace, if I could only trust him, not to let it get back to her. I must think about it for the time being.

In addition to this new sorrow, I began to be plagued by another worry in that I had to change trains near Hasselt.

With these troublesome thoughts, I did arrive at the small, but very crowded station where I had to catch the rural coach. Such provincial depots have the advantage of one level. Therefore, I did not have to lug the bundles, consisting of both my personal items and Mutti's "rags." The day was actually clear and bright. In fact, the sun was so brilliant that I could discern to my left another small station. As I was wondering why it was necessary to have two railroad stops within so short a distance—suddenly I halted because on the platform, people were milling about. Quite sharply defined in the foreground, thus closer to me, stood a tall lady with a chiseled profile. Wait a minute, I thought to my utter surprise, this is Erika from Erfurt, now moving in a most nervous manner, perilously at the rim. Did I or did I not wave to her to step back, for it was quite disturbing, as the black locomotive edged slowly and breathlessly closer to her. At that instant, oh, God!—I witnessed Erika jump or fall like a huge sack in front of it. Did I or did I not scream from horror and pain?—Then, I saw multicolored dots—men and women were leaning over me with concerned faces, when I found myself horizontally on top of two bundles.

"She is coming to, she is coming to!" I heard a woman exclaim with a touch of relief in her voice.

"So she is!" various voices were repeating, all seemingly glad. Momentarily, I relived the entire terrible scene, as I uttered to all the strangers, "I deeply appreciate your interest and worry about me, but what is a little fainting spell compared to . . . ?"

"Because, my dear, you still could be helped," the kind lady answered.

"Does this mean-?" Somehow, I managed to ask in dread.

"Yes, most unfortunately, that's what it means," was their response as they were all mournfully looking down, while trying to help me to my feet.

"Most likely a suicide." They consulted with each other.

The group waited with me for my coach. I got terribly sick to my stomach. My breathing became as heavy as the train-pulling engine. My feet felt like ice blocks. I was barely able to whisper to them, "I knew her!"

The train finally arrived. What a pity, that none of these supportive well-wishers had to board with me.

Again, the strangest emotions in the form of Tolstoi's heroine had flooded me, as the rural train whistled its way from this macabre scene of another Jewish persecution casualty.

What a traumatic experience! The sight of horror unfolding before my eyes overshadowed all of the previous miserable occurrences throughout this doomed voyage. It felt as though I were the only passenger to bear testimony before this frightful drama. After such a disaster, it seemed trivial now how to relate the truth about Simon to Mutti.

As I stared out the window, I saw the evening sun, with her last glow in the sky, forming a crimson cuff along the clear horizon. Only gentle, small clouds were floating above, just as the lyrics in Gounod's valse, the opera version of Abelard and Heloise. Oh, no, stop! I bade myself. For Simon likened us to them the last time I had seen him. Only their love was immortal after all. It was hard to fight off all of these tormenting thoughts, that descended upon me all at once, to no avail. In fact, the closer the train huffed to "my" village, the more nervous I became. I had more practical apprehensions about the tricky handle at my very brief stop. But then, there was relief after I managed to depart the train rapidly with the bundles, without any help. Once on the ground of Hoeselt, I looked at them with gratitude, for they eased my fall upon fainting. As I started heading to my abode, I absorbed the fresh country fragrance of the spicy early spring earth. Inhaling the balmy air for consolation I wondered how dreadful I felt at this moment. I started marching with more energy. The familiar sight of the square, with its cloister and the barrack, evoked anxiety anew, full force, mainly the prospect of facing Mutti as a loser. Also, it was strange that at this point, possibly the first time in my life, I had nothing, absolutely nothing, to anticipate.

Upon entering the large, brown gate, traces of the "Feldkommandant fears" took hold of me. Ironically, the song of "Mein Yiddishe Mamme" also came to mind. I thought any real mother of any religion could grant me the compassion, true love and, above all, acceptance that I direly needed. However, again the empty feeling that I had nothing and nobody. Perhaps Vati would make do, but of course, he would be stifled by Mutti. With a heavy heart, I entered through the driveway into the country kitchen. How dim and plain everything looked now after the Antwerp apartments of Gerstel and Holzer. But, it was warm as was Vati. After he embraced me with much tenderness, he busied himself, preparing an aromatic meal with meat which worked like magic on me, imparting a certain coziness, after all. Mutti gazed straight and sternly into my eyes. Not only wasn't she anything resembling the "Yiddishe Mama" song, she now appeared like the typical patriarch, a German authority figure. In her better moods, throughout my childhood and adolescence, we would laugh each time I pointed this out to her being rather suitable as a father image sporting a Bismarck moustache. For emphasis of her top hierarchy, she now claimed, "the rags," becoming terribly disappointed that the stack wasn't any higher. Immediately, she dictated a harsh letter to Mr. London. Feeling too weak and tired to contradict her, I complied with her demanding list.

"Leave the child be. She looks to me as though she suffered. Leave her be!" Vati tried to restrain her by coming to my rescue while keeping his eyes on the old-fashioned, steaming casseroles.

"Yes, the poor child, "she snapped, "who was probably wined and dined by the old man."

Here was my opportunity to escape of my original worry by explaining, "It's unbelievable how changed Antwerp has become! There is no Prager's, no "Café Riga", no "Bialistok Jewelry." Imagine, not even Sasha and soon, there won't be Mary nor the boys anymore. Of course, there's no uncle Manuel any longer." I went on to tell them about the relatives.

Upon tasting the scrumptious meat dinner, I was compelled to exclaim, "I haven't had a great meal like this for the longest time, Vati!" adding that this repast was the best event happening to me of late.

I would have enjoyed it fully would I not have observed Mutti scrutinizing the bundles. As she drew her breath for complaints, I cut her off by relating the long trek to Groenvinckstraat. Nevertheless, as she went on to dictate the grating letter to Simon, I gave in to her as well as to my fatigue. I would deal with the matter after a good night's rest, reporting the shocking scene of Erika's death.

I never had realized before how dull, poor and sad everything seemed. On the other side of the wall, little Joske started crying bitterly which reinforced my despair and hopelessness. As I was writing, something within me mourned, "Yes, little Joske, cry for me too. Go on, shed some tears for me also!" He did, crescendoing even more plaintively into a full lament.

Maybe I could get Mutti out of this "rag-letter kick" by telling my parents how while I resented these wretched *shmatas* they certainly eased my fall when fainting, by sheer luck protecting my head like pillows. The loss of inner constraint had me now reveal Erika's horror, the reason for my spell of unconsciousness.

After their being stunned and Vati's predictable reaction: moist eyes and sad nodding, he cleared his throat several times, then hesitantly said, "We, too, had some distressing news just a few days ago." THEY did come to take Abbuhl, the dentist, Bauman, the volunteer, and Beer, his young student of philosophy.

"Oh, my God!" was my outcry with my inquiry, "THEY" in the form of the brutes, the Feldgendarmery from Hasselt?!"

"Ja, ja, THEY were here and had left THEIR mark by taking these three men," Vati explained dolefully and worriedly.

Instantly, it occurred to me when I repeated Abbuhl, Bauman and Beer, that I was forced to scream out while repeating, "Abbul, Bauman and Beer! Oh, God! THEY seem to take the men alphabetically. Next THEY"LL come for Chelner, Conska and you! You must leave instantly!" I figured out and insisted. We took each other's hands as though to find strength and consolation.

"But then, what will happen to you, if I'm not here?"

"We'll think of something; anything! So far, THEY didn't take any women and won't in the future." I tried to soothe his worry about the Nazis' eventual reprisal.

After much deliberation, he said, most reluctantly, "So be it!" He added that his nephew, Maurice, was correct in that Brussels was much safer than Antwerp for various reasons. Therefore, it was suggested that Vati try Mutti's cousin, Gitta, in Brussels "the one I met when I was about nine—whose hand you kissed, gallantly, in the French style upon her arrival in our Köln apartment," making light of the present dismal situation.

Vati knowingly, yet sadly, nodded in bittersweet remembrance.

Getting back to the sorrowful present, I pointed out, "Since you did not visit the barracks regularly like most men or even Mutti, no one will notice you are missing."

"You see how smart our child is!" Vati said proudly. "We hadn't even realized the alphabetical order of the men."

Just to detour Mutti from her cloth obsession had elicited an immediate, major change in our lives. We had stayed up the entire night to plan, that if it should not work out with Brussels, our contact would be the Gerstels in Antwerp as long as they remained there. We were moving very softly while Vati was packing ever so lightly. It was an unexpected quiet, tearful "bye," when Vati left to catch the first train at dawn. Thus, it came about that we were left without him in the village for the sake of his safety.

I missed him terribly. Contrary to his usual lifestyle, he turned out to be quite a loner here, which was an advantage this time. As for me, I tried to go about my daily routine.

Tonight, I took my first "Bathsheba" bath in the tin tub. Then Mutti rinsed me off with the small bucket which made it appear like some sort of a ritual. Noises from above made me uneasy. Suddenly, in great distress, I had to scream.

"Mutti, look at that small opening! It is bigger, and listen! I hear something!"

Mutti, the usual alarmist, tried to calm me down by saying, "I always noticed it. It's the same size, I assure you. It's a cat!" she repeated as she was pouring the refreshing buckets of lukewarm water on me, while I was waltzing around haltingly in the primitive tub. I could hardly catch my breath from the water and the excitement as I screamed between pails: "It is such an eerie, weird feeling, Mutti!"

Hastening to wrap myself in a terry robe, I said, with some relief, "I really am much more comfy and well protected now."

The following day, Mutti and I acted as if Vati was still here. Hoeselt in April was most conducive to walking. Presently, it was clad in magnificent hues of green, embellished with trees in white and pink bloom, as though the entire village was dressed in its best gala to herald spring. We met other deportees and soon formed small groups. The ones who joined us remarked to Mutti, "Everything is blossoming, including your daughter!" Other couples and individuals added themselves. We hardly were aware of not being free people since all were in a jocular mood and, coincidentally, made the same remark about the budding nature and me.

Still hurting from Simon's rejection, their compliments surely perked me up until this fantasy ascended into reality. It was amazing how I finally reverted to my individual self. That's when I went to the cloister for the first time since my return from my fiascoed Antwerp trip. The nuns were thrilled to see me. There was lots of laughter and singing as they handed me their favorite music sheets, urging me to play the piano. I was saddened, though, when I continued my artistic darning of Vati's silk shirts, which they so admired.

Nevertheless, high in spirit as usual after having been in the company of the sisters, I returned home where I saw the three Molenaers children. As always, Lizy and Joske were happy to greet me, however, it seemed to be another story entirely with the middle child, Jani. She stared at me incessantly, but unlike in the past, her gaze was piercing, curious and most unkind. She had stayed on as her two siblings had left. I almost felt embarrassed under her scrutinizing me. When this mature twelve year old had gathered some courage, she asked me point blank, "Why did you kill our Jesus?" With this simple, but highly loaded question, it became suddenly crystal clear to me that I had witnessed, first hand, how it all came about: an innocent, sweet girl obviously coming from her religious class at school, where her young heart was inflamed with hatred, her child's mind poisoned with one of the most sinister, universal mental ills—ANTISEMITISM!

How fortunate we were feeling like free people. Shortly hereafter we were sent back: women to Antwerp men to Brussels because ovens weren't ready yet. The village of Hoeselt, Limburg Age 18.

At first I was stunned, but then I tried to sum up what I knew, mainly from what I had derived sporadically about catechism, when at times I arrived early toward the end of the bible studies at the Catholic public school which I attended in Köln.

I, the accused, had to prepare my defense with simple directness for the pre-teen: "The Jewish people were the very first to accept one sole God. Though invisible, their belief in him was unshakable. This was very holy to them, for religion was all they had left since enemies occupied their land. Their pride and joy Jerusalem, with its magnificent temple, was lost. Hence the Hep, Hep, Hep! (in the Roman mania for abbreviation) which had become, throughout the centuries, a mocking term against Jews, derived from 'Hierosolayam Est Perdita' (Jerusalem is lost!). Personally, I was tormented by this as a preschooler when all the bigger children would run after me, lynching style, with this menacing anti-Semitic singsong. It was very frightening and humiliating with their Jid! Jid! Jid!'s (derogatory German term for Jew) and 'Hep! Hep! Hep!'s. This 'Hep' had been used by the Roman Empire in a most hurtful way to remind the Hebrews of their losses, stripped of everything but their Torah. In fact, Jani, it was very much then as it is today. Do you Belgians have any say in your own country since the powerful Nazi occupation?"

"No, of course not!" was her correct answer, adding, "in fact, we are very suppressed!"

"That's exactly the way it was with the Hebrews under the mighty Roman conquerors, at the time when this young Jew, Jesus, presented himself as the son of God to the Israelites. They rejected that belief for the whole story seemed all too fantastic and abstract to them. They did accept him though as a prophet while his disciples insisted that he was King of the Jews. Well, the Romans surely did not take kindly to that idea, because not only did they want to be the sovereigns of the Jews but like the Nazis, their ultimate goal was to control the whole world. The Hebrews questioned his claims although they viewed him an instigator and a threat, they did not know how to handle the case of Jesus. After much deliberation between the Jewish tribunal and Pontius Pilatus (thus the expression: running from Pontius to Pilatus), the Romans finally decided to crucify him."

My other practical defense was my pointing out, "Crucifixion was the typical punishment by the Romans. Not that the Jews' method of ancient times was any kinder or faster: execution by being stoned—also lynching style was just as cruel and slow. But death on the cross clearly shows the Roman method. It is barely known that an entire road was lined with crosses upon which Jews were killed by Pontius Pilatus and other Roman notables. However, minorities are always accused of terrible things whenever matters don't run smoothly, or for the sake of fomenting dissatisfied people against a common enemy: Hitler is a modern-day perfect example of this!"

"If you were the first, how come you are a minority?" she wanted to know.

"Because Christianity throughout two thousand years had missionaries in the farthest corners on this earth often into the deepest regions of foreign lands. It is considered a good deed to spread Christianity while the contrary holds true amongst the Jews. It is extremely difficult to convert to Judaism. In most cases, it is strongly discouraged. A very valid reason of an idealistic nature is required. If finally accepted, the most rigorous methods to acquire Judaic knowledge are employed. That's basically how we became a people who were very few in number.

While I am at this, may I add that another Hebrew rule prohibiting the buying and selling of human beings had been established in the Talmud, an ancient scripture, which Hitler despised.

Also, the more modern and the newer religion one converts to, the better off one is. The Catholics, after their early struggle with the Romans and lions, fared better than the Jews. Then the Lutherans had and still have an advantage over the Catholics. Now, the Nazis—to many it's like a religion with their Pagan pomp and ceremony—are triumphing over all of them.

Then there is a different slant entirely: I was often an interpreter. Therefore, I am aware of the fact that a minute error may change the entire story from the original Latin and Hebrew into the ever-changing modern languages, as for instance, now, my Flemish." Smilingly, I asked, "So, Jani, was it really that terrible that we, meaning my ancestors of two thousand years ago did not become Catholics, and went on as they had been born? If they had converted, it certainly would have prevented my present suffering and fears, and I would not have been pinpointed as to have killed your Jesus and all of us would not have been deported to this place."

My defense seemed to have fallen on deaf ears. Either she was too young to comprehend or she did not want to understand. I felt quite crushed when she left without my side of the story having made any impact upon her.

Yet the entire Molenaer family continued to be just as nice as they had been from the beginning. In fact, when the brothers asked for Vati to help them in their métier, we felt compelled to confide the truth. Approving the idea of Vati's safety, they wanted to notify the mayor. Fearing this would generate a conflict between his heart and his duty, we all agreed to harbor the secret. The family regretted only that a farewell and "good luck wishes" to Vati could not have taken place in the light of his sudden departure. However, the Molenaers were happy for his being out of immediate danger, even though so far, no other men had been taken.

One evening they invited us to the village bar, a place filled with smoke and mirth, upon entering, everyone stared at us, we were greeted in a friendly manner. The owner barmaid with the protruding teeth welcomed us cordially, throwing me a special saucy glance. Each spare moment, she joined us, being full of fun and, yes, mischief. Many of the people especially the men, appeared elated that we were there, acknowledging this with a flirtatious nod. When she was a few tables away, every so often, the word "cat" got into my ear. At first, I did not give it any thought, but when the mentioning of said pet became more frequent, something dawned on me, and I looked at Mutti. But she in turn found so much enjoyment conversing in her sparse, cute Flemish with the Molenaer couple that it passed over her head. As the evening progressed, and the barmaid was less busy, she sat down in our corner, not taking her roguish eyes off me, she finally spat out with laughter: "De kat, the cat, ja, de kat!"

"Oh, God!" clasping my palm against my cheek in horror, I exclaimed: "Oh, God, my God!" Again I could not help repeating the same gesture, accompanied with outrage once more by : Oh, my God, de kat!" Feeling humiliated, embarrassed and very angry, in the light of all the onlookers, I did not know how to react publicly. My consolation was: King David did it to Bathsheba. But they were many and none of them was a Monarch, certainly not!

"I understand, you are enchantingly beautiful!" she exclaimed
coquettishly.

This infuriated, flabbergasted and flummoxed me even more.
In fact, endless adjectives expressing my shock and shame crossed
my mind, as all eyes were upon me.

Everyone in this bistro was observing me intently, listening to
each breath, each word, looking for any gesticulation.

Shall I sob, scream, scold them or cry and accuse? I controlled
all of these feelings while I was thinking and gazing at my half-
empty glass. Suddenly, my imagination conjured up the picture
of how Mr. Somers, the nice V.I.P. of Hoeselt jostled his
powerfully-built friend out of the way while the other Satyrs
were trying to catch a glimpse of me. I had an inkling as to who
was clandestinely fighting over the small opening, created by
them, for the best peek. But my visualizing Mr. Somers, shoving
his buddy's big head aside, made me burst into laughter. Mainly
the men followed, so did the barmaid, de Molenaers, even Mutti.
The entire house was brought down and the patrons turned into
cheromaniacs not unlike in the foodless restaurant at Ostende.
Only this time I was the catalyst and not a mere amazed onlooker;
having been glad it had taken this turn, with my being a good
sport instead of the hurt, ashamed ingénue. In the Shakespearian
sense: "All's well that ends well." On this note, our party left, all
in good-natured fun.

Later in the bedroom, Mutti and I talked about the kat, the
barmaid, the bistro and the impertinence of men. I felt flattered
when she confessed the following: "Your Vati and I agreed upon
one thing, when we commanded you: 'Be a guy!' True, both of us
wanted a boy—but mainly we meant: 'Be tough!' Yet tonight with
your feminine diplomacy and gentleness did you not only turn a
downright embarrassing situation—embarrassing—for the kind
of occurrence and our position here in the village—into gaiety—
and elegantly eased out of it, but you made a completely favorable
turnabout, thus saving our honor." With such enormous
compliments issuing from the one I always wanted to please so
desperately, I drifted into the wonderful world of dreams.

A beautiful, sunny morning greeted us. We rushed outdoors as fast as we could. Instantly, we were joined by the others. In a group we walked up the hill, about to pass the mayor's office. At this very moment he appeared. His soft, green eyes sparkled with excitement when he exclaimed in Flemish:

"Do I have some startling news to impart to all of you! I am going to the barrack in order to inform you that only minutes ago, I received orders from the Feldkommandant in Hasselt that all expelled women and children are to be returned, from where they were deported in the first place: Antwerp!"

I wanted to jump for joy and exclaim: how absolutely wonderful!— but refrained from fear of offending him. With the mayor, we all walked to our wooden meeting place where everyone present gathered around him to hear his speech given in a clear voice. He made this most important announcement, officially, ending on a somewhat apologetic note as he had done the very first time: "As usual this Nazi command appeared on such very short notice just to create more stress. You are not even left with a full week to liquidate your belongings." Then, looking at me, he added in a consolatory way: "It will be my pleasure to accompany you all the way to Antwerp."

The women were wringing their hands and clutching their husband's arms as if not wanting to let go of them. Mutti and I exchanged brief, meaningful glances. Occasionally, we were asked, how Vati was, but fortunately, not where.

Though our future was shaky, Mutti and I gladly got up early. The Molenaers had breakfast prepared for us, but we were happy just to enjoy the freshly brewed coffee to fully awake this spring dawn which promised a beautiful day in more than one way. Then the warm "Good-byes" and heartfelt thanks on our part and best wishes on theirs followed. Joske's eyes moistened when I bent down to embrace him for one last time. Since Lizy had a hard time bidding us "Bye!" she wanted to walk with us the long way on foot to the station for emotional and practical reasons, as well as help us carry our things. In contrast, Jani was just sitting there brooding. I merely waved to her as I had done in the past with my cousin Frima when I could not come to terms with her.

Indeed, the day had turned out to be lovely! The mayor sat in our compartment along with the Fass family. We chatted as fields and woods seemed to fly by. What a difference this westbound trip was from my last miserable voyage from Antwerp to Limburg! The mayor wished to meet us later for dinner. He gave me the local number, but since I would be at Gerstel's, I could not control my time. It was not possible to see Erna because she was in Germany now, whether for a visit to her family or permanently, her husband didn't know. When we bade "Farewell!" to the mayor at the Antwerp station, he offered to at least accompany us to a certain point which was Quellin Straat and de Keyserlei. Since we were unable to commit ourselves to anything, Mutti suggested to tentatively "take leave" from him while thanking him profusely since he had made our stay very pleasant. For five months we had not felt that we were Nazi prisoners, an emotion shared by each of the women and some children who were old enough to understand.

Then instead of our usual "Au revoir!" Betti and I knew that this time it was "Adieu!" since her plans were more shaky than mine. We embraced as she thanked me for my enriching idea of our English-French language swap.

Back in Antwerp, at Gerstel's doorstep, even, hard-to-please Mutti was impressed with the neighborhood, entrance, interior and, above all, the human warmth of a mere business associate to me, total strangers to her.

There was again that rare time when she and I understood each other without words when we spotted the fine table set in their elegant dining room, that in these foodless, hard times, we had not one, but two dinner invitations. I was glad about the loose arrangement with the mayor, so we saved face as not to look like ingrates to him. Anyway, it would have been impossible to leave the Gerstels in view of their hospitality and our animated conversation, and downright rude to interrupt with complicated phone plans.

We discussed their pending immigration to Cuba organized by street smart Moishe. Apprehension arose concerning their entry visas (especially remembering again the tragic fate of the "St. Louis.") Nowadays, there was in addition maritime war danger by German torpedoes. In fact, one of Mr. Weinstock's investors and acquaintance of both Vati and Simon, Mr. Stolz, had considered himself extremely fortunate to have been one of the last "well-to-doers" able to flee across the Atlantic. Their ship was hit by German U-boats and the entire Stolz family perished on the high seas.

We chatted till late and then had a wonderful night's sleep in their beautifully furnished guest room. "To leave all of this behind as we did three years ago." Mutti mused sadly. I recalled my recent conversation with Molenear's middle child Jani and felt compelled to murmur, still in utter disbelief, "Just because we were born Jewish or just because our ancestors did not convert to Christianity 2000 years ago—the lethal masses believe we are evil and they adore Hitler. Maybe some day in the distant future, these same idiots will laugh at him after they come to their senses when it'll be too late."

Following breakfast, we were to leave for Brussels, anxious to join Vati. I had missed him terribly during these few weeks of forced absence. My successful association with Gerstel was liquidated as of now, very much to my chagrin. When we bade them "Bye," as usual these days, one never knew, whether, when or where one would meet again.

Chapter 20

A streamlined, ultra-modern, blue, electric train took us to Brussels. This was a special 35-minute commuter from Antwerp to the capital with only one stop in *Malines* or *Mechelen* (in Flemish). Leaving la *Gare du Nord*, I realized how beautiful the Belgian metropolis really is. Thanks to poor *Yossel*, this lovely, sloping boulevard was not totally unfamiliar to me.

"Exciting as the city seems to be, I would rather be in another hilly town, namely San Francisco," I said to Mutti.

"Ach!" she waved me off with a dismissive hand gesture, "you, with your America, they never wanted us on their shores!"

By now, we were passing the Boulevard *Jardin du Botanique*, and up, up into a right curve, further up we went *into Ixelles*, a suburb of Brussels. After my French inquiry, we promptly found the house of Mutti's cousin. There, Vati stood in front of us as though he had wings on his heels after our first ring. The "*Wiedersehen*" joy was immense. He led us upstairs into an imposing drawing room, where lots of initial embraces, kisses, and tears marked this happy occasion.

The door flung open, and Gitta entered crying "*Siessel*" (Sweet one, Mutti's Jewish name) and Mutti replied "*Gietel*" (Good one, her cousin's Jewish name). "Little sweet one" and "little good one" had a lot to share. I couldn't help but visualize a huge turban filled with bananas, papayas, mangos, and exotic tropical fruits atop Gietel's head. She looked like an older, fatter, taller Carmen Miranda; even her glittering, dark eyes shifted wickedly sideways, and in my imagination I could hear: "Ayaya, I love you very much!"

Then her daughter Suzanne, a soft-spoken serious woman in her thirties entered. Her almond eyes strongly reminded me of

Lili's. Although I had met Gitta only once, I had vivid memories of Suzanne and Krijgstein, her gregarious blond husband in Cologne. When the need to flee arouse, Krijgstein chose suicide rather then leaving his country. Suzanne was left a widow and returned to Brussels with her five-year-old son Raymond.

She ushered me into her comfortable room where we chatted for hours on end, only to awake the following morning, after falling asleep on her wide bed. She confirmed what Maurice had said about the vast difference in anti-Semitism between Antwerp and Brussels. Since there was not a high concentration of Jewish people here, and also the Gestapo was extremely powerful in Antwerp, Jews here were not as persecuted here as there. My relatives here, for instance, were very successful in bag manufacturing business.

Just after lunch I set out to get acquainted with the capital! I hoped to enjoy the Boulevard *Adolph Max and la Place de Brouckère* as thoroughly as the *Keyserlei* and the *rue Neuve* as the *rue du Pelican*. The mountainous city was graced with old stately architecture. La Grand' Place was the most gorgeous Baroque square, showcasing the ornate City Hall. German officers frequented the picturesque sidewalk cafés.

The next day I ventured out, walking the long way downhill, from the *Porte de Namur* (my new abode, because we rented Gietel's upstairs) to the *Gare du Nord*, finally reaching the *Boulevard Adolph Max*, which indeed, I liked as much as *de Keyserlei* in Antwerp. However the stores, cafés and, above all, the people were unfamiliar to me. No sooner thought, as I was approaching the terrace of the majestic Hotel *Metropole* where all elegant wicker chairs and tables uniformly faced the entire plaza, I spotted Sofie and Norman. Though most incongruous in age and height, they seemed happy with each other. This was one of the very few times, I saw her smiling, and both were delighted to see me. They invited me to have coffee at their small table, while I told them all about my experiences in Limburg. They, in turn, informed me of today's refugees' trade trends.

With the help of a city map, I tried short cuts, which led me past the greeneries of the Royal Palace, the *Musee des Beaux-Arts*, and the *Palais de Congres* with its eternal flame to commemorate the fallen of the Great War. Each passing male, whether on foot, tram or car lifted his hat for a moment in a devout manner. But now what?! The map had forsaken me!—The Capital lay at my feet, but steeply downhill. How could I possibly get from this level, to the actual city below? I eventually found steps and small paths winding all the way to the heart of Brussels.

At first, I was confused as how to get here. The little, quaint, narrow streets with their overwhelming quantity of restaurants, boutiques, cafés and souvenir shops—displaying mostly facsimiles of their famous tiny *"Manneken Pis"*—had my head spinning. I felt very well compensated with this lively *"quartier"* having a charm all of its own, just the way I like it! At the end of my tour I came to *la Place de la Monnaie*, the internationally renowned theater and opera. This is when I exhaustedly dropped into a comfy wicker chair in "my new offices," the terrace of the *Metropole* Hotel. A suave waiter served me a *"filtre"*. I deserved this, especially, after my lengthy walk. It was oh, so long, since Simon, that I was deprived of all these little luxuries!

After frequenting "my" two business places, I learned that at the present, the vogue was trading in solid, heavy, 18-karat bracelets. Rapidly, I became reacquainted with former diamond associates from Antwerp and also met new people. Soon, I was part of that industry. Between deals, there was a "Tea *Dansant*," most conveniently located on the premises of the *Metropole*. I enjoyed the attention, the dancing, and was amused to watch the bassist—never having heard this big instrument used for jazz. He was plucking to that modern rhythm: *zoomm, zoomm, zoomm, zoomm,* which lent to the band a unique mellow sound. His swinging the huge fiddle, in a 360-degree turn, added to the visual excitement. As I was swept past him on the dance floor, he flirted with me, and I, of course, flirted right back.

In the spring of 1941, business was almost as successful as in the fall of '40. Only this time, I was nobody's protégée, and since my life was devoid of love, I plunged full force into my new "craft". On the Boulevard Adolph Max, I walked daily into every jewelry store to buy old 18k gold by the gram. Through Sofie and Norman's connections I found a contractor, who melted it down. Since I could not master the artistic technique, I explained my concept, and they were truly designed from my imagination. After wearing, thus modeling, my own creations the results were startling!

Once, just before closing time, I bought a collection of antique gold and was compelled to bring home this nice haul. As always, Mutti took great interest, and found among the many items two exquisite necklaces. In payment for her discovery, she kept one unusual piece. She generously endowed me with the still outstanding, but simpler jewelry, and the rest, I proceeded in my customary way: recycling old gold into fine bracelets. My trade was very much as that in Antwerp, dealing strictly with Jewish merchants. Why bracelets were the most sought-after articles at the moment, and where they wound up at the end, no one seemed to know. This business was en vogue and it was profitable even without Simon.

One mild evening, I walked with my parents past "my office," when a young man dashed breathlessly up the stairs from out of nowhere! He shook hands with Vati asking him whether he had heard the latest BBC transmission about Rudolf Hess, who was trying to persuade the British to form and alliance with his superior, Hitler. Of course, he was instantly arrested.

Willy, who conveyed this interesting news, was young, about my age, fair skinned with dark hair and eyes, which were shaded by long straight lashes. After talking with me he offered to meet me at "La Coupole" next Sunday.

Prior to entering this beautiful café, the wonderful euphonious wailing of Jewish-Hungarian strings filled my ears. Willy signaled to me while getting up to greet me. As I slid between the tables toward him, I bumped into a striking brunette. Before I could apologize, I touched a hard surface, realizing it was my own reflection in the mirror! Embarrassed, yet pleased, I continued my way through the seated well dressed crowd. When I met my own image on the other side again, I became aware that this charming place just appeared large because of the mirrored walls.

This was my first Brussels date and also my premier rendezvous *sans* Simon. Willy was a good looking, tall, slender man, far more befitting to my age than Simon, yet there was not anywhere near the impact that I felt with Simon right from the start. The conversation went on smoothly. The violin acrobatics, by Egon, added to the mesmerizing momentum. Besides of his talent, he was very impressive and when poised sideways, gliding the bow dramatically, his fascinating profile reminded me of Erika's. During a brief intermission, I informed Willy about her sad fate, but wanting to have an animated evening, I also told him about my first day in Antwerp and the Jewish girls. At first we conversed in German, because he originated from the Imperial City of Aix-la-Chapelle, which I only knew as the checkpoint and long stop at the Belgian border. Then our talks continued in French. While having these bi-lingual discussions, I developed the yearning to speak all the world languages, which I revealed to him.

He replied, "That certainly is an ambitious aim!"

"But where and how can I find the books? I am too busy at the moment to go to the *Berlitz School*." With a secretive grin, he failed to answer.

The vibrant Hungarian music resumed. Again, I was hypnotized. Many such lovely dates were spent with Willy. Though he was no Egon, he also played the violin well and rented a studio with a piano. Sometimes, he brought a friend who was great on the drums. Our Sunday morning musical trio was a delight. We also frequented the Jewish theatre or *La Gaiete*, to which I had been introduced by *Yossel*, where la petite, adorable Tomala still sang her heart out with: "*Tu m'apprendra, dis*!"—and of course, our evenings were crowned with the passionate sounds of Egon and his Gypsy band.

The mirrored room was always filled with the intensity of their music. The concert kept mounting, full of fire, into a furious finale. The brilliant performer was thunderously applauded, as though the café was a concert hall.

Throughout, I wished I had Simon by my side, for the entire rendition gave me a sensation not unlike his lovemaking! Though

Mutti condemned our relationship—this did nothing to diminish my longing for him—my relationship with Willy was condoned because I had no strong involvement with him.

When he accompanied me back to Ixelles and bade me "good bye" I discovered some excitement. After dinner "Carmen Miranda" invited us to her kitchen—where her husband composed funny limericks. They were mainly about the three of us, but were not offensive at all, *au contraire*, rather flattering. This mustached baldheaded man added his own melodies to his rhymes, and cherished the idea of entertaining us with a few different songs each night. His nocturnal "creations" would bring a lot of laughter to all of us. However "Carmen Miranda" seemed to despise her third husband. The more we were amused the more furious Gietel would become with her mate. What topped this parody was our amazement with how well the distinguished, aloof, prim and proper Jewish refugee maid eased right into the situation.

The difference between the two cities being so close together never ceased to amaze me: the utter desolation in one, and the total non-war-like atmosphere here.

Regularly we dashed into the salon to listen to the BBC's news in German. This was announced by the Morse code derived from Beethoven's 5th Symphony first bar. Though transmitted by the British—to me its sound was ominous, possibly caused by the deep bass of the broadcast tapping, or perhaps the connection with the death penalty. Most Jewish people tuned in nightly, despite the technical disturbances by the occupiers. Also, all kinds of Allied spy messages were sent across the Channel in such simplistic phrases: "Bring the milk!" "Take care of the cat!"

Fortunately my life ran a gentle course. My birthday, on June 15th, was first celebrated with my parents and then later at "*La Coupole*" with Willy. The highlight of my day, though, was receiving a neatly wrapped package with "Happy Birthday" printed in five languages. Not being of a destructive nature, as always, I carefully loosened the ribbon and paper. The contents revealed a brown mini *coffre*. With great curiosity and under the watchful, amused eye of Willy, I discovered a stack of thin books. They were Martin's

Fast Method to the Autodidactic Study of the Spanish Language. "What a splendid surprise!" I quipped with delight, while embracing him yet not daring to make my first move to kiss his well-shaped mouth, even though it and he had deserved some passion! It was a memorable Sunday birthday.

On exactly the following Sunday, June 22, 1941, the Nazis suddenly invaded Russia. Operation "*Barbarossa*" was a dark Nazi secret. Was it so called because of the German 12th century monarch Fredrick I, Red Beard, and the "Reds" I kept wondering.

One night Willy sighed, "Now, they are in the various corners of the globe attacking Russia, parading with the Italians for *Rommel* in Tripoli, North Africa, and they are certainly here!"

Most amazingly, all the German grandeur and occupation did not diminish my lifestyle. Again, it had taken business, private and social shape in Brussels. I never had imagined it possible, to be rather well off, once again, because in my mind the whole world had collapsed after Simon's split with me and the dwindling of the Jews in Antwerp. I was also so caught up in my gold bracelet manufacturing business, Willy and my latest hobby: studying Spanish I didn't realize that Greece and Yugoslavia had also been seized by the Nazis for some time now.

Willy was wonderful company and so was his family. Rosa, his sister, an exceptionally vivacious girl; her pretty face was dominated by her alluring—like her brother's—but very full lips. What's more, she was a magnificent soprano. Unlike her brother, she was small of stature, but vocally she produced a full range of powerful sounds. I was a first-hand observer of her when we formed a trio. We even rehearsed to record Zarah Leander songs, a film diva; I had enjoyed so much with Simon.

Rosa also became my friend, so did our respective mothers and sometimes we two girls would form a foursome to shop and then rest in a café. Mutti learned that their father was an early concentration camp victim even before Yossel. Most of the time, though, dates continued with Willy.

An amazingly wonderful summer had turned into fall. Each of these seasons though was marred by Nazi threats: shortly after having spent a splendid July Sunday with Willy at "*Le Bois de la Cambre*," we had to present our white IDs to be stamped by the authorities in both Belgian languages: "*Juif*" and "*Jood*." On a lovely October Sunday evening with a mild breeze when Willy brought me back from the theater, he said: "I guess, this is our last Cinderella date, after tomorrow, it's a shame, we must be home early according to the latest Nazi decree, which orders a 7 o'clock curfew for Jews. I need to bring you home around 6 pm so I can make it home, to my Bourse section, on time. Just imagine the severe penalties that could be imposed. They are just beginning with these ludicrous inconveniences." These were also the precise words used by Simon, when all the Jewish bank accounts had been Nazi-blocked. "This vexation, and then who knows!?" Willy sighed again.

"Therefore, we must enjoy whatever we can," I consoled and encouraged him.

Jews had to cut everything short or start earlier with the stress of rushing home on the dot; like obedient, frightened children or criminals in prison. The short-lived afternoons were warm and charming even though tribulations and insecurities were starting to manifest themselves.

Most fortunately, these long evenings were filled, though, with fun and fear, a most unusual combination. There was diversion because of the cute and sometimes naughty verses with Max's own "diseur" style tunes. Once my family was satired describing me as "*Pola Negri in the red frock!*" Gitta's husband, Max, really helped overcome our worries and anguish when we heard distressing and frustrating news on the BBC. It would be quite some time until the Royal Air Force could dream of becoming a match for the feared Luftwaffe. Also, that Roosevelt insisted upon remaining neutral. Two very shocking blows!

Nevertheless, my life continued its status-quo-pace. So did Vati's with Hans—being the latter's personal shopper. Therefore, Vati possessed a monthly train pass between Brussels and Antwerp, to facilitate travel on a daily basis. To him, getting there was half the fun, since he never failed to meet acquaintances on this 35-minute ride. These consisted of mostly refugees like us living in the capital now, with ties in Antwerp.

One morning, I received a letter from the Jewish community to be there in the Midi, (South Brussels) the "area Juive." I was more than amazed that they had my correct address. Though not having any idea what it was all about I was there on time, since, the neighborhood of *Anderlecht* was unfamiliar to me. To my astonishment it was "Paleface" who was trying to find me! For a split second I fantasized that Simon had sent him here, no, impossible, Simon had already been in the "Unoccupied Zone" close to a year. I found out that "Paleface" only wanted me to continue in my diamond business on an expert level. He conducted tests right then and there. He regretted that I lacked the visual skill to distinguish the minute differences between white, whiter, blue-white, bluer, clear, and clearer, impeccable under the lupe. Mutti would have passed with flying colors!

"Paleface" lamented, "I went through such trouble to locate you, for I wanted you to be my scout in Brussels. I knew you were here and thought of your trade-savoir-fair and above all I valued your trustworthiness . . . I am so frustrated!" He complained while folding the varied parchment packets containing the valuable diamonds into their original prescribed pattern. Without "*Mazel and Brache,*" he left, whereafter, I stopped at the office to inquire how they had my correct address. A tall secretary explained that the Nazis compiled the addresses of all the Jews in Brussels. It was called "*Association des Juifs en Belgique.*"

"In other words," I sadly replied, "the SS and Gestapo are capable of really getting their hands on any one of us in the entire city!"

For a while I sat there motionless, yet thinking and developing the idea of not registering, but where to find a cooperative landlord? When I finally came out of my daze, I spotted an advertisement for French stenography derivative of the "German Unity Shorthand," I was instantly interested. Even though I was pressed for time because of my gold trade, I had fun with learning. As I continued my autodidactic Spanish studies, and then added French shorthand, I wondered if I could apply the same methods to create my own English stenography, and it worked!

Every Monday afternoon, I managed to be there for my tiny class. Other than myself there were only three female refugees. After each lesson, we would walk home together and pause at the eclectic, yet, very imposing *Palais de Justice*, which, for its majestic, dominant position overlooking the city below, it is most impressive. Miriam, one of the girls in my class, a natural beauty, conversed a great deal with me. She could not stop raving about Paris, where she had lived right after her escape from the dreadful Crystal night. Miriam's descriptions made me see Paris through her eyes, always finishing with: "Paris is not just the greatest city, it's a feeling!" Even when it grew colder, we marched to our parting point, the Palace of Justice—court.

Usually, the frigid winter season is not my favorite, but Monday December 8[th,] a sunny day was invigorating, when I went straight from the apartment to my steno class. Upon arriving there the whole place was in an agitated state. It was hard for me to discern if it was happy excitement.

"Pearl Harbor, Pearl Harbor in Hawaii! The tall secretary spat, "It was attacked yesterday by the Nazi partners in crime—the Japanese". "It was in vicious, violent Hitler-style on the American fleet. We know very well in such raids human lives can never be spared," she lamented.

Nonetheless, a feeling of guilty satisfaction for self-preservation emerged, especially amongst us four émigrés, and we could read this in each other's eyes. Finally, there was a glimmer of hope for us, in that Roosevelt no longer could afford to remain neutral. We discussed this in the shadow of the Palace of Justice, hoping that at last justice would be done. Indeed, that very same week, the mighty US entered the war. We had high expectations. On subsequent Mondays, our studies and meetings continued. Instead of boys and fashion we discussed politics.

Miriam pointed out the irony in that "the Nazis are so fanatically race and religion-conscious, yet the Japanese are part of their Axis!"

"They don't even know how to distinguish race from religion, always referring to us Jews, as the vilest race, but we observe a faith whose antiquity is well over 5000 years old. Their Allies are lacking in Caucasian characteristics on the outside and inwardly. How contradictory can one get!?" I exclaimed in great dismay.

"May I take this a step further?" We were asked by our classmate of "Aryan" appearance, "the word *Aryan* actually means an Aristocratic tribe of Hindu-Persians!" Yet nobody ever questioned the "purity" of this "new and holy" Nazi term to distinguish Germans as superiors of the rest of the world: Aryans vs. us, the sub humans: the Non-Aryans. Look at the four of us!" I suggested and we all laughed.

The fourth steno student emphasized: "Well, that is the German problem, precisely. The Teutonic Patriarch dominance of never questioning, but blindly accepting, and believing, and above all else blindly obeying!—Which brought Hitler this far. I would love to immigrate to the US for this reason alone: The Declaration of Independence. "WE THE PEOPLE," meaning if I were American, I would have the right to dissent for I would be the people!

It became evident at the present time that the *Wehrmacht* needed gasoline desperately, mainly for the Russian front. Consequently more and more Belgians had to use public transportation. This created the apparent perilous human "grape bunches" hanging out of all the overloaded trolley exits. It was a droll, yet, strange sight. This had directly affected me, because my daily route was very long and time consuming, and the return uphill was quite tiring, if I had to do it on foot.

We were aware that Gietel wasn't so good nor Siessel so sweet. These two strong willed cousins got into more than one squabble. Because of this tension, Mutti wanted to move out. I looked upon this as a chance to better myself, by living closer to town. The next morning, Mutti was particularly fuming. After another argument with Gietel, she accompanied me by trolley to the city. Just before we got to our destination, Mutti suddenly insisted that we get off. I felt that this was probably her sixth sense at work again. This time, I shared her desire.

We found ourselves on *la Place Madou* and walked the hilly lively street, which took us to a rather large square with a charming small church, *la place St. Josse*. To our left, two streets were forking into the plaza. Half pulling me, Mutti said: "Just think how lucky we were with our place on *Groenvink Straat* in Antwerp, which we got because I suggested you ask the green-grocer with the red cheeks. Now, go over to that young big Huckster!" she urged, "and ask him about an apartment around here." I did just that and he, indeed, pointed out a three-story-house on the far side of *la rue Saxe-Cobourg*. "A Brussels's street with such a German name?" Mutti questioned in surprise.

It was a nice enough house. A tall, slim, middle-aged, stern-looking woman opened the door. After I inquired, in French, we were shown into a fine oak-furnished semi office-salon. His wife dwarfed Mr. Buts, her distinguished husband, who sported a trim, short beard and white smock. He was a manufacturer of genuine amber cigarette holders. The very first question posed by him was "*Vous etes des Juifs?*"

Just after thinking to myself with the greatest astonishment, "Oh!" I answered simply "*Oui, Monsieur!*"

"In that case you may see the apartment." He said in a friendlier tone, Oh?! I thought again, but this time with relief.

The furnished *quartier* was wonderful. "Look a piano!" I could not help exclaiming. We saw a sterile looking, lab-like, white kitchen. The bathroom was on the landing half a flight up. We signaled to each other that we would love to have it. Back downstairs we started negotiations. I recalled that the Nazi authorities had knowledge of each and every Jew in Belgium at their fingertips. Therefore, my urgent plea to the Buts was, renting without registration. Unfortunately, my request was denied. Although, I was persistent, it was to no avail. Mr. Buts pointed out that with our carte blanche we were perfectly legal and that there was no danger. "You are right, Mr. Buts. There's no peril, not just yet," I sighed.

We were enthralled with the flat. I had the additional thrill of being independent of transportation. When we went to register at the local precinct, Mutti and I were legitimate, but there was a discrepancy with Vati's papers. Naturally, for safety's sake, he was compelled to take off from the Limburg village. The police advised us that the only place that could remedy this would be none other, but the Gestapo headquarters. Again, as in previous and precarious situations, it was decided for me to take yet another courageous step into Ave. Louise at the feared and mighty Nazi stronghold. Accompanied by the usual panic, I ventured into the lion's den with Vati waiting only but a few meters away.

On the top of the elevator entrance, there was the same sign as in *Hasselt* stating clearly: "NO dogs, NO JEWS allowed." Then a lift arrived carrying an operator. He was not just an elevator man, but also served the dual job of being a caseworker. Briefly, I stated the purpose of my "visit" on our way up, then I was led through spacious offices. Shortly thereafter, a tall civilian in a greenish hairy felt hat, far too wintry for the season, entered. Instead of becoming more fearful, my anxiety diminished upon seeing this bespectacled man. I envisioned that he could have been Mr. Meskendahl, our jovial insurance agent in Köln. The mere resemblance allowed me to get over my initial apprehension. Facing me from the edge of the desk, I had his undivided attention. After my statement, he questioned exactly what I was afraid of. "Why didn't your father come himself?" What could I say?—That Vati felt a Jewish man's life is more threatened by the Gestapo than a young woman's? Instead I explained that he was too sick to present himself. Even though this was a simple matter, deep down, I expected him to push a button and then, one of his hoodlums would come get me. Therefore, Vati's idea of setting me in the path of peril plagued me.

When I got his consent for Vati to legally reside here, I challenged myself to boldly ask for this in writing for submission to the precinct. He replied: "The word of the Gestapo is good enough and carries a lot of weight." I wholeheartedly agreed upon the last part silently and took leave rapidly. Before I could find the staircase, the same elevator man once again dared me to step on to it, and stared down at me all the way from the top floor of the infamous high-rise to the bottom. Small pearls of perspiration were on my forehead. What happy relief it was to be free and breathe the fresh air, able to give Vait the "good" results.

"It would have been far better, Vati, if the trip would not have been necessary. If only the Buts, who seemed Jew-friendly, would not have been so adamant about our registration."

I hadn't heard his sad "*ja, ja,*" for quite some time now. He then admitted, "I'm so ashamed and so sorry that my cowardice resulted in sending you instead of presenting myself." Then he asked, as he was caressing my cheek, most fatherly, "weren't you scared to walk into the wolf's lair?"

"Yes, especially having to use the elevator with the threatening sign. Yet the "operator" made me get on, and when realizing that he was a case worker, I feared it was one of their mortal traps."

"Oh, I'm so sorry!" he sighed as tears filled his eyes.

For a moment I thought he should be, but I continued to tell him about "Herr Meskendahl," and that I had felt more at ease from the sheer resemblance, even though the thought of it all being a ruse, had never once left me.

After the very reluctant registration, living at 40 rue Saxe-Cobourg was a delight. Every free minute I played Puccini's and Verdi's arias, sometimes I had fun emulating a soprano, especially "*La Traviata*" in German, since I still had my sheet music from Köln. Also, I practiced with Zarah Leander songs that were intended to be made into a record with Willy, Rosa, and myself. Our big musical moment to create our disc had come. After the fait accompli everyone had to admit that the sound of our ensemble was professional and harmoniously delectable. In other times, we really could have tried to commercialize it, but this wasn't even discussed by our trio of Jews.

Soon, the disconcerting notice came for us to pick up the yellow Jewish Star of David. This was incredibly distressing news. Exactly on my birthday, June 15th, I went to "*L'association des Juifs en Belgique*" to fetch a bunch of these ugly rags. Until now, I had thought of yellow as being a cheery and sunny color, but these were a depressing shade. The sadness was emphasized by the inky edges and in its center the black Hebrew script spelled "Jew." It was such a doleful homecoming with this newly forced acquisition. We looked at each other and could not help concealing our tears.

Mutti, in her pragmatic way, got her composure together and figured out how each square of fabric could be formed into a star. This symbol of Jew-hatred and identification was thus born. Although my birthday was veiled in enormous tristess, it wound up being pleasant after all due to friendship, music, and the fact that I received literally buckets of roses.

The following day, I placed my yellow star as Nazi-prescribed near a Jewish heart, underneath my left breast, disgracing my beautiful summer dress and marring my overall appearance. Since I had a late start due to mourning this disquieting spot on my chest, I took the trolley. When I got on, all at once as though it was a command, from all corners people jumped up to offer me their seats. There were some German soldiers observing this silent rebellion of various passengers. It was a feeling of triumph and enormous warmth that there were still people on our side, even at the risk of endangering themselves. Fortunately, these military men were neither fervent Nazis nor did they want to make waves. Upon exiting, I nodded gratefully, but one alarming thought kept turning in my mind: to wear this star was so public, so vulnerable, and so dangerous. I enjoyed momentary comfort at a small table, and while the coffee was dripping into my glass, I developed an idea. Yes, the star had to be worn, come what may, for it was under severe or even death penalty not to, but under any circumstance, it must be shielded from all to see. Yes, I'll have my dressmaker tailor a bolero to go on top of each dress. Indeed, the short button-less jacket was a sound trick; for it made me feel much safer on the streets. This unsightly yellow patch served a double purpose: psychologically, as a symbol of shame and, pragmatically, to distinguish us, Jews, from the rest of the population.

One beautiful afternoon, while walking with Mutti alongside "*Le Bon Marche*" (the largest department store in Brussels) in heavy pedestrian traffic, a young blond *Luftwaffe* soldier in blue passed us from the opposite direction, and most angrily pointed at my star and complained that it was not completely visible. I felt aggravated and crushed; the only thing he noticed of my entire appearance was the ugliest aspect.

Mutti, however, after cursing him under her breath, advised that we must examine each garment to see that it naturally falls as we move, so that this will never happen again. "Don't feel hurt because of that '*Passkudniak*,' consider it a wise criticism. Who knows he might have done us a favor." I was moved that she viewed it this way, and in the process made me feel better.

Once, as Mutti and I walked down the slope I heard someone call us from behind. It was a gorgeous, tall, young woman who looked like a showgirl. She knew both of our names, yet neither of us recognized her. After she identified herself I candidly exclaimed "Sabine Berger! God, did you grow up beautifully!" She and her sister were in my religion class with Dr. Simons in *Köln-Mülheim*. I noticed that every so often she touched her shinbone in pain, whereafter she explained that a few days ago she was at the Gestapo on behalf of her boyfriend. During her plea, one of them kicked her while saying "*Du verfluchte arrongante Judenhexe!*" (You damned arrogant Jewish witch).

When I told her about my experience, she answered, "You always have such sweet manners, but I never could or would be servile to them. She insisted for us to visit her, and when we did she was in bed. The pain in her leg was so intense that she had to seek professional help.

At the moment, there was no time for Puccini or Verdi. We were busy with our wardrobe, making sure that the star was sewn as far left as possible. After that I saw my friends regularly again. Since Rosa had to do all the food shopping with the rationing stamps, we agreed to meet at her flat and go out in July.

The July day to meet Rosa had come. As usual I looked forward to seeing her, and hopefully her brother as well. I went to the tram stop and waited a bit, but then something from within alarmed me. Something completely inexplicable made me turn and hasten back home. Upon arriving back at the Buts, I used their phone to call and cancel our meeting, which is quite out of character for me.

Later on, Vati returned from his daily commute. This time, however, he was agitatedly gasping "Oh, weh! Oh weh!" just as he did two years ago at the coastal villa. He threw himself into a chair and his head into folded arms upon the table. In muted tones between sighs he managed to mutter, "At the Mechelen station the same type of brutes that brought us to Limburg entered the train in steel helmets with machine guns and murderous looks. Anyone wearing a yellow star or suspect of being Jewish had to get off the train! With a few exceptions, almost all of the passengers were asked for their "*carte d'identite.*" As they were passing, I had the *Brüsseler Zeitung* tucked into my left jacket pocket, concealing my yellow star! Just think of my poor heart! I was one of the very lucky few they did not bother at all, mistaking me for a German civilian."

"Oh, how awful, how terrible!" we all moaned while pacing the floor. At this moment, Mrs. Buts called from downstairs, in her stern way, "Mademoiselle, telephone!"

"Hello?!" cried Willy nervously. Then, while trying to control himself, he asked barely above a whisper, "do you have any idea what is happening? No one, of course, could have known, but I'm terribly curious why you called off our date?"

"It was just, well, an inner voice that absolutely forced me to turn back." I tried to share Vati's story with him, but he excitedly interrupted me.

"Something horrible happened here in Center City and around the entire Bourse section! They just swept anyone that was Jewish off the streets and drove them away in truck loads! An Aryan eye witness told me that one man pleaded that he wasn't Jewish " . . . please believe me, I'm not Jewish! I'm not Jewish . . ." he was commanded '*Zum Hosendoktor!*' (to the pants doctor), where he was to be checked if he was circumcised. The Wehrmacht's lorries just rolled away with men and women. How lucky you were with your premonition. You could have been taken away to God knows where! Bless your insight!" His voice then lowered an octave as he lamented, "Our lives are dismal now."

"There is more!" I finally spat. "The destination may be Mechelen. I told him of Vati's train ride. "The reign of terror has just begun here in Brussels."

After briefly reporting the terrible happenings to the Buts, I dashed up to inform my parents. I told them how people were amassed like stray dogs. Though gloating over my good luck, we were in agony because of today's horrors.

It was a warm sunny day when two men rang our bell. They were officially sent by "*L'Association des Juifs.*" to give us two forms; one was addressed to Vati and the other to myself—nothing for Mutti. Breathlessly, we read the printouts. Made by the virtue of the Jewish, not Nazi, authority! It dictated that we were to "*stellen*" ourselves within 48 hours and bring blankets and food for 24 hours. The last phrase had me up in arms. It made me visualize facing a life of poverty-stricken degradation, annihilating the last traces of human dignity and values that any freedom loving person stands for. Right then and there, my mind was made up, come what may, I would stick to my guns and be a forger of my own fate. What I had failed to do, when my future hung in balance with Simon, I'd rectify now, no matter what! Besides, one could only get so lucky once! I also had a certain arrogance; what? Me! Work for the Nazis! Ha! They had another thing coming! Plus, who knew what kind of labor I might be forced into. As these self-convincing thoughts went through my mind, Mutti fainted and suddenly dropped on to the floor. We all tried to revive her, since this occurred in extreme cases. I used my method of putting 4711 Cologne underneath her nose and pulling her feet and legs up to allow the blood flow to her head. When she came to, she could not stop, and understandably so, with "Oh, weh! Oh, weh!" accompanied by gestures of utter fear and despair. Watching her was extremely touching and dramatic. Our lives had taken a tragic turn, because we were despised in the entire world.

The two conveyers of this "Job's Message" attempted their utmost to persuade and convince us very calmly that there would really be nothing to it, and everything would be fine. "It's just to work for the Germans." The Jewish "Nazi tools" took off and left us with both summonses. As always, the more they persisted, the more I resisted, by conjuring up unknown terrors, which might give credence to my worst nightmares. No, I would not go down that road! My decision was crystallized.

Chapter 21

The following noon, after we received the chilling message, I was once more a fugitive, running from the law for my crime of being Jewish.

Mrs. Buts took me to the country, as she said: "I must rescue you from this chaos. The faster we act, the less chance you'll be captured—at least not yet". Ironically, the day was the brightest. Occasional laughter tinkled as we passed by peaceful villages on the long-distance trolley.

We walked from farmhouses to barns. Everyone seemed to know and respect Mrs. Buts. Nevertheless, again, it was apparent that I was the most undesirable alien in a hostile world. Mrs. Buts tried her best throughout these very long, warm hours to find a place for us.

In the shadow of a red sunset, we returned. There was no seat for me, so I stood wearily during the entire trip. My companion was more crushed than I. The pristine beauty we passed had a consolatory effect upon me, and also a practical thought: after having been there, it became clear to me that hiding in these rural districts would make us far more conspicuous than in a crowded city block with lots of pedestrian traffic. In a sense, we were beggars, yet also had to be choosers—carefully selective. I imparted my newest survival idea to my parents at once.

At any rate, we were staring at a sad reality: we could no longer stay with the Buts and had to move fast. These were tense moments when we were forced to leave our comfort zone instantly.

"*Ja, ja*!" Vati sighed. "The modus operandi of the Nazis is surprise in military strategy as well as their war against us Jews. I was so upset the other day on the train when they suddenly *chapped* (snatched) the Jewish passengers in Mechelen, I forgot to tell you I briefly saw the nephew of Manny Stern, the tax lawyer from Köln who committed suicide with his Dutch bride. The rather youngish Mendel Mandel had escaped concentration camp before. Now, on the train, he had to present his *carte d'identité*. Then— come to think of it—he was no longer there. Remember this tall, lanky blondish man? Just before THEY stormed the train, he gave me his address here, in the largest suburb of Brussels, Schaerbeck."

"We must go there immediately to find out from his very 'Aryan' looking wife what became of him, whether he, indeed, was taken by THEM. And who knows? We might find shelter there," we all agreed, and were soon on our way.

"It's a nice, lively neighborhood, the way I want it," I exclaimed upon arriving.

This naturally light blonde Meta, whom I knew slightly, was a most serious, fashionable woman in her late thirties. A giant golden cross was shining on her fair chest. She pointed to it, stating: "This was the last gift from Mendel. I feel safer with it because it emphasizes my Gentile looks. Plus it's practical in case of a financial emergency. Feel the weight of this 18 carat solid gold piece! No more will I see him, no more will he take care of me. He's such a go-getter, yet he can't escape THEM. We were each other's support system, though not officially married." She raved while looking down at her enormous symbol of Christianity. I could not help thinking about the irony of religion depicted by Hieronymus Bosch and how misunderstood and thus dangerous any faith can become if carried to extremes.

"So then THEY did take him off the train?" Vati could not suppress his astonishment as Meta could not suppress her tears. Yet she did not seem to be one to dwell on sentimentalities, and before she even knew the details of our calamity, she offered to have us stay at her large apartment. There was a long corridor branching into many rooms on either side.

"You can remain here a few days until you find some good souls willing to let a flat without registration. Very soon, I'll have to do the same. But right after breakfast, I'll take your daughter to my hairdresser. It's dangerous to be so striking and different looking. Another pretty blonde will be just fine," she advised while studying me like a portrait. "Does everybody agree?" she asked anxiously. As she touched my hair, looking at it carefully, she stated to my parents: "Tomorrow, both of you can rest for the hard hunt ahead, because this 'Aryanization' will need a double process. Many hours are involved."

Being a blonde was not unbecoming. The bit of green in my eyes was more prominent, projecting a lighter aspect. It was interesting to examine my image in the mirror. We were pleased with the startling results, which would hopefully add to my security.

The following day, my first as a blonde, we went earnestly flat hunting. Our desperate search for a *quartier* without registration around the *Bois* de la Cambre—where I had spent many pleasant hours with Willy, Rosa, or both—was regrettably unsuccessful, even though in Brussels there was not nearly as much anti-Semitism as in Antwerp. I learned this fact for the first time from Maurice. I now wondered about him and the family since there was no contact between us. At least I was confident of my cousins' safety because of their Belgian birth. After all, von Falkenhausen, the highest command of Belgium and Reeder, another Nazi satrap, pledged through Cardinal van Roey to spare the Belgian Jews to King Leopold's mother, Queen Elisabeth.

As a crimson sun was setting in back of this forest's lush beauty, Mutti stated: "Since it's impossible to find anything, maybe it would be better for you to *stellen* yourselves."

Appalled and shocked, I gritted my teeth with a crisp "NO!" and continued: "No one, but no one will lead me astray anymore! I have to follow the dictates of my own will and conscience. I have the youth, health and stamina—in fact, all three of us do—to escape this tragic condition! I'm prepared to live a Spartan life but not as THEIR prisoner. Tell me anything, Mutti, but never, ever mention or even think about *stellen*! I listened to you once, though lucky with Hoeselt, it still stirs dark emotions within me. It's an unusually beautiful summer. I would rather sleep here under the stars than give myself up. Here, there are no snakes nor wild beasts—except the Nazis—and our lives would be much safer."

When we came literally, but alas not figuratively, out of the woods, I noticed "Rosier's Real Estate" and said: "I'll try—it's all a chance. We've been surrounded by danger since the unforgiving occupying forces marched in here. I'll risk it and endeavor, for effort breeds success," I said, sad that in order to survive, I must forego my desire for the artistic creativity my soul craves.

After I brushed my blonde mane and looked into a mirror, I took heart and was about to walk into the agency, stopping short with: "But I don't know quite how to handle it. Do I put the cards on the table or is it preferable the 'underhanded' way? They will be closing any minute now."

Vati suggested I follow a Jewish saying which translates: "You must judge as you are confronting the bull! Good luck!" I threw them a kiss and with lots of courage, I entered.

Two middle-aged, well-groomed men were present. The one at the big main desk was big himself with a kind, chubby, jolly face. I liked him instantly, but the one at the roll-top, I wished I could conjure away. He was Gallic looking and picturing him in farmer's clothes, he resembled the mean Frenchman in the barn who kicked the woman. Whatever this "Grouch" was doing, he stopped cold in his tracks and listened. I felt he was observing my every move without really watching me. I feared and perceived him to be a threat. I definitely had to keep the truth from that Grouch so long as it was feasible. What a shame "Fatcheeks" was not here by himself, especially after he found a flat on his list. It must have been far away. I knew Brussels well by now, but was amazed that I had never even heard of this section. But then I thought, far away from what—midtown? I will not, if ever, see the gold ornaments of the fantastic Medieval Grand' Place glistening along with my 18 carat bracelets again, even being in the same city. After this reflection I said: "Fine, we'll take it!"

"Who is going to sign the lease?" Fatcheeks asked.

None of us had thought of this legality. From now on, I had no choice about revealing our secret or not, for my parents' language was a dead giveaway, but we were anxious to have a roof over our heads. I called them inside. The Grouch just kept thinking, brooding and staring at us from the corners of his eyes. This was most disquieting, but what could we do in our plight?

Returning to her place, we imparted the good news to Meta. The next day we went to that real estate firm. The Grouch showed us the way, which was, as I assumed, to be endless, and the walk from the trolley stop everlasting till we arrived at a small roundish plaza. On it, there were a few unpretentious houses forming a cul-de-sac. I thought this was great since there was no vis-à-vis at all.

The flat would have been fine, but it was in deplorable condition and needed an enormous amount of work. But again, what were we to do? Right then and there, we stayed. Right then and there, my poor parents started to work in that horrible dirt. Each movement they made caused us to cough and sneeze from dust. Oh, but I discovered one very nice thing: a balcony! I fled onto it and started my work—studying—as they performed theirs most efficiently and diligently. This continued over the entire weekend. On Sunday afternoon, looking in from the outside, I could hardly believe my eyes: not only was it immaculate, but also very cozy! After they freshened up, I ran inside to congratulate and embrace them. They were very proud of their domestic accomplishments.

I spent a great deal of time outdoors and did my self-assigned lessons. Every so often I paused to admire and enjoy the cleanliness and ambience of my parents' creation. The family harmony—prevailing now—was most gratifying and soothed my emotional turmoil.

One beautiful Sunday, I liked my fair reflection in the mirror and sported one of my fine custom-made dresses—from my diamond-Simon era, a green one. It indeed emphasized the emerald of my eyes. All the artistic endeavors I would have tried now, especially those requiring youth, beauty and talent, were going to waste, and I had to be grateful in the process, quoting a German proverb—"Turn on a happy face to a nasty game!"—or a song: "—though your heart is breaking keep on smiling!" How I wished to see, observe and be amongst people; also, to be seen and observed! I did the next best thing from a nearby phone booth. I called my sibling-friends, but could not reach them. So I wrote a letter to them without my address, hoping their spinster-landlady might forward it and they in turn would do the same with the Buts.

I was able to contact Meta though: "You reached me just in the nick of time. I must go into hiding like you, and guess what! I'll be so close to you that were I to carry a steaming cup of coffee, it would still be hot upon arriving at your flat. Please understand that no one is to know my address." We wished each other the very best and a miraculous escape of Mendel as he had done in the past.

We had brought along only the household items and clothes that were absolutely needed, leaving most of our meager possessions at the Buts'. One day, just as we were starting to feel settled and for the fun of it, I had been wearing my green frock so I could admire myself, narcissistically, in the mirror, the bell downstairs rang loudly and incessantly. There was a man outside wearing a hat. We consulted nervously about what to do and decided we had to open, for it was imperative for our safety to know why he came.

The stranger presented himself as the Gestapo without speaking a word of German, stating he was with the Belgian Gestapo, which I'd heard existed, indeed. Right away, I knew what he was after even before he asked for a huge amount of Belgian Francs. My suspicion had been confirmed: he was a blackmailer. I had left the house-door ajar so my parents would have an idea about what was going on. I had taught Mutti French and was now hoping she understood this heated shakedown. Fortunately she did, for she stepped out of the house all dressed up and with a smile greeted me with: "*Bonjour, Mademoiselle, comment ça va?*" "*Merci, ça va bien, Madame!*" . . . and off she went, this "neighbor" of mine! I had to suppress my admiration for her clever survival trick while negotiations continued. But when the stranger threatened that giving him the money was the only way for us to live in liberty, I felt compelled "to acquiesce."

"I shall accompany you," he offered in a somewhat softer voice.

"Oh, no *Monsieur*, this will ruin the whole scheme!" I vehemently objected, hoping Mutti had put my purse into her net shopping bag, for I sensed that this creepy person would follow me were I to look for it—and what about Vati?—so I just had to have faith in Mutti's efficiency. This was my moment to assure and reassure the extortionist that I would come back with a big haul of cash for which he, in turn, would keep quiet about our whereabouts.

So long as he watched me, I walked at a normal but fast pace. The second I was out of his sight, I started to run that endless distance toward the trolley stop in this unknown neighborhood. After all, I had been here only once before, led by the treacherous Grouch who I was sure had masterminded this chantage idea. I felt confident I was running in the right direction, but now I began to doubt it, for all I passed was brushwood and undergrowth. I was expecting to get closer to a more trafficked section and there was nothing but these ugly stick bushes. I was glad, though, to finally see a man walking a dachshund. I crossed over while constantly looking to see if I was being followed. I felt relief that this was the correct way, and when I stepped up my gait through the tall weeds, I finally reached a wide, lively avenue. Before I could see tracks or anything, there they were, both of my parents! I felt a miraculous joy not unlike the one when I found them on the *Flucht* underneath the crooked tree. The momentary elation of having escaped and been reunited made us forget our fugitive fear, even though we were now in its grasp. I imitated Mutti facetiously—"*Bonjour, Madame, comment ça va? J'éspère que vous avez pris mon sac* "—while embracing and kissing her, as she had indeed remembered my purse. "But *Monsieur*," I hugged Vati: "How in the world did you get here? I never saw you exiting the front door!"

"I never did," was his proud reply. "I played Renaldo Renaldini stunts from balcony to balcony."

"Of course he stumbled upon a half-naked woman," Mutti interrupted but this time playfully. He smiled, setting forth most seriously: "Index finger on my lips, I pleaded with her not to scream and felt in danger then, but fortunately she obliged, enabling me to continue my swashbuckling adventure until I wound up on a different street entirely."

"Absolutely fantastic!" I exclaimed in candid admiration. It was strange that at such a stressful time we each were overwhelmed with euphoria and harmony for we had managed to flee and find one another. At this moment, the usual crowded tram arrived. I had no idea about our destination nor where we would be sleeping now, for we never returned to that apartment. Although separated by many passengers, Vati must have sensed my concern, for he made a facial and hand-quieting gesture. Most people had gotten off and so did we, in order to change lines, when Vati said: "We'll go to Woydeslawski in Schaerbeck."

He seemed to know the whole nice residential area when we arrived. With great anticipation, we rang the bell of a sturdy three-story apartment building A stunning dark-haired beauty à la Hedy Lamar let us in and led the way to the second floor. It was great to be received by smiling, familiar faces. I recognized the interesting, good features of Mr. W., his tiny blonde wife and 11-year-old son Harold. For the first time, I came face-to-face with Mrs. Schwartz, and it all came back to me. The embarrassing moment with Simon when Mutti rattled on about this giant of a woman, Mrs. Schwartz, having a petite only child, Mrs. W. We were introduced to the gorgeous tall "door opener," an "Aryan" Luxemburger, her Jewish husband and his not very intelligent looking brother. They lived close by the Buts. Mrs. Schwartz was about to serve coffee with chicory, but it tasted amazingly good. The pastry was scrumptious, being some sort of cereal with raisins into which she had folded apples and baked, turning out the finest of crumb cakes. Then everyone but Vati and myself made a big fuss over the chocolate she served on the side. The knockout Mrs. Hakum and the huge Mrs. Schwartz were discussing where to get some good sweet stuff these days. I thought they were insensitive. Somehow, this put a damper on the pleasant afternoon and this lovely Kaffee Klatsch: They are concerned about candy, I thought, and we, as before in our refugee life, don't have a roof over our heads. They must have known why we had come. I saw Vati and Mr. W. walk into another room. When they returned, Mr. W informed everyone officially about our plight and added: "Of course, you will stay with us.

This house is built in a most unusual style: Just a few steps above, there is a separate concealed landing affording the utmost privacy. On the same level are the bath and my mother-in-law's very large room with several beds and couches. Well, she is quite a big lady," he chuckled. He had a charming way of winking both eyes, continuing his kidding with: "Good cake, fine chocolate—but give me just a *tricken stickel gans* without anything at all, just a dry piece of goose!"—and he let out a most nostalgic sigh.

The three Hakums left late and gave us their address for eventual future reference.

The flat was lovely, with two steps leading to a sunken living room. When it was time to retire, we went up for the night's sojourn. There was an alcove for the hostess, and I even had a bed all to myself.

Everything Mrs. Schwartz prepared allowed one to forget the Nazis. She and her daughter could have passed easily as Gentiles. Her build and face were masculine, yet in the kitchen and dining room she acted most feminine enjoying cooking and serving us meals. We even had eggs for breakfast and she wanted us back for lunch between apartment hunting. She could not do enough for us, possibly to compensate for the bum steer to Limburg a year and a half before, meaning they had lived here in hiding that entire time, yet their way of life did not seem clandestine.

Her soups were especially delicious, despite the warm weather. They represented a welcome break from my unsuccessful search. It was an emotional food which, some day, I wanted to prepare myself. While observing her, I recorded the recipes in shorthand. Mutti tried to restrain my doing so by reprimanding me: "Mrs. Schwartz hardly needs a reporter in the kitchen!"

This was the first time I saw the latter smile—making her appear even more like a man—when she gave me her full permission to jot down the procedure of her culinary talents.

Sometimes there was a variety of visitors. They tried to console me, saying that even if the war were to last another four years—judging from the way the Allies were lagging behind with their equipment and as long as there wouldn't be a Second Front—I would still be young, even though my best years, they admitted, were stolen.

The flat-hunting turned out to be a full-time job without any success in sight, because they were scarce. I did not quite know how to handle our main issue: To tell the truth or withhold it. I did have to act according to Vati's Jewish proverb: "While confronting the bull, judge and decide!" Either way, I felt rejected constantly as my parents waited "in the wings."

On the eighth day of our stay with the W. family, we returned as usual without any luck, but Mr. W.'s good humor and upbeat mood and Mrs. Schwartz's great food bridged our emotional hurdle.

Eleven-year-old Harold and his dainty mom had an uncommonly special bond. They were compelled to physically hold on to each other whether there was company or just the four of them.

One night over a light supper, Mr. W. took a loose five-carat sparkling diamond out of his vest pocket, using the same gesture Vati had with the half-naked woman, index finger on his lips, but with winking eyes. He said: "Business can be done even under these circumstances. People prefer their nest egg—if it's sizable—converted into something smaller like this. As you know by now, I like something little." He was smiling winsomely while looking at his wife, carefully unfolding the parchment to show us this exquisite single stone, advertising: "This can easily be hidden, taken along anywhere or sewn into garments. Who is to know? You can tuck it into one corner of the Jewish star, for no one will tear that yellow ugly *schmatte* (rag) off. It can even be swallowed. It's not as tasty as *tricken schtickle gans* but has its merits!" He winked again, and his handsome face became more serious when he confided: "A former diamantaire from Antwerp entrusted me with this beauty. You'll see it tomorrow over breakfast when, in daylight, you can appreciate it even more!" Back went the jewel into his vest pocket, whereafter he was patting it and grinning at us. He was such fun to be with. The four of us bade the three of them "Goodnight!"

I fell asleep promptly but awoke the moment night gave way to day, hearing Mrs. Schwartz going into the bathroom. A second later, in the still of dawn, I perceived a heavy motor idling and voices—German voices! Then the deathly frightening "*Aufmachen! Los! Los!*" followed by violent knocking.

"*Oh weh! Oh weh!*" we moaned.

Downstairs, louder: "*Aufmachen! Schnell!*"—accompanied by brute force front door-smashing.

My heart was pounding in my throat. I crawled underneath anything that was wide enough—not daring to breathe—

Now, heavy boots, marching up. Only a few steps separated us from them, outside the W.'s apartment, again thundering: "*Aufmachen! Los! Los! Los!*"

We heard the crashing of the door being kicked in along with screaming and screeching from Mrs. W. and Harold. Then the rough command "*HALT!*" closely followed by a single shot.

Oh my God! I sighed inwardly while listening intently. I realized that Mr. W. had been silent since the attack. Oh God, what disaster is happening now? Speech being absolutely *verboten* among us, we went into a petrified freeze. Any moment now, they would come for us, too.

"*Raus! Schnell! Los!* (Out, out, and be quick about it!)" they kept yelling, with their commands now getting closer as they were exiting. Had they left for good? No, impossible! This was the moment for them to come up and find us—*oh, weh! Oh, weh!* This is the end.

The whimpering and crying of the "two prisoners" could be heard on their way down. Then Mrs. W.'s begging: "Please, may I go to him?! Please, let me see him!"

"You'll be seeing plenty of him on the nice trip we'll all take together."

Something horrendous must have happened! We dared not guess! They might still come for us after they unload their prey, I agonized, hearing the words, now from the street: "*Los! Einsteigen!* (Hurry! Get in!)"

Then there was loud crying and screaming:

"Mommy! Mommy!"

"Harold! Oh, my Harold, my son!"

They returned indeed, just as I had anticipated. Now this was really the end! Being alone with my parents, enduring the wall of torturous silence which forbade any communication tore me apart.

If only I could have whispered or received one word of comfort, but the danger was incalculable. My mind shook my body into breathlessness. I knew THEY were still inside the house, but where the devil had THEY gone—fortunately not on the stairs leading up to our room. But where? What unbearable suspense!

Then there was a period of throbbing quiet, hysterical, heart-wrenching, lamenting screams—"Papa! Papa!" "Oh, Henri! My poor, poor love!"—followed by car doors slamming. With what sheer gratitude and relief we heard the motor turn over and at last, at long last, the Nazi vehicle leaving. A blessed but sad deliverance.

Suddenly everything seemed so peaceful again, as though nothing had occurred.

As I was trying to crawl from underneath the bed, which was considerably harder since the ferocious fear had propelled me there, I suffered another private fright—not being able to utter a sound—when I perceived the bedroom door was opening ever so slowly—it was Mrs. Schwartz, afraid to knock or call through this early morning stillness. Her reddish curls were disheveled, her face and eyes crimson—she could hardly catch her breath as she entered. Needless to say we were all beside ourselves. My parents pulled up the boudoir chair for her comfort. She could barely control her voice, sobbing: "My baby, my sweet *siebele* (seven-month premature in Yiddish)!" With her arms she made a cradling motion as she looked down at her imaginary infant: "Don't cry! Don't be afraid of anything for your Mama is young, big, strong and healthy. My lovely, frail *siebele*. I'll cherish and nurture you for the rest of my life. I swear I'll never, ever let you out of my sight, my tiny one! But now THEY have taken you away from me! My everything. THEY tore out my heart!" She crescendoed while rocking back and forth from pain still "holding her baby." "Then your handsome prince came along, helping me to pamper you and later on, so did Harold. All gone! All of them! My coddled only child working for the Nazis—heh!" Until she consoled herself with "But they are still alive!" I thought she had gone mad—and understandably so. Briefly, she pulled herself together while shaking her head endlessly. Then after some time, she sighed—"totally, completely gone!"—

and her hysteria took over again. She regulated her screaming to muted sounds: "This was the end—in front of my eyes—so abruptly—so dreadful, so bloody!" Her whole body shook as she pressed her burning face into her open palms, while rocking more vehemently: "In one swoop!" Suddenly, she stopped moving entirely, turning into a cryo sculpture. None of us knew how to handle such a tremendous tragedy. We gaped at her. So mesmerized was I that I didn't even realize I was still belly down on the floor. After a chilling silence, Vati timidly dared to ask: "The 'halt!' and the shot were intended for him? For Henri? They murdered him?"

She nodded while streams of tears rolled down her bright red face.

Still gazing at her, I felt something of the emotional turmoil she wanted so desperately to share with us. After having been taciturn, she decided to confide her innermost feelings. "In addition to all the unspeakable pain that hit me so unexpectedly, I'm experiencing such guilt because of my anger and disappointment toward Henri—for the first time. And this is how it all ended—between us?! He abandoned his wife and child, yes, my only, tiny *siebele* and grandson!" She let out such moans as she continued: "In order to save that diamond and his integrity to a former diamantaire, leaving his family behind, in the clutches of the Nazis?! Imagine so smart a man committing such foolishness, to jump off the balcony! I saw it all—oh, it was like a knife cut through me as I peeked out of a slit in the WC window. I cannot describe-" She clutched her robe closer in nervous anguish. "He prepared for his plunge when I was about to yell 'Don't! Don't!' But being in total shock, I would have done you another evil deed— as in Antwerp with Limburg. Also, it happened in a split second when I just heard "*Halt!*"—and as his foot left the balcony, he was shot with a revolver in mid-air. He actually would have made the leap, but instead landed lifeless and blood-spattered on the ground. I know he's dead because no one could have survived a bullet at such close range!" Her body was shaking uncontrollably again, and her crying continued throughout this dreadful tale.

"I don't feel blameless, either. I did not step forward when they took my everything," she repeated and again bawled into her hands. "But then they would have found you and I would have three innocent people on my conscience in order to prove my faithful motherhood."

"It's always better for someone from the family to be on the outside," Vati stated. "Also, they would not have kept you together anyway—just to the collection camp Mechelen, from what I heard."

"I still have goose pimples," Mutti said. "But we must get out of here. Who knows—they might come back in their mania for efficiency."

At last, Vati helped me up from the floor. He held and embraced me, repeating glowingly, "Fannichen! Fannichen!"

"If you can bear it, we'll all go to the terrible scene below," Vati offered Mrs. Schwartz. "I suppose there are important things you want to take, for of course, you won't ever be able to return here. Such is our fate, *ja, ja,* for we are Jews, thus criminals, thus fugitives, thus we must leave everything behind!"

"But where will we go? Where could we go?" we asked each other.

Carefully and fearfully, we proceeded down the steps to the cozy flat which they had turned into a horror chamber. Like frightened children we were all holding on to each other. Ever so slowly, Vati opened the door to the living room. Only one overturned chair facing the balcony bore witness to what had occurred.

"Let's stay away from the windows or wherever we might be seen and—betrayed. Who knows who squealed on you?" Vati warned. He then proceeded to the kitchen, while I returned alone to the upstairs bathroom to ready myself for the next unknown move to come. I wore the same green dress—on the ninth day— from our last runaway housing.

When I rejoined the others, Vati was passing hastily prepared cups of chicory-coffee to everyone, pulling out a chair for each of us ladies, the first for Mrs. Schwartz, who nodded gratefully while saying: "In the one-and-a-half years we lived here in secret, I grew so fond of this place. Each morsel I created was full of love. Now I realize this main ingredient made my dishes such a hit." Again she cried and continued talking to herself: "So happily and with such gusto I cooked for them." She glanced toward where she had last seen her son-in-law, bawling: "How can I ever get rid of this gruesome scene? How shall I ever manage to live with these feelings? How will I ever be able to exist without them, my everything, my *sieb* . . . !" Then, in a stronger tone: "I must learn to survive all by myself!" Indeed, she was able to gather her most precious items while suffering so deeply. Then she became more practical: "All my belongings must be left behind, because I would be frightened taking the tram and facing that many people all at once. Let's walk."

Very softly, Vati sang an extremely sad Yiddish song in a minor key: "*Wie ahien zall ich gen?*" (Where can I go?) Mrs. Schwartz answered: "To any of the friends who came to visit us during our time here. I feel safest with the Hakums. But their *quartier* is so small." With this word, tears welled up in her eyes again, probably recalling Henri's teasing about her large frame in a little place.

"Then you'll be in our vicinity," Vati stated.

"You mean you want to return to the Buts despite the danger that THEY might come for us?!" Mutti exclaimed indignantly.

Whereupon Vati asked: "You have a better idea?"

We all kept quiet. Mrs. Schwartz got her bearings and suggested: "I know a short-cut through this nearby park, but we should go singly or in pairs. It would be wise to call the Buts in advance. This is dangerous indeed, because the two of you were summoned already, and only one of you must proceed with extreme caution! Perhaps, *Madame?*" she paused inquiringly. No answer. "Maybe, *Mademoiselle*, you'll call them first, from outside, since they do have a phone." Busying herself with our problems seemed to soothe her somewhat. But watching her leave and look around one last time with so much love—and pain—was gut-wrenching.

The day was beautiful, with a blue sky overhead and everything as green as my dress when we crossed this lovely display of nature with its multitude of colorful flowers, calm ponds—petals gently flowing in them. And this was not meant for me to behold, to enjoy, because one man said so and the world listened and seemed to agree. I was boiling over with anger, but nevertheless appreciated the peaceful scenery to such a degree that the sensation turned negative: The birds are singing—I thought—but not for us. How long will I be able to savor these wonderful daily pleasures? I asked myself. With such feelings, we reached various small streets like *rue Smits, Monrose* and—how apropos—*Troost Straat*. From here I was able to phone the Buts. She answered with surprise: "I thought you were settled very far out in the rental from the realtors."

"No, Madame Buts. Very much the opposite. You are our only and last hope. Since the first couple of weeks, we have been on the run constantly."

"Where are you now?"

"Most appropriately, *on la rue de la Consolation.*"

"It's not very far on foot. Your apartment is available. We'll be happy to have you here, but all of us must consider the danger. So, come on!" She said it pleasantly enough, but I knew she was worried.

"Shall the three of us be together, or would it be more discreet if Vati or I were to enter alone?" I inquired, taking into account Mrs. Schwartz's earlier apprehension.

My parents could tell from my expression I had good news and they smiled faintly as I walked up to the corner. "It's alright for all of us to appear there, and what's more, we can use our former apartment," I informed them enthusiastically.

"Then you'll be at 40, *rue Saxe-Cobourg* and my temporary address is in care of the *Hakums* 12, rue de la Charité." Mrs. Schwartz dissolved into tears at the mere name of the street, lamenting: "Yes, charity, without my family, me, yes, I, being a woman all alone in the world so suddenly, no family, me, without a family! What has become of me?! What is yet to become of me?"

In the meantime, we had arrived at *la Chaussee de Louvain.* Fortunately, the way was downhill and easy walking. We finally reached the familiar small church *on la Place St. Josse* and before bidding "bye" to Mrs. Schwartz, Vati asked whether there would be someone present to let her in. She nodded ever so sadly, assuring us that his brother-butler was always there unless he had gone on an errand.

Now we were standing in front of our former abode, ringing the bell.

Mrs. Buts opened and with one look at me, it was obvious she was befuddled—barely able to keep a smile, a rarity for her, indeed. Just as uncharacteristic was the way she kidded me as we were walking down the familiar hallway together: "In addition to the Nazis you must beware of men in general, *Mademoiselle!*"

"Which means you like me as a blonde?" I did not expect an answer, nor did I get one.

From the large kitchen the scent of real brewed coffee smelled marvelous. The luncheon table was set for five. I noticed there were that many lusciously browned chickens. They too exuded the most appetizing aroma.

The Buts wanted to know all the details of our escapades since they last saw us after we'd been served with the two summonses. We obliged. My parents explained in Flemish and every so often I clarified in French. Then when it came to the gruesome, fatal morning at the W. family, I warned them: "Now we must relate something atrocious. I mean really sickening!"

Mr. Buts took the platter of mini-fowl saying: "These will get cold, so we'll pause and savor the pigeons. It's a *delicatesse!*" Most likely divining our uneasiness, he asked: "You've never eaten these before?"

Even though I was famished and the birds were most appealing, I needed some courage to dig into them. I guess the same happened to my parents for we exchanged brief, futile glances. We thus became "gourmet adventurers." The results were far better than expected. Mrs. Buts had also made a tasty crumb cake like Mrs. Schwartz's. The former told Vati exactly which box to get in order to prepare it. "It's the only kind of baked goods available, and in these hungry, rationed days, it's great to be able to 'nosh' on something," Mr. Buts pointed out while enjoying another cup of coffee with this "war time cake."

I mused upon the strong love which appeared to exist between these two people in spite of their childless marriage. Their important bond was a fervent devotion to the ideals of Communism.

We went ahead and told them the grisly experience with the W. family, when we were escaping to save our lives from the blackmailer. Their shock goes without saying. We thanked them dearly for sheltering us and for hosting this unexpected luncheon, which, for now, was a real sacrifice in addition to the usual treat.

They ushered us upstairs. Upon entering our former apartment, tears welled up. Instead of this place being our home, it now served only as a brief hiding place as again, we were fleeing the Swastika! Besides, to me it was déjà-vu—reminiscent of my last return to *Groenvink Straat* in Antwerp when I fetched Mutti's bundles prior to going back to the village. In both instances there were so many lost joys.

After two days of intensive flat-hunting, mostly in *Schaerbeck*, dragging ourselves up and down the city's hilly streets, we were dismayed not to have found anything. On day three, Mrs. Buts came running, yelling our names and knocking at the door. "*Mademoiselle!! Dépêchez vous! Dépêchez vous!* Quickly!" Still tired from yesterday's vain search, I climbed out of bed to answer her.

"No questions asked, throw on anything and come! Time is of the essence!"

We did just that and dashed across into 41, rue Saxe-Cobourg. That neighbor was only a nodding acquaintance. We occasionally glanced at each other while sewing the yellow stars on my garments.

We followed the two landladies all the way to the back of the cellar—and lo and behold, there were cages upon cages of rabbits. "This is where you'll stay until I come for you," Mrs. Buts advised most nervously and off she went. "*Au revoir!*" The other lady left with an uneasy smile.

Here we were, the three of us, with an enormous number of malodorous hares. Mutti suffered the most, for she had very refined senses, moaning constantly: "*Es stinkt! Es stinkt!*"

As always, I was prepared not to waste precious studying time and had Willy's birthday gift, my current Spanish booklet plus a pad with pencils on hand. Scared and confused, I auto-hypnotized my mind with conjugations:

tengo miedo
tu tienes miedo
el, ella tiene miedo
nosotros tenemos miedo
vosotros teneis miedo
ellos, ellas tienen miedo

I did this over and over again and, indeed, with fear as its translation is: "I have fear!"

It was another beautiful day, which we barely could discern through the bleak windows. We received some very meager food from the grinning woman, and though hungry, I continued to busy myself with my latest intellectual acquisition of this new language. There were some fascinating stories about Rosita, which I was able to read in my new tongue. My parents whispered a minimum of words. Vati had forever given me the spirit of constant productivity, for which I was always grateful, and quite especially today. He must have gotten extremely bored; yet Mutti copied me after I gave her writing materials, trying to improve her French, which I sporadically taught her, since it had served her so well with the blackmailer.

Through the dreary windows we saw this bright day turning slowly into dusk and then into a cheerless night. We received the same supper as did the animals: carrots. Vati fell asleep—and so did the four-leggeds. Mutti and I continued to widen our knowledge of our new Latin languages.

After midnight, our messiah arrived in the form of Mrs. Buts. She thanked the other lady, then ushered us straight to her house. In her big kitchen, she fed us prepared sandwiches, apologizing for the sparseness of provisions. "First enjoy these, and then I'll tell you the reason for the sudden rescue among the rabbits." Like obedient, famished children we didn't lose a minute nor waste a word, just devoured the snacks at this late hour.

"Now then," she started. "I'm not at liberty to reveal the exact source, but rumor had it the Gestapo would be looking for you here at our house. Well, don't you think that was reason enough to make you suffer a while?" she asked in her somewhat harsh manner. We were open-mouthed for quite some time, thanking her profusely. This actually seemed to anger her, because she replied indignantly: "You would have to be an outright murderer not to have done this. Wouldn't you know—" she said, growing more upset, "they did arrive only minutes after I had hidden you with the hares. I had a pat answer all prepared for these two miserable Gestapo killers. 'Oh, that family has left for the Unoccupied.' I tried to protect you."

Mrs. Buts continued. "They asked when you'd left. Fearing I might put my foot into the wrong time-slot, so to speak, I said I wasn't here since I often go to the country. 'About what month did the Jews leave? You're not a Jew-friend, are you now?' I ignored the last part of the question and replied to the first: 'You wouldn't want me to give you incorrect information, would you? I truly cannot pin-point the date. My trips are so much alike that I could easily be confused,' I answered firmly, knowing you were just across the street amongst the hares. 'Na, ja!' one of them said finally." She had finished relating her Gestapo experience.

"This is the best sound from any German authority, Mrs. Buts. It means THEY were yielding without quite believing your story, as if to say: have it your way!" I explained.

"In this case, THEY might return!" Mutti worried.

"Yes, indeed, THEY just might," Mrs. Buts agreed with a sorrowful, sad, affirmative nod and advised urgently: "You must get up early, for you never know when THEY will come back, those damned assassins! God how I hate THEM, les Boches! Nous les aurons, les Boches! (We'll get them!)" With a deep sigh and a tough hand gesture, she altered her entire demeanor, asking me: "Did you ever search around la Place Dailly, Mademoiselle? It is further up from where you arrived with Mrs. Schwartz, but keep on going east up, up *la Chaussee de Louvain* until you see a big building of military barracks on your right. Of course, before, our boys were there. Now it's THEM—the *Boches Wehrnacht*! Directly across is *l'Avenue Dailly* and many other residential streets. You never searched in that part of *Schaerbeck, Mademoiselle?*" she asked again in honest surprise.

"No, I haven't even heard of it, because we hadn't ventured that far."

On the following day, we did find *la Place Dailly* crawling with lots of Nazi servicemen. We turned into the tree-lined Avenue *Dailly*. Amazingly, there was an apartment for rent sign, but it said "For two people." I had to use all my power of persuasion on this elderly widower-landlord. He was startled at our wanting the flat for three and even more so when I insisted in Flemish that we'd move in at once. We told the all-important news over the phone to Mrs. Buts, who brought the most necessary items.

Again my parents worked hard to make this longish "*doorloopend kameren*" (straight through in Flemish) as clean and cozy-looking as they did the one from the realtor, where our most recent odyssey with the blackmailer had started. This one, though, was not quite as bad. At last, we could take care of ourselves. While I shampooed my blonde locks, there was a knock at the door. We held our breath while my hair was dripping—until we recognized the landlord's Flemish voice. He handed Mutti forms to fill out. She nodded and acted as though she was prepared to register. Our momentary good mood was replaced by miserable thoughts and worries. Our original dilemma came back to haunt us: should we reveal the dangerous fact that we were Jews or perilously conceal it from this harmless looking present owner?

Mrs. Buts had brought the long robe Mutti had packed four years ago in Köln. She could really use it, wearing it while puttering with the curtains, obviously content, humming her own little tunes as she did when I was a child in *Köln-Mülheim*. I was near tears from this memory—echoes of the past, filled with compassion for her—desiring so very much to be the lady of the house and just take care of that which she loved.

After a few weeks of pleasant living there, whenever he saw us, *Mijnheer* asked whether we had registered. It soon turned into downright nagging. We kept stalling. Thereafter, we were given a certain date, but now that we had to deal with a definite deadline, we were cornered and had to make one last effort with . . . the truth.

His answer was an instant, definite, devastating "NO!" Then: "*U moet weg gaan!* (You must go away!)" His decision was ironclad!

Immediately, I ran out of the house—and my parents after me. Running in step, I said: "Each minute counts, because he knows. Telling him was an enormous risk, depending on what he does with it."

There they were again, the many military *Boches*, indicating we had arrived at the barracks *à la Place Dailly*. Alright. To the left now, up, up, *la Chaussee de Louvain*! East, east! "Ha! Direction Germany!" was my sardonic remark.

After we had walked a few blocks, I saw an interesting corner. It consisted of a three-story rotunda ornate in its entirety with tiny filigree balconies reminiscent of Parisian postcards picturing some old *quartier*. Downstairs it was more mundane with a shoemaker and a produce store. I could only dream, wish and hope that there would be something free at this charming "roundhouse." Besides, it had a practical side, concealing its true address just as Mrs. Schwartz's landing which saved us. The street sign said "*Avenue du Diamant*"—lucky traces of Simon—and I saw #3 above the entrance; yet it appeared as though it was still *La Chaussee de Louvain* and another street, Avenue de la Topaz was forking into them, surrounded by all others with the lovely names of jewels, such as *rue du Sapphire* and Avenue *de l'Emeraude* or *Smaragdlaan*. "Let's cross this *trafficked Chaussee* and find out. It just draws me there as did the *Molenaers'* butcher shop in *Hoeselt*." Now, we were standing in front of the shoemaker's. I could barely see this baldish man, for he was encircled by laughing ladies as though he were Maurice Chevalier. He was clad in the same type of blue double-buttoned sweater as were the *Köbes* waiters in the *Kölsche Kneipe* tavern-restaurants typical of Köln. There was a happy Cologne Mardi-Gras song we learned in school: " . . . *un alle Schusterjonge han immer, han immer frohen Sinn.*" ("All the shoemaker boys are always in a good mood.") The man, who looked about 55, embodied happiness like his young colleagues. I was waiting for him to be alone while watching the jovial scene in front of me and thinking: here are all these images of Köln suddenly flooding my mind in a pleasant nostalgia. First, the garb of the *cordonnier*, and his apparent cheerfulness, reminded me of our singing class. My superego scolded me: Oh, Köln—where is your beloved Cologne? Does it not lay in the northwest of Nazi Germany? Is the location of your adored city not in the most loathed country causing you so much grief, misery and the loss of the foremost human treasure: youth with its chances and opportunities? Will this incongruity of the love for the city and the hate for the very same country continue the rest of your life? It made me think—

My parents were behind me when I briefly informed them: "I'm getting excellent vibrations from this *Schuster*. I'm not going to hesitate to tell him the truth!"

"You act as though you knew him and he had something for rent," Mutti said skeptically.

"On both accounts, you sized up the situation correctly," I answered and remarked with glee: "At last, there is nobody. Hopefully no one else will enter. Now that she is leaving, I'm stepping in." As I said this, I rubbed my palms together from being so very anxious. Since I overheard them speaking French as most *Brusselers* do, upon going in, I pretended as though I did not have a care in the world: "*Bonjour, Monsieur, comment ça va?* Is there by any chance an apartment for rent?" He laughed in a nice, somewhat hoarse way. "Yes, right above here there is a spacious one with all these balconies you see and in the back a huge lovely veranda with a marvelous view, like in the country."

I was delighted but pressed for time because any moment, someone might enter. "This sounds great, *Monsieur*. But can you keep a secret?" I asked.

"In these years of war one must certainly be most discreet," he answered.

"*Monsieur*." I wrestled stoically to stop my hands from wringing, this time from impatience that nobody would come in prior to my revelation. I ventured to whisper: "*Monsieur, nous sommes des Juifs!* (We are Jewish!)" There, I said it—as though I had committed a crime.

His reaction was not what I expected. "Wonderful, wonderful! I don't even live here. I just lease the shop from a fine, rich and very anti-Nazi landlady."

"Nowadays I would hardly refer to being Jewish as wonderful," I sadly joked.

"Yes, in normal times it is. But mainly I felt so enthusiastic about it because this owner will be thrilled to let the flat to you— yes—and I can imagine your most ardent wish: without registration!"

"Oh, *Monsieur!*" I cupped both of my hands on top of each other, knuckles up, in sheer gratitude. Then I jotted down this holy address.

"She lives very far out. It will take a good hour to reach her."

"*Monsieur, s'il vous plait*—tell anyone who might inquire that the flat has been taken already."

"Of course. Besides, it's not advertised," he assured me. As he gave me her information, customers poured in. How fortunate, I thought, that they arrived now instead of at the crucial moment of my confession. When I bade him "*Au revoir,*" he encouraged me: She is a very fine person and will be absolutely thrilled." He was careful with his wording.

I called to make sure that our future landlady would be home the next day. I told her the apartment was needed most urgently for my parents and myself. I had to impart the truth about being Jewish in person. Her line might be tapped—who knows? For the moment, again, we had nowhere to stay overnight. We would be in danger at the Buts, because of the Gestapo eventually returning, or with our present owner for what he might do. We just had to trust that man and continue to act swiftly.

The moment we entered our current place, the lawful widower opened his door, at which moment I volunteered: "*Wij zullen gaan, Mijnheer,* as soon as possible."

"When?" was his anxious question.

"It's a matter of days and we'll be happy to *vertrekken* (leave in Flemish)."

He sighed with relief.

This time on the out-of-town trolley, I felt so much better than with Mrs. Buts, when our efforts were hopeless. But now I had faith in the shoemaker and this landlady we were to meet. The ride was extremely long but pleasant. After getting off the tram, we walked around lush, rolling fields. In front of us, it looked like a movie set: country greenery surrounding a private estate with small bodies of water ornamented with gently curving little bridges, one of which led to a quite unusual mansion embellished with Corinthian columns, crowning the entire idyllic scenery.

I rang the shiny, huge brass bell.

A maid in formal attire showed us into a palatial interior. In the drawing room on a Burgundy colored Chippendale sofa sat a slim, white-haired friendly woman with a youthful face, who got up to introduce herself. She asked the servant to bring coffee outdoors on the back lawn. "After the refreshments are served, it'll be my pleasure to speak with you there," she suggested as she pointed to the most charming wicker furniture. "We'll have all the privacy we need."

This was the first time since the coastal villa that an invigorating brew was served in beautiful moss rose *Sèvres* cups and poured out from a matching pot. It was great to experience this kind of luxury again, if only for a fleeting moment, I thought wistfully, longingly.

After the maid had left, the lady said with an impish smile: "I have an idea why you came out here: You want to rent the apartment on Avenue *du Diamant* without registration, so you can live in hiding, because you seem a fine, small, Jewish family. I'd love to let you have it for—" She named an incredibly low figure. I thought this was just to help us and make life easier. We thanked her. Though we had met only minutes ago, I went to her with a sincere, grateful glance and a warm "*Merci infiniement, Madame.*" I shook hands with her as I gave her a peck on the cheek. She was most receptive.

Now that the *quartier* was ours, we could admire the beautiful August day as the trolley rushed back into the city. Our first stop was the widower in order to get the items Mrs. Buts had brought us just a few weeks ago. While the landlord was anxious to be rid of us, he now apologized for not being able to take such a risk. Nonetheless, we were looking around constantly—as I had when running from the blackmailer—to make sure we were not followed.

We had rented this flat unseen and after looking at it, we were absolutely enamored with our new abode. There were actually two entrances; one led to a huge kitchen whose French doors opened onto a large veranda complete with bathroom, overlooking multi-flowered green slopes. This outdoor beauty thrilled me as much as the piano *chez Buts*. The other branched into a corridor, forking into three furnished rooms, each provided with its own balcony, which had attracted me to this corner in the first place. Underneath to the right of this outdoor marvel, the veranda, there were all kinds of small projecting eaves in the shape of little flat roofs. I took note of this . . .

In the evening, we went to the Buts to share our good fortune and pick up more of our belongings; when they asked what we intended to do with our financial reserve; they suggested that it could be hidden in a tin box. Then they would bury it in their garden and, as needed, give us a piece of jewelry to be sold or else the cash. In our former, now very dangerous apartment, we were once more wringing our hands in despair as we consulted with each other when we were alone: "Suppose one or two of us survives. There will always be resources. Yes, we must be realistic! On the other hand, so called 'good Belgian Gentiles' had been known to 'hide' Jewish fortunes, and just because of it, betrayed the owners to the Gestapo. For not only would they keep the assets but would be further compensated with a certain amount per Jewish head."

But all of us, even skeptical Mutti, agreed that we could trust the Buts with everything we owned. It was a chancy, hard, tormenting decision. But we made it that very night, and left cash, diamonds and gold with them, taking only the amount we needed for immediate necessities.

We would live only thirty minutes walking distance away from them. Wanting to embrace her for tonight's "goodbye" and most of all out of gratitude for them being our "anchor," we realized that contrary to our latest landlady, this past one was hardly the person for affectionate demonstrations. However, if not for her and her husband, whom she so fondly called "*Jauke*," our lot would have been a precarious one. Thanks to their constant protection, we were able to escape the ensnarement of Nazi captivity and slavery.

Chapter 22

Once more in our lives, a new era had begun. We could only pray and hope for the Allies to start a second front rapidly, for the "fortunes" of war to turn in their favor—and for us to survive here in this lovely place. We trusted them despite their doomed attempt in Dieppe, where fifty percent of the mostly Canadian troops were lost. This invasion might have proven a rehearsal for the eventual attack of redemption.

On the same evening, minutes after we had arrived at our new flat, I shampooed my blonde hair. As I was marveling how totally different it felt to suddenly have all that fair wet bulk in front of my face as opposed to the very dark tresses I'd had all my life, a tremendous blast went off very nearby, shaking the whole house.

The following day, while bringing our first business to that wonderful shoemaker, he told me that there was a Gestapo quarter right in the next block which had been bombarded by *la Guarde Blanche*, the Belgian counterpart of the French *Maquis*, both anti-Nazi underground movements.

"This is interesting news. Would *la Guarde Blanche* call on me, I would not hesitate to join. As you know, I'm in danger anyway, so I might as well accomplish something for our cause, *n'est pas, Monsieur?*" I volunteered to inform him.

Aiming for a productive lifestyle, I got up every day when the night had turned into morning and retired in early evening, for I felt that should I survive, I would need a lot of strength, and the same held true if I should ever be under THEIR control for THEIR work. Thus, my Spartan habits were comparable to those of the pre-Edison period.

Since Limburg, I had been seized by household ambition. Each Friday I cleaned the apartment thoroughly including the adorable balconies. I washed them with liquid soap, and cleaned the windows of the French doors leading to them with the *Brüsseler Zeitung* and vinegar. Every Wednesday I did the light work. Once a week the stairs were scrubbed and the balustrade dusted. While my parents were still asleep I set the breakfast table on a white cloth and had the chicory coffee ready for when they arose. Awaking before Vati was a new experience for me.

Some afternoons I would go to bookshops and buy the classics in each of my languages: Goethe in German, Shakespeare in English, Flaubert and Anatole France in French and Maeterlinck in Flemish. Of course, I continued to study Spanish. Not unlike my idol, Winston Churchill, I had to be my own university. Mutti was right when she stated that I was an eternal student—I love to devour all knowledge. I also continued to teach Mutti French. When Vati noticed that I went through a lexicon like most people would read a novel, he thought it too extreme. For once, Mutti took my side in an argument. She agreed that it was a sound idea and explained to Vati that word power makes a person. He shrugged in defeat. In the morning I would sit on my marvelous terrace with the first cup of coffee, book, dictionaries, pad and pens and mark down any unknown word of the tongue at hand to widen my vocabulary.

Vati, as always, had left right after our first meal and did all the rationed food and general shopping. He had returned with a German haircut, and told us apologetically: "I did not know how to behave at the barber's. It's a real risk with many of those men around, some of whom even seem to be German civilians, like Hans from Bad Godesberg. So I was afraid to open my mouth with my foreign Flemish. On impulse and to protect myself, I spoke plain German and was treated with respect, and this was the result. In the future, I won't have to worry. I'll just go there," he concluded as he was unfolding the *Brüsseler Zeitung* with its clever, cute caricatures. It was evident that the Nazis weren't very fond of the Italian Prince Umberto and his tiny father, King Victor Emanuel despite their great friendship with Mussolini, for they had the little one in full uniform complete with fancy hat and plumes in the waste basket. No matter what the political artistic satire was about, they always managed to find a lowly, ridiculous spot for the mini royal papa.

My parents' marriage could now be described as a happy one. Mutti was by nature a homebody and that Vati was around a lot seemed to please her. They played chess and checkers. The only fights they had were during these games, which were cute, especially when they were taken so seriously, while I recited aloud *"Count Egmont"* by Goethe. Vati admired this and stated: "I can hear now why Johann Wolfgang is so famous. There is true beauty and sense in this work."

Mutti hadn't left the apartment since we lived here, and was actually apprehensive about facing the world. We had to persuade her that it was just as dangerous inside as on the streets. Either way, one could get *chappt* (snatched) by THEM. It's truly a matter of luck. Even though Mutti needed only reading glasses, just to look somewhat different, she felt safer wearing them outdoors for the first time ever to hide behind them. We decided that the hour had come—now that we were settled, never losing sight of the fact that we were in constant danger, no matter how comfy it felt—to inquire about Mrs. Schwartz.

It was a Sunday afternoon when we went down *la Chaussee de Louvain* passing *la Place St. Josse,* practically looking into *rue Saxe-Cobourg,* where our "anchor" and assets were. It seemed strange not to stop *chez Buts.* A bit further, on the left, we were now ringing the bell at 12, *rue de la Charité.* In a moment of *déjà-vu,* the beauteous Mrs. Hakum opened the door in a silk multi-colored house-suit. Surprised and cordial, she showed us upstairs. Even though it was tea time, there was a heavenly smell coming from the kitchen. "The creator of this must be Mrs. Schwartz," I said smilingly, sniffing.

"Who else?" the beauty asked in jest.

Mrs. Schwartz wiped her hands and greeted us—friendly as she could manage.

The flat was small but filled with unusual treasures without looking cluttered. My two favorites were an artistic photographic study of the glamorous hostess in an antique gold frame, hanging above a large piece of fruitwood furniture, which was one of these ultra modern radio-phono combinations. As soon as I'm free and have money again, I told myself, these are two possessions I wish to own: a blown-up photo like this in which I'll cradle fresh lilacs wistfully, posing my chin over my bare shoulder and this large, wooden object, which doesn't just stand there, but plays great music with a soothing full sound.

While I was dreaming about liberty and the wondrous things it would bring, the table was set by the brother-butler and Mrs. Schwartz, the eternal housekeeper.

"One could go crazy from the various wonderful aromas. First the cooking and then the brewing!" Mutti exclaimed. The coffee and the "cereal pie" were also a *déjà-vu* just prior to the "horror experience."

"Mrs. Schwartz would like to look for some quarters of her own, but I think it would be a downright disadvantage for her to be alone," Mr. Hakum related. Here, she makes us happy with her culinary skills and her company instead of being all by herself," he stated and added: "True, our flat is small but adequate, since Mrs. Schwartz uses my brother's room, while he sleeps here on the couch."

"It's no inconvenience at all!" the sibling attested. In a way, there is the same number of people and even gender of her own lost family, it occurred to me. But not wanting to stir up emotions from this recent terrible memory, I kept silent.

"You act and talk as if it were up to Mrs. Schwartz, as though there was a choice. It is nearly impossible to find a hiding place with owners who have non-registration tolerance," Mutti explained.

"Besides, it's enormously dangerous!" Vati exclaimed and he set forth to tell all present of our ordeal-odyssey.

"But now, at long last, we have been compensated. But look what we were exposed to until then!" I sighed.

While Mrs. Schwartz was in her domain, the kitchen, the Hakums quickly revealed this macabre story: They had visited Henri W. at his resting place. They would give us the address, in case we were interested. "It's near an out-of-town trolley stop."

"He actually lies in a cemetery?" we anxiously inquired.

"In a way it is, but indoors, in a drawer-type stone coffin," Mr. Hakum described while giving us directions, warning: "But keep in mind that this is most likely Gestapo territory on which to bury their fallen enemies in singular cases like our murdered friend!"

To get me over this newest sad story I gazed at the impressive photograph and concluded that the following three women could have been triplets: Hedy Lamar, Joan Bennett—the only known Hollywood blonde to turn into a dark-haired beauty—and of course, Mrs. Hakum.

When we said goodbye, all of them, including Mrs. Schwartz, insisted we visit them on a regular basis. This was the first outing together since we could not recall the last one, other than apartment hunting or being hunted.

Now that Mutti got a taste of the outside world, or maybe because the late Mr. W. was from her hometown, she was the one to suggest we pay our respects to him. We all agreed.

On a lovely September Sunday, we dared to take this trip. The ride, the scenery and nature were very pleasant, since the weather was still warm. The out-of-town tram took us past miles of fields looking like monochromatic hues of beige and soft green carpets interspersed with farmhouses. Upon some of these "rugs" were large, cone-shaped bundles of grain and corn. Unlike during the *Flucht*, when dead cattle covered the pastures, live cows were grazing peacefully, enhancing the Indian summer countryside. The villages exuded their characteristic scent of earth and hay with a faint odor of manure. Birds were flying in flocks.

We got off in one tiny town and walked and walked the quaint streets leading us to a menacing flat building, where people were entering.

Once inside, a foreboding, musty darkness and still solemnity in stark contrast to the sun filled idyllic images which had just rolled by was startling and awe-inspiring. My throat got dry. After my eyes became accustomed to the dense obscurity, I was able to discern a rather narrow corridor where some men and women were passing or stopping in front of these sarcophaguses, tiered rows of each simply bearing a last name. It looked ancient, eerie and Arabesque as though straight out of Egyptology. The macabre atmosphere added to the fear that at any moment, someone might grab my shoulder. We were prepared for this. Walking single file, we just scanned over the names in this strange burial site with tombs stacked on top of each other—forming the entire left wall space. Despite the double anxiety of being caught and facing the reality of Henri W. indeed being in his grave, something—perhaps a sense of duty mixed with curiosity—had compelled us to go through with our plan and come here. While ambling through this gloomy passage, we glanced at the inscriptions. Vati detected the long W. name first and touched us as a signal, when we followed his glance. Henri's stone coffin was located in the center. My upper stomach got into circling knots from shock, sadness and compassion.

Now we knew exactly where he was, but where were his wife and child? There he lay in his crypt, this handsome joker, who'd been so full of fun and joie-de-vivre. He never got to taste his *stickel tricken gans* nor did he ever get to show us the diamond on the following clear morning. Instead, he was shot to death. Our "procession" of three continued to the other end when we made a turn-about to pay our respects by just catching one final glimpse of "*Woydeslavsky*" for the very last time. We left this deposit of the dead and Nazi mysteries.

On the way to the trolley stop and while waiting, we were moved to silence. Inside the tram, we continued to have our own thoughts. Besides, it was not wise to converse. Being followed or observed was a possibility, especially from a place of Nazi territory.

I thought to myself: how heart-wrenching to die way before one's time had come, and so violently. In these days it was a miracle—quite particularly for a Jew—to wind up in any kind of cemetery as opposed to remaining at the site of the killing. It was amazing, though, that any obsequium existed for Woydeslavsky. May he rest there in peace!

Mutti was facing me in the trolley. Uncharacteristically, she was totally withdrawn. Her fine features expressed extreme pain.

She held her stomach and then her jaw. Vati was just nodding to himself in sad disbelief. I tried to console myself by observing the picturesque scenery of rustic life while taking notes. As I was doing so, I suddenly remembered the "recording lady" from the *Flucht*, who was so busy jotting down the current events. I watched her, and swore to myself that I too must report some day of these horrific happenings. Now the time had come. Our beautiful veranda was especially suited for this kind of project. During my household chores it came to me that I should, through my writing, create a large family—since I was always in awe of such. Why not show through each member the various terrible tragedies, originated by one man, then by one nation, and thus dedicate one chapter to each character's suffering? My life and readings inspired me to set forth this idea and get started, while nevertheless continuing my studies of philology.

I needed more literature. Of course, dealing with the nearby public library, with my name and address, was out of the question. Buying reading material was a big expense. I took all the classics I had and marched to *la Place St. Josse*, where I recalled a book and art gallery on the opposite side of the church and *rue Saxe-Cobourg!* Naturally, the peril prevented me from visiting the Buts. In one of the shops was a kind-looking middle-aged lady. I offered her my books for sale, and she seemed glad to buy the stack for a nice amount of Belgian Francs, part of which I reinvested in five volumes. One of them was Mark Twain's "Voyage of the Innocents." The store owner told me in French that this was a pseudonym for Samuel Langhorne Clemens, and she set forth "My parents took me on a trip to America. I still remember New York and Philadelphia, especially its suburb, with quaint houses on Maple Street in Langhorne. I recall having so much fun there with my American cousins. Those were the days!" she sighed. "If you would like to experience his report, written in that inimitable humorous style of his, about travel adventures in the Middle East, I recommend this English original. As for French, here are two by Emile Zola: 'Nana,' *la coquette cocotte* and '*J'accuse*!'" She looked around and said in a low voice: "This one may not be circulated at the moment because of the Jewish officer Alfred Dreyfus." Shades of Simon compelled me to grab Goethe's "*Faust*" off the shelf. "This is our very own still living best Nobel prize winner Count Maurice Maeterlinck's '*Pélleas and Mélisande*' in Flemish, of course."

I could only talk Yiddish, not read. A big "joke" would be if I were literate in this language, it not being found anywhere in these Nazi occupied regions. I was surprised that "*J'accuse!*" existed here.

Feeling good about myself and the little book deal, I arrived loaded with excellent international classics. Mutti, though, seemed to be in pain. "Ever since we paid our respects to Henri, which was quite risky and frivolous—and especially upon our return from that macabre place—my tooth hasn't stopped hurting. I don't even know exactly which one it is. I tried to cure myself with hot compresses and holding schnapps against them for as long as I could, but this only helped for the moment, and the ache returned. The bad news is, we must see a dentist."

"It is surely very daring to go to any professional. These days one doesn't know what their political view is, even though they are Belgians. There are two of them in the Rue Victor Hugo: one just at the tram stop and the other in the next block," I informed her.

"You talk as though we were regular people and not fugitives of the Nazi law," she reprimanded.

She was obviously in pain, so I shared this idea with her: "Look, Mutti, it's as dangerous right here at our comfy apartment as it is when we dash to the public bath place each Saturday. The attendant with his sour expression could easily give us away, and how more helpless could a woman feel than in the nude? With the dentist, we must do the following: As soon as he leaves his actual office, we must take off as well, no matter what, even in mid-work. If he wishes to make an appointment, we refuse. In other words, we give him no opportunity for betrayal time. Just let me do the talking. Your sparse French might reveal our identity" I advised.

The next day her discomfort persisted requiring a dentist after all. Both of us were extremely nervous. In order to reduce the risks involved, we went at the end of his hours to avoid other patients.

The short visit was an all-around success. Mutti was thrilled with her now painless mouth and no return was necessary.

On this peaceful evening my parents were playing chess with their cute little fights and I enjoyed my newly acquired world literature. My idea to retire at dusk and arise at dawn not only saved electricity but, more importantly, gave me more working hours in which to read, study and write my book. My parents were pleasantly surprised at this, for me, unusual lifestyle. Amazingly, I was able to fall asleep soundly, drifting into pleasant dreams—what is this?!—for heaven's sake—a motor idling—men's voices—in a most familiar language. Oh, God! This is it! Now indeed, THEY are coming for us! This time my pounding heart was keeping time with the running engine. Fear would not allow the pulsating beat to lessen. Pressing both palms forcefully over my mouth, so my total focus was on my hearing. At last I was able to discern: "Is this the correct road to the city of *Louvain*?" It was actually a car full of Nazis asking directions from a local passer-by (their confusion caused by the forking streets). "What wonderful, miraculous relief!" I marveled to my equally frightened parents. The release of tension allowed us to continue our slumber.

In the midst of an interesting dream, there was the intrusion of an all-German male choir with accompanying marching heavy boots, singing: "*Wir haben den Krieg schon gewonnen; für uns war's ein grosser Sieg! Wir werden weiter marschieren bis alles in Scherben fällt: denn heute gehört uns Deutschland und morgen die ganze Welt!*" (We already have won the war. For us it was a great victory! We shall continue to march until everything falls into debris, for today Germany belongs to us and tomorrow the whole world will be ours!) Facetiously I thought, how the Wehrmacht dare awaken me this early, recalling slowly the nocturnal fright of the idling motor and the German voices.

Daylight was peeking through the curtains. As of late, I was the first one to be in the big kitchen, preparing the chicory and setting a perfect breakfast table for the three of us, while my parents slept. It was still warm enough to savor my first cup on the terrace while continuing to write my book in German shorthand. As I busied myself with the various characters of the large fictitious family, my glance fell onto the right on the little roofs. My creative imagination was interrupted in favor of these. Unlike Mr. W.'s fatal, huge leap, these would be short jumps from the veranda to the bigger square one, then carefully to the triangle and afterwards to the last large one which would bring me to a different house altogether. Closing my eyes, I actually could see myself executing this scheme, hoping fervently I would never, ever have to put it into practice.

It was still morning after my chores were done, so I took my daily errand walk. There was a long line in front of the butcher's. I took a spot at the tail end and discerned for the first time that there existed such a product as frozen meat. "Frozen meat, uh?" I tried to make sure.

"It's not as good as regular beef because of its aftertaste. But expert preparation will take care of it," the housewives next to me contended.

As the queue proceeded toward the inside, I barely caught a glimpse of a very good-looking, young, fair butcher, dressed from head to toe in stark white. Instantly, there was eye contact. Like an old friend, he ran up to me, grabbed my arm and to the tune of Lohengrin's "Here Comes the Bride," he was humming and walking me in this fashion to his work room in back while complimenting me and saying: "I never saw you before, but hope this will change in the near future. Especially with this." He gently piled a huge bundle into my shopping bag. This happened so quickly it left me speechless. I could only admire his swiftness and vivacious, excellent French speech and fine features that actually were more those of a poet than a butcher, when he advised with a warm smile: "Whenever you see a line in front of my shop, please, don't hesitate to come in. I'll be happy to see that pretty face again and gaze into those beautiful, big, dark, eyes."

"Yes, sir, Mr. Flatterer, I will and thank you ever so much!" was my reply as I left through a different door. When I saw the crowd from afar, I thought there was still enough meat to go around for everyone.

On the short way home, I had to grin about this pleasant, surprising interlude, especially now, since my romances had run dry. But seriousness took over, as my departure through the different exit made me think of my emergency escape plans, designed so that I would wind up at a different house or better still another street, as did Vati to escape the blackmailer. This is so vital, as in most cases the "clever" Nazis always had one standing guard while the others amassed THEIR prey.

Upon entering our apartment, Vati was just about to add some finishing touches to his project: In my "cozy corner" where I had displayed my books and did my studies when the weather prevented me from doing this at my pet place, the veranda, he had attached a huge map above the adorable, dainty flowery couch. He was about to affix a red wool thread to demark the Russian front with colorful pins. After admiring his own job, beholding it with a few steps backward, as though it was a Rembrandt, he was thrilled—as was Mutti—with my nice haul. When they both proceeded to clean, store and prepare the meat, I told them how it had come about. We were all giggles.

"We hope you remembered to pay him," my parents asked.

"Of course," I smiled.

Mutti and I were invited the following day to a first birthday. Her acquaintance was the grandmom of that sweet, dressed-up baby girl. The elder, willowy lady was another *Landsmann* of Mutti's. She had two married daughters: the Golas, who were the happy parents and another tall, blonde, 'Aryan-looking' one, who was there with her equally well-built husband. Of course, they were all in hiding almost right next to the charming church on *la Place St. Josse*. Since this was near the Hakums, we saw both families frequently. In everything and everywhere, there lurked danger for us.

One day, the very tall couple made a surprise call on us, stating that this was a farewell visit, since they were going to *stellen* themselves. "Oh, no, don't say that! Don't even dare think it!" we all besought them.

"No, there's no use. We can't live this way. The fugitive, dishonest style is not for us." They tried to convince themselves and us, even after Mutti gave Limburg as an example and told how she had felt similarly, as did the dentist Abbuhl, who was never heard from again.

"Sorry, for us there are no other means." And with that, they sadly shook hands with us and left. I ran after them and caught them at the landing for one last try: "Please don't do it! You two quite especially with your very 'Aryan' looks. You have so much to live for, obviously having each other's love. Don't do it. For heaven's sake! You are sinning against yourselves!"

They repeated: "We just can't live dishonestly. So we'll work for the Germans. Most Jewish people do *stellen* themselves and 'hiders' like you are really the exceptions, for it takes special stamina and fortitude, which unfortunately we were not blessed with. We deeply appreciate your concern." was their stubborn reply. I finally rested my case.

My life continued amazingly ordered in these turbulent times. I bought and sold books, so the shopkeepers thought I was a representative. I never would have guessed that buying rationed meat could be such fun since it resulted in contact with the handsome butcher. Visits to the Golas were now sad since, indeed, this nice "honest" couple had gone to *stellen* themselves. Mrs. Hakum seemed to be a big money maker with the *Wehrmacht*'s purchasing department. With their staff at hand, the brother as butler and Mrs. Schwartz, the cook, their life bordered on luxury despite the small size of their apartment. During one visit Mrs. Hakum gazed at me and said, "I understand your hair is as dark as mine. I'm trying but can't picture you that way, for you look like a true, natural blonde."

"I'm very glad. It makes me feel much safer. I sometimes pass acquaintances who stare at me, but don't recognize me as readily. In fact, today on my way here, there was a classmate, Margot Nürnberger, from the Jewish school in *Lützowstrasse* in Köln, who did not recall me. I left it that way, because these days, you don't know anymore who you are dealing with. This is great for now.

But looking at you, the desire to have my own color is stirring within me," I explained to the beautiful Luxemburger.

The tremendous nocturnal fear of idling *Wehrmacht* vehicles that were lost because of the forking streets was repeated with frequency. So nightly, prior to falling asleep, my mind rehearsed the escape from the terrace over the rooftops should THEY—may it never, ever happen—come for us.

Gradually, the summer turned into fall. Slowly, nature was changing into copper, golden splendor. The fortunes of war turned equally bright for the Allies, since GENERAL SIR BERNARD MONTGOMERY BECAME THE COMMANDER OF THE BRITISH 8TH ARMY ON 10-42. When two weeks later, on November 8th—a fine revenge for the eve of the *Kristallnacht* four years earlier—THE AMERICANS UNDER GENERAL CLARK AND THE HIGH COMMAND OF GENERAL EISENHOWER were reinforcing this military enterprise, the cold night winds must have roared across the desert to its Fox, Rommel: "*Achtung! Raus, raus!*" Indeed, our axis enemies, the Germans and Italians, were chased through the sweltering sands across Egypt and Libya and out of North Africa altogether.

ROMMEL, WHOM THE GERMANS REVERED AS THEIR INVINCIBLE MYTHOS-MYTH, WAS AT LAST DRIVEN OUT OF THE VERY MUCH FOUGHT FOR EL ALMEIN, near Alexandria, not far from the Nile, BEFORE THE END OF 1942! The French-language BBC reported this proudly, signing off as they always had since the time when Simon and I had imitated in unison—with this hate-spiked verse: "*Nous les écraserons!* (We'll crush and squash them!) *Nous les aurons, les Boches!!*" With even more passionate emphasis on the end: We'll get them!! I gathered plenty of material for my own chapter about North Africa and the fictitious younger son, Alfred, a volunteer pilot with the British fighting the Afrika Korps.

For the first time ever, the *Brüsseler Zeitung* depicted the extent of the suffering during their own retreat in the unforgiving heat. How stiff their underwear would become in the contrasting chill of the nights from dirt and sweat. I collected these dramatic articles

for future reference to my book, which I kept at the bottom of a
huge traveling basket, so no one would find it.

For quite some time now, each individual and nation wanted a
swift end to Hitler's war and desired, most fervently, the Second
Front. It was the battle cry from the East, Russia, and the West,
England. Of course, we all expected the great saviors to be the
U.S. Most unfortunately, it remained an unanswered prayer. To
that effect, facetiously, the *Brüsseler Zeitung* showed the following
caricature: Roosevelt as a nanny, his chin huge as a beard with two
immense breasts holding a suckling on each. "Baby" Stalin was to
the left and "Baby" Churchill to the right, whose big cigar was in
the corner of his mouth so he could do the job at hand effectively.
Clearly showing Roosevelt's preference, he gazed dotingly at
Winston. Both "babies" were screaming: "Second Front! Second
Front!!" Thus, the Germans were poking fun at the Allies—

About one month later, on December 12th, 1942, Vati's red
wool thread finally budged to the west.

ANOTHER UNCONQUERABLE GENERAL VON
PAULUS, JUST PROMOTED TO FIELD MARSHAL, DARED
TO OPPOSE HITLER AND WAS ABOUT TO SURRENDER
TO THE RUSSIAN GENERAL ZHUKOV, was reported in the
media. Von Paulus led the most powerful Army, the 6th, which
up to now had never known defeat. Irony upon irony for Hitler: In
order to absolutely strengthen his "military virtue," he upgraded
General von Paulus to Field Marshal, which was the former's last-
minute idea because Field Marshals were never, ever conquered!
Zhukov choked Stalingrad with a noose in concert with ground
and air attacks. At great length and with many sacrifices the
embattled city was turned into Dante's blazing inferno.

I had resented some Jewish furriers for manufacturing unlined,
primitive rabbit vests in their own hiding places for contractors to
the *Wehrmacht*'s Russian front. Of course, their funds were running
out and this was the only way they knew how to make a living.
Vati had bought one for me. It was amazing how practical these
warm, lightweight, thin garments were. Now that the weskits didn't

help the Nazis any, my bitterness was gone. Also because of the Buts, I'm sure the hares we were hiding with didn't go that way.

Despite my admiration for Mrs. Hakum as a business woman—I even intended to emulate her, but with the Allies, should I survive—it bothered me. Even though her merchandise was of a naïve nature, thus for no war efforts whatsoever, her dealings did not meet with my approval.

It was Christmas 1942. During my four-year stay in Belgium, I had never had the opportunity to realize that this high holiday was celebrated in a most boisterous, happy fashion. It was just the antithesis in Germany, where it was truly "Still Night, Holy Night." I recalled how on this Christian festivity, my neighbors and friends would pile up a special pretty plate with those wonderful goodies. Now these were the very people I was hiding from, leading this abnormal life in deathly fear of them. How could this be possible?

For us it was, indeed, a still night. In the warmth, looking at the crackling fire, we were glad to be here, peacefully and together.

Chapter 23

Vati came running up the steps breathlessly—but this time from joy—showing us the headlines of the *Brüsseler Zeitung*: "1-14-43 : CASABLANCA CONFERENCE BETWEEN UNITED NATIONS LEADERS TO FINALIZE TUNISIA CAMPAIGN."

"What's so great about that?" Mutti asked, adding: "They'll start discussions and the time it'll take to put their plan into action. Besides, they are talking about Tunisia. A lot of good it will do us!" she speculated sarcastically.

"But Sofiechen. Don't you see? Once they have freed themselves of the North Afrika Korps, they will be able to fight for bigger and better things, such as creating the much-desired Second Front. Or do you think Eisenhower and Clark will just take their troops back to America after driving Rommel out of Africa?"

With a shrug, she sighed: "In the meantime the Nazis might come to deport us, first to Malines for a few weeks and then—who knows where?"

"*Ja, ja,*" Vati sadly agreed.

Only days later, on January 18th, 1943, he was happy to finally move the red thread on his Russian map, for THE 17-MONTH SIEGE OF LENIGRAD WAS CRUSHED.

At about this time, rationing got tighter and food more scarce. We were most fortunate with the Buts around. Mrs. Buts got our official stamps, which was astounding and it was kept secret even to us how she could obtain my parents' rations. However, there was a most pivotal turn concerning my I.D. They contacted a Belgian girl, my age, who dutifully claimed the loss of her green *carte d'identité*. I was blessed to feel safe with this "lost" I.D. Also most amazing was Mr. Buts' skill in putting half of the legitimate cruncher and stamp onto my blonde photo and the other half on the actual green all-important *carte d'identité*. Even with a magnifying glass, a demarcation line was undetectable. Should I, God forbid, get into THEIR clutches, I could still hope that, thanks to Mr. Buts' great art work bearing my new "Flemish" name, I might be released. This also made fetching my rationing legal for Mrs. Buts.

By now there were long lines for everything. Vati or I would join them without knowing what they were really for. Nowhere was I as lucky as with the handsome butcher. I had followed his advice many times over whenever there was activity in front of his store. It had never failed to be the highlight of my present Spartan life.

Was there an attractive fish woman somewhere? Vati also was fortunate to bring home a nice haul of "green herrings." They had to be prepared immediately. This was quite a rare treat, because other than the Jewish, sweet-tasting carp prepared by Vati on Friday nights, no fish was allowed in our household because it offended Mutti's nostrils. These days, though, nobody had any objections, least of all about food.

Just as we were about to sit down to enjoy our fried dinner, there was a knock at the door. Our breath and appetite abated instantly. A stronger knock followed. With a pounding heart and quivering voice, I inquired from within: "*Qui est là?*"

"*La Police!*"

Pulsating all over from throat to fingertips, I had no choice but to open. It was bad but not total despair—depending on the attitude of this Belgian uniformed individual. A very lean Belgian policeman entered. The Bobby-style helmet made his face appear gaunt. Looking from us to the hot fish, he excused himself—an excellent sign. In perfect English, he addressed me apologetically: "Sorry, but it's my duty to check up on you. Suspicious people wanted to know what strange family is living here."

My heart was still thumping, but I was relieved by his kind behavior and now forbidden English speech.

"Personally, I advise you, *Mademoiselle*, to shop downstairs, here with your own neighbors at the green grocer's store. The fat lady and her thin husband are good people. Also, their son is about to open his own dairy adjacent to his parents' shop, and you can get your *fleutje melk* (newly invented skim milk) and other rationed items there. Why don't you go there tomorrow in order to lift your mystery? There's nothing to fear. They're a fine couple and are on our side. They will understand and no questions will be asked. In turn they can reassure their customers that you are regular people. Enjoy your fish!" and with a slight military salute, he left.

Though dinner was no longer hot, we could now savor it with joy after the anxiety of the alarming visit had passed. I took the policeman's advice and found out that he was right in every way. I bought the necessities and detected three boxes whose contents created the delicious apple crumb cake. Vati had complained about not being able to find this great product anymore. Instead, Mutti baked with the flour from the country, which Mrs. Buts had brought us for black market prices. The cake tasted good, but upon swallowing, it scratched the throat. Most likely, the grain was not ground finely enough. "This is a very wise choice, *Mademoiselle*. I ought not give you my last three. They won't produce them anymore for lack of ingredients. But since you are our neighbor and honored us with your first purchase—welcome! You may have all of them," the heavy-set lady said with a broad grin. We were glad that we could take a short leave from our "scratch snacks."

On January 27, 1943, the *Brüsseler Zeitung* announced with open bitterness and horror: "U.S. KILLER BOMBERS OVER GERMANY!" Then, on January 30th: NAZI FIELD MARSHAL VON PAULUS, AT LONG LAST, TOTALLY SURRENDERED AFTER 5 MONTHS OF FEROCIOUS BATTLE FOR STALINGRAD. This enormously important news was not printed in the *Brüsseler Zeitung* for von Paulus' capitulation was a disgrace and, therefore, too embarrassing to be reported in a German paper. It was just common knowledge.

As usual, I was taking my long walk to la Place St. Josse. While window-shopping, I caught glimpses of my reflection and was pleased, when I heard a congenial male voice: "*Mademoiselle, comment ça va?*"

If it wasn't the policeman observing my complacence, making me feel somewhat embarrassed. I thanked him for his advice, which had turned out so well. Softly, we conversed in our favorite forbidden language. "How did you know to address me in English that night, *Monsieur*?"

"You don't realize how many Anglo-Saxon books and *feuilletons* are at your apartment. I detected them the minute you let me in," he explained.

After I took leave of him, I continued down la Chaussee until I arrived at la Place St. Josse, where I entered another dairy store. From the back came the very good-looking boy with wavy blonde hair and handsome profile. I enjoyed his wonderful smile and fantasized it being a different place and another time. Of course, any period, any location would be far better than the here and now, I thought, while the blushing young man in the white smock was giving me generous rations of eggs, cheese and butter, without taking his blue stare off me. I paid as fast as I possibly could to avoid his overprotective parents. I saw them approaching from the rear in order to shelter him from me—the evil woman. He must have been a virgin, too, I speculated as I took off like a thief in the night.

My parents were pleased when I got home—especially with the tiny amount of "good butter," as it was called. Later Mutti asked Vati: "So what use was the Casablanca Conference of the Allied leaders? Nothing is happening."

"As I always said, even in Antwerp, decisive, earnest fighting takes place in spring. Look at my red thread on the map!" He got up and showed us proudly: "I had to move it quite a bit to the west after Stalingrad, which was the biggest defeat not only for Nazi Germany but in all of Teutonic history. Do you know what the letters 'CL' mean? It's the international code for 'This station will no longer transmit.' That's what happened at Stalingrad, and Hitler's laughable ruse of promoting von Paulus and other generals to field marshal because they never, ever surrender—ha, ha! The big joke on the Führer was that von Paulus disobeyed and he and his famous Sixth Army—or what was left of it after death and capture—was now in Russian hands. Believe me, this is a big turning point for us. Besides, the real heavy fighting in Tunisia has just begun now, in February." He tried to convince us, but this was unnecessary. It became a known fact that TENACIOUS BATTLES AT SEA AND ON LAND PREVAILED IN TUNISIA AND RUSSIA THROUGHOUT THE WINTER.

Our immediate concern was staying safe from Nazi claws. Our second worry—and we were not alone—was to have enough food. We usually did—and if worst came to worst, I would alternate cooking red, white and green cabbage or my parents would prepare a typical Polish piping hot sauerkraut soup.

In the meantime, the war against the Jews—snatching them wherever THEY could—went on here relentlessly, lately even at cinemas. Nevertheless, we did go to see films, because most Jews were caught at their own flats. The movie house was across the street from us. The first picture we saw was with a very young Rossano Brazzi as Cavaradossi. The libretto of Puccini's "Tosca"— shown in beautiful *directoire* costumes—was relative to our struggle but by no means quite that extreme. As much as we enjoyed this and subsequent Italian, German and French films, all Goebbels-controlled, with pounding hearts, what sheer relief we felt to be walking out without being stopped!

One sunny, brisk Sunday afternoon, Vati and I turned up the Avenue du Diamant, admiring the pretty houses which led us to a new journey. He was fascinated by my retelling the Spanish stories I was studying. At the end of this long, healthy walk we stumbled upon a huge drill ground. "Aha!" I exclaimed in utter surprise. "They swagger and sing from the barracks of la Place Dailly just marching around our house in order to get here and be trained for the Führer's fresh cannon fodder!" I calculated my logical discovery.

Indeed, the next morning they awoke me again with a song I might have heard before. I was too sleepy to realize the lyrics, except: "We landed! We landed!"

On Tuesday we read about the Belgian traitor Léon Degrelle amassing a fortune collaborating with the enemy. It was snugly tucked away in kilos of solid 18-karat gold. "Can one *platz* (burst)?" we cried.

In 1938, the sad year I had become a refugee, ubiquitously one heard the very *triste* song, "*J'attendrais.*" Now, this seemed to be happening with an equally melancholy melody: "*Je suis seul ce soir.*" Analyzing my feelings from the past, I concluded: Then, there was more depression and we were in a cloak of utter hopelessness, while now, constant fear accompanied us at all times. As to fate, there were only two ways about it: either to survive by continuing our clandestine lifestyle or be caught by THEM—

We finally got out of that "winter tunnel." My favorite season had just started. Daily, I went onto our beautiful terrace to work on my book and improve my self-imposed classes in philology, while admiring my treasured time of the year which to me represented youth and hope. Violets were in bloom again, so were all things of nature. The pleasant chirp of birds made me look skyward when I realized their return. It was a happy combination: my endeavour while enjoying this idyllic scene.

Occasionally, Vati would run into other hidden acquaintances from his Antwerp days. They even invited him to their places.

Some time later, he jubilantly ran upstairs announcing: "Didn't I tell you?! Didn't I tell you?!" On May 12th, 1943, the BBC proudly announced: "AXIS SURRENDER AT TUNISIA. ALL GERMAN RESISTANCE ENDED!" "Isn't that wonderful?" he asked, his eyes beaming. "Now the Allies are free to go on to bigger and better things!" he added with joy.

We could hardly catch our breath when Vati entered with the *Brüsseler Zeitung* from May 16th, in which the Germans complained again of "DAY RAIDS BY AMERICAN BOMBER KILLERS OVER KIEL."

One early morning, while savoring my writing in the lovely surroundings, I was compelled to look upward—not by the merry twitter of the migrant birds, but its contrary sound: a basso profundo of American planes soaring through the sky in outstretched finger formation, escorted by their squadron leader,

looking like tiny silver toys. Their humming had a soothing effect
upon me, contrary to a couple of years before, when Stukas were
aiming at us and THEIR roar was the most frightening, panic-
evoking noise ever! Why did we have to become such mortal enemies
of those I grew up with, I asked myself, and the answer was: THEIR
enthusiasm, devotion and unbridled allegiance to Hitler!

Looking up at the glittering mini-appearing Flying Fortresses,
I wished the American pilots, navigators and bombardiers "Good
Luck!" in their mission—and a safe return to their base. My only
hope for the German side was to leave the *Kölner Dom* (Cologne
Cathedral) unharmed. During their first mighty try-out-
bombardment of all cities, the British had picked my birthplace,
Köln, on May 30th, 1942. And indeed, even though the main
station, a key strategic target, was only a few steps across from the
Dom, it remained untouched. What precision! I knew that the
planes now flying above were American, because they flew by day,
while the RAF's were on night missions.

Again, the Nazis were protesting: THE NIGHT RAID OF
THE ENGLISH ON DORTMUND WAS DEVASTATING, THE
WORST EVER! Vati said indignantly: "What did the Germans
expect?! That they have the right to bomb any European city without
it ever boomeranging on them?! That others should just keep taking
it forever without any repercussions?!"

I had all the research for my chapter on the RAF and U.S.
Flying Fortresses and the suffering of the German population at
my fingertips, from on-the-spot reports in the *Brüsseler Zeitung*
showing what Hitler's own people were going through and
remembering my horror of their Stukas on the Belgian coast. Yes,
I could relate very well to that, reliving my excruciating experiences
of three years prior. Erna, who was believed to be back in Germany,
was the heroine in this part of the novel. I went to work on it right
away in the early morning spring splendor on the veranda, not
neglecting to point out that the air warfare was their Führer's idea
and not that of the Anglo-Americans. After all, this book was
entirely about the global pain brought about by Hitler in various
ways.

For the time being I felt blessed—even more so when Vati
arrived not only with edible goodies but with military ones. He
ran up two steps at a time, mocking the *Wehrmacht* song: "We
landed! We landed! Didn't I tell you so?! Didn't I tell you?!" He
cheered as he unfolded the German newspaper, proudly showing
us: "6-12-43: ISLAND FORTRESS PANTELLERIA AFTER
INCESSANT BOMBARDMENTS BY ALLIES—FROM 5-29
UNTIL THIS DAY—SURRENDERS TO THEM. THE ISLAND
OF LAMPEDUSA WAS CAPTURED BY THE ALLIES AS
WELL"

"I've never even heard of these places," I stated.

"Both are Italian islands. Pantelleria is located between Tunisia
and Sicily and Lampedusa between Tunisia and Malta. At any
rate, it's just as I predicted: Once out of Tunisia, the Allies would
go on to bigger and better things. Now, with the capitulation of
these small islands, the road to Sicily has been paved. Hurray!"

One afternoon, we were invited to Vati's former business
friends, the Perlmans. This was an intellectual family of four. Their
youngest son was about my age and I could talk with him in many
different languages. I made my speaking debut in Spanish, in which
he seemed to be fluent—a rarity here. He was amazed at my almost
accent-free Spanish, but suggested I still had a lot of studying to
do in the grammar department, especially the conditional, which
I was overusing. It was a pleasure to converse with his elder sister,
a school teacher. Mrs. Perlman gave Vati lots of exotic, interesting
vegetarian recipes.

The entire family went prematurely into hiding. The parents
were the first Jewish people I ever met of the very few privileged,
naturalized Belgian citizens. The Perlmans did not trust the solemn
Nazi pledge to the dowager Queen Elisabeth to spare at least the
"handful" of Belgian Jews.

"We landed! We landed!" Vati entered singingly with his
German paper on the sunny morning of July 10th, 1943. "WE
LANDED ON ALL SIDES, EDGES AND FROM ALL
DIRECTIONS ON SICILY, THE SOUTH GATEWAY TO
EUROPE! HURRAY!" We embraced in one happy heap, but when

Mutti let go, she said worriedly: "Now it's going to be our karma, what comes first—our Allies' success pushing up north or THEM finding us." "This will truly be our destiny," we agreed. "But let's savor each enjoyable event that crosses our path!"

When we saw the Perlmans again, the four of them seemed extremely upset. "Is today *Tisha b'Av*?" Vati tried to make light of it, at the same time gently pressing for an explanation.

"Yes," Mr. Perlman answered. "A modern one at that. Last night, we heard on the BBC that the endless convoys and trains filled with Jews are being led to their slaughter in annihilation camps. That they were shipped to work or even slave-labor are all Nazi lies."

"This is far worse than the biblical *Tisha b'Av*, because it's not just the rampage upon a holy architectural marvel, Herod's Temple of Jerusalem, but the extermination of the most precious creation on earth: human lives!" Mrs. Perlman detailed.

"'Destruction of the entire European Jewry' were the British announcer's exact words." The son wanted to clarify this earth-shaking broadcast.

We were stunned, open and dry-mouthed, just flopping down onto the closest chairs. All of us sat there in mourning, aghast and utterly dejected. They were losing, but for us, they were still the attacking colossus, dominating our lives—but, most fortunately, I did not accept it. Shall we call it arrogance, this attitude of mine? Ha, me work for the Nazis? They have another thing coming! This viewpoint had saved my life—so far.

Lately I'd been having good feelings for Mutti, but at this moment, her words from the forest, exactly one year before, echoed: "Since we can't find a flat, it might be best that you should *stellen* yourselves after all!" How I hated this phrase then and even more so now—in fact so much that as before, I doubted her, which in turn made me feel terrible. She, of course, was totally unaware of my very private inner struggle. Should I survive, will I ever resolve this? I certainly would not owe it to her, but to myself. Would she have received the summons to *stellen* for "work" also, my resentment would not be that overpowering.

On July 19th, 1943, the BBC reported: "AIR AND RAILWAY INSTALLATIONS WERE BLASTED BY U.S. B-26 IN PREPARATION FOR INVASION ON THE ITALIAN MAINLAND AND TO CUT NAZI REINFORCEMENT AND SUPPLIES FOR THE PRESENT FIGHTING ZONE, SOUTH ITALY."

"The Americans must have been as careful with the many churches of the Eternal City as the English in Köln with the Dom. The situations were the same: the holy architectures being so close to the all-important train terminals. The Basilica di San Lorenzo was the only exception," Vati pointed out.

When Mrs. Buts brought us the black market food supplies, her face was even more stern than usual. "Listen carefully, *Mademoiselle*! The mother of your two musical friends called us briefly and nervously, saying: '*Madame*, you must warn that family to use extreme caution. Rumor has it that after THEY have caught and taken us to the collection camp, Malines, THEY ship us like cattle to the east, not to work but to gas chambers, then ovens and finally crematoriums. There are really mammoth killing industries for mass murder. I, for one, who lived in Aachen all my life before Brussels, can't believe such extreme atrocities. Nevertheless, warn the friend of my children and her parents! *Merci, Madame.*' Then she hung up." Madame Buts relayed this grisly, ghoulish tale—a message of death—and added with great bitterness: "She is Jewish and doubts THEIR unspeakable cruelty, and I, who am not, don't put any horror past THEM, those *Boches*!"

I didn't say anything, but such unprecedented brutality went beyond my imagination, too. We hadn't yet got over Perlman's BBC information news, but now this unthinkable method of genocide?! What an ingenious system toward assassination of such magnitude!—THEY are after us—me, that THEY want to do these nefarious things to—

After a self-tormenting weekend, on July 24th-25th, 1943, despite the terrible news, Vati came running up the steps as though there was joy, exclaiming: "As of yesterday, a Sunday yet—Benito no longer has the benediction of his Italy. No longer can you find the daily demeaning caricatures of HRH Victor Emmanuel, royally outfitted with medals and fancy plumed hat in the waste basket, because now that Mussolini is ousted, the King placed Marshal Pietro Badaglio at the head of his government. Why, oh why hasn't this already happened with the Führer as it did with his good, old—and now, at sixty, seemingly senile—buddy, Il Duce?!" Vati asked in a praying gesture, adding: "With this bastard, Hitler, it's so much more urgent for all mankind and mostly for us."

Now, due to the constant peril, in addition to my "roof escape" nightly mental rehearsals, my mind also practiced that—God forbid!—should THEY catch me on the street, though it would be difficult for me, I would create such a commotion that THEY might, just might, release me. Would this occur in Poland or Russia, THEY would machine gun me on the spot, while here in the west, THEY do keep THEIR murderous ways secret. That's why we were hearing about this only now, even though the general killings had been going on since December of 1940, when indeed, THEY had summoned us. We'd been sent to Limburg in January 1941 for that reason, but obviously, some miracle had occurred.

Like everybody, I had always believed the camps were for hard labor. Again I was complacent about my "Nazi-work-attitude." Of course, my greatest protection was the green Belgian citizen's I.D. without the stamps *Juif* and *Jood*, but with THEM, one always had to imagine the worst and hope for the best, should everything else fail—

The news in the *Brüsseler Zeitung* on July 26th, 1943: "BRITISH HORROR BOMBERS OVER HAMBURG DISRUPTING ARMAMENT PRODUCTION AND KILLING CIVILIANS!" Only three nights later: "A REPEAT TERROR ON HAMBURG WITH THE MOST CATASTROPHIC CONSEQUENCES!"

On the first Sunday in August 1943, Vati took us to visit yet another acquaintance. Prior to this, we had weighed our present, very sad and perilous situation thoroughly: "Danger looms inside and out, so we might as well live as normally as possible, since we saw, without realizing, that we had been observed by our 'strange behavior,' the policeman, this Belgian angel, being a warning, and serving as an example to prevent suspicion, thus avoiding eventual squealers."

Our decision was made: We set out into a different direction than the usual *Chaussee de Louvain*, because that family was hiding further than *Schaerbeek*.

A dark, very friendly middle-aged man, whose politeness belied his rough looks, answered the doorbell and led us up into a plain furnished, but clean two-room apartment. I was stunned at the flashy showgirl type with red, long hair and longer legs whom he introduced as his wife. She was a beauty and very young—my age. This incongruous couple was extremely courteous, their hospitality bordering on servility, as though they were most honored to have us.

As we were finishing the coffee and well-prepared cake—though another throat-scratcher—we heard a child 's gurgle from the next room. They brought in a precious girl with very dark curls and black eyes. Her already feminine appearance was marred by her left, turned-in eye. While the young mom took care of her, the father explained that they still had a special desire upon liberation: to see an ophthalmologist, which was too risky at this time.

Mr. Alesky wanted to know exactly which streets we took to get here, and applauded our explanation. We thought this strange until he warned: "No more streets with heavy traffic for you, please! There is a mean fellow, Jewish, mind you! He is known only by the name of 'Jacques' and I'm told he resembles the *Brüsseler Zeitung*'s caricature of Churchill. Since one Jew is apt to recognize his own better than the Germans do, he drives with THEM all over Brussels. Now that it's summer, he is actually hanging out the car window to get a very close look at each passer-by—and unfortunately for us, he is extremely successful. Most likely he has been promised freedom. But we know the value of a Nazi vow."

Totally shocked once again, I stated: "Each pleasant visit brings more and more dark emotions."

"This relentless flow of ups and downs." Vati shook his head sadly. "High from our Allies and a continued low, low for us, the Jews!"

Now we returned through all the small streets consciously. "RUSSIANS ARE UNSTOPPABLE AFTER LENINGRAD!" was the news. Vati kept moving his red thread to the left accordingly. "8-17-43: CONQUEST OF SICILY COMPLETED!" was the wonderful news. As he was doing this, he informed us of the following: "The Nazis are losing on all fronts; their defeat in North Africa is recent history already. Now, they are being chased to the north from Sicily, enabling the Allies to continue their European entry from the south. The Russians are making great strides in the east, regaining their lost territories and unpronounceable cities. Only last year the German Navy had the upper hand in the Atlantic. This year, the tide has turned against them, plus the air war above Germany. "But *ja, ja.*" His face grew gloomy as he finished on a sour note. "*Ja, ja,* only THEIR fight against us Jews is stepping up in ever increasing proportions, because our Allies never came to our rescue, *ja, ja*!"

At this point, no one knew if we would ever be liberated, and if so, by which of our glorious Allies, the Anglo-Americans or the Russians? In the latter event, I thought, what use would all my languages be? Therefore, at my next book-gallery visit, instead of selling, I swapped my French language "Madame Bovary" by Gustav Flaubert for a slightly used Russian-German autodidactic book. It was a compact, lacquered hardcover.

Vati, as before, entered with great glee, chanting: "-and we landed! We landed!" On September 3rd, 1943, he read: "'MONTGOMERY WITH HIS BRITISH FAMED 8th ARMY CROSSED THE MESSINA STRAIT, THUS THE ALLIED INVASION ON THE ITALIAN MAINLAND HAS BEGUN!' This is great news! But what's even more important: not only are they now in the Italian 'boot,' but imagine, on this very same day, without any further fights, hardly a shot, the Italians surrendered unconditionally." Just five days later, on September 8th, it was officially announced by Eisenhower.

I heard Vati running up with his usual double step, singing as had become customary for him: "-and we landed! We landed!" The news in the *Brüsseler Zeitung* on September 9th, 1943: "ALLIES

LANDED AT THE SEAPORT OF SALERNO FACING STRONG RESISTANCE BY US! (Germans)"

It was still warm enough to do my new study of the Cyrillic alphabet on the terrace. I was counting all the symbols I knew chronologically, to write and/or read: Gothic, Hebrew, solfège, phonetics, German and French shorthand and now adding the invention of St. Cyril, the 9th-century Apostle to the Slavs.

ON September 12th, 1943, the *Brüsseler Zeitung* proudly announced: "MUSSOLINI WAS RESCUED DARINGLY BY OUR BRAVE GLIDER!" On September 16th, the news was: "THE 7th DAY OF THE BEACHING, THE ALLIES FINALLY SECURED THE BRIDGEHEAD AT SALERNO."

"ON SEPTEMBER 25th, GERMANS WERE CHASED 300 MILES NORTHWEST AND DRIVEN OUT OF SMOLENSK!" Vati informed us after he kept moving his Russian victory thread steadfastly to the west.

We saw the Aleskys again. Upon arriving, Mrs. Alesky was not quite ready yet, and I was amazed how different she looked sans skillful make-up. While she finished, her husband revealed that since the traitor Jacques was on the loose, they didn't dare leave the house other than for the bare essentials because of his very dark, foreign appearance and her striking beauty. Then he told us what he went through during what was actually the very first mass deportation of Polish Jews in Germany at the end of October 1938—five years ago to the month at this point. This, of course, preceded the *Kristallnacht*, the night of smashing glass and hurling Jewish property through their windows onto the streets. "You were most fortunate that you remained untouched by these savage actions," he finished.

"May we all be free of the Nazi ruthlessness until our liberation!" Mutti exclaimed.

"*Omein*," the good-looking young woman, now entering, said and we answered with "*Omein!*" lifting our chipped coffee cups.

"Please tell me about your dreadful experiences and I shall take it down in shorthand for my manuscript. This is another disaster created by THEM which should be in my book. I want to impart this knowledge for the descendants of all the world. This is what my docu-fiction is all about!"

After expressing their astonishment at my setting out with such an ambitious plan while in hiding, Mr. Alesky answered: "One afternoon is not long enough to relate all the cruel sufferings and ferocious evils we had to endure. We'll be happy and honored to have you here any time," the couple assured me.

"It's a deal!" I agreed.

"Another morning, another victory," Vati entered happily on October 1st, 1943. "TROOPS OF THE AMERICAN GENERAL CLARK OCCUPY NAPLES: THEN CONTINUE UP NORTH ON BOTH COASTS, THE MEDITERRANEAN ON THE WEST, THE ADRIATIC ON THE EAST!"

We also visited the intelligentsia, the Perlmans. They were the antithesis of the Aleskys, though the latter would not have been our prime choice for friendship in normal times. Nonetheless, there seemed to be mutual enjoyment with each get-together. The same could be said of the Perlmans, and for me, it was additionally gratifying because I could converse with the son in seven different languages. What a shame that with my romances run dry—other than the butcher and the young dairy man—I felt no physical attraction to Perlman, Jr. He told me in Spanish of his family's continuing desire to leave for Switzerland, especially now with this nightmare Jacques! "Just think how fast our lives can be taken away!" he warned.

"Though the Allies are doing extremely well this year, there is still no Second Front," Mr. Perlman pointed out. "Meanwhile almost 1000 Jews arrive in Malines each month and are shipped to annihilation camps."

Mutti repeated her question from before: "Whatever comes first—the liberation by the Allies or the unspeakable?"

"The Nazis seem to be made of a very special, cruel fibre," the daughter stated. "We obtained the following information: Just before THEY were driven out of Naples, THEIR usual, natural style in THEIR animalism debauchery of executions, explosions, destruction and terror climaxed in the premeditated killings at the new post office. THEY had placed a time-bomb to go off one week later at the busiest time and the most active place. This was the communication center of Allied-occupied Italy, where mostly women and children were hit and died. On this October day at the post office alone, over one hundred civilians were killed instantly. Many hundreds were slain at the various sites of explosives set by the retreating Germans for their 'buddies,' the Italians of their own Axis. Of course, let's not forget THEIR brutish book burning style—first, Jewish books and now, 200,000 of the Royal Society were burnt. So much for Nazi culture! No wonder the thrilled Neapolitans welcomed their former enemies, the Allies, with open arms, literally!"

The news on November 6th, 1943: "KIEV 'RECAPTURED' BY RUSSIANS!" Shortly thereafter, we took a walk through small trafficless streets as advised. When I told Vati my last Spanish story of a prince who was perpetually melancholy. In order to cheer him up, they had the most beautiful dancers perform for him. After the curtain fell, the young royal wept. When asked why he was so touched by the performance, his sobbing answer was: "Their lovely faces and smooth, svelte bodies will be wrinkled and fat, nor will they be able to move about—if they are alive at all—forty to fifty years from now."

"Vati, it makes me so sad that I am losing these precious, young years. There is such tremendous importance to youth, especially for a woman. Of course, every day, I am grateful for being alive as a very old person would be. It still gives me the desire to save myself by going to Switzerland. I will inquire at the Perlmans as to what is my first step to get there," I told him of this moment's innermost wish.

"But it does look so close to an Allied victory," he objected.

"True. Yet on a daily basis, Jews are being caught regardless of age or sex, no matter whether in their own dwellings, on the street, in stores or cinemas. It's going on notwithstanding THEIR losses. Indeed, the Jewish Final Solution is THEIR sacred task, German Racial Supremacy is THEIR priority number one, no matter what! In the meantime, I have turned from a girl into a woman, and churn with longing for life. The years are passing with fear and nothing else. One season is flowing into another, while it gets more dangerous by the minute and still, the liberators do not come!" I got so angry I did not realize I had quickened my step as I continued: "We are constantly in the path of violence. Fall is turning into winter and we are still in hiding. I no longer see things through rosy glasses. But at this moment, I feel a soul-elevating consolation: we are defying death by hiding—that's sort of a fight also. But it's becoming long-term, an existence in a world from which we are excluded." I elegized while even the wind was crying with me. In my mind, I heard the strings of a deep, sad cello.

Vati, being most sympathetic, said after a mournful *ja, ja.* "Just be patient and appreciate each morning upon waking that you are still free instead of being in THEIR deadly clutches."

Lately, a family of three had been visiting us frequently. Otto, Meta's brother, whom Vati knew through Mendel in Antwerp, his Gentile live-in mate and her daughter, my age. Even traitor Jacques would never be able to recognize this very big, tough, German-looking red face (like Vati's) as Jewish, believing instead he was a pure rustic Aryan in the constant company of two tall, fair ladies. Of course, there was a pang of jealousy in me when the young one rushed off to a dinner dance date. I was under the impression that the whole world had come to a standstill while living my Spartan existence with an indefinite hold on life's youthful joys.

In the meantime, winter was upon us, and soon it was Christmas, 1943. On the second day of this holiday, December 26th, the *Brüsseler Zeitung* read: "THE ALLIES FINALLY REACHED MONTE CASSINO ON THEIR PAINFUL ROAD BETWEEN NAPLES AND ROME: OUR BRAVES ARE DIGGING IN AND WON'T BE DEFEATED!"

Heavy fighting continued on all fronts after these "holy days of good will and forgiveness to all mankind." Yes, what happened to this piece of morality? How can this be unified with all the slaughter? Where are all the good Christians of the world, of Germany, and those of Cologne, who took me by the hand to show me into their homes, filling a special heaping, pretty plate with goodies underneath their wonderfully decorated tree? I could scream out loud!

Chapter 24

By now, Vati had made his Russian map more interesting by adding a new green thread to mark the start of the German retreat in November 1941 (at the time I was with Willy). The Nazis had reached, in an amazing three months, the gates of Moscow. Now, in 1944, the Red Army was going into their third year of fighting ferociously to chase our common enemy out of their country. Nevertheless, the gap between the two demarcation lines (where the Nazis had been and were presently) was quite respectable for the steadily advancing Russians.

Throughout the winter, the *Brüsseler Zeitung* was still teasing about the absence of a Second Front—to our dismay! Despite his consenting, sad "*ja, ja,*" Vati never gave up hope, advocating the Allies' cause with: "They are battling against another shrewd enemy on the other end of the world, the Japanese. The expenditure in manpower, military equipment and supplies it takes to transverse the Pacific is unimaginable."

Vati was my all-around support system in emotional, private, political and, at this moment, even military matters. I came to agree and uttered what we French steno-students discussed in December 1941: "Were it not for Pearl Harbor, the Americans would not have entered the war." Roosevelt had said repeatedly: "The U.S. remains neutral, but we cannot close our mind, conscience and heart!" Yet, in 1938, he and his State Department did just that with us Jews. Now that I knew of the annihilation camps, I dared not think what fate may have met so many I knew after the Belgian collection camp Malines . . . and what might yet happen to me?!

I was torn from this macabre thought by Vati's continuing effort to defend our brave Allies for the absence of the much-desired

Second Front: "They are also fighting in the Balkans, connecting with guerrillas of those various countries."

IN THE LIGHT OF THEIR SUCCESSES, THE QUEBEC CONFERENCE TOOK PLACE LAST AUGUST 1943 AMONG CHURCHILL, ROOSEVELT AND THE CANADIAN HEAD McKENZIE KING TO DISCUSS FURTHER ACTIONS OF THEIR ARMIES, NAVIES AND AIR FORCES.

Though there were very few noteworthy headlines in the *Brüsseler Zeitung* nor on the BBC, the local Jew-hunt continued to be ferociously active. Nevertheless, there was ongoing fierce fighting from the air, in the south, Italy, the east, Russia and the west, and the Nazis did prepare by watching the Channel and beyond from Antwerp to La Loire—THEIR "Atlantic Wall." We were thrilled with the smallest Allied victory or any advance that brought them a few kilometers closer to us, for the sake of world's morality and, undeniably, for our own cause, since each day we were engulfed in anguish, duping ourselves, leading as normal a life as possible under the clandestine circumstances.

February 1944: GENERAL MONTGOMERY OF THE FAMED 8th ARMY BECAME COMMANDER-IN-CHIEF OF ALL THE BRITISH ARMIES UNDER GENERAL EISENHOWER.

During this time I often thought that I was not only hiding myself and my being, but also burying the plague of fear behind my autodidactic studies. It was an excellent antidote to my emotions; I consoled myself by thinking that should I survive, I would need to be literate and cultured despite having been forced to miss out on the formal education I so eagerly desired. Should I be caught now . . . knowing the truth—no, the unthinkable must not even enter my mind.

These winter days, Vati appeared joylessly at the apartment with the *Brüsseler Zeitung*, which boasted news like: "AROUND THE ROCKY MOUNTAINS OF MONTE CASSINO, TORRENTIAL RAINS, MUD, HEAVY SNOW AND SLEET AND ABOVE ALL OUR BRAVELY FIGHTING TROOPS WITH FLAMETHROWERS AND BOOBYTRAPS ARE

PREVENTING THE PANZERS AND HEAVY ARTILLERY OF MONTGOMERY'S PUSH TOWARDS ROME."

"I always think of Goethe's Italy, with lemon blossoms, sunshine and warmth," I exclaimed in surprise.

"It's as I always contended," Vati now said optimistically. "Wait until the spring, after this very difficult terrain dries up. The Allies will continue their offensive despite the territory, and the unshakable rocks—the Nazis—who are still dying on all fronts for their worshipped Adolf!"

"TREMENDOUS STRIDES WERE MADE IN FEBRUARY 1944 BY THE RED ARMY PUSHING NAZI TROOPS OUT TOWARD THE WEST AND SOUTHWEST TO RUMANIA!" announced the BBC—and Vati's yarns on the map. Also a *Wehrmacht* tragedy of an immense scope occurred at *Shanderovka* at the *Dnieper* River's bend, where 75,000 with their heavy equipment were wiped out by the Russians. Troops that tried to break free were mowed down by pursuing Cossacks' swords, the classical, antique warfare; only 3000 officers were air-lifted and thus saved, we had heard.

It was common knowledge that for quite some time now, the Nazis had been losing on the high seas and in the air; certainly, German cities were being smashed. There were big, bitter, bloody battles, sometimes at bayonet point. "BOTH SIDES ARE FIGHTING BRAVELY AND SUFFERING ENORMOUSLY IN THIS BITINGLY COLD SEASON," was even admitted by the *Brüsseler Zeitung*. Although it was apparent that Nazi Fortuna was going downhill and haywire, they incessantly proved their pledge of Holy Allegiance to their beloved Führer and to THEIR Holy war against us Jews.

"So far, so good!" we might exclaim during these winter months. Avoiding *La Chaussee de Louvain* for its car traffic, I used only small, overseeable residential streets—except to get meat from the handsome butcher, whose store was on the main road. Besides, how could I possibly give up this double pleasure?

In order to stay informed about the local situation and to avoid becoming isolated, we kept in touch with acquaintances, Mostly I went to the *Aleskys*, sometimes accompanied, other times by myself.

There, I felt like a reporter, jotting down tragedies such as the story of the many deportees who had committed suicide at the barbed wire during the fall and winter of 1938. How lucky we were to be spared these horrible experiences of being without food and shelter in the Polish no-man's-land, later referred to as *Zbonzyn*, or *Bentschen* in German (ironically meaning the opposite in Hebrew: to bless). Were it not for Mutti's sixth sense and her undaunted determination to leave Köln for Belgium immediately (also supported by our landlord, Mr. Jung's early warning) exactly one month prior to the first mass deportation, we would have been amongst the wretched, for the action was strictly against Jews of Polish nationality living in Germany. These terrible tales would amount to one full chapter in my book.

The intellectual Perlmans grew more restless with each visit. They still wanted to save themselves by going to Switzerland. To me, this was very infectious, especially after learning from them how relentlessly the Jew-catching was going on and even accelerating. The daughter, who still would have been teaching were she not Jewish, got all her local information about the various districts through her school. She could no longer establish contact with an ever-increasing, staggering number of children, students and colleagues of the Jewish faith who had disappeared from the face of the earth.

Anguished after hearing this, I asked indignantly: "Doesn't the League of Nations exist anymore?" This turned out to be a silly question. So I tried again, inquiring about the first steps I could take to escape to Switzerland, despite Mutti's strong objections.

Until now, Junior—with his seven languages—had been speechless. At last he uttered one phrase: "The impossibility of defying THEM had me crushed." He handed me the address of a certain Motke, also near us in *Schaerbeek*. As we were leaving, Mr. Perlman warned us about THEM stepping up THEIR security.

Notwithstanding Mutti's protest, we intended to meet Motke. As I was closing the balcony doors after airing the rooms, I looked to the right of *la Chaussee* as usual, but this morning, I was compelled to hide behind the curtains. Open-mouthed, I could almost hear my blood pulsating in my temples from the sudden warrior scene before me: across the *Chaussee* was the terminal of the out-of-town trolley from the city of *Louvain*. At that moment, all the passengers, including some children, had to face the wall with flat palms and straight elbows. On either side of the large group stood a *Feldgendarme* with breastplate in steel helmet, machine guns poised to shoot, while a third one searched each person, helping themselves to the travelers' identification as though they were prisoners. They must have been looking for Jews. Since, fortunately, there weren't any, the lucky ones were free to leave. Here was living proof of Mr. Perlman's alert. After witnessing such militant action first-hand and realizing we were now in the wolf's lair, we went to find Motke the same afternoon as a threesome, with Mutti now a willing participant.

Even though his was only a basement apartment, it looked cozy and interesting with Persian carpets, a rarely seen silver samovar and other heirlooms. At its center sat the fortyish, smart-looking Motke in a huge *fauteuil* as if it were a throne and he, Pharaoh, ruling in it. Seated majestically at his feet was a huge German shepherd looking more like a proud lion carved out of stone. The dog was the subject of Motke's endless praises about his amazing deeds. At the start of a new phrase of his sharp rrr's: "*Derrr Hund—*" Mutti cleverly interrupted with: "Enough about the wonders of your priceless pet—*tacheles*! We came here—"

With a slightly arrogant edge to his voice, he broke in by saying: "I know, I know. But I didn't want to be so blunt as to say in my dog's language: You are barking up the wrong tree concerning Switzerland. I understand you—we all—want to get out of this deadly trap. But the entire train ride has become extremely, I repeat, extremely dangerous. Before, there were only strict controls at the various borders, which was perilous enough. Now, THEY board at almost any station. THEY indeed catch THEIR prey, Jews, like wild animals." Every so often, he patted his well-behaved pet. "Being caught on such an express means to be sent back to certain death. Beware of my so-called competitors! They'll take your money and that of their Swiss contact, then go directly to Ave. Louise, to the Gestapo, who in turn deal with you: first to Malines, from there to the east. Sorry I can't help you. I'd rather lose the money you would have given me than to have you on my conscience for the rest of my life—may it last till tomorrow or, if I'm very lucky, to the end of my natural one. Perhaps this can serve as a consolation: don't think for a moment you'd be free people there. Hardly! Upon arrival, the Swiss take you to an internment camp, just as in the Unoccupied. We are not a popular 'tribe' with them, either," he hinted facetiously and with that, Motke and his "wonder *Hund*" got up simultaneously. He wished us the best and left us with one last bit of advice: "*Je regrette*, you'll have to tough it out here!"

Routinely, several times a week, across from us, THEY checked each passenger, poised with THEIR machine guns and wearing THEIR helmets deep onto THEIR brows. Something about the Nazi steel helmet made you tremble with fright. Of course, that's what THEY wanted. As terrifying as it had been to see the passengers against the wall the first time, the more I saw it—perilously close as it was—it no longer had that life-threatening effect on me.

Neither did THEIR comrades wearing caps, Adolf's cannon fodder, singing and marching around the curb of our house on the way to the drilling fields. "*Oh, du schöner Westerwald*! (Oh, you beautiful W'woods)," a benign evergreen hiking song. Though it came out of many throats before Hitler and might be heard in the post-Führer era should I survive to hear it, the song will always evoke these sad days just the same. Now, the officer commanded: "*Aufhören*! (Stop!) Start with '*Volk ans Gewehr*! (Nation, On To Arms!)' "From row to row it went: "Nation, On To Arms!" This one was most familiar to me for we had been taught this interesting, militant melody and its "inspiring" lyrics in elementary school: "*Siehst Du im Osten das Morgenrot*! (Do you see the red dawn in the east? A sign to freedom and the sun . . .)"—each verse ending with "Nation, On To Arms!"

All of this had filled my winter months.

Once more, my beloved season sprouted with all that was beautiful in nature. Birds were twittering so sweetly. I was thrilled to be able to study on my darling veranda. Above, all the way up, directly overhead, there they were—our longed-for liberators, the Americans, in their tiny silver toys, in reality the famed Flying Fortresses. I took a deep breath to behold our saviors, these glittering finger formations with one plane separate like the dog watching its herd. Forgetting the consequences, I took it all in, the soothing bass humming. As this sound was tapering off toward the east, I thought: Why in the world can't the Germans stop NOW and prevent the further bombing of their beautiful cities?! I wished the U.S. pilots and navigators luck for a sound return to their base in England, where the Nazis had started these kinds of terror tactics in the first place. But could my conscience totally relax, when I had to admit I pitied the innocent children in my homeland, who would suffer? Despite this, I asked myself: Will this morning be my last? This wonderful spring—is it my final one?

On April 10th, 1944: ODESSA WAS RECAPTURED AFTER FIFTEEN MONTHS OF PAUSELESS, BRAVE FIGHTING BY THE RUSSIANS SINCE STALINGRAD! was reported.

Lately, many afternoons, I'd seen a very pretty blonde in her thirties passing me. We made eye-contact. She must have lived nearby, in one of the little side streets of my *Ave. du Diamant*. Each time, we just exchanged glances, until I realized that her fair hair was of the same variety as mine. Surely we were in the same situation! We would amble by silently—not daring to utter a word because of suspicion toward strangers. Nevertheless, one time we approached each other with a look of mutual compassion, floating by like "two ships in the night, for we were in the same boat."

NOW IN THE FOURTH MONTH OF HEAVY FIGHTING—FROM THE END OF 1943 THROUGH THIS SPRING, 1944, AGAINST OVERWHELMING, DANGEROUS ODDS, THE VICIOUS, BLOODY STRUGGLES FINALLY PAID OFF, FOR THE ALLIES TO CONQUER CASSINO! was the news on May 18th, 1944. The Nazis had turned the ancient Benedictine monastery into a veritable artillery fortress atop *Monte Cassino*. Not a day had passed during the past four months without an article in the *Brüsseler Zeitung* about the embittered combat for Cassino.

One afternoon, Mrs. Buts arrived at the apartment with our ration stamps and staples, saying: *Mademoiselle*, you'll have to make a sacrifice! Black market food is about to get very scarce, especially flour. Now, *à la campagne*, they don't even want money anymore, but as you told me, when you were at the coast in France, *quelque chose à rouler* (wheels). They most likely need them for our cause against *les Boches*, for messengers I assume, since gasoline cannot be obtained. Therefore, you can barter a large supply of flour for your bike."

A crushing sense of sadness befell me, even though I hadn't used it since I'd left Hoeselt, because of the hilly, trafficked, often narrow streets here. How I loved it in *Köln*, cherished it in Antwerp—shades of Simon came over me. The true romance started when I was holding on to it in the cloakroom, plus its partnership in business. In Limburg, riding my bike in the country helped make my life sweeter as a deportee. I now felt as Mutti did when she sold her first beloved piece of jewelry to Mr. Bialystok in Antwerp, caressing it one last time. I couldn't even dare do this with my magnificent all-chrome frame and its thick red rubber, for I would not risk showing myself at the Buts, where it was stored. my feelings might lead to disaster! How I adored it the first minute I laid eyes on it on my 12th birthday. A pang of mingled resentment and pain shot through me—a smaller tragedy amidst those of dramatic scope. "Farewell, my beautiful, metal baby. You have served me so well and brought me so much joy!" How I would miss petting it one last time! Tears must have welled up in my eyes, for Mrs. Buts and my parents seemed moved.

Exactly one month after the Russians' recapture of Odessa on May 10th, 1944. Vati's map announced: THE CRIMEA WITH THE BONUS OF SEBASTOPOL WAS CLEARED OF GERMANS AS WELL! His information came from reliable sources.

Then he asked me for advice with his French. "What should I say to the strangers—mostly women—who approach me, since they always seem to single me out in a crowd?"

"Despite your German haircut, your face is so friendly and sunny. So say '*Oui, oui, c'est la guerre*! Any casual conversation amongst Brusselers winds up with this exasperating remark," was my tip.

A few days later, he complained: "It doesn't always work! True, many times it's positive and the accosters actually echo my . . . your exact words. But others seem to get angry or deem me to be dimwitted."

"If '*oui, oui, c'est la guerre*!' doesn't help, try: '*Je regrette, je ne sais pas*! (Sorry, I don't know.)' The latter might be more prudent in any situation," I recommended.

Unfortunately for the Allies and ourselves, the rough weather, rocky terrain and tough fights for *Monte Cassino* had put a four-month hold on the original drive from Naples to Rome. As Vati's spring predictions would have it, the rest of May 1944 was used to destroy the German Armies and their defense line in Italy. In the process, the 5th Army joined efforts with the forces that had been stranded since January on the Anzio beachhead. From now on, the road to Rome was clear. On to the Eternal City! The following headline was the happy result on June 4th, 1944: THE U.S. 5th AND THE BRITISH 8TH ARMIES GLORIOUSLY ENTER ROME. THE FORMER ENEMIES, THE ITALIANS, ALSO WELCOMED THEM WITH OPEN ARMS AS THEY DID IN NAPLES!

The next afternoon at 2:30 P.M., Vati still had not returned from his errands for lunch. This was highly unusual. As the hours passed, our worries grew. Mutti tried to play it down by using his German looks as consolation. "Not even a Jacques would be suspicious of him." In a way, I felt flattered for Vati's sake that she did feel concern. In light of the fact that he loved her so much more than she loved him, and in their youth it was he wanting to wed her in the worst way and she had refused him repeatedly until his persistence succeeded—would she ever pardon his philandering? Would I ever truly know what came first, her rejections throughout the years or his womanizing? Nevertheless, in my opinion, his love for her was greater than any I had read about in all these multi-lingual classics or seen on stage or screen. What irony! As for me, my life would feel empty without him. What mighty relief when I heard him run up at 6:00 P.M., hastening his double step. I flung the door open and hugged him even harder than usual. He responded in like manner, kissed Mutti and sank onto the little flowered couch, sighing, "I worried I'd never see you again nor live to tell you this story: During my visit at the Hakums"—Mutti grimaced—"and Mrs. Schwartz," he added, "lucky once more not to be at home—his brother went for the rationing stamps—both siblings also possess a falsified Belgian green *carte d'identité*. As I was about to leave, a Belgian Gestapo came to the front door. He identified himself—the genuine article, unlike the blackmailer from the realtor. He must have trailed the brother from the rationing office. I was about to be taken to Malines, when in the nick of time, it occurred to me that some Belgians, unlike the German Gestapo, can be bribed. I remembered the antique 18-karat gold watch with cover and heavy chain which was not 'canned' and buried in case of emergency. I felt terrible to get the Buts involved, but my life was at stake and—thinking of you—"

Vati wept when he got up, forming a loving circle, to embrace us. He continued: "I led him to the Buts and rang their bell. No answer. I tried over and over again and still nobody appeared. Finally the Gestapo growled: 'Let's go!' 'One more try,' I pleaded. This time I did not let go of the buzzer. After a while I heard footsteps from within. What alleviation from disaster when Mrs. Buts opened the door in total shock. When we got inside, she regained her composure and rapidly produced the article in exchange for my life, handing it over to that evil traitor of his own country. *Ja, ja,* I ran in the opposite direction through the narrow, hilly streets and kept turning around to see if I was being followed. How delighted I am to have lost him and found you, my dearest ones in this whole wide world"—precisely Mutti's words when she was anxiously awaiting our return from the flaming city of Dunkirk four years earlier.

"This time, we really landed at the right moment and right place!!" Vati entered wide-and-bright-eyed, proudly spreading the *Brüsseler Zeitung* in front of us, jubilating and imitating "babies" Winston and Joseph: "Second Front! Second Front! At long last! The Second Front, our salvation!" Vati's thrilled voice broke for joy like that of a Bar Mitzvah boy when he read of this earth-shaking, happy event in the newspaper: "ON 6-6-44, THE VASTEST ARMIES IN HISTORY STARTED BY ALLIES ON THE BEACHES OF FRANCE'S NORMANDY—BUT WE HAVE OUR ATLANTIC WALL!" We literally jumped for joy and arranged a small, private celebration to mark this long-desired American-English invasion to finally get rid of the Nazis once and for all. Beethoven's "Ode To Joy" from his "9th" thundered in my ears—

Two days later I went downstairs to get the *melk*. Upon entering our neighbor's store, I arrived in the middle of a conversation between his married girlfriend and Jeff: "Yes, THEY caught her, I saw it with my own eyes, Jeffke. THEY dragged her out of her abode, loading this pretty, screaming blonde, who always passed here by herself, onto THEIR truck into which other Jewish victims had been collected already, as though she was a reluctant, poached animal. How could I help her, what was I to do with THEIR machine guns in hand? Such a good-looking woman, too, and young, not much older than myself!"

"And this only one day after the Allied landing in the west!" Jeff bemoaned, shaking his head.

"How awful, Jeff. It never occurred to me that she could be Jewish. I admired her when I saw her ambling by, always coiffed and dressed so fashionably and immaculately," she sighed, truly moved, grabbing his hand. Other customers entered the shop, all bearing witness and having genuine compassion for this attractive, elegant stranger.

I just listened, and once my utensil was filled with milk, I silently and carefully went up. I hated to spoil my parents' wonderful, festive mood by imparting this sad news. Unlike the Gentiles downstairs feeling mere commiseration, the continued catching of the Jews was—despite the Allied western breakthrough and the promise of imminent liberation—a personal threat to our lives. Making a scene won't help—and it happened so close by, I reflected. Thus, never shall I pass her "like a ship in the night" nor ever have the pleasure of personally meeting this lovely lady. I knew, it was her—

On June 15th, 1944, the three of us celebrated my birthday "in style." The toast was: "May this be the last one under the Nazis, and the next in liberty—which we hope will be very soon anyway!" "*Omein!*" prayed Mutti and added with some skepticism: "If THEY don't catch us before, as happened to the young woman in the neighborhood."

On June 23rd, Vati's map clearly showed: THE RUSSIANS NOW WERE SYNCHRONIZING THEIR RAPIDLY MOVING CAMPAIGN TO THE WEST WITH THE ANGLO-SAXON DRIVE TO THE EAST. His threads distinctly outlined as though they were aiming to meet some day—like the lyrics of an English song with a lovely, wistful melody: "Don't know where, don't know when but someday—"

I walked the little streets. There were some stores, whose windows I used as mirrors. Again, I was complacent with my blonde reflection. Feeling such euphoria which led me to believe ever so firmly that I would survive!

On June 27th, 1944, the London-based French broadcast reported: "U.S. TROOPS CAPTURED CHERBOURG, THE THIRD LARGEST PORT IN FRANCE." They signed off with an even more profoundly passionate declaration, almost growling with hate: "*Nous les écraserons les Boches*!!! (We'll crush them! We'll get them!)"

Lately, I'd been running my errands on other narrow sidewalks for safety—God, oh God, what sounds am I hearing?! Those deadly WH boots and rough German voices commanding: "*Ausweis*! (I.D. card)" Quickly, I had to act against my own impulse to make a complete turn-about. Were I to continue, I would run into one of THEIR ever-increasing checkpoints. Instead, I used my own control and quick concentration to think fast, yet move slowly, to avoid giving myself away through any sudden "run away reflex" to other pedestrians—Nazi sympathizers. I unhurriedly crossed to the other side, which took me into a different section. What a close call— with death!"

One magnificent July morning—the kind of perfect day that makes you want to live, live, really live—Vati entered breathlessly, the *Brüsseler Zeitung* under his arm. His face was missing its usual beam.

"Vati, what's the matter? Did the Allies lose?"

Shaking his head, he sighed mournfully, "Oh, no, but the Germans did!"

"And that is so sad?" I questioned in deep concern.

"The very scarce, enormously brave top-ranking aristocrats lost. Here, read about the Nazi joy and triumph yourself!"—throwing the paper onto the table with disgust.

The headline from July 20th, 1944 read: "ATTENTAT ON THE *FÜHRER'S* LIFE A FAILURE! HE EMERGED UNSCATHED! WILL GET EVEN WITH OFFICER TRAITORS! LATER ON THIS SAME AFTERNOON, OUR *FÜHRER* HAD TEA WITH TODAY'S DARINGLY RESCUED MUSSOLINI."

"Imagine. Europe and we would have been free as of today, for the German high brass had planned to create a democratic government after Hitler's death. Such Nazi luck!" He went on. "Colonel Brandt was engrossed in the map the generals were studying. The bag containing the bomb underfoot of the other colonel was in his way, so he moved it. The briefcase belonged to Colonel von Stauffenberg, the catalyst of the coup. Thus, unwittingly, Brandt shifted the explosive. This cost him his life and saved the *Führer's!* Now, the three of us could 'platzen (explode)'!"

Because of traitor Jacques, I even used side streets to get to my butcher on *la Chaussee*. While making the detour, again I heard the miserable, leaden sound of Nazis boots. Oh God! I shrank. It was sunny, but in the shadow stood two *Feldgendarmes*, THEIR steel helmets deep into THEIR eyes, which made them look even more frightful. THEY made me shiver as I saw them from afar. By now, I could discern in the distance that THEY were checking the papers of passers-by. I was filled with such hatred because clearly, THEY were on a final losing streak, yet THEY wouldn't let up on us. All these controls were mainly to catch another Jew, still snuff out another Jewess' life—like mine.

Once more, I had to use my bravura and iron will to slowly change course without turning around—which was my first impulse. In a moment filled with peril, I hadn't lost my humor by thinking: Let THEM eat THEIR murderous hearts out; if THEIR boots were less noisy, THEY would have caught even more Jewish prey. Surely, I couldn't have been the only one who'd been saved by the clatter of THEIR footwear. I hope it'll be a joke on THEM for the ones that survive. Most fortunately, I'll be one of those! I can feel it!

Where could I go? In car traffic, there was the threat of traitor Jacques, while on little side streets, one would run directly into THEM, the bastards!!! But triumphantly, I had escaped my second brush with death in the last three weeks!

I was forced to change my plan, trusting the handsome one would save some meat for us, come tomorrow. Instead, I went into a totally different section. There was a fine, large one-man grocery, which was about to close. After the last customer left, the grocer found all kinds of goodies for me in addition to the regular staples. As I was about to pay with both money and ration stamps, an endless flow of beautiful French sprang from his lips. I was amazed how free he felt with his anti-Nazi statements. Noticing my astonishment, he said with a sort of apologetic smile: "I'm a true Wallonian. THEY hate us French and Wallonian-speaking a lot more than the Flemish, whom THEY consider in THEIR racial mania 'Germanic-related.'" Slight as my accent was in a long conversation, he may have guessed the truth, I gathered. He made other comments: "THEIR awe-inspiring idol Hitler's fierce determination to save the world by devastation is finally choking THEM." At this moment—I could not believe my eyes—Vati entered, visibly angry at me.

"How in the world did you find me here, since I'm making my debut in this fine establishment?!"

Obviously still mad at me, after a brief while, nonetheless, his embrace was especially strong. We paid and left with a friendly "*Au Revoir, Monsieur!*" As we walked home, Vati could not stop reprimanding me for being away those hours. Again, throwing his arms around me on the street, he said: "How happy I am that my hunch led me into this neighborhood and then, how thrilled I was to pass the store and see, quite unexpectedly, my daughter inside. We were tormented by worry of the unspeakable. And here I found you!" he exclaimed with beaming, moist eyes, adding: "Nowadays, one mustn't stay away too long!"

The BBC announced: "Hitler did get even, 'dealing' with his traitors within 11-1/2 hours: von Stauffenberg and many of his co-conspirators were caught. This time, he was true to his inner circle threat that they would meet a fate even harsher than the SA plotters, led by the Nazi satrap and friend Roehm at the 1934 coup. The vengeance came to be known as the "Night of the Long Knives"; today's revolters suffered a slow excruciating death by being hung with piano wires on meat hooks. THROUGHOUT JULY 1944, A VERITABLE ORGY OF NEFARIOUS TORTURE AND EXECUTIONS AGAINST AN ESTIMATED 5000 OF THEIR OWN HAS TAKEN PLACE was announced on the air and in print.

Finally, though late in the Nazi game, they had dared a rebellion, which unfortunately turned out to be a fiasco. This had us really down, plus reading Victor Hugo's "*L'homme qui rit.*" These days I felt mostly euphoric—particularly and strangely, while walking through the dangerous outdoors while delighting in complacence upon meeting my reflection. I actually felt intoxicated, taking an oath of survival for myself; especially after the last two close brushes with the *Feldgendarmes*. Yet this book caused me to be sad about the cruelty of man. The English circus people had this poor individual's face operated on so his appearance resulted in a constant smile—just for people's amusement. There were always cruelties committed somewhere in the world. But just to catch humans—men, women and children of all ages in their flats and on streets in all European cities, towns and villages en masse for annihilation because they were Jewish—was an absolute first in all of history. Don't THEY have any compassion for others, as I have now for brave von Stauffenberg and the 5000 believed to be involved? Even Hugo's fictional tragic figure is causing me to have a sensation of tristesse, just reading it!

On July 25th, 1944, AN ALL-OUT CONCENTRATED TOUGH ATTACK BY THE ALLIES EXTENDS ALL OVER FRANCE AND BELGIUM! was the thrilling news. We wanted to share it with the people living closest to us, so we visited the *Aleskys*. She seemed desolate (without having read "The Man Who Laughs"). My parents suggested inviting their little Tanya to a great meat dinner (my fair butcher always saved our portion). The parents bade her farewell as though they would never see their offspring again and added, one never knows where and when our death sentence can fall, at home or outside. An almost festive table reminiscent of peace time was set for the little, well-behaved, lady-like guest. We passed an enjoyable couple of hours, then brought her home. Upon doing so, we saw her mother outside, looking very distraught. My parents and the child went upstairs, while Mrs. Alesky asked me to lend her a certain amount of change. I was about to comply, when I realized that these few centimes were carfare. Dumbfounded, I questioned her half in jest whether she wanted to go anywhere, and if so, where?

"To the Avenue Louise!" was her sobbing answer.

"Don't tell me to the Gestapo?!" I inquired suspiciously. "Oh, no. For this I won't give you the money," I almost yelled.

"But I'm so unhappy with him!" she lamented.

"And your adorable little daughter?"

"Tanya is the reason I endured him these four long years," she assured me.

"Stick it out a little longer!" I exclaimed, having to control my voice as I took the liberty of shaking her shoulders. "We are so close to being delivered from this oppression. A major event in our favor is bound to occur sooner than we think. And you want to commit suicide—and in the most horrible way imaginable, by THEM somewhere in the east?!"

"I deserve this chastisement for having married him!" she answered with pathos.

I repeated my sobering gesture to bring her to her senses, but her reaction was that of a rag doll. My very first impression flashed through my mind: The Showgirl and the Brute. I continued my pep talk: "Just because your life is in shambles right now, you needn't take such a drastic step. We're almost there! Then you'll be able to alter your life for the better. You are young—like me—beautiful and striking."

"Only you are free," she objected in a tone of envy.

"Give yourself a chance! And remember: unlike me you were really and truly cooped up. This fact alone lends itself to depression."

"This too is his doing. Or should I say: his command. Today is the first time in two years that I 'ventured' out of the flat—if just to stand here in front of the house. And it's only because of the excellent excuse of anxiously awaiting you with my baby. Even this came about despite his violent objections," she explained.

My parents now came outside and we returned home. I was glad I had calmed her down, at least for the time being. On the way, I filled my parents in about her state of mind. When they questioned me, I answered that details were hardly discussed between her and myself, but the quivers of her mouth revealed her inner turmoil.

Ever since Anzio and Cassino, the Allies were at the heels of the fleeing Germans. The hunters became the hunted: the BBC reported the liberation of Florence on August 22, 1944, of course with the ensuing, passionate: *"NOUS LES ÉCRASERONS! NOUS LES AURONS, LES BOCHES!!!"* Such incongruity : war and Florence? I conjured up the stone and marble miracles by Michelangelo, such as the Slave, the Tomb of Lorenzo, the enormous Statue of David, the bas relief of the Centaurs, Detail of the Satyr from Baccus and the universal artistic works of *la Renaissance*. This imagination inspired me to continue my German shorthand manuscript. I was in a rush with my chapters because I doubted, once I was no longer forced to hide, if I would have patience, time and above all discipline to stick with it. I wanted the world to be aware of the European "Nazi Fortress" as soon as possible. My ardent literary desire was for my "docufiction" entitled "The Susskinds" to be the first publication of its kind, created by the youngest author: me. While sketching this in my mind, I strode to one of my balconies and was absolutely stunned—but this time in an especially wonderful way: across the street at the tavern, I saw the Belgian flag and boldly (after all, we were still under "Nazi management"), the British Union Jack unfurling proudly in the mild August breeze!

One day later, August 23rd, was a wonderfully sunny morning. Entering the kitchen from the back terrace, where I could still observe, to my delight, the "U.S. silver toy planes" in finger formation—almost daily—I got a refill of chicory-coffee. I casually turned on the BBC. "La Marseilles"! My hand began to shiver from sheer joy causing me to spill the beverage. A tremendous sense of warmth filled my body, hearing, so unexpectedly, the rousingly passionate patriotic sound of *Nous Marchons! Nous Marchons!* At the same moment I recognized the familiar French voice, close to screaming with incredible elation, fire and zeal: "NOUS LES AVONS ÉCRASÉS! NOUS LES AVONS EU! NOUS LES AVONS EU, LES BOCHES!!! (WE CRUSHED THEM ! WE HAD THEM! WE HAVE GOTTEN THEM!)"—as opposed to the future tense used throughout these tough, undeservedly miserable years. Just one day earlier, we'd heard: *"Nous les écraserons! Nous les aurons, les Boches!* (We'll crush them ! We'll get them!)" I was so moved by this magnificent BBC announcement. PARIS LIBERATED BY THE ALLIES!!! It filled me with wonder and goose-pimples! "My cup runneth over"—literally. I burst into the bedroom, shouting: "PARIS IS FREE!"

Vati could be audacious with his German looks and go the longer way deep into Schaerbeek to check out the spirit of the Perlmans. Upon his return, he reported that of course the family was euphoric, but cautioned to be extremely careful, because despite THEIR retreat, THEY were loyally filling THEIR deportation quota as diligently as before. It would continue here and mainly in

Antwerp. THEY would be loading Jews, at last count well over 20,000, now using THEIR latest method by shipping them in huge furniture vans to the Belgian collection camp Malines. "Damned THEM!" we cursed.

One late evening—was I dreaming?—or—I looked at my parents to detect whether they also heard something. It recalled the time a good four years earlier in Dunkirk, when the sounds turned out to be those of British soldiers, when we could not distinguish imagination from reality. Tonight, it was no different. There seemed to be enormous cheering (so strange to us—and long forgotten). Though faintly audible in the far distance, it aroused our curiosity. We ran to the front balconies. Once outdoors, we could define—like *a fata morgana*—a single voice stirring tremendous jubilation. There was silence—then the same exchange, getting a bit nearer, between a spoken phrase and a group of people in a frenzy—another pause—then, a young female, saying one single sentence—once more, met by fervent enthusiasm. The verbal enigma was getting closer and closer . . . ever so slowly—this repetition approaching—our frustration and suspense—not being able to grasp the still too remote, yet so significant words got us to the explosive point—until at long last it was within earshot—against the very dark background like a vision of light on a bicycle—a woman, stopping every so often, made this hair-raising announcement: "I come from Uccle." That was south of the city, quite a way from here, the east. An octave higher, she declared with great verve: "Our Allies—our Allies are at the gateway of Brussels!"

Open-armed and speechless, we fell on each other's necks—choked up with joy—tears of happiness welled in our eyes—right after this very brave and good-hearted female messiah had created the most touching moment of my life. Her message set me free!

The news on September 2nd, 1944: PISA, FAMOUS FOR ITS LEANING TOWER IN NW OF ITALY, NEAR THE ARNO RIVER, WAS CAPTURED BY THE ALLIES, NOW FINALIZING THE LAST NAZI HINDRANCE IN FEVER PITCH.

In the front part of the flat from the balconies, I saw, but could not trust my eyes: disheveled, some even downtrodden Nazi servicemen on retreat. There, from a front row seat, I watched the most important historical event of all times unfolding: the swan song of the once proud WH. Naturally, they were on their way back to the beloved fatherland, flattened by Allied bombs. No longer did they swagger, but were exhaustedly hiking. No longer were they in smart uniforms, but dragging themselves slovenly and unkempt up "my" *Chaussee de Louvain*. All of them were bedraggled, hatless, unbuttoned, trying desperately to get out of here, whichever way they could. Even the once-elegant officers were "having their dinner"—out of a can on their eastbound refuge road.

I took extreme delight in this extraction of vengeance, as did my parents. "No longer can THEY hurt us!" I uttered with glee.

Vati objected, pulling me gently in back of the curtains. "Just observe without being observed." As he had done in May 1940 with his comparison to the Great War, he now spoke about their withdrawal: "They are very sore losers and in their proficiency for wreckage, they shot some innocent souls on their march back. And mind you—they weren't even Nazis then!"

Finally, on September 3rd, 1944: BRUSSELS LIBERATED BY ALLIES! I didn't hear this news on the BBC nor read it in the *Brüsseler Zeitung*, which was defunct—I lived to watch this marvel. I experienced, savored and relished the rapture. Sensing all along I would survive, again, I was all choked up from bliss and felicity. Imagine U.S. tanks passing by right at my corner, "my" *Chaussee de Louvain*!

The Americans were besieged by cheering, elated crowds. When I appeared at the front door, there were never-before-heard wolf whistles and smiles from these wonderful, great and glorious liberators. I was thoroughly absorbed and exalted in the joy of my newly found life with its physical and spiritual triumph over the banner of hate.

Indeed, we were victorious in—

FLEEING THE SWASTIKA!!!

Epilogue

The Immediate Aftermath

On the first evening of our long-awaited freedom, the Boulevard Adolphe Max was an ocean of deliriously happy Brusselers. Though living in the capital, we hadn't seen mid-City for two years. It was wonderful to be part of a huge, ecstatic crowd. September 3rd should become a Belgian national holiday to forever commemorate this auspicious event.

The following noon, immediately after leaving the flat, we noticed a shouting mad group of people. Upon coming closer, we saw a man with facial lacerations, being led prisoner-style by two stocky, young males wearing white armbands, indicating they were *La Guarde Blanche* (the White Brigade), the underground counterpart of the French Maquis. Almost every civilian punched the man with a fist or flat palm, while a small, very angry gang was closing in on him, cursing: "Damned collaborator!" Women were also hitting, scratching, slapping him hard in the face, spitting and verbally blasting the traitor. Some of the local avengers "accompanied" the philo-Nazis. Walking on, we encountered quite a few such human clusters. Next, there was a woman in the middle. Since only long hair was the style, her uneven match-long cut looked weird, spiking up every which way. As we went along, there were more such bunches—each of them surrounding a female. The booers went a bit easier on them, but still they were struck, scratched and spat upon while enraged retaliators swore: "*Poule, Poule du Luxe des Boches!*" There seemed to be quite a few such German-friendly "chicks".

A tall fellow, dressed impeccably, was tugged by others. The Belgians' released even more fury against him. He also had open wounds on his head and face and was receiving more by the minute, dripping blood on his fine clothes. As the throng kept yelling, "*Boche! Boche! Gestapo!*", I understood the unbridled wrath. It was open season on THEM as it had been on us for endless, hard years. We three just gaped at these varied spectacles.

We passed the huge, multi-storied building of the barracks, a.k.a. *la Caserne*. Only the two guards and the prisoner evidently had permission to enter the gate, which had been the billeting place of the WH Nazi Army only a couple of days earlier.

For the time being, Brussels was a lawless city. No Belgian or any other government existed. There was no public transportation, no newspapers were being printed, and only the BBC was available since no local stations could be tuned in. The few open stores had only meager merchandise. Vati already started to worry about obtaining food. Nevertheless, we continued happily down la Chaussee de Louvain, when I remembered Mrs. Hakum. "Perhaps we might help her, attesting that she dealt in toys and other non-essentials?" I asked.

Mutti answered: "Then they will say: 'Ah, to bring happiness to German children, thus boosting Nazi morale.'"

Cringing, I visualized her luscious, long, thick, black hair being snipped off and that exquisite face being scratched and punched upon. As we were about to pass the narrow *Rue de la Charité*, another shock: It was dark with people, visibly disappointed, yet to our delight, the Hakums had left in time. Of course, since Vati's Belgian Gestapo arrest at that house, we had had no further contact with them. His eyes got moist and he said his sad "*ja, ja*" to himself, obviously remembering the harrowing day his own life was about to be taken.

It was wonderful to move freely, especially downtown, where we went almost daily to make up for lost time. Only once did we splurge—to celebrate our liberation with *filtres* at the Métropole Terrace, searching inside for acquaintances and former business associates, but none of these Jewish people were to be found. I had not seen one familiar face in the crowd. Not only was this deeply distressing—the practical side of trading was gone, so I was forced to find work.

The euphoria hadn't quite calmed down when future openings of Allied offices were announced. Armed with many languages—mainly my favorite one, fluent English—I applied indiscriminately. I learned that the pay was very low but there were generous benefits of good lunches plus food and soap to take home. The latter part sounded promising, since merchandise of any kind was rare. A couple of weeks later, cards for interviews came pouring in. I was free to choose whichever interpreter executive secretary job I wanted.

Once during this time, it was almost evening and Vati had not come home yet. We knew he'd been in need of a haircut, at which time he intended to share his true identity with the barber. When he finally returned, he flopped down on the sofa, exclaiming: "I never thought I would have a riveting adventure like this after the liberation. Entering the barber shop, I wanted to set them straight about who I really was. Before I could do so, the owner quickly exchanged his white smock for a jacket. Instead of his almost sycophant amiability, he grabbed me forcefully, commanding me in a rough manner: 'Let's go, *Boche*!' 'But I'm Jewish! I can prove it!' I violently objected. This was met with laughter from the customers and employees alike. 'Sure, look at him. This *Boche* dares to claim to be Jewish!' Another big ha, ha came from all corners. 'Here is my *carte d'identité* with the *Juif* stamp!' I protested. 'How do you like that? Now the Nazis want to be Jews! It's true they do adhere these same *Juif* stamps on their passports. Let's go!' he repeated before identifying himself as a Guarde Blanche auxiliary. I was very lucky not have needed a trim before. They would have dragged me through the streets like a Nazi sympathizer. Even though the way from the shop on the Rue Dailly to Place Dailly is very short, the angry populace would have lynched me. I worried and wondered: how will I get out of this one?

After waiting in the barracks with all the accused Nazis, my turn finally came. They brought me into a vast hall. Chairmen and judges were seated at banquet-style tables. The moment I entered, before I could discern any of the faces, I heard a voice exclaiming: 'What bungling is going on here? This is Cukier! My apologies, Monsieur Cukier!' To my delight, it was Motke!" Vati had finished his tale of suspense.

I had chosen a British purchasing office with the intention of following in Mrs. Hakum's footsteps—but with the Allies—should I survive. Being Mr. Tomkin's executive secretary and English-French-Flemish interpreter, with an office facing le Jardin Botanique, was very pleasant, as were the two-hour hot lunches served in a fine restaurant at the head of Rue du Progres. I also had rare goodies to take home: the pungent disinfectant American LifeBuoy soap and toilet paper. None of these items existed elsewhere.

Not having continued writing "The Susskinds" did plague my mind during the scarce free moments between business and celebrating. So I wanted to gather some of my research. When I looked into the huge wicker traveling case, where I knew I had hidden the stack about Rommel's Afrika Korps—to my dismay—it had disappeared. Upon informing my parents, Vati sheepishly admitted to having used it as toilet paper. It had been cut in the perfect shape, he said. I was fuming!

I found a manufacturer of stuffed toys, which I presented proudly to Mr. Tomkin—whereupon I was given notice with two months severance pay. After having lived "lawlessly" for so long, I was no longer familiar with business ethics—an employee cannot do merchandising!

That very morning, I found the same kind of job at the Hotel Atlanta, an Allied Officers' Club. Two secretaries worked for me. During my breaks, I played the baby grand located on stage in the elegant dining room (All of which still existed just as it was then as recently as 1996). I played from sheet music I had never seen before, such as Judy Garland's "You Made Me Love You" and others. The dining Allied officers applauded even though I was just practicing. Since I had played "Jealousy" at the Buts', the keyboard skill came easily. Once, a middle-aged British Captain, after flirting, walked up to compliment me on my performance. He told me I played better than he and "with so much feeling." Captain Jimmy, as we called him, became a friend of our family. After quite a while—to our surprise—we learned that Jimmy Kennedy was the foremost composer in the UK, having written "Siegfried Line," "April in Portugal," "On the Isle of Capri," "My Prayer," "South of the Border," "Red Sails in the Sunset," "Harbor Lights" and countless others.

Later on that month, coming home from work on the trolley was extremely pleasant. The passengers were mostly English servicemen. Though for us the war was over, it was raging in the still-occupied areas of Europe and in the Pacific. Of course, I had no way of knowing that there were even blackouts inside because of my "hiding status". I had never heard a male choir or any kind of singing in a tram before. How soothing to my ears and my soul, hearing in my favorite language: "Long Ago and Far Away," "White Cliffs of Dover" and "I'll Be Seeing You." What lovely chansons I listened to for the first time after this glorious liberation, emerging from the darkness with such wistful longing . . .

On one such trip in the first spring in liberty, I spotted the real estate traitor and thought myself most fortunate that two Guardes Blanches were present also. When I quickly pointed out this miserable man who had caused us so much grief, they fired a barrage of questions at me about my own background, giving the "mastermind of the blackmailer-false Gestapo" time to escape. Though I had been sure all along it was "the Grouch," his flight was just confirmation of my suspicion. My frustration reached the boiling point.

Since the pay at the Atlanta was low, I took an evening job, barely making it from the end of my day shift and the start of the evening one near our first Brussels abode of "Gietel" at *la Porte de Namur*. I was exalted, filling what was usually a man's position of maitre d'. Desiring the Allies presence so desperately all these years, I literally rubbed elbows with them in this huge, crowded bistro-restaurant with a big band. It amazed me that the Yanks and Limeys, as they called each other, were cordial up to a point, but I quickly learned that when the place was especially mobbed, not to seat them together.

One pleasurable lunch hour, I was strolling down the Boulevard Adolphe Max when a dark-haired man addressed me by name. I was startled since he did not look familiar to me. He promptly suggested the current trade done amongst the few slowly returning survivors might interest me, since this business was a success. Also, I still had to rid myself of the toys to other Allied buyers, but what a problem: the doggies did not want to sit. They had to be reshaped.

During one meeting at the Métropole, my new associate said with glee: "Do I have a surprise for you! Please come with me!"

"But what is it?"

"If I told you, it wouldn't be a surprise, would it?"

I went along reluctantly. Upon entering the pre-hiding Jewish café where deals were made, he led the way toward the back. There was a group of men. When the circle opened, there stood before me, in the flesh, Simon London! It was more than a shock. Amidst the onlookers, we were gaping and gazing at each other in silence for the longest time—until he smiled, exclaiming "You still look like you're eighteen" and then, in a higher tone: Then they were right in Antwerp. You are alive, thank God! At the Unoccupied I was told THEY had taken you. I came especially to Brussels— knowing you would be wherever trading could be done—to find out for myself. The Unoccupied turned out to be a disappointment. I was interned under poor conditions and got sick. Whatever—the bottom line is that we made it! Yes, we made it!

Unlike me, he had grown much older and bigger. If I'd had the same impression four years earlier, we would have remained business companions, perhaps friends, but nothing more.

I had certainly matured in these four years. Nevertheless, he seemed to have remained, magically, my mascot. This brief encounter brought me luck, being most successful, indirectly, with *la Bourse*. Post-war opportunities, together with my good reputation and business sense, made me a young multi-millionairess—in Belgian Francs (ca. $30,000). I refurbished the apartment and yes, I smiled, glancing coyly over my bare shoulder, cradling a bouquet of purple lilacs in an exquisite frame on top of a fine piece of furniture which talked and played American hits . . .

A couple of years later, on Pelikaan Straat, when my US fiancé was pointing out diamonds in rare settings he wanted to manufacture for me, we were interrupted from behind. It was Simon and his entourage also offering us jewels and congratulations. This was the very last time I saw him, even though he lived to a ripe old age.

Later, in Antwerp, a very interesting, good-looking lady dressed ho lá lá! Haute Couture, although just food shopping, was pointed out to me as Simon's woman. I was told that while ill, he had become her tenant and then later brought this roughly 35-year-old from the Riviera.

NOTEWORTHY AFTER OUR GLORIOUS LIBERATION

Ch. 24: Only after returning the precious tin can containing our complete worldly fortune did the Buts reveal that one flight up, they had Communists hidden. My faint suspicions (because of toilet flushing) were correct. We could profoundly sympathize with the extreme fright experienced by Mrs. Buts after she finally had opened the door (the delay was to shield her other protégées) and then the Belgian Gestapo stood before her. By letting him enter and then saving Vati's life in exchange for the gold watch, she had threatened the lives of the others in hiding.

Ch. 8: The tremendous fear of the Luftwaffe that overwhelmed me at the Belgian coast was more than justified, for they had equipped their Stukas with a special screeching device for the specific purpose of intensifying the dread felt by the enemy.

Ch. 20: Until this day I still enjoy my antique gold necklace and have been complimented on it throughout the years. Though it was her idea not to melt it down, Mutti's intricate one along with "quite a lot of precious jewelry had disappeared in the most mysterious and baffling way," Vati informed me in a letter to Philadelphia.

I became very saddened walking back to my Jewish roots in the cities of my upbringing. In Antwerp, the whole hub of Yiddish

Life looked as though erased from the earth. In Brussels, the area around *la Gare du Midi* is void of Jews except for a few shop windows of children's clothing stores. How lucky we were to survive in that city.

The Belgian Quarter in Köln is so named because its streets point in that direction and are therefore named after Belgian cities. Cologne's well-to-do Jews once lived in these huge luxury apartments, but ever since meeting their dreadful fates, the same dwellings have been occupied by non-Jews. The residents of the poor Jewish section in back of today's main library, on Neumarkt (where the wretched round-ups took place—amongst them, many we knew), were just eking out a living. During the reign of horror, when discussing these pitiful souls, the mere mention of their address (mainly Alexianer and Thieboldgasse) was just above a whisper. The entire section has been reconstructed in pleasant stark white neo-modern architecture—the only place in Cologne where I have seen such alabaster purity. It is *Judenrein*. In fact, we are few and far between in the entire city. My presence in Köln ruins Hitler's master plan.

I never have resolved the warm feeling I have for the city of my birth with the terrible actions of that country—or have I? I continue to return on a regular basis twice a year for two months each spring and fall, to visit my beloved Köln.

The following must have contributed to our survival: despite the lack of harmony in our family, we were united, passionately, in climbing the economic, social and cultural ladders. After having been stripped of everything, our sole aim was to stay alive. All our efforts were devoted to this one goal with the same fervor plus Mutti's sixth sense, Vati's food provisions and my languages and youth.

Though not very religious, I advocate strongly that there must be a truly biblical Jewish holiday! As much as I always loved Purim, I get a pang of jealousy because as the result of a minor Hitler, such as Haman, threatening the Jews in only one country (Persia), there is an annual traditional feast. Why not pick the end of World War II or the freeing of the camps or the end of Nazi tyranny, the death of Hitler or any such auspicious date to honor the vanished humanity with dignity? This will help greatly to establish the naked truth after all of us are gone—!

I have had my share of losses and have made wrong decisions, and above all I regret two of the latter: never having tried my luck in Hollywood and not continuing my German shorthand manuscript "The Susskinds." Because of my frequent transatlantic trips, it got lost in New York. This has always bothered me tremendously

During the 1980s, I called the University of Pennsylvania Press, who advised me strongly to forget about rewriting my novel and to start a new autobiography. "Unfortunately," my story contains less anguish, agony and suffering than those of many others who survived the Nazi horror. I wanted to be the first and youngest! It has turned out to be one of the last and mildest true stories, but one of only a few written directly in English by a Holocaust survivor herself, who until doing so was convinced it could not be done for lack of death camp experience.

My parents: Vati had visited the U.S. several times during the 1960s. My return, after many years and raising two children, took place in the glorious summer of 1968, when I first reunited with Mutti since 1953. I found Köln as magical as Vati had when he saw it for the first time. In August of 1970, I took a trip to Germany with my husband. That same year, my parents attended my son Curt's Bar Mitzvah in Philadelphia. From then on, my voyages became more frequent and Mutti's behavior more difficult and arrogant, even though she was in excellent health in body, quick in mind and tongue. She had remained vivacious and witty, retaining her amazingly youthful, good, if very stern looks.

At about the same time I came to the U.S., they returned from Belgium to Köln and lived there for thirty-nine years.

Ch. 24: Mutti never forgave Vati for being a womanizing *charmeur*, so he wound up spending his last few years at St. Heribert's, a Catholic home for the aged. They called me right after New Year's of 1987, and I barely made it from the U.S. to Köln just in time for my beloved Vati to die in my arms.

This was the end of our threesome together

This pleasant, woodsy-smelling home on the right bank of the Rhine River was within walking distance of the "Steps of Tears"—the Köln deportation point to Auschwitz. Ironically, the fact that Vati had lived a long life could be attributed to Mutti's insistence that we leave Köln in 1938. Strangely and chillingly enough, even though Mutti did not relent enough to be at his deathbed, his very last word, pressed out with a voice from the beyond, was "Sofiechen". This was a first for me ever having witnessed death. And it had to be my dearest Vatichen . . .

On January 5th, 1987, I saw both of my parents for the very last time—Vati laid out in the plain pine casket according to Judaic tradition, and Mutti taking great strides in her fine boots to his funeral—and later to the entrance of her apartment building, which is now mine. (I kept the flat Vati had rented during its construction in 1973 as a sort of shrine.) Though still in good health, only two months later, Mutti suddenly passed away of an acute heart attack. She was pushing ninety, and Vati lived to be ninety and ten days. So far, I'm grateful I inherited their genes.

In August of 1986, arriving in Köln from Madrid, I booked a room in the hotel-like atmosphere of St. Heribert to spend one week with Vati. I told him then about writing this book, and he answered with an expression full of compassion: "Oh, Fannichen, this is such a hard undertaking with a lot of work you really don't need. It is too tough a project for you!" He was right. It is a most arduous creation born out of love and devotion.

Five months later, when Mutti arrived by cab, I invited them to a restaurant—the finale of our threesome together.

Ch. 10: When I informed Mutti about my manuscript, she said: "Oh, I really could give you a world of helpful information. For instance, do you recall the French peasant on the Flucht with the *Schimmel* (white horse), green wagon and the exchange of burlap sacks for the pigskin suitcase thought to be lost?" As soon as she mentioned it, I relived it!

Ch. 23: The Belgian traitor Léon Degrelle dwelt happily in Spain with his heavy kilos of gold.

Quisling "Jacques"? No one ever found out. He was never heard from. Did the Nazis finish him off or did he save himself? To the regret of all Belgian survivors and in the name of all the ones slain through him, nobody learned his fate. He remained an enigma.

Another miracle for their generation: I can visit them at the Jewish cemetery in Köln-Bocklemünd, where they are together for eternity—my dear parents.

Ch. 22:

>Crushed, the young years, the sweet
>with heavy booted feet—

We, The Few Lucky Ones
The Survivors

IN BELGIUM

I was to become the toast of two cities, but without realizing this, I continually made my own survivor's-guilt remark: "Yes, since the greatest beauties of both Antwerp and Brussels never returned . . ."

I only stopped using this statement after it had been pointed out to me many times: "Must you always ruin it for yourself?" . . .

Ch. 2: . . . and yes: In my mind, I repeated the same comment when I was crowned Esther Hamalke of the Purim Ball 1946. The men voted for us girls wearing numbers on our backs. The most popular young lady was secured the greatest number of trees for Israel (still Palestine for two more years) and became queen.

Ch. 1: I had been presented at this intoxicating ball by the Horowitz family. That's where I met my U.S. diamond dealer fiancé, who was my stepping stone to the U.S. (New York). Directly after the liberation, our great friendship with them had survived, just as we did. They succeeded in the Unoccupied and the boys there and in Switzerland. Through Marcel I learned later that when the Nazis eventually occupied the "Unoccupied," each Jew had to go into hiding like us. Yet when the Italians took over, they felt safe enough to roam the streets. It was an alternating game of hide under the Nazis and being free under the Italians.

When I returned to Köln with my husband in the early 1950s, Marcel Horowitz was a soldier under the Belgian occupying forces. Twenty-five years later he treated me to fine Jewish meals at his own restaurant in *Ostende* at the same location, *Lange Straat*, where I "ate" the paintings during the *Flucht*. As of 1987, we would meet twice a year when I came to Köln. In 1989, this was crowned by my trip to the charming Israeli seaside resort of Natanya. Upon arriving at midnight at the Tel Aviv airport, where both brothers picked me up, I saw—for the very first time in 48 years—Julien, who fathered no less than five children. If not for Marcel and Julien, I would never have toured our fascinating State of Israel.

The Köln meetings with Marcel continue to the present. He is one of the few I can converse with in seven different languages, but English was our primary tongue—which brings me to the Perlman family in Brussels, who were amongst the smart Belgian Jews not to have heeded another Nazi promise—and thus lived! Unfortunately, very few were that clever.

Ch. 20: One of the first survivors I found in Brussels after coming out of hiding was the French steno student Miriam, a cutie sans make-up with naturally shiny lips, who was still raving about Paris. She became my girlfriend. Each time, she showed deep concern when she asked: "Do you think it's possible anyone will ever return alive from THERE?"

My answer was more of a consoling guess: "A very few strong ones, heroes in body and mind, just might."

A couple of years later, the reason for her worries became clear to me. While strolling with my U.S. fiancé along the beach, she was there with her mom and husband—one of those rare suffering braves.

Ch. 6: On a drab, cold evening in late autumn, after the liberation, I took my first trip to Antwerp. The moment I got out of the station, I ran into two well-to-do diamond dealer brothers, the Fremds. One of them had proposed marriage to me upon my arrival here from Köln, and he repeated it now with the same fervor, when a good-looking couple entered the elegant restaurant we were in. The stunning dark-haired, blue-eyed girl in gray fur coat and matching hat smiled beamingly at me just as she had on the eve of the Nazi attack on May 9th, 1940, when our glances and giggles (caused by our resemblance) met in her aunt's mirror. I had given my very last English lesson to this nice diamond washer. She and her son were among the very lucky ones. Miss Zandmeer succeeded in getting to England through her fiancé, who had joined the RAF.

Ch. 2: I learned later in like manner that Lili had also been fortunate. She was a very happily married woman living in comfort when I was occasionally her dinner guest.

Ch. 3: My dancing partner, Ben, and I were just nodding acquaintances when he sat with his wife at the various terraces on the *Keyserlei*.

Ch. 16: A few years later, Moishe, the brother of Mrs. Blum, owner of the *Vesting Straat Café*, returned from Cuba as a wealthy gem trader. He also kept proposing to me, but I already had a fiancé in the United States.

Ch. 19: As late as 1995, on a very rainy spring day, I looked up Raymond Krijgstein, "the boy," now a 60-year-old grandpop, who graciously met me at my favorite Hotel in Brussels, the *Métropole*. He told me all of them had survived, but each in a different place. The child had been separated from his mom, Suzanne, who was in hiding somewhere in France, while he spent two years with a Gentile Family. His grandmom, Gietel, hid in a small town in Belgium and the "Limerick Creator" in yet another city. Later on, they died of natural causes. Raymond was successful in Gietel's bag-manufacturing.

Ch. 23. Through the grapevine, Vati heard about Mrs. Alesky—in short, most unfortunately: "The Fall of a Showgirl!" There was no news about Mr. Alesky nor Tanya, except the most important: They had survived and were in the process of finding an ophthalmologist.

IN THE UNITED STATES

Ch. 3: The first Belgian acquaintance I encountered was on West 47th Street, the New York diamond counterpart to Pelikaan Straat. I spotted a shiny bald head in the window of a jewelry booth—lo and behold, it was Mr. Bialystock! As one of the very few naturalized Belgian citizens, he was granted a U.S. visa without any waiting period.

Ch. 2: I ran into Rosa Stern at Macy's in New York. She had made a very wise choice in Antwerp before the war.

Ch. 3: In the heart of Manhattan, I saw Meusch, my would-be boyfriend of the foursome at *St. Anneke.* He was married.

Ch. 16: In the early 1950s in sunny Miami, I met Mr. Gerstel coincidentally through one of his diamond employees. Their Cuban move was a smart one. All of them were fine, and his daughter was a well-known equestrienne in Kentucky.

Ch. 15 In one of the fancy stores on Lincoln Road in Miami Beach, through a conversation about Belgium, the shopkeeper revealed that one of her customers, a big elderly lady, was often there with her husband, bemoaning the loss of her family: her only daughter, son-in-law and grandson—the former Mrs. Schwartz.

IN GERMANY

Ch. 4: I often saw my school chum, Inge Kasper-Ehrlich, from Rektor Kahn's class, in Köln and once in Chicago. Her Jewish father had wound up in Auschwitz. On a daily basis, her Gentile mom was nagged by the Gestapo to divorce him so THEY could gas him. Since she did not, he returned. Inge wasted away in one of the tiny cells at the horrible Gestapo headquarters, the infamous EL-DE-Haus, which today serves as a museum of the Nazi time in Köln.

On one of my trips, I went with her to pick out a room at the Köln Jewish Nursing Home, where she lost her fight against cancer on a New Year's Eve in the early 1990s.

Ch. 21: Since I had heard that the Hakums ran directly from Brussels to Frankfurt, I telephoned from Köln in 1952. When she begged me to visit, I had to decline.

Ch. 1: On my very first trip to my roots in ruins in 1947, I saw Vati's friend Hans, Nellie and his sister many times, enjoying each one enormously, especially when we got together with my Belgian buddies at "*La Redoute*" or the *Dreesen Hotel*. Under the U.S. administration in *Bad Godesberg*, the *Brunnen Allee* became just that: Americanized, with all its charming houses gone except "*La Redoute*," no longer in its former splendor, but a cute, smaller place at the same site. The *Hotel Dreesen*, one of the Chamberlain/Hitler meeting locales, now appears like a dilapidated old lady.

Ch. 8: I looked up my babysitting family—the oasis amidst much anti-Semitism. It was a stirring moment when I finally found Thea at the same house where she had watched over me from the time I was four. What memories! Since then, we've had many great get-togethers. Her husband, whom I never met, and the youngest of this large family, Walter, my dear big friend, both fell in the war, in Rumania of all places. The strangest feeling overcame me—to think that my wonderful anti-Semite-protector died for the WH—thus for Hitler.

Ch. 1: I don't quite understand why I waited until 1994 to finally return to my real roots in *Mülheim* on the right bank of the Rhine. Our very last Köln domicile, where Mutti had the life-saving "Antwerp tantrum," stood there just as we had left it in 1938. The freight depot, Vati's business location, where the boys threw stones at me, was now owned by the cable maker Felten & Guillaume, to whom Vati delivered 20 tons of train-wagon loads almost daily. I hadn't realized the entire German Reich was one big labor camp, as each large mill was provided with foreign slave laborers. In the beginning, they were lured there with false promises of work; later, they were snatched off their own Nazi-occupied streets as we might have been. Amongst these was none other than Vati's business connection, Felten & Guillaume located just steps from his place. Though this slavery had occurred much later, it was quite a shock!

444FAYE CUKIER

I walked right back into my childhood, to where Vati made his start as a scrap dealer and kept his horses, Lisa, Fritz and Rex. The now-cemented yard is operated by a large English firm. Visions of 1933 returned, when two brown-uniformed SA men were planted in front with the sign: "*Kauft nicht bei Juden!* (Don't buy from Jews!)" This alone showed the stupidity: on a little industrial street *Langemaßstrasse* on Saturday, when no one even came by anyway, Vati had to beg them to enter his own warehouse and stable to feed the animals, reassuring them (inwardly in jest) that the horses were not Jewish. The dumb brutes insisted—in earnest—that they were because their owner was.

Upon my return to our last Köln residence, I now noticed a brass plate: Law Offices of Jung & Partners. It was an unexpected surprise to meet Dr. and Mrs. Alfred Jung, whose great parents owned the bicycle store in times gone by (which is even bigger and better now). He recalled us only vaguely, but remembered clearly the Nazi pressure his father was under because he had rented his brand new apartment to Jews—us—his dad's advice: to leave the country.

On a lighter note: As a child, Alfred practiced on the same piano as I had, since his family had bought it from us. His nice sister-in-law had her own Holocaust exhibit and wrote a book about the Jews who had vanished from her small hometown of *Schmallenberg*. I met her several times.

The fate of the ones not mentioned here is unknown.

50 years later Hoeselt, Limburg revisited. To my left the handsome, great mayor and to my right 5 years old Joske, here a 55-year-old grandpop.

In Memoriam

In memory of my relatives, friends and those who crossed
my path between September 1938 and September 1944,
along with all those who perished and vanished,
nameless, in history.

Ch. 1: My Antwerp relatives: Aunt Hella, cousins Frima, Sara
and Maurice. He escaped from a concentration camp, back to
Antwerp, and was described as though he'd arisen from the dead—
like Lazarus. His freedom was short-lived. Betrayed by a Flemish
girlfriend—said to resemble me—he was recaptured, never to
return.

Ch. 18: What tragic irony: Maurice perished and I survived!

Ch. 23: My cousins, like most Belgian-born Jews, relied too
heavily on the honest promise of the King's mother, dishonestly
given by the German Satrap Reeder; therefore, they took no
precautions. The first ones were deported on August 3, 1944,
exactly one month prior to Brussels' liberation! The Caravan of
Death—which sent 2,500 souls to the Mass Killing Industries in
the east—occurred as late as September 19th, 1944, composed of
mostly Belgian Jews, an especially refined group, from German-
occupied Belgian cities.

Ch. 1: In 1946, I was on top of the world in every way! At this
moment, I sat in the back of a cab making its way through the
crowd in the busiest street of *Blankenbergh*, a Belgian seaside resort.
A tall man, outstanding, though balding, with movie star good
looks, caught my eye. Curious to see the lady he accompanied—I
got goose pimples—"*Attendez! Attendez!*" I instructed my driver,
dashing out of the taxi to embrace this familiar woman. I exclaimed,

excitedly: "Mitzi, Mitzi! You survived! You are actually standing here before me! How wonderful!" Trying to curb my overwhelming emotion, I asked kiddingly: "No more bobbing curls?"

My joy was met with a stony stare. Surprised, I pressed on nevertheless: "True, it has been over six years since we saw each other last. People change. Perhaps you don't recognize me?!"

She nodded in a profoundly sad way. "Yes, I do."

"Handsome" stood at a respectable distance. He was not introduced to me.

In my exuberance, I wanted to jolt her from her apathy, but held back. "How is Fred and tell me about your lovely children! They must be big by now!" I tried to encourage her to speak—to react! In an even more heartbroken manner, she answered—barely audible: "All gone! All four of them and my husband," she moaned above a whisper, without shedding a tear. Obviously she had none left. This former dazzler seemed so dazed, so completely spent, physically and emotionally. Slowly I began to understand her total inertia. Maybe she was drugged to blot out her pain. I told her my parents had survived. She couldn't even smile, but there was a faint nod. She still had her fine features and good bone structure, but that "paprika" was gone.

"I guess you live here by the seaside." I hoped she would mention to meet again, but answered faintly, "To recuperate."

I hated leaving her in such an unstable condition but she seemed to be in good hands. What this poor, young woman must have suffered in so many ways: her losses and—only she and God know what happened to her own body and spirit—! Most reluctantly, I felt her hand, cold and lifeless, for the last time.

Back in the car, the chauffeur turned around twice to see if I was the same person. In my ears I heard Tschaikovsky's very dramatic sounding "Pathétique." How pathetic, indeed, that these horrible events had turned the vivacious Mitzi into a tragic figure. I could never get her out of my mind.

Ch. 2: Our Hungarian neighbors from *Berchem*: The youngest two daughters lost their lives. She was the first one to knock at our door and also the "baby" of the family, the Orthodox Yeshiva scholar who advised me where to study French. The mom and all three sons survived. The middle one made it across the Channel (we failed) after we briefly ran into him during that chaotic time in *Ostende.* The husband of the eldest, the Spanish freedom fighter who helped me with my French pronunciation, was captured, never to return. His tall, charming millinery wife and son Eddie survived, and she remarried. The second eldest sister made it to the U.S. in the nick of time.

Ch. 2: Marika, the violinist's beautiful wife I'd met at the New Year's party, with fine olive skin and a contrasting boa-trimmed white dress, fared disastrously. When THEY came for this young Hungarian couple, she was pregnant. To protect her unborn child, she just refused THEIR command to come with THEM. Thereupon, THEY dragged her forcibly, head first down two flights of hardwood steps. As much as THEY despised all Jews, THEY seemed to have an especially violent hatred toward the Hungarian ones in their dark, diabolic hearts.

Ch. 3: My favorite teacher of all-time, Rektor Emil Kahn of the Jewish Lützow Str. School in Köln, perished in one of the first transports after languishing for months in a death camp. As did most Köln Jewish victims, he left from the huge hall of International Fairs (Messe) in Köln-Deutz, where as a child I watched my parents dance so happily—the bandleader flirting with Mutti. Today it's called the *Tanzbrunnen* ("Dance Fountain"). In my native city, two collection camps—like the Belgian Malines—were needed. The Müngersdorf Sporthalle was another. Everywhere, only mammoth places could accommodate the masses deported as part of the sinister plan. The old Deutz Station was conveniently located for THEM on the right bank of the Rhine River so "passengers" could be shipped straight to Poland—"Destination Death." These steps are still called the "Treppen der Tränen" (Steps of Tears), but are no longer in existence. There is supposed to be a memorial plaque at the site, but as recently as 1995 I searched there in vain, so it must be so inconspicuous that one can easily overlook it. Thus, it was a grand consolation to find an engraved reminder of

Principal Emil Kahn on the outside wall of the Lützow Str. School, today called the Rektor Emil Kahn Schule.

Ch. 3: My dear friend, Rosalie Lipshutz: In 1946, under glamorous circumstances, I saw the big, distinguished good-looking diamantaire Mr. Lipshutz with his red-haired bride. (Not related to my first cachet buyer.) Years ago, he was introduced to me by Rosalie. I briefly left my U.S. fiancé, also a diamond dealer, to ask about his cousin Rosalie's whereabouts.

"Whereabouts," he repeated sardonically. "She succumbed to typhoid in a concentration camp! So did her friend, Charlotte!"

I was barely able to nod a thank you.

Ch. 4: The Waiting Wives with children in *Berchem* never were issued a U.S. visa to join their husbands in America. Their hopes and English studies went up in Auschwitz smoke.

Chs. 10 & 17: I actually was pleasantly surprised as I peeked into the *Leuwerickstraat*, Antwerp's Jewish hub of life went on as late as 1941. There was a definite Nazi reason for this: When the time was ripe, the sudden round-ups took place from where there was no escape! Our *Flucht* companions—the father of five and family—were thus trapped as the standard "catching" method all over Nazi-occupied Europe (in addition to THEIR "random" snatching) continued relentlessly.

Ch. 4: Michel, Maurice's friend who moved us from *Berchem*, was also caught with his family here. So was the beautiful dancer to Chopin's Valse at my first rhythmic class and the waiter, "*Schmendrick*."

Ch. 14: The *restauranteur Prager* and his entire large family were loaded onto THEIR trucks and later furniture vans. Along with the entire neighborhood, they were shipped to *Malines* and from there, in freight trains, to Auschwitz and other Mass Murder Mills.

Ch. 13: Mutti's furrier *Landsmann*, Mr. Chmurra, who kept exclaiming, "Ash, ash, ash, everything will turn to ash!": Unfortunately, so did he and most of his family. His spinster sister, who once lived very poorly in a furnished room, not only survived but was financially successful as a sort of paralegal obtaining restitution for fellow survivors.

Ch. 16: With the exception of Betti Fass and a handful of others, all the Limburg deportees were eventually killed. The dentist and the two others taken out of Hoeselt were never heard from. Though no further men were nabbed, they were later amassed in the four Belgian big cities where Jews were allowed until . . .

So were the Holzer brothers—I hope sweet Erna survived the Allied bombs.

I had met Betti coincidentally during my honeymoon, traveling from New York to Brussels where she was an exhibitor at that European city's big fair. She was single.

In the early 1990s, I paid various visits to Hoeselt and was surprised to find Mayor René Nartus, pushing 90, looking well and driving his own car. He lived comfortably at his villa, and remembered me and my last name instantly. He took me to the cloister where I played for him and different nuns on the same piano of my youth.

Five-year-old Joske was, in 1991, a 55-year-old grand-pop with a wonderful family. "Our" country kitchen had been turned into elegant rooms as was "our" bedroom and the rest of the house. With the mayor present, they treated me royally. Joske was the only one to survive his sisters, family and friends, including the peeping toms and barmaid. (They all died a natural death.) He recalled me ever so faintly. There was still laughter concerning "*de kat* "!

They deemed my request to see the young, slim doctor funny and strange. After I'd met this now old and fat physician in his same office, Joske and the mayor revealed the irony: Unbeknownst to me, the doctor was Hoeselt's biggest Nazi, thus a Belgian traitor who spent two years in prison.

The mayor, now Honorary Delegate, had furnished me with lists of all our Antwerp co-expulsees. Most perished later. It was assumed the dentist and the two other men had been taken to nearby mines and from there to the final solution.

I also encountered one of the "gawking boys." He continued his admiring glances—even after 50 years.

In a book called "*Oorlog* '40-'45 in *Zuid-Oost Limburg*" (The War '40-'45 in Southeast Limburg) by former Mayor Mathieu

Rutten of the village of *Tongeren*, pages 184—185 were devoted mainly to me, with photos of me taken in 1941 and 1991.

The whole mystery behind our having been returned to Antwerp/Brussels was revealed: The ovens were not ready yet.

Ch. 20: There was great joy at first when I ran into Willy near *la Place de Brouckère*—after being liberated he imparted the following: his older brother Léon had been caught again and escaped successfully once more. Through him, Willy had learned about the fate of Egon, the handsome violin artist of *la Coupole*. Léon was at the same Killing Factory when the musically talented prisoners were summoned up front. They stepped forward to audition for the SS murderers. As each musician played a few bars, he was "compensated" with an enormous blow to the base of his skull. The youngest in the group, who seemed to carefully think it over until his bow touched the fiddle with the "Blue Danube," was spared punishment. When it was Egon's turn, he played in his irresistible, enchanting manner. Not only was he hit like the others, but flanked by two of THEM and dragged away. Then the inmates heard gut-wrenching screams as only a man could howl from physical pain. THEY had broken all of Egon's fine, wonderful, artistic fingers.

Though shocked, I thought quickly: So much for Nazi culture!—and their very special hatred of Hungarian Jews! Absorbed in this ghoulish tale, Willy continued: "It was the last time this gifted group, except for the young "Danube" player, was seen in that horror camp, which suggests that shortly thereafter, they were led to the gas chamber. I had a lot to contemplate on my way back to the Atlanta Hotel. I saw Egon's graceful hands giving joy to my heart and many others. And in *"Le raconteur"*—Willy—there had been a change, too. Or was it me? That certain cozy warmth of his company was missing. At subsequent times, he surprised me by pacing in front of the hotel and taking me to their richly furnished apartment nearby. Rosa had turned into a different, withdrawn personality, having lost her vivaciousness. Her desire to sing and even make up had vanished. A case similar to Mitzi's—but why? I could not relate to her at all. I was glad they had survived and sad that our friendship had not—!

Ch. 21: The biggest amazement of all was that scum of the earth, Jacques, did point out Otto to his Nazi bosses. This rustic, Teutonic-looking Jew, Otto, was so sure of himself that he dared going downtown. Even the Nazi catchers were so dubious that a "*Hosendoktor*" (pants doctor) was needed to confirm Jacques' finding. Thus it came about that a strong man like Otto wound up at one of the Mass Murder Mills. He never wanted to utter a single word about his experiences. Only once did he talk about his comrade-in-suffering, Tibor, a virile, big man like himself who was resilient enough to have survived there for almost two years. (This was highly unusual, but THEY needed him for the gruesome job of "gravedigger.") Tibor spoke about the time he was shipped from *Malines* to the east—at first to Auschwitz, near Krakow, Poland. As usual, the cattle-wagon was packed to over-capacity. He saw a tiny blonde woman holding onto a pre-Bar-Mitzvah boy for dear life. He recognized Mrs. W. and Harold. Since they were shorter than the rest of the wretched standing "passengers", they were suffocating. Otto's friend then carried the featherweight Mrs. W. high above his head to the freight car's sliding doors so no one would obstruct her breathing. Though moving through the car was practically impossible, he managed to do the same with Harold. The woman was unable to utter any sound. She was in visible agony. Then, only silence—

Upon arrival at Destination Death, the heavy train gate was opened from outside by the SS. Mrs. W., still holding onto her son, rolled down lifelessly with Harold onto the Killer Earth of Auschwitz. Even in their last gasp, this uncommon bond could not be severed. With machine guns pointed at the doomed "cargo" as they jumped down from the cattle train—"*Schnell! Raus! Los, los!* (Let's go, come on, be quick about it!)"—it was impossible to give them as much as one last glance. Otto knew the W.s from their store on Pelikaan St., where fine English worsteds were sold to tailor custom-made suits. Even this masculine man had tears well up in his eyes, recalling this and most likely his own experiences.

Ch. 23: To think how easily we could have wound up in that carload. A few months later my parents were invited as Otto wed his loyal live-in Gentile German woman, who had stood by him through the hard times, enduring misery out of pure love.

Ch. 21: Meta, Otto's sister, was there, too. She was engaged to a well-to-do survivor who, coincidentally, had proposed to me right after the Liberation. He got a flat "no"!

My parents said it was downright uncomfortable for Mendel to be present there. But he was capable of heroic efforts—he had escaped from Killing Camps several times. Obviously, Meta preferred the richer man to one who must start from scratch.

Ch. 4: It was a picture perfect day when I was on the train from Brussels to Antwerp. I felt two big roundish eyes staring at me. It was Anette, my Parisian student, owner of the millinery shop on *Provintie Straat* in Antwerp.

"Oh, Anette. Isn't it great that we made it?!" I chirped while inquiring about her husband, lost during the *Flucht*, when I had run into her just prior to finding the heavenly "bed" of wood shavings. She shook her head in sorrow: "No, he has never been found."

"This is surely the strangest case. Many a family member disappeared in the chaos. After the Nazi assault and bombardments, they did emerge, though. I too had lost my parents briefly—it was a terrible feeling! There was so much love between the two of you and all that laughter at your private jokes whenever he paid you a short visit from his hat factory to your store while I taught you."

Now, she switched effortlessly from French into English. It was nice to have given her something lasting and even more so when she pointed out that she always thinks of me when speaking in that tongue. She giggled when remembering the impossibility of pronouncing "h" . . . as a last resort I had tried to force the silent "h" in French by belly dancing rapid diaphragm vibrations. She was the one responsible for my stage rhythmic studies.

Ch. 14: After taking leave from Anette with the promise to meet again, I crossed the street from the station to my still-favorite corner of times gone by and saw Mrs. Friedman. With her most charming, good-looking husband, the now Mrs. Salik related that her first mate—whom she'd nagged through the "cannon" night with "La Panne!"—also was caught with her young sister Rachel at the round-ups. "Yes, they both joined my poor brother!" she sighed.

The last time I had seen her on this same Pelikaan Straat, she and her teen sibling were devastated about Yossel's arrest. This was prior to THEIR Jew hunts. Simon tried to rescue him, but too late. Shortly thereafter, his ashes were delivered—for a fee yet.

What I saw now was a far cry from then. She nestled her head happily and wistfully against her husband's shoulder, inviting me and my parents to her spacious apartment, similar to Erna's as it was a neighboring house, located so conveniently that we saw each other quite often during my frequent visits there.

It became customary for one surviving spouse to wed another concentration camp widow(er).

Ch. 22: The happy Gola family with child and mom survived, bemoaning their tall "honest" sister/daughter and husband, who never returned, as was the fate of all those caught in the early stages.

Ch. 20. The gorgeous Sabine Berger, her sister Helga, mom and father, who was our bookkeeper in the 1930s, perished. The girls were in my religion class in *Mülheim,* taught. by Dr. Julius Simon, who also was murdered by THEM.

> Once upon a time, there was a white butterfly,
> the queen of them all.
> At dawn, she flew from lilacs to violets.
> The little, beautiful butterfly was so happy . . .
> One spring morning,
> when she was sitting coquettishly atop a jasmine flower,
> a collector took our queen prisoner, brought her to his museum
> and threaded her onto a black velvet board,
> where there were other white butterfly beauties—dead ones . . .
> The survivors missed their queen so very much
> when they never saw her again,
> enjoying life each dawn.

Acknowledgements

Special thanks to Leona Abrams, my most talented and dedicated editor who believed in this book from the very beginning.

Tanja Nesterenko for her swift finalization. Nanette Arndts for her passionate ideas. Libby Schwartz, Stanislav Onischenko, Sunshine Werbock, Peter Hannon, Ruth Jachertz, Steve Nobles, Vincent A., Wayne, Jordan and Melody Arndts for their great help and Curt Goldman for his moral support.